Human Differences

Human Differences

Lewis R. Aiken
Pepperdine University

 LAWRENCE ERLBAUM ASSOCIATES, PUBLISHERS
1999   Mahwah, New Jersey   London

BF
697
.A55
1999

Lawrence Erlbaum Associates, Inc., Publishers
10 Industrial Avenue
Mahwah, NJ 07430

Cover design by Kathryn Houghtaling Lacey

Library of Congress Cataloging-in-Publication Data

Aiken, Lewis R., 1931–
Human differences / Lewis R. Aiken.
    p.   cm.
    Includes bibliographical references and index.
    ISBN 0-8058-3091-X (hardcover : alk. paper) — ISBN
0-8058-3092-8 (pbk. : alk. paper).
    1. Individual differences.   I. Title.
    BF697.A55 1999
    155.2'2—dc21   99-11092
                                                            CIP

Books published by Lawrence Erlbaum Associates are printed
on acid-free paper, and their bindings are chosen for strength
and durability.

Printed in the United States of America
10 9 8 7 6 5 4 3 2 1

Not ev'ryone's the same as some,
For folks are good and bad.
And once in a while you'll see a smile
On someone who is sad.

'Cause people are alike and not;
They are both right and wrong.
And if you come near, you may see fear
In someone who is strong.

To you I may look mean as sin,
But gaze at me anew,
And then you may see that old mean me
Is as kind as that old mean you.

So let's forgive the us we don't
And like the us we do,
Then time will soon tell if all goes well
With the not us and me and you!

—*Lewis R. Aiken*

Contents

Foreword

Research on human differences is a double-edge sword. On the one hand, a preoccupation with the differences among people can lead to stereotyping and provide support for prejudice and discrimination. This was the trap into which certain early pioneers in the mental testing movement fell, a trap set and sprung by those with an ethnocentric philosophy of life and a political agenda rationalized by eugenics. Of course, modern thinkers, whether liberal or conservative in their social and political viewpoints, are not immune to ethnocentrism. This is not surprising when one considers the universality of group pride, social competition, and outgroup hostility. It often seems, as some have argued, that humans have not really grown much in wisdom since Cro-Magnon times and each generation must rediscover tolerance and philanthropy.

On the other hand, it can be argued that a knowledge of human diversity is important in understanding and appreciating individuals and cultures that are different from one's own. In fact, a defensible point of view is that, because heterogeneity and hybridization have greater survival value than homogeneity and cloning, they should be encouraged and applauded rather than dwelt upon as causes of social friction.

This book is a mixture of concepts and findings from biology, sociology, economics, psychology, and many other natural and social sciences. But because the author is a psychologist, much of the book is about psychology. American psychology developed in the early part of the 20th century in the context of a socioeconomic system that was based on the principle of equity. According to this principle, the goods and services obtained by people should be commensurate with their abilities and efforts. In contrast to the principle of equity, adherence to the principle of equality results in the division of resources equally among individuals who perform many different, but necessary, tasks. Historically, Americans have seemingly straddled the fence between these two principles, a gymnastic exercise that might be simpler if all people were truly created equal.

A generation ago Leona Tyler (1978) proposed that we move away from psychological assessment mode based on the equity principle toward one based on differentiation among people in terms of their complementary role skills. In this psychometric model, tests are used primarily for diagnosis and placement rather than selection and screening. People are assigned tasks that they perform best, but all occupations are accorded equivalent social status and rewards.

Civil rights legislation during the 1960s and 1970s helped to end discrimination in employment, education, and other social contexts, and efforts were made to achieve equality rather than continuing to adhere to the traditional notion of equity. In an attempt to compensate for the injustices and inequalities of the past, the government instituted affirmative action policies. In recent years, however, affirmative action programs have been severely criticized and rolled back in various quarters because of alleged inequalities in the treatment of different racial and other demographic groups.

Be that as it may, from a sociopolitical prospective few will deny that progress has been made in ensuring the civil rights of all American citizens, regardless of race, ethnicity, gender, nativity, religion, physical disability, or sexual orientation. Obviously the degree of progress has not been rapid enough to please everyone and perhaps too rapid for some. Few would probably deny, however, that minority groups and women are, on the whole, economically and socially better off today than they were two or three generations ago. Nevertheless, confusion and uncertainty remain with respect to how social justice can best be attained while maintaining intergroup harmony in an increasingly multicultural, pluralistic society.

No doubt there is comfort and security in stereotyping and ethnocentrism; everyone has an ego and we tend to think of the groups to which we owe allegiance as better than others. Like many other animal species, humans appear to be naturally aggressive and competitive, characteristics that are reinforced in games, school, work, and other endeavors throughout our lives. But whether we like it or not, the increased interaction among people with different psychical and psychological characteristics and different cultural backgrounds will demand ever more that we do our best to cooperate and attempt to fashion some kind of community from our diversity. As people of different nationalities, races, and backgrounds draw closer together, it may be that the differences between them will, to a large extent, disappear. Perhaps in a thousand years or so our descendants will all be of similar color, shape, and size. In a sense this may be desirable, in that it should make conflict less likely. For the present, however, we can delight in our diversity, and accept the fact that the world is generally a more interesting, and certainly a less disturbing, place when we tolerate, interact with, and learn from each others. We cannot, however, settle for mere tolerance. Rather, we must come to sincerely appreciate and like people who are different from ourselves while realizing that we are more similar than different in our needs, abilities, and aspirations.

Speaking for professional social scientists in particular, Jones (1994) summarized the current attitude toward individual and group differences and his proposition of *affirmative diversity* in this way:

We have given much lip service to the notion of human diversity as a value and a good in society and in the world. But we have not, through disciplined inquiry, demonstrated exactly how diversity confers strengths to us as individuals and as a society. The goal of affirmative diversity is to legitimate and promote this inquiry and the values underlying it. (p. 43)

If this book makes some small contribution to the realization of this goal, then the author's time will have been well-spent.

—*Lewis R. Aiken*

Preface

It is arguable whether people are more alike than different, but they obviously differ from each other in many ways. Biologically, they differ in gender, race, size, strength, speed, agility, sensory acuity, endurance, health status, longevity, body chemistry, and attractiveness. Psychologically, they differ in general and specific cognitive abilities, creativity, interests, and in a host of personality variables. Sociologically, they differ in social standing, economic status, ethnicity, culture, religion, and politics. In terms of productivity, they differ in school grades, degrees earned, occupational/professional accomplishments, and other measures of success. Some of these variables are causes and some are effects of each other, but for the most part they are intermingled in a complex, multidimensional and multidirectional web.

The systematic investigation of individual differences, traditionally referred to as *differential psychology*, was inaugurated by Sir Francis Galton during the late 19th century. Galton viewed the study of individual differences in mental abilities and temperament as a natural outgrowth of his cousin Charles Darwin's research and theorizing on the evolution of species differences. The influence of Darwin's evolutionary biology was not limited to the biological sciences, but it had an effect on psychology, sociology, and other disciplines as well. Comparative psychology, developmental psychology, and the study of individual differences in general all bear the stamp of evolutionary thinking. Investigations in these fields have been conducted with an understanding that, although both physical and psychological variations among people are to some extent inherited, individual initiative and opportunity make definite contributions to the fulfillment of one's potentialities and help in overcoming limitations imposed by biological constitution and unfortunate experiences.

The study of the origins and outcomes of individual differences in psychological characteristics has been greatly facilitated by the construction and standardization of tests of intelligence, personality, and other psychological constructs. However, research on individual differences in cognitive abilities, personality traits, and psychomotor skills has been unsystematic and often a reflection of convenient measuring instruments and methodology rather than sound thinking and appropriate research design. There has been no scarcity of hypotheses and theories concerned with human differences, but such speculations have not been very successful in predicting and explaining research findings and everyday observations. For this reason, this book is primarily an empirical treatise dealing with facts and statistics rather than theories. Brief overviews of theories of cognition and personality are given in chapter 6 and chapter 8, but readers who desire a comprehensive exposition of psychological theories must look elsewhere (e.g., Aiken, 1996b; Ewen, 1998; Ryckman, 1997; Flanagan, Glenshaft, & Harrison, 1997; Maddi, 1996).

Many conclusions derived from research on individual and group differences in psychological characteristics, particularly those concerned with the relationships of race and gender to cognitive abilities, have been highly controversial and widely debated. However, a spirit of forbearance and open-mindedness, together with the application of more sophisticated multivariate statistical procedures and data processing techniques, have increased the scope of such studies and yielded more defensible conclusions. Nevertheless, the nature–nurture debate and other topics of contention with respect to the origins and effects of human differences continue to be pursued.

There is a massive amount of popular and professional literature on the topic of individual differences, in journals such as *Learning and Individual Differences* and *Personality and Individual Differences*, in dozens of scholarly books, and in more popular sources. The International Society for the Study of Individual Differences serves as a forum and clearinghouse for such research. The majority of recent books on individual and group differences are, however, not integrated texts but collections of readings by multiple authors (e.g., Gale & Eysenck, 1992; Jonasses & Grabowski, 1993; Lubinski & Dawis, 1995; Trickett, Watts, & Birman, 1994). Unlike these sources, the present book is a unified compendium; though broad in scope, it is written by a single author, hopefully with clarity and continuity. Preparation of this volume has involved a great deal of selection and condensation of source material, but hundreds of references from a research literature consisting of thousands of published articles have been retained.

Many scholarly books concerned with individual differences in characteristics, such as general intelligence, are essentially summaries of studies concerned with the relationships of hereditary and environmental factors to the development of the characteristic. Other books focus on a particular background variable, such as heredity, nutrition, or restricted experience, and attempt to trace the effects of the variable on assorted psychological characteristics. The research methods employed in these two approaches may involve selective breeding studies, controlled experiments, correlational analyses, and other procedures.

The structure of the present book represents a combination of the approaches just mentioned. Not only is every human being viewed as the product of a complex interaction between heredity and environment, but human characteristics are seen as being influenced by and in turn influencing what have been referred to as biological and experiential "background factors." Behavior is determined by the biological makeup and experiences of a person, but those experiences, as well as the person's physical structure and functioning, are affected by how he or she behaves.

The purpose of *Human Differences* is to examine and attempt to make sense of the mass of information and interpretation pertaining to the various ways in which individuals and groups differ from each other. A review of research findings and interpretations is provided in each of the areas defined by the various chapters. Before launching into a description of the research literature on individual and group differences, an overview of the historical and conceptual foundations of the topic is presented, along with the traditional and more recent methodological tools that have been brought to bear in such studies. In addition, a synopsis of genetic and other biological and biochemical factors that are important in shaping individual differences is provided. Chapters 1 through 4 deal with basic background material, setting the stage and providing perspective for a consideration of individual and group differences in the physical, psychological, and social variables discussed in chapters 5 through 10.

As the author of a number of books in psychology and related fields, I know that a first edition is immeasurably more difficult to prepare than a revision. This is particularly true when the author has to do it alone. With this volume, however, I have been lucky to receive the assistance of four outstanding professionals. To begin, my thanks go to Judi Amsel, whom I have known for years and always appreciated, for "signing me up." Not only did Judi make many cogent suggestions for improving the book, but she was instrumental in having the first draft reviewed by Robert J. Sternberg of Yale University. Although I did not do everything that Professor Sternberg advised, I tried to do enough to make the manuscript acceptable to him. I hope that he approves of the finished product. Also deserving of acknowledgment are Kathy Scornavacca, my understanding and considerate production editor, who accomplished the laborious tasks of shepherding the manuscript through the production process and tolerating my idiosyncrasies, and Sara Scudder for proofreading the manuscript and finding most of my mistakes.

—Lewis R. Aiken

CHAPTER ONE

Origins and Developments

Human beings may look alike, act alike, and think alike, but in one way or another everyone is different from everyone else. People differ not only in physical characteristics such as weight, height, hair and skin coloring, and facial features, but in their abilities, personality, and behavior as well. Even identical twins, who have identical heredities, are not exactly alike. They may appear initially like two peas in a pod, but on further acquaintance the two peas are seen to possess a number of dissimilarities. People are born different, and in many ways they become even more dissimilar as they grow older.[1] These differences enable us to distinguish among people, thereby serving as a basis for differential treatment of friends, acquaintances, and strangers.

Some futurists fantasize a world populated by armies of clones that would presumably be easier to train and control than the masses of individuals now inhabiting our planet. But in addition to being uninteresting, such large-scale conformity of appearance and action might very well result in mass extinction when conditions or circumstances changed radically and the clones did not possess the physical structures or abilities to deal with the changes.

From a Darwinian perspective, some individual differences, such as birth defects or physical disorders, decrease the chances of survival and reproduction. Other differences contribute to the individual's likelihood of surviving and perpetuating his or her own kind. The occurrence of severe climatic or environmental changes may pose a test of the survival value of individual characteristics. For example, introduction of a new strain of viruses or physicochemical conditions that individuals lack the necessarily equipment to deal with can easily decimate a population. This would seem less likely to occur, however, in a population consisting of individuals possessing a wide variety of physical and behavioral characteristics.

---

[1] Furthermore, many of these differences are related, or appear in clusters. According to Berg's (1967) deviation hypothesis, for example, people who deviate from the norm in one way are likely to deviate in other ways as well.

A vast array of individual differences in structure and functioning can be found both within and between various plant and animal species.[2] From single-cell organisms at one extreme to whales and giant sequoias at the other, a wide range of sizes, shapes, and other characteristics can be observed. For example, there are both inter- and intraspecies differences among mammals in speed, strength, agility, emotionality, intelligence, and other behaviors. A common pastime among boys is to rank different animals on their aggressiveness and which ones would be most likely to win in a fight. Are lions better fighters than tigers? Are grizzlies better fighters than Texas longhorn steers? A similar game played by comparative psychologists has been to rank different animals on their intelligence. Over 2,000 years ago Aristotle attempted to rank different animal species on a scale of intelligence—a so-called *scala natura*. Many centuries later, G. W. Romanes (1883), the father of comparative psychology, made extensive comparisons of the learning abilities and other psychological characteristics of different species of animals. The intelligence of a variety of animals (crabs, fishes, turtles, dogs, cats, monkeys, human infants, etc.) was also studied by E. L. Thorndike (1898/1911). Thorndike initially believed that earthworms have absolutely zero intelligence and hence are at the bottom of the intelligence scale. However, after observing that earthworms could learn a simple maze after many trials, Thorndike concluded that they have some intelligence after all. Many other interspecies comparison studies of the abilities of animals to perform cognitive tasks such as problem solving and thinking were subsequently conducted by psychologists and biologists.

As interesting as comparisons of animals' abilities may be, this book is limited to the description and discussion of human differences, both within and between demographic groups. Within this restricted domain, attention is given to biological, psychological, and social differences and how those differences affect human behavior. The approach, however, is holistic, recognizing that the physiological, cognitive, and behavioral characteristics manifested by individual humans do not act alone but rather interact in shaping a particular person.

First and foremost, this book emphasizes the uniqueness of the individual. Although the body and mind of a given person operate according to the same natural principles or laws as those of other people, everyone is a unique whole in his or her own right. Consequently, the uniqueness or individuality, as well as the general biological and psychosocial principles that apply to all people, must be taken into account to obtain a clear understanding of why a person behaves in a certain way.

INDIVIDUALISM

The social theory of *individualism*, which maintains that the highest political and social value is the welfare of the individual, goes back at least to an-

---

[2]The longevity, or length of life, of animals varies from a few hours in adult mayflies and a few days in fruit flies and houseflies to more than 100 years in some humans, tortoises, and certain large birds. Even greater longevity occurs among plants: Italian cypress trees can live for 2,000 years and bristlecone pine trees for 5,000 years or more.

cient Greece. According to this doctrine, people should be free to exercise their self-interests through independent action. In contrast, advocates of *collectivism* believe in centralized socioeconomic control.

Greek philosophers such as Plato (c. 427–347 B.C.) and Aristotle (384–322 B.C.) advocated individualism in thought and action and had much to say about human differences. As described in the *Republic,* Plato's ideal state was one in which people are selected, perhaps by means of aptitude tests, to perform tasks for which they are best suited. Aristotle's interest in individual and group differences was revealed in his comments in the *Ethics* and *Politics* concerning gender and ethnic differences in mental and moral characteristics. Like their successors, however, Plato and Aristotle realized the need to place limits on human behavior. Whenever the goals of the individual conflict with those of the society of which he or she is a member, social disharmony is the result. The writings of 20th-century psychologists also point out the problems of unbridled individualism. Although it is not synonymous with egoism, or extreme self-centeredness, individualism can lead to feelings of alienation, loneliness, worthlessness, depression, and other symptoms of mental or behavioral disorders. Psychologists recognize that a stable sense of individual identity develops not from preoccupation with the self but rather from cooperative and supportive interactions with other people.

The emphasis on individual abilities and rights that characterized Athenian democracy did not persist through the Middle Ages in Europe. Until the revival of Greek culture and thinking during the Renaissance, prevailing political, social, and religious forces emphasized autocratic control. The individual was seen first and foremost as a member of a group or class (e.g., the peasantry, clergy, nobility, artisans, etc.) and inseparable from it. Rather than being a person who happened to perform a particular occupation, an individual's identity was viewed as synonymous with the role prescribed for members of that occupation (Fromm, 1941).

The Middle Ages was a time of unquestioning faith and a struggle to survive and do one's duty toward the church and state. Earthly existence was merely a preparation for Heaven—a reward that would come only from neglecting the self and practicing obedience toward God and accepted social institutions. However, the 16th century witnessed the beginning of a gradual return to the ancient Greek perspective on the value and worth of the individual. The growth of capitalism and the attendant Protestant ethic stimulated the belief that every person is to some extent separate from others and self-sufficient. Unlike the deterministic "veil of tears" perspective that prevailed in the Middle Ages, the philosophy of life during the Renaissance and the Enlightenment periods was that individuals can influence their situation and circumstances. Freed from the constraints of intolerance and censorship, people can use their abilities to understand themselves and the world in which they live. Such knowledge can then be applied to improve one's situation and that of other people.

Traditional, nativistic theological doctrine had held that life is a battle between good and evil—that people are born in sin and hence basically evil with only a hope and not a guarantee of salvation and a happy afterlife. In contrast, philosophers such as Jean-Jacques Rousseau, John Locke, and Voltaire saw human beings not as innately bad but rather as being made bad by the social circumstances in which they exist. According to this idea, if you want to shape or change an individual's behavior, you must control his or her social environment.

Individualism flourished particularly in 18th- and 19th-century Britain, France, and the United States of America. The democratic political structures of these countries, which emphasized freedom and equality (in theory if not always in fact), contributed to that growth.[3] Sustaining this individualism by freeing people from the shackles of poverty and disease were the industrial, scientific, medical, and educational advances of the time. These advances put health, wealth, and wisdom in the hands of more people, allowing them to realize their desires and achieve whatever they would. The self-made man, who attained wealth by his own efforts rather than by inheritance, became more common and widely admired. It was thought that, given sufficient drive and ambition plus a bit of luck, all things were possible.

SCIENTIFIC BEGINNINGS

The 19th century was a time of rapid developments in the natural sciences—notably astronomy, physics, chemistry, biology, and geology. Furthermore, developments in mathematics and engineering provided methods and tools for the growth of both pure and applied science. Emerging from progress and issues in the physical and biological sciences was a new scientific psychology.

The Personal Equation and Reaction Time

In 1795, Maskelyne, royal astronomer at the Greenwich Observatory in England, became concerned when he discovered that his own observations of stellar transit times did not agree with those of his assistant, Kinnebrook. When Kinnebrook failed to correct this error, Maskelyne concluded that his assistant lacked the ability to make accurate determinations of stellar transit times, and so poor Kinnebrook was discharged. The matter might have rested there if it had not come to the attention of the astronomer Friedrich Bessel at Königsburg two decades later. After examining the data from the Greenwich Observatory and making additional observations of his own, Bessel concluded that rather than being due to simple mistakes by Kinnebrook, the disagreement between the two astronomers was caused by individual differences in their response times. In other words, each man

---

[3]Intermingled with the social atmosphere of freedom and individualism was a moralistic tone that stressed proper social conduct, obedience to God, and conformity to the will of the community. This Puritanism was especially pronounced among early New Englanders, but also permeated other areas of the nation and often came into conflict with an equally strong libertinism.

was filtering his sensory experiences—in this case, the time required for the passage of a star between cross-hairs on a telescope—through his own unique personal equation. Correcting for the personal equation of an observer became the practice in astronomy during subsequent decades. Invention of the chronoscope did away with many of these errors of observation in astronomy, but the concept of a personal equation continued to be of interest to physiologists and psychologists during the latter half of the 19th century. Numerous studies of variations in the personal equation with sense modality (vision, audition, touch, taste, smell, etc.), stimulus intensity, and other conditions were conducted.

Investigations of the personal equation by psychologists took the form of reaction time experiments, studies of so-called *mental chronometry*. These studies were concerned with determining the time required for various mental processes by application of a subtractive procedure. As described by the Dutch physiologist Frans Donders and illustrated in Fig. 1.1, the procedure involved the measurement of three different kinds of reaction time. To measure Donders' A (simple) reaction time, a single stimulus (S_1) is presented; the subject is told to make a specified response (R_1) to the stimulus as rapidly as possible. To measure Donders' B (choice) reaction time, one of two different stimuli (S_1 or S_2) is presented; the subject is told to make one specified response (R_1) to one of the stimuli (S_1) and another specified response (R_2) to the other stimulus (S_2). To measure Donders' C reaction time, one of two stimuli (S_1 or S_2) is presented; the subject is told to make a specified response (R_1) to only one of the stimuli (S_1) and ignore the other stimulus. After completing a number of trials using each of the three procedures, three mean reaction times—A, B, and C—are computed. Next three derived times are determined: baseline, identification, and selection. Reaction time A is referred to as *baseline time,* the difference between reaction time C and reaction time A is *identification time,* and the difference between reaction time B and reaction time C is *selection time.* These three times vary with the individual, the sense modality, and other conditions under which they are determined.[4]

Innumerable investigations employing Donders' procedure were conducted at Wilhelm Wundt's (1832–1920) Leipzig laboratory and elsewhere during the late 19th century to determine the time for certain mental events. Unfortunately, these studies, which also employed the method of introspection (a "looking into" one's mind and reporting on subjective impressions) failed to confirm the validity of Donders' method for this purpose. However, the Donders method and extensions of it are still widely employed. One extension is S. Sternberg's (1969) additive factors method, which breaks down total reaction time (RT) into a series of successive information-processing stages (also see Biederman & Kaplan, 1970).

---

[4]A computer program for measuring Donders' A, B, and C reaction times and then deriving baseline time, identification time, and selection time is available from the author. Send a self-addressed stamped mailer and 3¼ inch diskette to: Lewis R. Aiken, PhD, 12449 Mountain Trail Court, Moorpark, CA 93021.

$$S_1\text{----}\text{>}\text{----}R_1 \qquad S_1\text{----}\text{>}\text{----}R_1 \qquad S_1\text{----}\text{>}\text{----}R_1$$

$$S_2\text{----}\text{>}\text{----}R_2 \qquad S_2\text{----}\text{>}\text{----}X$$

(A) (B) (C)

FIG. 1.1.　Diagrams of Donders' Type A, B, and C RT experiments: S_1 and S_2 are Stimuli 1 and 2, R_1 and R_2 are Responses 1 and 2, and X is no response.

Sir Francis Galton

Psychology was formally established as a science in 1879, the year when Wundt founded the first psychological laboratory in the world in Leipzig, Germany. Rather than psychology being devoted to the study of individual differences, Wundt maintained that it should be concerned with the discovery of general facts and principles pertaining to the functioning of the normal, conscious, adult human mind. As a pure scientist, Wundt was concerned more with theory and the formulation of general psychological laws than with individual differences and applications. He viewed individual differences in RTs not as interesting in their own right, but simply as a source of error in experiments. When one of his most famous students, the American J. M. Cattell (1860–1944), announced to the "Herr Professor" (Wundt) that he wished to write his doctoral thesis on RT and its applications, Wundt reportedly remarked that it was *ganz Amerikanisch* (completely American). Other students of Wundt also conducted RT studies, but these were oriented toward the theoretical question of how long it takes mental events such as sensing, perceiving, feeling, attending, and association to occur. As noted previously, however, experiments using Donders' procedure were never very successful in answering this question.

After receiving his doctoral degree from Wundt, Cattell stopped over in England for a while to work with Sir Francis Galton (1822–1911) on the research Galton was conducting at the South Kensington Museum. Galton, a Victorian genius of wide-ranging interests and a cousin of the famous naturalist Charles Darwin, believed that all human characteristics—physical and mental—could be measured. Stimulated by Darwin's theory on the evolution of interspecies differences Galton became interested in intraspecies differences, and in investigating differences among people in particular. He attempted to apply the Darwinian evolutionary principles of accidental variation and selection of the fittest to human populations.

In his book, *Hereditary Genius* (1869/1962), Galton dealt at length with the genetic transmission of mental abilities and the relative contributions of heredity and environment to those characteristics. One of the proposals made in this volume was for studies of monozygotic and dizygotic twins to estimate the relative importance of nature and nurture in determining mental abilities. A finding from his studies of eminent men (that as the degree of genetic kinship increased, the percentage of eminent relatives also increased) led Galton (1874) to conclude that general mental ability (intelligence) is determined more by heredity than by environment. He subsequently applied the same research technique to 150 families from the British population. Another of Galton's (1883/1907) investigations was concerned with comparing different races of humanity in terms of their hereditary characteristics. The results of this study indicated that different races evolved by adapting to particular environments in which groups of people found themselves. As a result of his findings concerning the role of heredity in determining intelligence, Galton became an outspoken advocate of eugenics (i.e., improving the human species by discouraging the breeding of persons with genetic defects or undesirable inherited traits).

Among Galton's many methodological contributions are the *pedigree method* of investigating human abilities, the *method of correlation*, the *free association method*, and various psychometric instruments (questionnaires, rating scales, etc.) for measuring human characteristics. Also of importance to the study of individual differences is Galton's *law of filial regression*—that the physical and mental characteristics of offspring tend to be less extreme than those of their parents. According to this principle of regression toward the mean, measurements made on children tend to be closer to the mean than those made on their deviant parents. For example, very tall parents tend to have children who are shorter than they, and very short parents tend to have children who are taller than they.

Because of his extensive methodological and empirical research on individual differences, Galton is generally viewed as the father of quantitative and differential psychology. Following Darwin, he stressed the importance of individual differences in the behaviors and evolution of all animal species. Galton certainly had an influence on J. M. Cattell, who brought the former's tests and methods back to the United States and pursued his own research with them in this country. Through these efforts and his own research with Galton's mental tests, Cattell saw the field of individual differences become a part of scientific psychology.

Differential Psychology

By the end of the 19th century, psychology had become fairly well established as an empirical science. In addition to Cattell, pioneers such as G. Stanley Hall and William James had provided it with a solid foundation in the United States. In Austria, Sigmund Freud was establishing the theoretical groundwork and practice of psychoanalysis; in France, Alfred Binet was studying and theorizing about mental abilities. Binet and Henri's (1896) article on *la psychologie individuelle* (individual psychology) and William Stern's book *Über Psychologie der individuellen Differenzen: Ideen zu einer "differentielle Psychologie"* (On the Psychology of Individual Differ-

ences: Ideas on a "Differential Psychology")[5] described the goals, range, and methodology of differential psychology.

Binet and Henri (1896) examined many different tasks as potential measures of intelligence, including sensorimotor tests such as tactile discrimination and more complex tests such as recalling a series of digits, mental addition, suggestibility, and moral judgment. They even considered the possibility of using cranial capacity, lines in the palm, and handwriting as measures of intelligence. Binet and Henri also tentatively proposed 10 different mental functions of intelligence: memory, imagery, imagination, attention, comprehension, suggestibility, aesthetic appreciation, moral sentiments, muscular force (will power), and motor skill. This list, however, did not restrict their later, empirically based research on mental measurement. Rather than adhering to a particular theory of intelligence, Binet was a pragmatist who discarded ideas or procedures if they failed to work and readily turned to new possibilities.

Binet, Stern, and other people and events led to rapid developments in applied psychology during the early 20th century. Particularly noteworthy for the psychology of individual differences were advances in psychological testing, genetics, developmental psychology, and cross-cultural psychology, all of which contributed to the methods, concepts, and data of differential psychology.

PSYCHOLOGICAL TESTING

The formal assessment of human abilities goes back at least 4,000 years. Around 2000 B.C., the Mandarin rulers of China established a civil service testing program in that country. This system of examinations continued into the modern era and served as a model for selecting candidates for government jobs in the United States, Britain, France, and Germany during the 19th century. The expansion of public education and the rise of scientific psychology during the late 19th century were accompanied by an interest in developing a variety of measures of educational achievement, special abilities (aptitudes), and personality. Standardized tests of achievement in specific school subjects (spelling, arithmetic, language, handwriting, etc.) were devised, in addition to tests of intelligence, personal adjustment, personality characteristics, and vocational interests.

The test that gave the greatest impetus to the study of individual differences—the Binet–Simon Intelligence Scale—was published by Alfred Binet and his colleague Théodore Simon in 1905 and revised in 1908 and 1911. Adaptations and extensions of the Binet–Simon Scale in Britain, and Germany in particular, were administered in numerous investigations of demographic differences in mental abilities during the ensuing decades. Rather than being experiments, the vast majority of these investigations were correlational studies in which measures of relationship between test scores

---

[5]Later editions of this book, entitled *Die differentielle Psychologie in ihren methodischen Grundlagen* (Methodological Foundations of Differential Psychology; Stern, 1921/1911), formally established the field of differential psychology.

and demographic variables such as chronological age, gender, ethnicity, and nationality were computed. Following Galton's lead, a primary question concerned the extent to which the obtained relationships were due to genetic and environmental factors.

Many other individual and group-administered tests of intelligence were published and employed in research on individual and group differences in mental abilities during the first half of the 20th century. Among the pioneers in this enterprise were E. L. Thorndike, Frederic Kuhlmann, Lewis Terman, and Arthur Otis. In addition to measures of intelligence or general mental ability, studies of variations in specific abilities (aptitudes) from person to person and group to group were conducted. The development of specific aptitude tests was prompted in large measure by the practical problem of selecting the most productive workers for many of the newer technical jobs created by rapid industrialization. An overview of research on general and specific cognitive abilities is given in chapters 6 and 7.

Almost as widely administered as tests of intelligence and special abilities have been measures of adjustment and personality. Both objective and projective tests of personality were constructed and administered to large numbers of people throughout the world. Robert Woodworth is credited with constructing the first standardized personality inventory, and Hermann Rorschach devised the most popular projective test. Like tests of achievement, intelligence, and special abilities, these tests proved useful in counseling, selection, and other applied contexts, as well as in research in differential psychology.

The advent of inventories of vocational interests occurred somewhat later than the first standardized measures of personality. The first published inventories of vocational interests, which were constructed by E. K. Strong, Jr., and G. F. Kuder, were used primarily in vocational counseling and research on the development of interests.

A number of tests of perceptual and motor skills were also constructed, but they were not as popular as measures of intelligence, special aptitudes, personality, or interests. But the most widely administered of all standardized tests were and still are those designed to measure academic achievement. By the 1950s, the research literature on individual and group differences in cognitive, affective, and psychomotor characteristics was so extensive that Anne Anastasi (1958) had no difficulty filling the pages of her now classic volume, *Differential Psychology.*

Even more extensive than their uses in research are the applications of psychological and educational tests in educational, employment, and clinical contexts. Tests of educational achievement and performance are administered to evaluate the extent to which students have attained the objectives of instruction. Tests are also used in school situations to (a) determine a child's level of cognitive or perceptual development, (b) identify and diagnose problems of learning and adjustment, (c) select or place students in programs that are appropriate for them, and (d) evaluate educational programs and curricula. Particular attention is focused on educational diagnosis and planning for exceptional (special) children—mentally retarded, gifted and talented, physically handicapped, learning disabled, and emotionally disturbed. In industrial/organizational and military/government situations, tests are used for selection and placement purposes and to evaluate the effectiveness of training. In clinics and institutions for children and adults, psychological tests are used to identify or diagnose particular disorders and to plan treatments or other intervention procedures and evaluate their outcomes. The effectiveness of these applications of tests depends on the range of individual differences, as reflected by variations in test scores both within and between persons. Comprehensive descriptions of the uses of tests in various applied contexts are provided by Aiken (1995, 1997a, 1997b, 1998) and Anastasi and Urbina (1997).

OTHER DEVELOPMENTS

For older adults who have lived most of their lives during the 20th century, the scientific achievements and improvements in the welfare of the general population have been truly awesome. In many ways, however, the changes that occurred during the 19th century—in production, public health, transportation, communication, and overall living conditions—were even more impressive. These changes were accompanied by a rapid growth of the population and a need for both public and private organizations to keep account of people and their characteristics, possessions, attitudes, and comings and goings.

Demography

Psychology was not the only discipline that contributed to the growth of interest in research on individual differences. Rapid expansion of the populations of European countries, combined with growing nationalism, during the 19th century brought with it an increased need for keeping track of the population and its characteristics. Censuses of populations had, of course, been conducted since Biblical times, but the descriptive analysis of census data was placed on a more scientific footing in the 19th century. This was the science of *demography*, which is concerned with examining structural (distributions by age, sex, marital status, etc.) and dynamic (births, deaths, crime, migration patterns, etc.) factors in human populations. The efforts of Adolphe Quetelet, Benjamin Gompertz, and others led to the establishment of some of the first databases for scientific studies of populations—the civil registries of births, deaths, marriages, and other demographic events. These civil registries had a number of practical consequences as well, among which was the growth of insurance companies. Most nations now have a bureau of demography or a health statistics department that conducts surveys and prepares reports on vital statistics and other data pertaining to the national population. For example, the National Center for Health Statistics of the U.S. Department of Health and Human Services collects nationwide data on births, marriages, divorces, and deaths by chronological age, gender, ethnicity, and geographical region and publishes summaries of the findings in the *Monthly Vital Statistics Report.* Similar data for the entire world, by country and as a whole, are compiled by the Statistical Office of the United Nations (see Table 1.1).

Statistics

Research on individual differences and most other matters of concern to social scientists is facilitated by descriptive statistical procedures of the sort used by demographers. However, the development of inferential statistical procedures, which permit making probabilistic inferences from samples to populations, substantially increased the power of the statistical approach. These procedures allow scientists to collect data on relatively small samples

TABLE 1.1
Some International Superlatives

Country	Highest or Largest
China	Population (1.24 billion)
Finland, Italy, Sweden	Percentage of population 65+ years (17%)
Gaza	Rate of population increase (4.6%)
Gaza, Niger	Total fertility rate (7.4 per 1,000 women ages 15–49)
Japan, Macao	Life expectancy at birth (80 years)
Kuwait, Singapore	Percentage of urban residents (100%)
Libya	Percentage of population under 15 years old (50%)
Luxembourg	Per capita annual Gross National Product (45,360 US$)
Macao	Population density (59,700 per sq. mile)
Niger	Number of births per 1,000 population (53) Percentage of women ages 15–19 giving birth (23%)
Russia	Land area (6,520,656 sq. miles)
Sierra Leone	Deaths per 1,000 population (30)
	Infant mortality rate (195 per 1,000 live births)
Slovenia	Percentage of married women using all methods of contraception (92%)

Source. From data compiled by Population Reference Bureau (1998).

of individuals and generalize the results to larger populations of which those samples are a part. Methods developed by pioneer statisticians such as Karl Pearson and R. A. Fisher have been employed extensively in correlational and experimental studies conducted in both the natural and social sciences. These methods are reviewed in some detail in chapter 2.

Social Problems

During the 19th century, increased social and political attention to the welfare of the individual in society led to a variety of sociological studies of populations. The reform movement of the late 19th and early 20th centuries encouraged social surveys of cities and communities with the objective of instituting reforms. Among the problems emphasized by these surveys were low wages, poor housing, inadequate public health facilities, and unsafe working conditions for the laboring classes (Hoover, 1993).

Although the melting pot concept of assimilating people of different nationalities, races, and religions into a democratically based, harmonious whole served as a sociopolitical credo in the United States and certain other countries, social problems associated with group differences persisted.[6] Scientific studies of these social problems and ways of dealing with them were conducted and led to new disciplines.

One social problem, the exploitation of children in the workplace and other walks of life, received attention from both sociologists and psychologists. Prior to the 19th century, little differentiation had been made between children and adults in terms of the behaviors expected of them or how they were treated. Young children were often dressed in the same type of clothing as adults and were required to assume the responsibilities of adulthood at a fairly early age. If they strayed from the straight and narrow, they were punished in much the same way as adults who had committed similar crimes.

Increasing concern with the health, education, and welfare of children during the late 19th century—a concern stimulated by writers and social reformers—led to legislation and public programs regarding the treatment of children. Associated with this child welfare movement was the new discipline of developmental psychology. Developmental psychologists conducted scientific studies of the physical, cognitive, emotional, and social characteristics of children. At first developmental research was concentrated on infancy and early childhood, but three chronological age groups—childhood, adolescence, and old age—were subsequently identified for special attention.

Problems associated with social class, ethnicity, gender, and religious differences were present long before the civil rights movement of the 1960s. However, concerted action with respect to these problems during the

---

[6]In recent years, the melting pot concept has been replaced in Canada by the perhaps more realistic notion of society as a mosaic consisting of different racial, cultural, and religious groups that retain their unique identities while living in peaceful coexistence with the larger society and simultaneously contributing to and benefiting from it (Moghaddam, Taylor, & Wright, 1993).

1950s and 1960s prompted legislation related to equal treatment of minority groups and women in employment, educational, and other social contexts. An important consequence of these legislative actions was an upsurge of research on gender and race in particular. An undercurrent in many of these studies was the nature–nurture controversy and the related question of the receptivity to change of behaviors associated with group differences.

Professionalism

The professionalization of research and practice in any area of human endeavor is signaled by the formal establishment of a professional association and professional publications of various kinds. Research on individual differences is currently conducted primarily by psychologists, the two largest organizations of which are the American Psychological Association (APA) and the American Psychological Society (APS). Each of these organizations has an extensive publication program, but the official journals of the APA and APS are *The American Psychologist* and *Psychological Science,* respectively.

Oriented specifically toward research on individual differences is the International Society for the Study of Individual Differences (ISSID).

> The purpose of this Society is to foster research on individual differences in temperament, intelligence, attitudes, and abilities. The aim of the Society is to investigate the major dimensions of individual differences in the context of experimental, physiological, pharmacological, clinical, medical, genetical, statistical and social psychology, and to seek the determinants, causes, and concomitants of individual differences, using concepts derived from these disciplines. To promote this purpose, the Society produces scientific papers and organizes scientific meetings to discuss and exchange information and ideas relevant to the measurement, structure, dynamics, and biological bases of individual differences. (The International Society for the Study of Individual Differences, 1997, p. iii)

The official journal of the ISSID is *Personality and Individual Differences.* Some of the other psychological journals that publish research articles on individual differences are listed in Table 1.2. Many journals in sociology, statistics, biology, chemistry, and other sciences also publish methodological and substantive articles concerned with individual differences.

SUMMARY

Individual differences in physical structure and functioning are present from birth, and many of those differences become more pronounced with maturation and development. Exposure to different environmental conditions, both physical and cultural, may increase the distinctions between individuals and groups. However, social pressures for conformity, in addition to similar living conditions, contribute to a certain sameness in behavior and appearance.

Concern with the freedom of individuals to express themselves and fulfill their own potentials received attention in ancient Greece from philoso-

TABLE 1.2

Some of the Professional Journals Publishing Research on Individual
and Group Differences

American Psychologist
Applied Cognitive Psychology
Child Development
Developmental Psychobiology
Developmental Psychology
Educational Psychologist
Educational Psychology
Intelligence
Journal of Abnormal Psychology
Journal of Consulting and Clinical Psychology
Journal of Counseling Psychology
Journal of Cross-Cultural Psychology
Journal of Educational Psychology
Journal of Personality
Journal of Personality and Social Psychology
Journal of Personality Assessment
Journal of Research in Personality
Journal of Social Psychology
Journal of Sport Psychology
Journal of Sports Medicine and Physical Fitness
Learning and Individual Differences
Neuropsychology
Perceptual and Motor Skills
Personality and Individual Differences
Personality and Social Psychology Bulletin
Psychological Bulletin
Psychology of Women Quarterly
Sex Roles
Social Behavior and Personality

phers such as Plato and Aristotle. During the Middle Ages, however, duty toward the church and state was the dominant social philosophy. Beginning
about the 16th century in Europe, progress in technology, science, medicine, and general living conditions was accompanied by a reawakening of
individualism.

Although 19th-century science was primarily concerned with determining
general laws that apply to all physical and biological events, individual differences in the time required to respond to a stimulus led astronomers to study

the personal equation and so-called *mental chronometry*. This research was continued by scientific psychologists during the late 19th century. Two men who helped establish psychology as a legitimate scientific enterprise were Wilhelm Wundt and Sir Francis Galton. Wundt, who founded the first psychological laboratory in the world, was the father of experimental psychology. Galton, who devised many mental tests and methods for studying individual differences, was the father of quantitative and differential psychology.

During the latter part of the 19th and early 20th centuries, standardized psychological and educational tests were constructed in growing numbers for uses in schools, clinics, business and industry, and military and government service. Achievement tests, intelligence tests, and personality tests, in particular, were designed for purposes of evaluation, selection, diagnosis, and counseling. In addition to their practical uses, such tests served as criterion measures in research studies on individual and group differences.

Studies of individual differences have been conducted mainly by psychologists, but demographers, statisticians, sociologists, and biologists have also made methodological and substantive contributions to the field. Increased social concern with the rights of children, older adults, women, and minorities has also led to a multiplicity of investigations on individual and group differences during the 20th century.

SUGGESTED READINGS

Anastasi, A. (1982). *Contributions to differential psychology*. New York: Praeger.

Boring, E. G. (1950). *History of experimental psychology*. New York: Appleton-Century-Crofts.

Bowman, M. L. (1989). Testing individual differences in Ancient China. *American Psychologist, 44,* 576–578.

Breslin, F. D. (1994). Individual differences. In R. J. Corsini (Ed.), *Encyclopedia of psychology* (2nd ed., Vol. 2, pp. 196–197). New York: Wiley.

Darwin, C., Richards, R. J., Galton, F., & Diamond, S. (1997). Darwinian influences: Adaptation and individual differences. In L. T. Benjamin, Jr. (Ed.), *A history of psychology: Original sources and contemporary research* (2nd ed., pp. 203–239). New York: McGraw-Hill.

Diamond, S. (1988). Francis Galton and American psychology. In L. T. Benjamin, Jr. (Ed.), *A history of psychology: Original sources and contemporary research* (pp. 261–269). New York: McGraw-Hill.

Kimble, G. A., Wertheimer, M., & White, C. (Eds.). (1991). *Portraits of pioneers in psychology*. Hillsdale, NJ: Lawrence Erlbaum Associates.

Kreppner, K. (1992). William L. Stern, 1871–1938: A neglected founder of developmental psychology. *Developmental Psychology, 28*(4), 519–547.

Stern, R. M. (1994). Differential psychology. In R. J. Corsini (Ed.), *Encyclopedia of psychology* (2nd ed., Vol. 2, pp. 374–378). New York: Wiley.

Wolf, T. H. (1973). *Alfred Binet*. Chicago: University of Chicago Press.

CHAPTER TWO

Measurement and Research Methods

As implied by the term, *research* is a process of repeated searching for information to answer questions or solve problems. Research may be exploratory or confirmatory, and theoretical (pure) or applied. *Exploratory research* is usually conducted when the domain of interest is not well understood and the investigator is merely curious to see if anything interesting happens when various procedures or manipulations are applied. In contrast, *confirmatory research* is a more formal, systematic process of testing scientific hypotheses so they can be either confirmed or disconfirmed. Whether exploratory or confirmatory, research is often conducted to solve some immediate practical problem, in which case it is referred to as *applied research*. Research may also be conducted with no immediate practical application in mind, but rather as an effort to understand nature and the relationships among events. Such research is designated as *theoretical* or *pure*.

Research on human behavior can be and is conducted almost anywhere—in the home, school, clinic, place of business, the street, or wherever people congregate and interact. A distinction is usually made between laboratory research and field research. Conducting research in a laboratory setting typically permits tighter control over conditions. Consequently, the results tend to be freer from the effects of extraneous variables or errors of measurement than research conducted in more real-life settings. Such research is said to possess high internal validity. However, because of the artificiality of the environment in which it is conducted, the results of laboratory research are often less generalizable to real-life situations than those obtained in field situations. For this reason, field research is said to possess greater external validity than laboratory-based research.

The internal validity of field research is not invariably lower than that of laboratory-based investigations. It is possible, although admittedly more difficult, to conduct highly controlled experiments in the field and hence obtain results with acceptable internal validity. It is also possible for the results of laboratory investigations to be generalizable to real-life situations (i.e., to possess high external validity). This is more likely to occur when the research task is realistic (it possesses mundane reality), individuals are selected at random from the target population, and the effects of the independent variable are quite strong and relatively unaffected by the particular situation or environment in which they are expressed.

In some ways, research on human behavior is more difficult than research in the physical sciences. Behavior is complex, and the instruments designed to measure it are not nearly as accurate and the theories of behavior are not as good as those in physics, chemistry, and biology. However, the very openness and lower technical level of research in the behavioral sciences is reassuring to students who want to understand people but react negatively to the complicated instrumentation and quantitative methodology of much scientific research. Almost all students can be taught to be better observers and to take a questioning, patient, and systematic attitude and approach to natural phenomena such as human actions and cognitions. In short, students can become scientists as well as practitioners in their interactions and dealings with other people and perhaps even make significant contributions to the understanding of individual differences in the ways in which people behave and think.

This chapter is an overview of the various methods and procedures employed in research on individual and group differences. It considers various research methods and designs and the statistical techniques that are most often used in conjunction with them. Although attention to the statistical procedures to be used in the analysis of data should be given in the overall design of a research investigation, research design is actually a separate issue from the choice of an appropriate statistical procedure. Certain statistical procedures are used more often in connection with particular methods or designs, but, depending on the nature of the research questions and hypotheses and the type of data generated, more than one statistical procedure may be appropriate. The appropriateness of both the research design and the statistical analysis depend on the questions that need to be answered or, more formally, the hypotheses to be tested. In addition, the design and analysis of a research investigation depend on the nature of the variables and how they are defined and measured.

VARIABLES AND MEASUREMENT

According to tradition in psychological assessment, anything that exists at all exists in some amount and consequently can be measured. The heart and soul of measurement, not merely in the behavioral sciences but in all scientific disciplines, are variables. *Variables* are static or dynamic properties of objects or events; unlike constants, they have more than one value. Certain variables are *discrete* (i.e., their values are discontinuous or detached from each other). Examples are categorical variables such as sex (male, female), race (African American, White, etc.), and social class (working, middle, upper). Other variables are *continuous* (i.e., at least in theory, measurable to any desired level of accuracy). Examples of continuous physical variables are height and weight, which, depending on the accuracy of the measuring instruments, can be measured as finely as one wishes. Certain psychological measurements, such as scores on tests of cognitive abilities or inventories of personality, are actually discrete but often treated for purposes of analysis as if they were continuous.

Constructs

In addition to being discrete or continuous, a variable may be either directly observable (concrete) or unobservable (abstract). Abstract variables such as anxiety, depression, or achievement motivation, which are measured indirectly, are referred to as *constructs*. Psychological constructs may be purely hypothetical and not directly connected with observables but definable only in terms of other concepts. In the most effective science-making, abstract constructs are ultimately tied to observable objects or events. To reduce the ambiguity of certain constructs (e.g., anxiety, hunger, etc.) and make psychological theories and research more publicly communicable and interpretable, behaviorally oriented psychologists in particular have emphasized the importance of defining constructs operationally. An *operational definition* of a construct is a precise statement of what to do (i.e., what operations to perform) to experience the construct. Most operational definitions of constructs such as intelligence are objective statements of the procedures used in measuring the construct.

Theories

Constructs play an important role in the theoretical conceptualization of a research domain. Most psychological theories consist of multiple constructs and specifications of their interrelationships. *Theories* are systematic, organized sets of explanations of why specified events take place. In psychology these events consist of the behaviors and cognitions of people or other animals. By providing a condensed description of such events, a good theory serves as a kind of scientific shorthand that encapsulates and explains the results of numerous observations. By means of an interlocking set of assumptions, combined with logical reasoning, a good theory enables a scientist to make predictions about future events. These predictions can then be confirmed or disconfirmed by research.

Good theories are parsimonious, precise, testable, and heuristic. They are *parsimonious* in that they employ only a few concepts. They are *precise* in that the predictions made from them are accurate. They are *testable* in that they can be confirmed or disconfirmed. They are *heuristic* in that they can assist in the formulation of interesting scientific questions and prompt suggestions concerning the answers. A good theory of human behavior, for example, summarizes available data concerning the origins, development, dynamics, and disorders of behavior in an accurate, efficient, and fruitful manner and can be applied in a variety of ways to answer questions and solve practical problems concerning behavior and cognitive processes.

Compared with theories in biology, chemistry, and physics, psychological theories of behavior, cognition, and personality are not very accurate or precise in the explanations they provide or the predictions made from them. Rather than being comprehensive conceptions of certain aspects of the natural world, as is the theory of evolution or the theory of relativity, most psychological theories are better viewed as microtheories or pretheories that serve as possible guides to understanding a limited domain but are a long way from detailed maps. Nevertheless, propositions of the sort provided by psychoanalytic theory, reinforcement theory, self-theory, trait theory, and information theory have provided assistance in generating hypotheses and interpretations about psychological phenomena. In addition, findings stemming from research in neurophysiology, biochemistry, and computer technology are laying the groundwork for theories of cognition and personality. These will undoubtedly replace older, more purely psychological explanations, which have their roots less in the laboratory than in the arm chairs of yesteryear's philosophers (see Loevinger, 1996).

Descriptive and Explanatory Research

A psychological research investigation is often concerned with many different constructs or at least their overt representations in the form of variables. The values assigned to the variables in research are observed, related to the corresponding values of other variables, and often directly manipulated to determine their effects. Research may be purely *descriptive,* in which case the investigator merely makes observations of some phenomenon and records or catalogs the results of those observations. More powerful, and potentially more useful, however, is *explanatory research,* in which the goal is to clarify one's understanding of some phenomenon and the conditions under which it takes place. Understanding leads to better prediction and control, which are valuable consequences of explanatory research studies.

Independent and Dependent Variables

In explanatory research, a distinction is made among independent variables, dependent variables, and extraneous variables. Strictly speaking, the terms *independent variable* and *dependent variable* should be reserved for the variables in an experiment, in which the effects of an independent variable (or cause) on a dependent variable (or effect) are being examined. The independent variable is manipulated, extraneous variables that interfere with a clear understanding of the results are controlled, and the effects of changes in the independent variable on changes in the dependent variable are determined.[1] The terms *independent* and *dependent variable* are

---

[1]Independent and dependent variables are also commonly designated as the X and Y variables, respectively. This refers to the fact that they are usually scaled on the horizontal (X) and vertical (Y) axes, respectively, of a graph depicting the functional relationship between them.

also used, somewhat loosely, to refer to the variables in correlational studies, surveys, and developmental investigations. For example, in a study of sex differences in mathematical abilities, biological gender (male vs. female) may be referred to as the independent variable and scores on a test of mathematical ability as the dependent variable. Clearly, however, sex per se is not a cause of mathematical ability but only a correlate or concomitant of some other causal factor.

The independent variables in behavioral science research are typically situations, or stimuli, and the dependent variables are responses of some kind. In this case, the aim of the research investigation is to determine the relationships between the stimuli and the responses. The stimulus variables in research studies include the type of task to be performed, the situations or conditions in which they are performed, and the characteristics of those who are doing the performing. The characteristics of individuals who participate in research studies are referred to as *subject variables, person variables,* or *organismic variables.*

The effects of several person, situation, and task variables may be of interest in a multivariate investigation. Furthermore, many of these variables may be accompanied by other, *confounded variables* that disrupt a clear understanding of the relationships between the independent and dependent variables. To take a simple example, suppose that we are interested in comparing the test scores of two classes of students meeting at two different times of day and the tests are administered by two different teachers. In this case, teacher differences are confounded with the independent variable (time of day), therefore a significant difference between the test scores of the two classes may be due to the former rather than the latter variable. There is, of course, another obvious source of error in this study: If the students were not randomly assigned to the two classes, differences in their test scores may be due to initial differences between the two groups rather than the time of day or differences between teachers. As with other extraneous variables, confounded variables must be controlled if one is to obtain a true picture of the relationships between independent and dependent variables in a research investigation.

Other designations for variables in both experimental and correlational research studies are intervening variables and moderator variables. *Intervening variables* intervene between stimuli and responses and affect the extent to which the responses are predictable from or caused by particular stimuli. An example of an intervening variable in a learning context is motivation. In general, a person's cognitive ability (independent variable) has an effect on the efficiency with which he or she learns (dependent variable). However, the ease of learning and its amount are also influenced by the person's motivation to learn the assigned material or skill. Similar to intervening variables are *moderator variables*, which moderate the relationship between independent and dependent variables. For example, personality variables such as compulsivity or obedience can affect the relationship between cognitive ability and performance. However, that relationship may be lower for compulsive or obedient learners than for noncompulsive or nonobedient learners. In other words, the degree of compulsivity or obedience can have a moderating influence on the correlation between ability and performance.

Levels of Measurement

Not all variables or attributes of objects or events are measurable in the sense of being assigned numerical values to designate their quantity or quality. The status or categories of certain attributes of things are designated by nonnumerical, descriptive labels. However, it can be argued that these descriptive labels constitute a crude form of measurement. Of course, it is not measurement in the strict scientific sense, according to which variables are scaled on a numerical continuum. In the behavioral sciences, this *nominal* level of measurement, in which the numbers represent arbitrary labels or categories, is considered to be the lowest level of measurement. For example, in the first panel in Fig. 2.1, three players on an athletic team—Bob, Meg, and Jim—are assigned the numbers 1, 2, and 3. A player's number is not a measure of how well he or she plays the game but merely another way to identify players and keep track of their performance. Demographic variables such as sex, race, geographical region, and serial numbers or identification codes of all kinds (social security numbers, driver's license numbers, etc.) are other examples of nominal numbers. The nominal number designations of a large group of people can be grouped into a frequency distribution or plotted on a corresponding bar graph. However, because nominal numbers do not represent magnitudes of anything, only a few statistics—modes, ranges, etc.—can be computed on them.

Somewhat higher than nominal numbers on the measurement hierarchy are *ordinal* numbers, or rank orders, on some scale of merit. As illustrated in the second panel of Fig. 2.1, Bob finished first, Meg second, and Jim third in some contest. Ordinal numbers such as first (1st), second (2nd), and third (3rd) represent a fairly crude form of measurement in that equal differences between the numbers do not correspond to equal differences in the attribute being measured. Thus, like nominal numbers, ordinal numbers cannot be added, subtracted, multiplied, or divided in any meaningful way. It is appropriate to compute statistics such as medians, percentiles, and quartiles and to conduct various nonparametric tests of significance on ordinal numbers, but there are definite limits in what can be done with such numbers from a statistical viewpoint.

At the next level on the measurement hierarchy are *interval* numbers. Although an interval (or equal-interval) scale has no true zero, equal numerical differences correspond to equal differences in whatever variable or attribute is being measured. The most popular examples of interval scales are the Celsius or Fahrenheit scales of temperature. The equal-interval property of such scales is seen in the fact that the difference between a temperature of 60 and a temperature of 40 is, in the sense of being the same difference in heating, equal to the difference between a temperature of 40 and a temperature of 20. Likewise, on the deviation IQ scale represented in the third panel of Fig. 2.1, the difference in intelligence between Bob (150) and

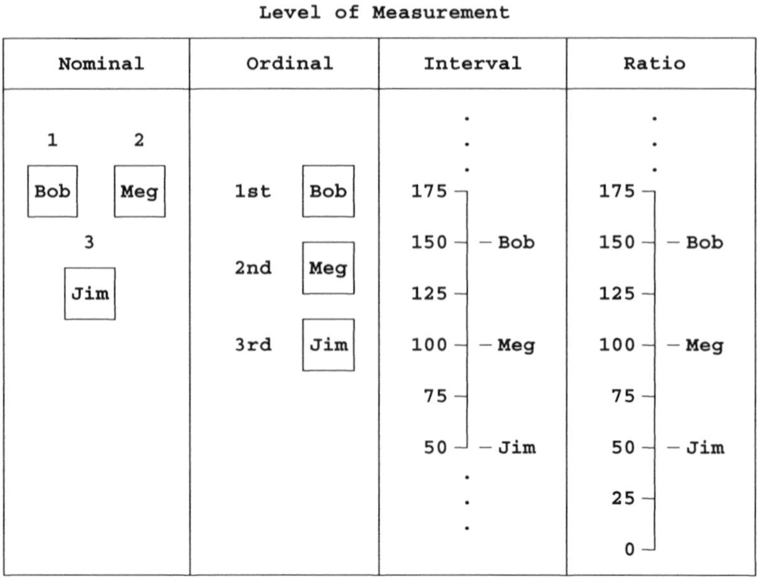

Level of Measurement

Nominal	Ordinal	Interval	Ratio
1 2 [Bob] [Meg] 3 [Jim]	1st [Bob] 2nd [Meg] 3rd [Jim]	· · · 175 ⌐ 150 ⊣ — Bob 125 ⊣ 100 ⊣ — Meg 75 ⊣ 50 ⌐ — Jim · · ·	· · · 175 ⌐ 150 ⊣ — Bob 125 ⊣ 100 ⊣ — Meg 75 ⊣ 50 ⊣ — Jim 25 ⊣ 0 ⌐

FIG. 2.1.   Four levels of measurement.

Meg (100) is equal to the difference in intelligence between Meg (100) and Jim (50). Almost all statistical computations can be performed on interval-level numbers, and such numbers represent the highest level of measurement attainable with most psychological variables.

At the *ratio* level of measurement, the highest level of all, not only do equal numerical differences imply equal differences in the attribute being measured, but equal numerical ratios also correspond to equal ratios of the attribute. This equal ratio property is a consequence of the true zero on a ratio scale, indicating an absolutely zero amount of the variable. Ratio-level measurement is most common in the natural sciences, as represented in physical measurements of distance, mass, energy, and the like. If it were possible to devise an instrument to measure a psychological variable such as intelligence at a ratio level, as depicted in the fourth panel of Fig. 2.1, we could conclude the following: Not only is the difference in intelligence between Bob and Meg equal to the difference in intelligence between Meg and Jim, but Bob is three times as intelligent as Jim, and Meg is twice as intelligent as Jim and two thirds as intelligent as Bob. All statistical procedures can be performed on numbers at a ratio level. Furthermore, any statistical procedure that can be performed on numbers at a lower level of measurement can also be performed on numbers at a higher measurement level.

Psychometric Instruments

The variables in investigations of individual and group differences are measured in a variety of ways—not only by what the participants say or do but also by their physical and physiological state and what other people say about them. Psychological data are obtained from observations of behavior, interviews, and measurements of physical structure and functioning. Among the physiological measures are muscle tension, skin resistance, heartbeat, blood pressure and volume, respiration rate, response time, and indicators of brain functioning and blood composition. However, the most popular measures of behavior and mental processes are psychological tests, questionnaires, inventories, rating scales, checklists, and projective techniques. These psychometric instruments may be administered and responded to in written form, orally, or by computer; in the case of nontest instruments, they must be completed either by the participants or other people who are acquainted with them. The instruments may measure achievement, general cognitive ability (intelligence), special abilities, personality traits, attitudes, opinions, values, and vocational interests, or they may simply provide demographic or identifying data on the participants.

Traditionally, psychological tests have been constructed primarily to evaluate individual differences in cognitive abilities and personality traits. People obviously differ from each other in their abilities and personality, and psychologists have attempted to measure these differences by means of various types of tests and other psychometric devices. When the differences between the scores of individuals and groups are large enough, the test scores may be used to predict and explain the behaviors of people.

Detailed descriptions of psychometric measures obtained in studies of individual differences are described in several books by the author (Aiken, 1996b, 1997a, 1997b, 1997c, 1998). Of the various instruments discussed in these volumes, those designed to assess cognitive abilities and personality characteristics are the most commonly employed in research on individual differences. Tests of general and special abilities, personality inventories, and ratings of personality and behavior, in particular, have served as dependent variables in thousands of research investigations during the past century. Many of these instruments have been standardized and published, whereas others are nonstandardized, ad hoc devices constructed by researchers for specific investigations and never made commercially available.

A list of 22 of the most popular psychometric instruments is given in Table 2.1. Some of these instruments are administered individually (i.e., to one person at a time), whereas others can be administered simultaneously to any number of people. Many published psychometric instruments have been standardized, yielding *norms*—grade, age, percentile, standard score—for comparing and interpreting the raw scores. However, the norms are often unrepresentative of the population corresponding to the sample of people who are examined in a particular investigation.

In addition to determining whether the norms for a psychometric instrument are representative, care should be taken not to be misled by the name of the instrument. Tests with the same name do not necessarily measure the

TABLE 2.1

Most Frequently Used Psychometric Instruments in Individual Differences Research

Adjective Check List
Basic Personality Inventory
Bem Sex-Role Inventory
Differential Aptitude Tests
Eysenck Personality Inventory
Eysenck Personality Questionnaire
Jackson Personality Inventory
McCarthy Scales of Children's Abilities
Millon Clinical Multiaxial Inventory
Millon Index of Personality Styles
Minnesota Multiphasic Personality Inventory
Myers–Briggs Type Indicator
NEO Personality Inventory
Primary Mental Abilities Test
Rorschach Inkblot Test
16 Personality Factor Questionnaire
Stanford–Binet Intelligence Scale
Strong Interest Inventory (all forms)
Thematic Apperception Test
Trait–State Anxiety Inventory
Wechsler Adult Intelligence Scale (all editions)
Wechsler Intelligence Scale for Children (all editions)

same variable (*jingle fallacy*), and those having different names do not necessarily measure different variables (*jangle fallacy*). Furthermore, researchers need to make certain that the selected instrument has enough range for the purposes of their investigation—both at the high and low ends on the scale. An instrument with a low ceiling or a high floor may not be an accurate measure of the dependent variable and hence fail to reveal the true effects of the independent variable (floor and ceiling effects).

Validity and Reliability

Selection or construction of a psychometric instrument for a particular research purpose requires a clear description and definition of the individual difference variables to be measured. Then an instrument is selected or constructed that matches the description. In addition to such content validity information, evidence for the criterion-related and construct validities of the instrument is important. *Criterion-related validity,* which is of most interest on aptitude tests, is concerned with the extent to which scores on a psychometric instrument are correlated with performance criteria that are conceptually relevant to the variables that the instrument was designed to measure. These criterion measures may be obtained at the same time (*concurrent* or *congruent validity*) or at some time in the future (*predictive validity*). Even more important for an understanding of the variables or constructs in research on individual differences is evidence for the *construct validity* of a psychometric instrument. This is obtained from a network of demonstrations that the instrument actually measures the construct of interest.

One source of evidence for construct validity is a *multitrait-multimethod matrix* of correlations between scores on instruments designed to measure the same construct by the same and different methods as well as scores on different constructs measured by the same and different methods. By inspecting the correlation coefficients in such a matrix, it can be concluded that the instrument has good construct validity if it has (a) high correlations with other instruments designed to measure the same construct, by both the same and different methods (*convergent validity*); and (b) low correlations with instruments designed to measure different constructs by both the same and different methods (*discriminant validity*). Additional evidence for the construct validity of a psychometric instrument is obtained from demonstrations that high and low scorers on the instrument behave in ways that high and low scorers are expected to behave according to theoretical predictions. Finally, an analysis of the composition of the instrument, by means of systematic inspection of its content as well as statistical analyses of the relationships among its parts, can provide information relevant to construct validity.

In addition to the validity of the selected or constructed instrument for the purposes of an investigation, some attention must be given to the extent to which the scores are free from errors of measurement. This is a question of the *reliability* of the instrument for its intended purposes and to whom and in what situations it is to be administered. Traditionally, psychological tests were designed to differentiate among people who possessed different amounts of a specified ability or personality trait. The greater the range of individual differences in scores on the test, the higher its reliability. More heterogeneous and, consequently, more reliable tests tended to have higher correlations with other measures of the characteristic being measured. Therefore, they were more accurate predictors of behaviors of which the characteristic formed a part.

Information on the reliability of a psychometric instrument can be obtained in various ways: (a) administering the instrument to the same persons on two separate occasions (*test–retest reliability*), (b) administering equivalent (parallel) forms of the instrument to the same individuals (*parallel forms reliability*), and (c) a statistical analysis of the extent to which scores on the various items comprising the instrument are measures of the same variable (*internal consistency reliability*).

As important as it may be for a psychometric instrument to be reliable, reliability does not guarantee validity. A test or any other psychometric device may be reliable without being valid, but it cannot be valid unless it is reliable. It is also important to stress that reliability and validity are not general properties of a psychometric instrument, but rather they vary with the sample of persons and the context in which an instrument is administered. Thus, a test may be reliable and/or valid with some individuals and in some situations but not in others.

RESEARCH METHODS

The purpose of a research investigation is to obtain valid information to answer questions or test hypotheses. Research information in the behavioral sciences is collected in many different ways—by observing, interviewing, surveying, and experimenting, to name some of the most popular approaches. Of the various research methods, observation—whether formal or informal, controlled—is the most basic.

Observation

Observations of human behavior consist of looking at, listening to, or in other ways attending to and recording what people say and do. Much of our information concerning human behavior and our ability to anticipate what other people will say or do is based on informal observations. In more professional clinical contexts, observations of the verbal and nonverbal behaviors of people in psychodiagnostic and psychotherapeutic situations form the bases of many personality theories. Most of these observations are informal, unplanned, and uncontrolled. They take place in naturalistic or field contexts and frequently involve situations in which the observer is a participant. One simply notes the behavior of people as it occurs, with no attempt to control who or what is being observed or the conditions under which it takes place. Despite the fact that these everyday observations are uncontrolled and, for the most part, not very objective, most people make some attempt to be objective in their perceptions of behavior. These perceptions are colored by the past experiences, expectations, and sensory limitations of the observer, but some degree of logical questioning is usually involved in interpreting and evaluating them.

Whether conducted for personal, clinical, or research purposes, observations can be made more objective by separating what is observed from the interpretation placed on it. For example, this should be done in an anecdotal record of a child's behavior kept by a parent, teacher, or health worker and certainly by a researcher. The objectivity of observations can also be enhanced by clearly communicating to the observers what they are supposed to look for and training them in the use of formal methods of recording their observations (e.g., rating scales or checklists). Objectivity of observations is typically greater if the situation in which they are made is structured or controlled, as in staging an encounter or interaction between two people. It is also best to record observations immediately and electronically for later review and reevaluation.

Observational methods are used extensively in psychological research and practice. Reports of case studies and counseling/psychotherapy sessions are replete with notes on observations of the behavior of examinees, clients, or patients. Observations of what people say and do during an interview are also recorded, evaluated, and compared with information obtained from other sources.

Interviews

Like most observations, the majority of interviews are fairly informal and unstructured. There is no finite set of prepared questions to be asked, but rather the interviewer simply interacts with the interviewee, letting the conversation go where it may. However, applicants for employment, clinical or educational admissions, or training are typically asked a series of preplanned questions concerning their background experiences, current situation, and perhaps their attitudes and aspirations. Likewise, when conducted for research purposes, there is some direction and structure in an interview. The prepared questions and interviewing guide are sometimes deviated from, but in the interest of efficiency and objectivity an effort is made to obtain clear and complete answers to the questions. Frequently, the questions presented in either an applied or research context are answered in writing, as on an application blank or pre-intake form. Such written answers to questionnaire items are also quite common in mail surveys.

Surveys

The questions on a survey form may be asked in person or over the telephone, but more often respondents fill out a questionnaire that has been given to them in person or mailed. Designing a survey to elicit true, relevant, and complete information is not an easy task and typically requires many hours of careful design, pretesting, and redesign (Aiken, 1997c). However, a well-designed questionnaire administered to a large sample of individuals who are representative of a specified population can provide a great deal of demographic, background, and opinion information in an efficient manner. Understandably, the validity of the results of a survey depends on the clarity of the questions, the motivation of the respondents to answer the questions conscientiously and return the completed questionnaires promptly, and the extent to which the returns are representative of those that would have been obtained if the entire target population had responded. When the percentage of returns is large, an analysis of the relationships between responses to the demographic and personal opinion questions can yield a great deal of information concerning individual and group differences.

Planned observations, interviews, and surveys may be used in either prospective (forward-looking) or retrospective (backward-looking) research studies. For example, in *prospective* epidemiological studies, health researchers follow up people who have certain symptoms or characteristics and those who do not have them to determine which individuals subsequently develop a certain disease or disorder. Alternatively, a researcher may begin by identifying a group that has a certain condition and another group that does not have it and then examine their personal histories to identify precursors of the condition. This is referred to as a *retrospective study*. In most cases, retrospective studies are viewed as less desirable though obviously less costly and time-consuming than prospective studies.

Archival research, in which archives or repositories containing large amounts of data on activities and events that occurred in previous times are examined, is a type of research that is sometimes conducted to study individual and group differences. Archives are also consulted in biographical studies designed to isolate the events and experiences that influenced the lives of individuals. This approach, which is referred to as *psychohistory* or *psychobiography* (Wrightsman, 1994) and is typically based on a psychodynamic theory of personality, is intriguing but obviously quite subjective and often of questionable validity.

Developmental Studies

Prospective studies in which chronological age is the independent variable and selected physical and psychological measures on individuals are the dependent variables are known as *developmental studies*. In developmental studies, interest centers on determining how people change across time and what age-related variables are associated with those changes. As in any research investigation, interpretation of the results of developmental studies are often muddied by the presence of confounded variables such as cohort differences, carryover effects of retesting, and sample attrition.

The most straightforward of the various developmental research methods is a *longitudinal design*, in which a sample of people of the same chronological age is followed up over a period of years and periodically reexamined (Design M–N–O–P in Fig. 2.2). In addition to being time-consuming and expensive, longitudinal designs have the disadvantage of mortality or attrition of the participants and carryover effects of testing from one time period to the next. More efficient and hence more popular than a longitudinal design is a *cross-sectional design*, in which different age groups of people are examined at the same point in time (Design A–E–I–M in Fig. 2.2). Unfortunately, the different age groups, or cohorts, examined in this approach may differ in other ways as well as age. To begin with, one or more of the age group samples may not be truly representative of that age group in the population. In addition, because they were born in a different cultural era than other age groups, people in a given age group may have been different from another age group when both groups were of the same age. Initial matching on the various age groups on variables related to the criterion measure can assist in controlling for the confounding of age and cohort effects, but the basis for matching is seldom clear cut. Thus, longitudinal designs confound age and time of measurement, whereas cross-sectional designs confound age and cohort differences.

More complex developmental research designs have been devised to control for the confounding effects of age, cohort, and time of measurement in longitudinal and cross-sectional studies, but they are expensive and time-consuming. Among these are the time-lag, cohort-sequential, cross-sequential, and time-sequential designs. In the *time-lag design*, each of several cohorts is examined at a different point in time (e.g., measurements on Groups M–J–G–D in Fig. 2.2 are compared). However, like longitudinal and cross-sectional designs, a time-lag design does not permit evaluation of the effects of aging separate from cohort differences and time of measurement.

Efforts to control for the confounding or interactions of age, cohort, and time of measurement led to what Schaie (1977) designated as the *most efficient design*. This design consists of three parts, or rather three types of analyses: cohort-sequential, cross-sequential, and time-sequential. A *cohort-sequential analysis* is concerned with the interaction between cohort and age, a *cross-sequential analysis* with the interaction between cohort and time of measurement, and a *time-sequential analysis* with the interaction between age and time of measurement. In a cohort-sequential analysis, successive cohorts are compared over the same age ranges; for example, changes from ages 45 to 55 in a group born in 1945 may be compared with changes over the same age range in a group born in 1935 (differences between measurements C and D are compared with differences between measurements F and G in Fig. 2.2). In a cross-sequential analysis, changes from one year to another in a group born at a particular time are compared with changes over the same period in a group born at another time (in Fig. 2.2, changes from B to C are compared with changes from F to G). In a

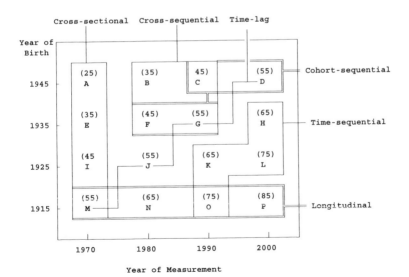

FIG. 2.2. Designs for developmental research.

time-sequential analysis, the difference between measurements on two different age groups at one time is compared with the difference between measurements on two other groups of those same ages but at another time (in Fig. 2.2, the difference between K and O is compared with the difference between H and L).

Experiments and Correlational Studies

Of all methods used in scientific research, only one—the *method of experiment*—allows the investigator to draw cause–effect conclusions. The results of all other scientific methods are likely to be confounded by extraneous variables that the researcher was not aware of and/or could not control. In some cases, the effects of extraneous variables can be minimized by the application of appropriate statistical techniques, but only a carefully controlled experiment leads to results that can be attributed to manipulation of the independent variable.

The earmarks of a true experiment are manipulation and control (i.e., manipulation of the independent variable(s) and control over extraneous variables). Extraneous variables may be controlled by randomly assigning the selected individuals to the various treatment conditions or by a matching procedure. The matching strategy consists of forming n subgroups of g persons each; the individuals in each subgroup are matched on extraneous variables that might affect the outcome of the experiment. The g persons in each of the n subgroups are then randomly assigned to the g treatment conditions.

Because behavioral scientists are seldom able to move people around like chess pieces, quasi-experimental designs are employed more often than true experimental designs. In a *quasi-experimental design*, the treatment groups are not formed by random assignment or matching, but rather they exist even before the experiment begins. The existing groups may consist of different classroom groups, work groups, therapy groups, or any other preconstituted collection of people. Efforts are usually made to ensure that the groups are comparable in age, sex, and other relevant variables before the different treatments are imposed, but this does not guarantee that the groups are identical at the start, thus the term *quasi-experimental* design. As with true experimental designs, quasi-experimental designs lend themselves to the use of multiple independent variables (i.e., presenting different combinations of treatments to different groups of people). In addition to the manipulated independent variable or variables, one or more subject or organismic variables such as age, gender, ethnicity, socioeconomic status, or intelligence, may be made a part of the research design and evaluated in terms of how they affect the relationship between the independent and dependent variables.

Variance due to subject variables that are not explicitly a part of the research design is treated as error and included in the denominator of the t or

F ratio for testing the significance of the difference between the means of the various treatment groups. Individual differences in response to the treatments and their interactions with other treatments are viewed as errors of measurement in traditional research designs, in contrast to research that focuses on identifying individual differences and their specific effects.

In true experimental designs, people (or animals) are assigned at random to the various treatment conditions and the independent (treatment) variable is manipulated by the researcher. The independent variable is also manipulated in quasi-experimental designs, but individuals are not randomly assigned to treatments. In correlational research investigations, neither manipulation of the independent variable nor random assignment of individuals to treatment groups occurs. Rather, the researcher simply determines whether there are significant relationships between two or more measures obtained on a group of people. For example, one may be interested in the relationship between delinquency and body build, between child personality and parenting style, between childhood trauma and adult behavior, or between any other pair of variables. Although any of these investigations may be worthwhile or productive in terms of confirming theoretical predictions and providing ideas for further research, in no case can a causal conclusion be drawn from the results. Finding that two variables are significantly related may facilitate the process of predicting an individual's standing on one variable from his or her standing on the other variable, but it does not justify the conclusion that one variable is the cause of the other.

STATISTICAL ANALYSIS

Statistics is concerned with the description and analysis of data obtained from measurements on variables. The oldest and simplest statistical procedures involve the construction of frequency distributions of data and the computation of measures of central tendency, variability, percentages, and other descriptive statistics on the data. For theoretical and interpretative purposes, raw scores and frequencies may be converted or transformed in various ways before making further comparisons with them. For example, raw scores can be changed to standard scores,[2] and frequencies may be converted to percentages, proportions, rates, or other convenient values. Rates are particularly useful when there is interest in plotting changes in vital or other socially significant variables (births, deaths, marriages, divorces, crime, etc.) over time. The following is a brief overview of statistical methods for the analysis of data from studies of individual and group differences. For more in-depth coverage, the textbooks by Pagano (1994) and Shavelson (1996) are recommended.

---

[2]A raw score is transformed to a standard *z* score by subtracting the mean from the score and dividing the remainder by the standard deviation. The resulting *z* scores can then be linearly transformed to another standard score scale (T, CEEB, deviation IQ, etc.) by multiplying them by an appropriate constant and adding another constant to the products.

TABLE 2.2

Items on a Similarities Test

1. In what way are an orange and a banana alike?
2. In what way are a dog and a lion alike?
3. In what way are an eye and an ear alike?
4. In what way are an egg and a seed alike?
5. In what way are a table and a chair alike?
6. In what way are work and play alike?
7. In what way are a fly and a tree alike?
8. In what way are praise and punishment alike?

Note. Responses to each item are scored as 0 = Incorrect, 1 = Partly Correct, 2 = Correct.

Comparing Frequency Distributions

As an illustration of descriptive statistics, the frequency distributions of the scores of two groups of people on a Similarities Test consisting of the eight items in Table 2.2 are given in the first three columns of Table 2.3. Responses to the items on this test are scored 0, 1, or 2 so the total scores range from 0 to 16. Because the two groups are unequal in size, interpretation of the differences in the scores of the two groups by simple inspection of their frequency distributions is tedious. However, the comparison process is facilitated by converting the frequencies to relative percentages and then plotting the results for the two groups separately as *relative percentage polygons*.[3] The relative percentages corresponding to the frequencies in Columns 2 and 3 are given in Columns 4 and 5 of Table 2.3. These percentages have been plotted against the corresponding raw scores in Fig. 2.3. A comparison of the two polygons indicates that Group A contains a relatively larger percentage of high scorers and a relatively smaller percentage of low scorers than Group B.

Central Tendency and Variability Comparisons

The pictorial representations of the frequency distributions in Fig. 2.3 are enlightening, but a more analytic approach is to compare the two groups of raw scores with respect to their central tendency and variability. These statistics are given in Table 2.4. Note that the mode, median, and mean of Group A are higher than the corresponding values in Group B. However, simple inspection of these values cannot tell us whether the differences are statistically significant. This determination requires conducting an independent groups *t* test, a between-groups analysis of variance (ANOVA), or a

---

[3]The relative percentage corresponding to a particular score is computed as $100(f/N)$, where f is the frequency of the score and N the total number of scores in the group.

comparable nonparametric statistical test (e.g., Mann–Whitney U test). Assuming that the population distributions corresponding to these two samples are normal in shape and that their variances are equal, tests of the hypothesis of equal group means reveal that $t = 6.43$ and $F = 41.34$. Because either one of these values is significant at the .05 level, it can be concluded that the population mean of Group A is larger than the population mean of Group B.

In addition to testing the null hypothesis of equal group means, and actually more meaningful if our focus is on individual differences within

TABLE 2.3

Frequency Distribution of Similarities Test Scores of Two Groups[*]

	Frequency		Relative Percentage	
Score	Group A	Group B	Group A	Group B
0	21	4	1.1	1.8
1	13	8	.7	3.6
2	40	6	2.1	2.7
3	52	15	2.7	6.8
4	73	14	3.9	6.3
5	95	23	5	10.4
6	151	23	8	10.4
7	179	26	9.5	11.7
8	228	21	12.1	9.5
9	222	23	11.7	10.4
10	242	18	12.8	8.1
11	198	17	10.5	7.7
12	154	11	8.1	5
13	131	4	6.9	1.8
14	61	8	3.2	3.6
15	25	1	1.3	.5
16	7	0	.4	

[*]Scores from Davis & Smith (1994).

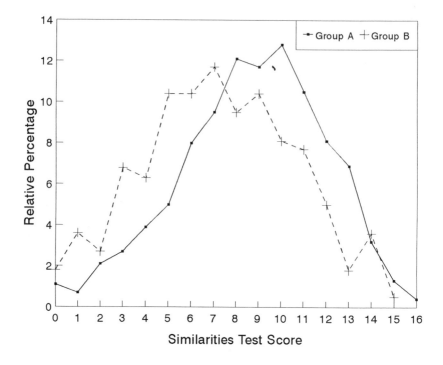

Similarities Test Score

FIG. 2.3.   Relative percentage distributions of scores of two groups on a similarities test (Based on data from Davis & Smith, 1994).

groups, is a statistical test of equal group variances. The ratio of the variances of the two groups, $s_2^2/s_1^2 = 1.13$, is distributed as the F statistic with $n_2 - 1 = 221$ and $n_1 - 1 = 1801$ degrees of freedom. From this result, it is concluded that the hypothesis of equal group variances cannot be rejected.

Correlation and Regression

Historically, the most popular of all statistical methods for analyzing individual differences have been correlational and regression procedures. Linear regression and correlation focus on prediction rather than explanation of individual differences in scores on tests or other measures. In linear regression analysis, interest focuses on determining a linear equation for predicting scores on measure Y from scores on measure X. This equation has the least squares property, in that the sum of squares of the observed Y values from the Y values predicted from the equation (Y') is as small as possible for the given data. In algebraic symbols, $\Sigma(Y - Y')^2$ is a minimum. The general form of the linear regression equation for predicting Y from X is $Y' = bX + a$, where b is the slope and a the Y-axis intercept of a straight line describing the functional relationship between the X and Y variables. The slope parameter is computed as $b = (\Sigma XY - \Sigma X \Sigma Y / N) / [\Sigma X^2 - (\Sigma X)^2 / N]$ and intercept parameter as $a = \bar{Y} - b\bar{X}$. In these formulas, Σ means "take the sum of," $\bar{X}$ and $\bar{Y}$ are the arithmetic means of the X and Y variables, and N is the number of paired X, Y values.

The Pearson product–moment correlation coefficient, an index of the linear relationship between the X and Y variables, is computed as $r = (\Sigma XY - \Sigma X \Sigma Y / N) / \sqrt{[\Sigma X^2 - (\Sigma X)^2 / N] [\Sigma Y^2 - (\Sigma Y)^2 / N]}$. This index, which ranges from -1.00 to $+1.00$, is a measure of the predictability of the Y scores from the X scores. The closer the value of r is to either $+1.00$ or -1.00, the more accurately can Y be predicted from X (or X from Y). Also useful in the analysis of individual differences is the *coefficient* of *determination*, r^2. This statistic is the proportion of variability (individual differences) in the Y scores that can be accounted for by variability in the X scores or, alternatively, the proportion of variability in X scores that can be accounted for by variability in Y scores. For example, if X is a measure of cognitive ability and Y a performance criterion, r^2 is the proportion of variance in the performance criterion that can be predicted or accounted for by variance in scores on the cognitive ability measure. The remaining, unpredicted variance in scores on the performance criterion, computed as $1 - r^2$, is known as the *coefficient of alienation*. The magnitude of r^2 may be influenced by such measurement errors as the examinees' failure to understand the test instructions, lack of motivation, external distractions, or other unaccounted for variables.

TABLE 2.4
Measures of Central Tendency and Variability for the Scores in Table 2.3

Variable	Group A	Group B
Measures of Central Tendency		
Mode	10	7
Median	8.91	7.19
Mean	8.71	7.25
Measures of Variability		
Range	16	15
Variance	10.12	11.42
Standard Deviation	3.18	3.38
Sample Size	1892	222

Other Statistical Methods

As diagrammed in Fig. 2.4, a variety of statistical procedures can be applied in analyzing individual and group differences in scores on tests and other measures. If our goal is simply to provide a brief quantitative description of the data, we can compare the averages (mean, median, mode), measures of variability (ranges, variances, standard deviations), and indexes of skewness (asymmetry) and kurtosis (steepness vs. flatness) of the frequency distributions of different groups of people.

In addition to frequency distributions and measures of central tendency and variability, we can compute indexes of the skewness and kurtosis of the frequency distributions and compare them across different groups of people. We can also compute correlation coefficients between pairs of variables and compare the coefficients obtained for different groups. However, most researchers go beyond the examination of data samples and make inferences about the nature of the populations from which the samples were se-

FIG. 2.4.   General outline of descriptive and inferential statistical procedures.

lected. Consequently, they conduct statistical tests of hypotheses and draw inferences or conclusions from the results.

The appropriate statistical test of a research hypothesis depends on the number of independent and dependent variables, the number of samples (groups) to be compared, whether the samples are independent or dependent, and whether the assumptions underlying a particular statistical test can be met. In most investigations of individual and group differences, it is assumed that, in the populations of which the treatment samples are representative, the scores are normally distributed and have the same variance as the scores in the other populations. Nonparametric procedures that do not make these assumptions but are less powerful than comparable parametric procedures are employed less often than the latter.

Although one-factor and multifactor ANOVAs are commonly used in the analysis of data obtained in psychological research, even more popular are correlational procedures such as tests of the significance of the difference between correlation coefficients, multiple-regression analysis, and multivariate techniques such as discriminant analysis and canonical correlation. As shown in Fig. 2.4, multifactor analysis of variance (MANOVA; between groups, within groups, and mixed designs), multiple-regression analysis, and chi-square tests of independence may be applied to the data when there are two or more independent variables but only one dependent variable. However, multivariate techniques (discriminant analysis, canonical correlation, MANOVA, etc.) are used when there are multiple dependent variables. These more complex statistical procedures have definite advantages over the simpler *t* tests, single-factor ANOVA, and correlation coefficients, but the assumptions underlying them are even more stringent. An introduction to multivariate statistical analysis procedures is given by Manly (1994).

Univariate research designs, in which there is not only one dependent variable but two or more independent variables, can provide a great deal of information. For example, MANOVAs permit an evaluation of the effects of several between- and within-groups factors and their interactions. Multiple-regression analysis provides estimates of the contributions of many different continuous and discrete independent variables to the prediction of a single dependent variable.

An extension of multiple-regression analysis to data consisting of several dependent variables, as well as several independent variables, is *canonical correlation*. A canonical correlation analysis consists of correlating two derived variables, one of which represents a weighed combination of one set of variables (e.g., a set of predictors) and the other represents a weighted combination of another set of variables (e.g., a set of criterion variables). A more widely employed multivariate procedure for differentiating between two or more groups on the basis of their scores on multiple dependent variables is *discriminant analysis*. The goal of a discriminant analysis is to determine the discriminant function(s) or equation(s) that best differentiate between two or more groups. For example, we may wish to differentiate between two or more demographic groups (sex, race, age, socioeconomic status, etc.) on the basis of their scores on several tests of abilities and personality characteristics. The resulting discriminant function would permit us to determine whether a weighted combination of scores on these variables results in accurate assignment of the individuals to the several groups.

Another multivariate statistical procedure that has been employed extensively in research on individual and group differences is *factor analysis*. A factor analysis of the scores of n individuals on p tests reveals what factors the tests have in common (i.e., the basic variables or constructs underlying the scores). There are essentially three stages in a factor analysis: (a) extraction of the factors, (b) rotation of the axes of the extracted factors to a simpler structure, and (c) interpretation of the loadings of the tests on the axes of the rotated factors. A variety of procedures are available for factor extraction and rotation, the most popular being the principal axis method of factoring and the orthogonal procedure of rotation. Applying these methods to the scores of the individuals in Group A on the eight items constituting the Similarities Test in Table 2.2 yields the results in the first three columns of Table 2.5. The numbers in Columns 2 and 3 of this table are the loadings of the eight test items on the extracted factors for Group A. Inspection of the loadings reveals that, for Group A, Items 1 and 2 have high loadings and Items 3 and 5 have moderate loadings on Factor 1, whereas Items 7 and 8 have high loadings and Items 4, 5, and 6 have moderate loadings on Factor 2. By referring to the items in Table 2.2, we can interpret these loadings as indicating that Factor 1 is a measure of more concrete reasoning and Factor 2 is a measure of more abstract reasoning. The last two columns of Table 2.5 show that the pattern of the factor loadings for Group B is somewhat similar to that for Group A.

TABLE 2.5
Loadings of Similarities Item Scores
of Groups A and B on Two Factors

Item	Group A		Group B	
	Factor 1	Factor 2	Factor 1	Factor 2
1	.793	−.016	.754	−.028
2	.776	.085	.803	.040
3	.438	.337	.266	.575
4	.204	.514	.170	.626
5	.477	.423	.664	.239
6	.040	.575	.023	.606
7	.197	.606	.476	.381
8	−.021	.660	−.028	.648

SUMMARY

Research on individual differences may be exploratory or confirmatory, descriptive or explanatory, theoretical or applied, and laboratory-based or field-based. The results of a research investigation possess internal validity if they are relatively free of errors of measurement; they possess external validity if they are generalizable to a specific population.

Behavioral science research involves defining and measuring relevant concrete and abstract variables. These variables, or constructs, may be discrete or continuous and measured on a nominal, ordinal, interval, or ratio scale. They may also be classified as independent, dependent, or extraneous and by other designations (intervening variables, moderator variables, confounded variables, concomitant variables, covariates, etc.). Independent variables in psychological research are typically stimuli or stimulus patterns, and dependent variables are responses. The goal of a typical research study is to determine the relationship between independent and dependent variables while statistically or experimentally controlling for the effects of extraneous variables. Uncontrolled extraneous variables that influence the relationship between the independent and dependent variables, and thereby confound the interpretation of the results of an investigation, are referred to as confounded variables. Related to confounded variables, but usually more controlled, are intervening and moderator variables.

Various kinds of psychometric and psychophysiological instruments can provide measures of the variables in behavioral science studies. Especially popular are individual and group tests, questionnaires, inventories, rating scales, and checklists. The reliability and validity of such instruments are affected by the context in which the instrument is administered and the individuals who take it. Reliability information may be obtained by test–retest, parallel forms, and internal consistency procedures. Validity information is obtained by careful, systematic examination of the content of a psychometric instrument, determining the relationship between scores on the instrument and performance on a criterion measure of interest, and a series of investigations designed to determine whether the instrument measures the construct that it is supposed to. In selecting or designing a psychometric instrument, attention should be given not only to information pertaining to its reliability and validity, but also to the score range(s), availability of norms, and efficiency with which the instrument can be administered, scored, and interpreted.

Methods of researching individual differences include objective observations, interviews, surveys, developmental studies, correlational methods, and experiments. Determination of cause and effect is only possible by means of an experiment, in which the independent variable is manipulated by the experimenter, extraneous variables are controlled (typically by randomly assigning persons to treatment groups), and changes in the dependent variable are measured. Correlational and quasi-experimental procedures permit researchers to predict changes in dependent variables from

40	CHAPTER 2

changes in independent variables, but not to draw conclusions concerning causal links between the variables.

The appropriate procedures for analyzing the results of a research study in the behavioral sciences depend on the hypotheses to be tested, the number of independent and dependent variables, how individuals were assigned to the various treatment groups, and whether the assumptions underlying a particular statistical test can be met. An outline of the various descriptive and inferential statistical procedures that have been applied in studies of individual differences is given in Fig. 2.4. Correlational methods have been especially popular for analyzing individual differences in both physical and psychological characteristics. Among univariate inferential procedures, *t* tests and ANOVA designs have been employed most often. With multivariate data, in which there are several dependent and independent variables, factor analysis and discriminant analysis have been used extensively.

SUGGESTED READINGS

Aiken, L. R. (1994). Some observations and recommendations concerning research methodology in the behavioral sciences. *Educational and Psychological Measurement, 54,* 848–860.

Anderson, E. R. (1993). Analyzing change in short-term longitudinal research using cohort-sequential designs. *Journal of Consulting and Clinical Psychology, 61*(6), 929–940.

Lietz, P., & Keeves, J. P. (1994). Cross-sectional research methods. In T. Husén & T. N. Postlethwaite (Eds.), *International encyclopedia of education* (2nd ed., Vol. 2, pp. 1213–1220). Tarrytown, NY: Elsevier.

Lubinski, D. J. (1996). Applied individual differences research and its quantitative methods. *Psychology, Public Policy, and Law, 2*(2), 187–203.

Lubinski, D. J., & Dawis, R. V. (Eds.). (1995). *Assessing individual differences in human behavior: New concepts, methods, and findings.* Palo Alto, CA: Davies-Black.

Magnusson, D., & Casaer, P. (Eds.). (1993). *Longitudinal research on individual development: Present status and future perspectives.* New York: Cambridge University Press.

O'Connor, K. (1992). Design and analysis in individual difference research. In A. Gale & M. W. Eysenck (Eds.), *Handbook of individual differences: Biological perspectives* (pp. 45–79). New York: Wiley.

Reynolds, C. R., & Willson, V. P. (Eds.). (1985). *Methodological and statistical advances in the study of individual differences.* New York: Plenum.

Snow, R. E. (1991). Aptitude-treatment interaction as a framework for research on individual differences in psychotherapy. *Journal of Consulting and Clinical Psychology, 59*(2), 205–216.

Biological Foundations

Throughout the history of philosophy and science, an enduring question has been concerned with the relationship between physical and mental functioning. A dualistic position, as enunciated by Rene Descartes in the 17th century, holds that the soul (spiritual, mental) and the body (physical) aspects of a person are separate and distinct. Descartes, the father of the mechanistic tradition in France, believed that animals are reflexively acting, machinelike creatures and that only human beings have souls. According to this dualistic conception, which has been advocated by most religions, the soul exists without the body in a noncorporeal state after death and even at times during life. In contrast, the monistic philosophical position holds that the mind and body, the mental and physical components of a person, are inseparable.[1] To a monist, there is no such thing as a spirit world—a spiritual state separate from a living body. Mind and body, psyche and soma, are combined as a psychosomatic unity in human functioning and experience. To a monist, the construct of mind is not a distinct entity, but simply a function of brain dynamics. The brain is seen as the center of cognitive, affective, and psychomotor processes. It is the seat of consciousness and behavior and the regulator of the nervous system, the musculoskeletal system, the endocrine system, and other body structures.

At the beginning of the 20th century, the older dualistic definition of psychology as the study of the mind was replaced by the definition of psychology as the science of human and animal behavior. A similar move toward monism was seen in medicine with the holistic concept of *psychosomatic medicine*. Psychosomatic medicine is based on the notion that thoughts and emotions can exacerbate and precipitate physical illnesses, and physical illness, in turn, can affect psychological functioning.

---

[1]A compromise philosophical position advocated by David Hartley is *psychophysical parallelism*. This doctrine maintains that the mind and the nervous system are separate but synchronized—that they run alongside each other on parallel tracks, so to speak. Psychophysical parallelism was espoused by Wilhelm Wundt, the founder of experimental psychology, but is now only of historical interest and not seriously advocated by any behavioral scientist.

Precipitated in some measure by advances in computing machines and neuropsychology, recently there has been a further modification of the definition of psychology to include cognitive processes. *Psychology* has been redefined as the study of behavior and cognition—a change that has been viewed by some as a return to mentalism or dualism. In any event, modern behavioral scientists recognize that behavior, cognitive processes, and personality are shaped and regulated by the structure and functioning of the human body. Understanding these influences and how they occur is the goal not only of modern psychology but also of many biologists, neurochemists, and health scientists.

The purpose of this chapter is to provide an introduction to the ideas and findings of researchers in the natural sciences as they bear on our understanding of individual and group differences among people. This material is important to an understanding of the biological and biochemical substrates of cognitive, emotional, and psychomotor processes and, more generally, human personality. Because several of the remaining chapters of this book draw heavily on this material, the reader may wish to go beyond what is included here and refer to more detailed treatments of these topics in books on neuropsychology and behavior genetics (e.g., Kalat, 1998; Kolb & Whishaw, 1996; Plomin, 1994; Vernon, 1994).

PHYSICAL VARIABLES AND SYSTEMS

How do we recognize one person as different from another? Initially we do it on the basis of a complex of physical characteristics, nonverbal behaviors, and speech patterns. As time goes by and the number of encounters with the person increases, fewer and fewer elements of the complex stimulus pattern that is representative of the person are needed to trigger a recognition response. How many times have you thought that you recognized a certain individual simply because something about him or her reminded you of someone whom you did know? This process, which is referred to as *redintegration,* has been interpreted by certain writers as evidence for the transmigration of souls from one planet to another. The underlying assumption of this viewpoint is that we respond to a stranger as if he or she were someone whom we know because we actually were acquainted with that person in a previous existence on a distant planet. However, this explanation is probably too fanciful to be taken seriously, and an interpretation of redintegration in terms of the principle of stimulus generalization is more reasonable and parsimonious: We mistake a person for someone else because something about the former—some physical feature or behavioral characteristics—triggers the recognition response that was originally conditioned to the latter person.

Be that as it may, many physical and behavioral characteristics go into making up a person. A sample of these characteristics is listed in Table 3.1. In addition to external structures and functions, there are internal substances and processes involving body fluids, organs, tissues, and systems. For example, the structure and functioning of the various systems of the

TABLE 3.1

Some Physical and Functional Characteristics of Persons

Physical Appearance	Psychomotor Functioning	Sensory Functioning	Internal Functioning
Arm length	Athletic ability	Auditory acuity	Blood type
Body shape	Gait	Pain sensitivity	Blood chemistry
Dress	Grip strength	Smell sensitivity	Blood pressure
Eye color	Handedness	Taste sensitivity	Brain activity indicators (EEG, CAT, MRI, PET, etc.)
Facial features (shape of nose, mouth, cheeks, ears)	Manual dexterity	Temperature sensitivity	DNA
Foot size	Pedal dexterity	Visual acuity	Heart rate
Girth	Reaction time		Neurotransmitters
Grooming	Rhythm		Pulse rate
Hair color	Speech		Respiration rate
Hair texture			Saliva composition
Hairiness			Skin resistance
Hand size			Urine chemistry/ composition
Head shape			
Head size			
Height			
Length of arms			
Length of legs			
Muscularity			
Skin complexion			
Weight			

body (e.g., cardiovascular, respiratory, musculoskeletal, gastrointestinal, genitourinary, nervous, and immune) are, to some degree, unique to the individual. This uniqueness varies with age, sex, ethnicity, socioeconomic status, and other genetically and environmentally determined variables.

Of particular interest to psychologists are changes in the skin, muscles, blood, and other tissues that occur during states of excitement or stress. Among these are: (a) change in the composition of the blood (blood sugar increases, epinephrine increases, blood coagulates more rapidly, acid–alkaline balance changes), (b) redistribution of the blood supply to the surface of the body, (c) increases in blood pressure and heart rate, (d) an increase in the ratio of the volume of oxygen inhaled to the volume of carbon dioxide exhaled, (e) inhibition of gastrointestinal movements, (f) pilomotor response (i.e., goose pimples), (g) inhibition of saliva secretion, (h) increased perspiration, (i) enlargement of the pupils of the eye, and (j) increased muscle tension and tremors. The magnitude of these reactions, referred to collectively as the *emergency reaction* and mediated by the autonomic nervous system, varies from person to person. Some people are more labile, whereas others are more stable in their emotional reactions to stimuli and situations. For example, one person may show little or no physiological response when telling a lie, whereas another person becomes intensely upset by even a suggestion that he or she may not be telling the truth. For many years, an apparatus known as the *polygraph,* which typically measures respiration rate, blood pressure, and the galvanic skin response (GSR),[2] has been used by law enforcement officers and personnel managers to detect lying. However, the polygraph has been criticized as inaccurate, and alternative procedures have gradually replaced it.

Other specialized apparatus, including the following bioelectric indicators, have also been used to measure the associated physiological reactions in investigation of stress and emotion:

- Electrocardiograph (EKG) and stethoscope: heart rate
- Electroencephalograph (EEG): brain waves
- Electromyograph (EMG): muscle tension
- PET scan: activation of different brain areas
- Photoplethysmograph: vaginal blood volume
- Pneumograph: respiration rate
- Psychogalvanometer: electrical resistance of the skin
- Pupillometer: pupillary diameter
- Sphygmomanometer: blood pressure
- Telethermometer or thermistor: skin temperature

In addition, changes in the chemistry of the blood, saliva, and other body fluids during emotional states can be determined by chemical analysis. Unlike the old days when physiological measurements necessitated connect-

---

[2]The GSR is a gradual decrease in the electrical resistance of the skin that occurs a second or two after the onset of a startling stimulus; it is an indicator of increased bodily activation level.

ing the immobile subject to imposing apparatus, there are now special transducer/recorders that can be worn like a watch on the arm or leg to record limb movements during activities, miniature transmitters that can be swallowed to report on the condition of internal organs, and other microelectronic devices. The output of these devices can then be fed into a computer and quickly analyzed.

Several of the measures of psychomotor and sensory functioning listed in Table 3.1 were employed by Francis Galton (1883/1907) in his pioneering studies of mental abilities. Among Galton's tests were measures of movement speed (speed of moving the hand 50 centimeters), muscular strength (pressure exerted on a dynamometer), two-point touch sensitivity, pain sensitivity (amount of pressure on the forehead required to produce pain), weight discrimination (just noticeable difference in heaviness), and reaction time to sound. The design and use of these tests as measures of mental ability were based on the associationistic or empiricistic philosophy that all knowledge, and hence mind itself, is the result of mental associations among elementary sensory impressions. Consequently, it was argued that persons with greater sensory acuity are more intelligent and knowledgeable than those with less sensory acuity.

HUMAN NERVOUS SYSTEM AND ENDOCRINE GLANDS

Individual differences among human beings are a function of all systems of the body, but in particular the nervous system. Our cognitive and psychomotor abilities, our emotions and personalities—things that make us different from other animals and from each other—are all consequences of the operation of our nervous systems. Perception, consciousness, language, learning, memory, thinking, and the social and creative behaviors engendered by them are the results of actions of the human nervous system. Consequently, to understand the origins of individual differences in behavior, cognition, and personality and their dynamics, it is important to know at least some basic facts about the anatomy, physiology, and chemistry of the nervous system.

The basic building blocks of the nervous system are neurons and glial cells. Glial cells are mainly supporting structures and are of less interest to us than neurons. Neurons, which consist of dendrites, cell body, axon, and end bulb, receive and transmit electrochemical impulses throughout the body. Sensory (afferent) neurons carry impulses from sensory receptors to other neurons and eventually to the central nervous system (brain and spinal cord). Motor (efferent) neurons carry impulses from the central nervous system to muscles and glands. A third kind of neurons—internuncial or association neurons—carry impulses between other neurons.

The propagation of a nerve impulse, or action potential, is a one-way trip from dendrites to cell body to axon to the end bulbs of neurons and then across the synapse to another neuron. Transmission of a nerve impulse from neuron to neuron is a biochemical event dependent on the release of chemical substances known as *neurotransmitters* (see Table 3.2). By influencing the magnitude of the membrane potentials of postsynaptic neurons, neurotransmitters either facilitate or inhibit the passage of nerve impulses across the synapses. Other chemical substances, such as addictive drugs and medicines, can also affect the occurrence of a postsynaptic potential. Among the drugs that affect nerve impulses, and hence mood and behavior, are the following:

- Sedative-hypnotics: barbiturates (Luminal, Nembutal, Pentothal)
- Nonbarbiturate hypnotics (Quaalude)
- Antianxiety agents: Librium, Valium
- Alcohol
- Bromide
- Paraldehyde
- Ether
- Chloroform
- Behavioral stimulants and convulsants: amphetamines (Dexedrine)
- Clinical antidepressants: MAO inhibitors (Parnate, tricyclic compounds such as Tofranil and Elavil)
- Cocaine
- Convulsants: strychnine, picrotoxin
- Caffeine
- Nicotine
- Narcotic analgesics: opium, heroine, morphine, codeine
- Antipsychotic agents: Thorazine, Serpasil, Haldol, Lithium Psychedelics and hallucinogens: LSD, Mescaline, Psilocybin, MDMA, bufotein, phencyclidine, cannabis

Divisions of the Nervous System

In terms of gross architecture, it is convenient to divide the nervous system into central and peripheral parts. The central nervous system (CNS) consists of the brain and spinal cord—structures that are encased in bone. The peripheral nervous system consists of neurons lying outside the CNS—and in particular the autonomic nervous system (ANS) and the peripheral nerves. Sensory impulses travel from sensory receptors to the spinal cord by way of the spinal nerves or from the cranial nerves to the brain. Motor impulses travel from the brain to the spinal cord and then to the motor nerves and effectors (muscles and glands)—or, in the case of reflexes, directly from the cord without. The spinal cord consists of clusters of sensory, motor, and connecting nerve tracts that carry neural impulses to and from the brain and from one side of the brain to the other. The sensory, or ascending, spinal tracts are on the dorsal side of the cord; the motor, or descending, spinal tracts are on the ventral side. Both ascending and descending tracts cross over to the opposite (contralateral) side at the brain stem level, resulting in the sensory and motor representations of a particular side of the body being localized on the opposite side of the brain.

In addition to sensory and motor areas that are responsible for sensations, reflexes, and skilled movements, the brain contains many association areas that regulate communication, memory, perception, problem solving, and other complex functions. Vital functions such as heartbeat and respira-

TABLE 3.2
Major Neurotransmitters in the Human Body

Monoamines	Amino Acids	Neuropeptides	Other Neurotransmitters
Acetylcholine	Glutamate	Leukenkaphalin	Adenosine
Serotonin	Glycine	Metenkephalin	ATP
Histamine	Aspartate	Beta-endorphin	
Catecholamines	Gamma-amino-butyric acid (GABA)	Substance P	
Dopamine		Cholecystokinin	
Norepinephrine		Vasopressin	
Epinephrine		Vasoactive intestinal protein	
		Gastrin	
		Galanin	
		Neuropeptide Y	
		Oxytocin	
		Somatostatin	

Note. From *Biological Psychology* (pp. 55–58) by J. W. Kalat, 1998, Pacific Grove, CA: Brooks/Cole. Copyright © 1998 by Brooks/Cole. Reprinted by permission.

tion are controlled by structures at the lowest level, or myelencephalon (medulla). At the next level, or metencephalon (cerebellum, pons), are structures whose primary function is the regulation of movements. At a somewhat higher level from the metencephalon is the mesencephalon; it consists of structures such as the inferior and superior colliculi and associated sensory nerve tracts, which mediate responses to visual and auditory stimuli as well as containing motor tracts. At the next level is the diencephalon, which is a region containing the thalamus and hypothalamus. In addition to its other functions, the thalamus acts as a relay station for visual, auditory, and other sensory impulses going to the cerebral cortex. The hypothalamus, which is located just under the thalamus, regulates a vast complex of behaviors, including feeding, sleeping, sexual activity, expression of emotions, and the regulation of body temperature and endocrine secretions. At the highest level of the brain is the telencephalon, which includes the cerebral cortex, the basal ganglia, the limbic system, and the olfactory bulbs. Each of these structures has its own particular functions. The olfactory bulbs are responsible for the sense of smell, and the basal ganglia are important in movement. The functions of the limbic system, which consists of the hippocampus, septum, and cingulate cortex, are not well understood, but its role in memory, in particular, has been extensively researched.

Cerebral Hemispheres

Although subcortical structures such as the limbic system, hypothalamus, and reticular system play important roles in initiating and controlling behavior, the crowning jewel of the human brain is the cerebral cortex. This structure, which covers the cerebrum like the peel on an orange, is divided for convenience into frontal, parietal, occipital, and temporal lobes in the two cerebral hemispheres; these hemispheres are connected together by the corpus callosum and certain other neural structures. The four lobes of the cerebral cortex possess a certain degree of localization of function for specific sensory and motor functions, as well as more complex functions such as perception and language. However, the largest portion of the cortex consists of so-called *silent* or association areas that function in complex behavioral and cognitive activities.

One method used in early neurophysiological research consisted of clinical studies of people and animals that had sustained specific brain injuries and losses due to accident or disease. Experiments were also conducted in which parts of the brains of animals were surgically removed or stimulated with electricity or chemicals. Cerebral stimulation of patients who were undergoing surgery for brain tumors or other neurological conditions was also employed.

By the early 20th century, some areas of the brain in which specific functions are located had been identified. Textbooks on neurophysiology and physiological psychology of the time contained illustrations of sensory and motor homunculi. These dwarflike pictures showed how voluntary motor functions are controlled by the precentral gyrus of the frontal lobes and how the sense of touch or pressure is localized on the postcentral gyrus of the parietal lobes. Furthermore, the occipital lobes were known to be important in vision and the temporal lobes in audition. However, sensory and motor functions were not found to be restricted to single areas of the brain; multiple brain sites are involved in sensation, perception, and movement.

One of the first higher order abilities to be associated with specific brain areas was language. In 1861, Paul Broca discovered a region in the left frontal lobe that is important in the production of speech and the comprehension of grammar. A few years later, Carl Wernicke found another area in the posterior temporal lobe that is important in language comprehension and naming. The roles of these areas in communication and speech are, however, not fixed. There is a great deal of plasticity in the way the brain operates, and the functions of the language areas, and other areas as well, vary to some extent with age, gender, and other individual differences.

The methods employed in early neurophysiological research included clinical studies of people and animals who had sustained specific brain injuries and losses due to accident or disease, extirpation and electrical and chemical stimulation of the brains of animals, as well as cerebral stimulation of patients undergoing surgery for brain tumors or other neurological conditions.

Of particular interest to contemporary neuropsychologists are the findings of studies of differences in the functions of the left and right hemispheres. The two cerebral hemispheres certainly work together and, depending on the age of the individual, are capable of compensating for a loss of function due to damage to the other hemisphere. Nevertheless, in most people, verbal/linguistic functions are controlled primarily by the left hemisphere and spatial/perceptual functions by the right hemisphere. With regard to cognitive abilities, it has been demonstrated that the frontal lobes play an important role in problem solving and thinking, that the hippocampus has a role in the storage of memories, and that other areas of the brain also contribute to cognitive processes.

The question of whether mental disorders are caused by physical disease processes or unfortunate experiences has been debated for over 100 years. It has been known since the famous 19th-century case of Phineas Gage that organic damage to the brain can produce profound psychological changes and even psychotic behaviors. However, approximately 50% of the cases of mental disorder are associated with no demonstrable physical changes in the brain. For this reason, more recently the search for an organic basis for schizophrenia, bipolar disorder, and other functional mental disorders has assumed a biochemical direction. Thus far, the search has met with no more than middling success, although the belief in a neurochemical basis for these conditions remains strong.

Questions concerning the relationships among variations in cerebral organization and individual differences in cognitive abilities, temperament, personality disorders, and other psychological functions continue to challenge neurophysiologists and neuropsychologists. The ancient Oracle at Delphi advised those seeking his advice to first "Know thyself." However, it often appears as if the functioning of the three pounds of spongelike tissue known as the human brain is as complex as that of the universe itself and may defy complete understanding. In fact, it sometimes seems as if humanity may attain a thorough understanding of the origin and nature of the cosmos before we understand precisely how our brains function.

Autonomic Nervous System

The autonomic nervous system (ANS), which regulates the activities of the visceral organs and other involuntary reactions, is part of the peripheral system. The implication of the term *autonomic* is that the motoric functions of the ANS are independent of those of the somatic system, which controls the skeletal muscles. The functioning of the ANS, however, is affected by the hypothalamus and other brain structures, and its activities are coordinated with rather than separate from those of the CNS. For example, the vagus and other cranial nerves play important roles in what are usually considered functions of the autonomic nervous system: beating of the heart, digestion, pupillary responses, and so on.

The ANS is divided into parasympathetic and sympathetic components, which affect the actions of smooth muscles, cardiac muscles, and secretions of certain glands. Connections of the parasympathetic division arise from neurons in the cranial and sacral regions of the spinal cord, whereas those of the sympathetic division arise from chain ganglia in the thoracic and lumbar regions of the cord. The neurotransmitter acetylcholine is involved in the transmission of nerve impulses in parasympathetic nerve fibers, but noradrenalin (noreinephrine) is found more often in sympathetic fibers. For this reason, the parasympathetic system is often referred to as the *cholinergic,* and the sympathetic system as the *adrenergic* system. Drugs that stimulate the action of the sympathetic system are designated as *sympathomimetic;* those that inhibit its activity are *sympatholytic.* There are also parasympathomimetic and parasympatholytic drugs.

The parasympathetic system has nonemergency, vegetative functions and is typically more active when the body is in a relaxed state. In contrast, the sympathetic division becomes more active during violent exercise, extreme temperatures, situations that provoke fear or rage, and other emergencies in which the "fight or flight" reaction occurs. Activation of the parasympathetic system causes the heart rate to decrease and digestive activity (salivation, secretion of gastric juices, elimination, etc.) to increase, whereas activation of the sympathetic system has the opposite effects. Although most visceral organs are innervated by both parasympathetic and sympathetic neurons, only the latter have connections to the adrenal and sweat glands and to muscles responsible for the constriction of blood vessels or the pilomotor response (erect skin hairs). When the sympathetic system becomes overactive, the parasympathetic system usually swings into action to compensate for it. This reaction, referred to as *parasympathetic compensation,* is responsible for certain delayed physiological reactions to *close calls* and other emergencies. Because the relative activity of the two divisions of the ANS varies appreciably from person to person, the role of the ANS in emotion has led personality researchers to describe some people as being more emotionally stable and others as more emotionally labile, depending on the degree of autonomic reactivity.

Endocrine Glands and Hormones

In addition to variations in autonomic reactivity, individual differences exist in the functioning of a related system—that of the endocrine glands. In contrast to duct glands, which deliver their secretions directly into the body cavities, the hormones produced by endocrine glands are secreted into the bloodstream. The master controller of the endocrines is located in the hypothalamus, but the various glands also regulate each other through a complex feedback system.

Seven endocrine glands in the human body are the pineal, pituitary, parathyroid, thymus, adrenal, islets of Langerhans, and gonads (female ovaries, male testes). The *pineal gland,* which is located at the base of the brain, assists in regulating the sleep–wakefulness cycle. The *pituitary gland,* which is located just below the hypothalamus and connected to it by a stalk known as the infundibulum, consists of anterior and posterior lobes. The anterior pituitary secretes the hormone somatotropin (or GH), which controls growth of the skeleton, muscles, and internal organs. Under-secretion of somatotropin during childhood results in dwarfism, whereas oversecretion causes giantism. Oversecretion of somatotropin during ado-lescence produces acromegaly—a disorder that results in overgrowth of only certain parts of the body (e.g., the hands, arms, jawbone, and chest). The middle-man hormones (ACTH, TSH, FSH, LH, prolactin), which are se-creted by the anterior pituitary, regulate the secretions of other endocrine glands—the thyroid, cortex of the adrenal glands, and gonads. Two hor-mones secreted by the posterior pituitary lobe are vasopressin, which con-stricts blood vessels and raises blood pressure, and oxytocin, which con-trols uterine contractions and milk production in females. An excess or de-ficiency of pituitary hormones can have physical as well as psychological ef-fects. Oversecretion is associated with irritability and distrustfulness, whereas undersecretion is related to forgetfulness and chronic drowsiness or fatigue.

The *thyroid gland,* which is comprised of two lobes situated on either side of the windpipe, secretes the hormones thyroxin and triiodothy-ronine. Thyroxin regulates metabolic rate and helps control the rate of growth and maturation. An oversecretion of thyroxin is accompanied by hy-peractivity, emotional agitation, and insomnia. An undersecretion of this hormone during early childhood can lead to cretinism, which is a disorder marked by stunted growth, lowered metabolic rate, and low intelligence. If diagnosed early enough, these symptoms can be reversed through thyroid treatment. A deficiency of thyroxin later in life can cause myxedema—a dis-order accompanied by lowered metabolic rate, heart rate, temperature, and activity level, but not changes in intelligence.

Humans have two pairs of *parathyroid glands,* which are situated in the neck near the thyroid gland. Parathyroid hormone, a hormone that regu-lates the calcium–potassium balance of the blood, is secreted by the parathyroids. An oversecretion of this hormone elevates the calcium level in the blood, whereas an undersecretion raises the potassium level. By means of its sensitivity to the calcium–potassium level of the blood, the parathyroids indirectly control calcium deposits in the bones. Because a de-ficiency of blood calcium due to insufficient parathyroid hormone in-creases the excitability of nerves, parathyroid-deficient individuals tend to be irritable and manifest uncontrollable impulses, muscle spasms, and even convulsions.

Located just below the thyroid gland is the *thymus gland.* The hormone thymosin, secreted by the lateral lobes of this gland, contributes to lympho-cyte formation and consequently the immune response of the body. The thymus gland is also involved in nutrition and growth and in the inhibition of premature development of the reproductive organs.

The *adrenal glands,* which are located on top of the kidneys, consist of two parts—an inner layer or medulla and an outer layer or cortex. The effects of the hormones epinephrine and norepinephrine secreted by the adrenal medulla are similar to those of the sympathetic branch of the ANS. Increasing amounts of the adrenal medulla hormones are secreted during emergencies, affecting the transmission of nerve impulses and causing a rise in blood sugar level. Epinephrine also leads to accelerated heartbeat, whereas norepinephrine causes the blood vessels to constrict. Hormones secreted by the adrenal cortex include aldosterone, cortisol, and corticosterone. The first of these hormones controls the excretion of salts by the kidneys, whereas the last two cause increases in blood sugar level and the metabolism of proteins and fats.

The *islets of Langerhans,* which are specialized cells situated in the pancreas, secrete the hormones insulin and glucagon. These hormones help maintain the blood sugar level by controlling the storage and utilization of sugar and fats by the liver. An insulin deficiency can lead to diabetes mellitus, whereas an excess can lead to hypoglycemia (sugar deficiency). Among the behavior symptoms resulting from disturbances of insulin secretion are mood fluctuations, irritability, and decreased mental activity.

The ovaries of females and the testes of males are referred to collectively as *gonads* or sex glands. These glands produce both sex cells and hormones (androgens, estrogens, and progesterone) that affect sexual development and behavior. The gonads of both sexes secrete androgens and estrogens, but the former are secreted mainly by the testes and the latter by the ovaries. Androgens (testosterone, androsterone) promote the production of sperm and secondary sex characteristics (hairiness, lowered voice pitch, etc.) in the male. Estrogens promote ovulation and secondary sex characteristics (pubic hair, breast development, etc.) in the female. Progesterone, which is secreted by the corpus luteum of the ovaries as well as by the placenta in pregnant women, assists in the maintenance of fetal viability.

The male hormone testosterone assumes a critical role in sex differentiation quite early in the developmental process. The gonads of every human fetus are identical, containing both Müllerian and Wolffian ducts. The Müllerian and Wolffian ducts are early precursors of female and male reproductive structures, respectively. Whether the fetus becomes a male or female depends on the level and duration of the hormone testosterone present during the third and fourth months of prenatal development. A gene contained in a Y chromosome causes the gonads to become testes, the testosterone produced by the testes increases their growth, the testes secrete more testosterone, and so on. Testosterone also causes the Wolffian ducts in the testes to develop into semen-storing sacs known as *seminal vesicles* and to the *vas deferens,* a duct extending from a testis to the penis. Finally, the release of Müllerian-inhibiting hormone leads to the degeneration of the Müllerian ducts. Although a genetically female fetus exposed to a sufficient quantity of testosterone for a sufficient period of time will develop male sexual organs, female gonads normally become ovaries. In contrast to the situation in the male, in the female the Müllerian ducts develop into oviducts, uterus, and upper vagina, and the Wolffian ducts degenerate. As implied by this description of the sexual differentiation process, every human fetus would become a female if sufficient testosterone were not present. The production of androgens by the testes is controlled by two hormones secreted by the pituitary gland: follicle-stimulating hormone (FSH) and luteinizing hormone (LH). In males, the maturation of sperm depends on FSH and the production of testosterone by the testes depends on LH. In females, the growth of the ovarian follicles, in which ova mature, depends on FSH, whereas ovulation and the production of estrogens and progesterone depend on LH. The pituitary gland and the testes form a closed feedback loop, in which a decline in testosterone by the testes causes the pituitary to increase its secretion of LH and an increase in testosterone level causes the pituitary to decrease its secretion of LH.

EVOLUTION AND GENETICS

During the 19th century, biology, like chemistry and geology, began to acquire the theoretical and empirical foundations of a systematic science. Not only was it a century of breakthroughs in neurophysiology, but also in the understanding of how living things develop and change. Two major unifying conceptions arising from 19th-century biology were evolution and genetics, which, following the pioneering research of Charles Darwin and Gregor Mendel, directed the study of human and animal origins in the 20th century.

Evolution

The organs that make up the human body, including the brain, have changed dramatically during the past 2 million years. In fact, only in the last 200,000 years have we been recognized as the same sort of living creatures that we are now. These changes were not limited to human beings, but took place in other species of animals and plants as well. What factors were responsible for these changes, and what have been their effects?

The question of the origins of the multiplicity of existing species that could not possibly have fitted into Noah's ark, even when limited to mating pairs, has puzzled observers for centuries. Barring the creation of entirely new species by a divine being, the similarities among various living creatures and the fossil record of extinct animals suggested that some species evolved from others. A reasonable hypothesis was that more complex forms of life evolved from simpler forms, but how and why did this evolution take place? This was the question that faced Charles Darwin (1809–1882) during the mid-19th century.

The belief that characteristics or abilities acquired during one's lifetime can be transmitted genetically to one's descendants was defended by the French naturalist J. B. Lamarck in the 18th century and in our own time by the Russian geneticist T. D. Lysenko. For example, Lamarck maintained that giraffes have long necks because generations of giraffes stretched their necks to reach leaves in the tops of trees. The vast majority of biologists no longer believe that acquired characteristics can be inherited, but rather adhere to the theory of evolution proposed by Darwin.

In a sense, the theory of evolution propounded by Darwin was an obvious extension of the knowledge gained from selective breeding experiments in previous centuries. Even if the study of evolution did not begin with Darwin, it was his patient, pain-staking observations and investigations in the Galapagos Islands and several other geographical areas that led to the first systematic treatise on the subject—the monumental *Origin of Species* (Darwin, 1859).

The basic premise of Darwin's theory of evolution is that new species arise as a result of chance genetic variations and the survival and transmission of some of these variations by the process of natural selection over many generations. The chance-produced variations in structure and function, in anatomy and behavior, that contribute to an organism's survival are more likely to be selected for transmission to subsequent generations because they increase the likelihood of survival and reproduction. Individuals with certain characteristics are more successful than others at finding food, attracting mates, protecting their offspring, and simply living long enough to do those things.

Both mutation and genetic recombination contribute to chance variations in genetic transmission. A *mutation* is a sudden change in a gene, such that the gene duplicates itself in a new form. Among conditions that have been shown to produce mutations—many of which are associated with abnormal or harmful characteristics—are radiation (X-rays, cosmic rays, ultraviolet rays, gamma rays, etc.) and certain chemical substances. A second factor that can lead to genetic variations is *recombination*, which is the occurrence of new combinations of genes that yield characteristics not possessed by the parents. The new variations within populations produced by mutation and recombination may be either advantageous or disadvantageous to a species. Those that are advantageous (i.e., that have survival value) are more likely to enhance reproduction and hence be passed onto subsequent generations. Consequently, they become more common in the population and a new species evolves.

Another factor in evolutionary change is *speciation*, which is the evolution of different populations of species in different environments leading to their independent development. Also important is *adaptation*, in which the environment remains fairly constant and natural selection produces a species that is better adjusted to that environment.

The theory of evolution has continued to develop and change since Darwin's time. Advances in geology and genetics, for example, have provided a foundation for interpreting naturalistic and fossil findings that was not available to Darwin. Furthermore, understanding of the manner in which genetically based variations take place has grown, leading to the current belief that recombination is more important than mutation in the process. Another modification in the theory of evolution is concerned with the speed at which the process occurs. Darwin saw evolution as a slow, gradual process that takes place over millions of years. More recent theorists maintain that evolutionary change can be rather abrupt in terms of the geological time scale and that the search for missing links in the fossil record may be misguided in some instances.

Genetics

The story of how an obscure, 19th-century Austrian monk named Gregor Mendel (1822–1884) became recognized as the father of genetics, although somewhat belatedly, is told in many school books on biology. Mendel's research on flowering plants revealed that offspring are not mere blends of their parents, but that some inherited characteristics are dominant, some recessive, and that the physical appearance (*phenotype*) of an organism is not necessarily the same as its underlying genetic structure (*genotype*).

The history of genetics in the 20th century began with the rediscovery of Mendel's work, progressed through Watson and Crick's (1953) model of DNA (deoxyribonucleic acid), which led to contemporary research on a variety of inherited characteristics and the genome project. The concept of *gene* as the unit carrier of genetic information has undergone some change since it was hypothesized early in the 20th century. Genes act in pairs; one member of each pair is located on a chromosome contributed by the mother, and the other member at the same place on a chromosome contributed by the father. When the two genes are identical, the resulting trait is *homozygous*; when they are different, the trait is *heterozygous*. In most cases of heterozygosity, one member of a gene pair (the *dominant gene*) suppresses the other member (the *recessive gene*), although blending can occur. A recessive gene is usually expressed phenotypically only when paired with an identical gene, whereas the effect of a dominant gene is expressed whether the remaining gene is the same or different. Dwarfism, cataracts, and white forelock are examples of characteristics that are due to dominant genes, whereas color blindness, albinism, and (presumably) bipolar disorder are recessive and necessarily homozygous characteristics.

Different genes determine different characteristics, but genes also differ in the extent to which they are expressed in their corresponding phenotypes (*penetrance*). A single gene can also have multiple phenotypic effects (*pleiotropy*), and genes located near each other on a chromosome may be transmitted together (*linkage*). Furthermore, two genes may interact in producing a phenotypic effect that is not predictable from knowledge of the effects of one gene alone (*epistasis*).

Some hereditary characteristics are caused by defective genes located on X chromosomes. Of the 23 pairs of chromosomes in human cells, one pair—an XX (female) or an XY (male)—is the sex pair; the remaining 22 pairs are autosomes. A *sex-linked defect* is manifested in a male who inherits a defective X chromosome from his mother or in a female who inherits a defective X chromosome from either her father or mother or from both parents. The expression of a sex-linked characteristic depends on whether it is dominant or recessive. If dominant, the characteristic is manifested in more females than males; this is because the chances of a female inheriting at least one defective X chromosome is twice that for a male. If a sex-linked characteristic is recessive, the chance of a female inheriting a defective X chromosome from both parents is substantially less than that of a male inheriting a defective X from his mother. Consequently, the characteristic is more likely to be present in males. When a condition is sex-linked recessive, a female who inherits only one defective X chromosome will act as a carrier of it and her male offspring will have a 50–50 chance of developing the condition. Examples of sex-linked recessive characteristics are hemophilia, pattern baldness, red–green color blindness, and muscular dystrophy.

Genetically based conditions due to major genes may also be *sex-limited*—occurring in only one sex. They may also be *autosomal*, in that they are caused by genes carried on autosomes (non-sex chromosomes). As indicated in Table 3.3, rather than being caused by genes carried on X chromosomes, many genetic disorders are autosomal in nature. Other disorders can occur when something goes awry during sex-cell development, causing a daughter cell to be an inexact copy of the parent cell. An example is Down's syndrome, in which the cells contain a third chromosome in the 21st position.

Certain physical characteristics are due to the dominance and recessivity of major genes, but most human characteristics are determined not by single genes but rather by the interaction of many different genes. Two examples of these *polygenic* conditions of particular interest to psychologists are familial mental retardation and schizophrenia.

Even when a person has a genetic disorder, it may be possible to control the symptoms by changing some aspect of the prenatal or postnatal environment. For example, interference with normal brain development and the resulting mental retardation caused by recessive disorders such as phenylketonuria (PKU), Tay-Sachs disease, and galactosemia can be controlled by special diets.

Much information concerning genetics and related disorders was available before Watson and Crick's discovery of the structure of the DNA molecule, but that event launched a genuine revolution in biology. It is now known that the unit carriers of heredity designated as genes are portions of DNA molecules, which carry the blueprints for inherited characteristics in coded form. A DNA molecule consists of two helix-shaped strands of alternating phosphate and deoxyribose units wound around the same axis and held together by four chemical bases connected by hydrogen bonds. There are approximately 3.3 billion ways in which these four bases—adenine, thymine, cytosine, and guanine—can be arranged as adenine–thymine and cytosine–guanine pairs into a double-helix-shaped molecule. Each of these arrangements constitutes the genetic code for the creation of a particular hereditary characteristic. Approximately 99.9% of the same base pairs are found in each cell in the human body. They are the codes for characteristics that most humans have in common—1 nose, 2 eyes and ears, 10 toes, specific chemical secretions from endocrine and exocrine glands, and so on. The remaining .1% of the base pairs contain the codes for characteristics differing from one person to another (see the appendix).

TABLE 3.3

Examples of Genetic Disorders

Disorder	Genetic Cause
Achondoplasia (Dwarfism)	Autosomal dominant gene
Amyotrophic lateral sclerosis (ALS)	Autosomal dominant gene
Ataxia	Autosomal recessive gene
Cleft palate	Recessive gene, possibly polygenic
Cooley's anemia	Autosomal recessive gene
Cystic fibrosis (CF)	Autosomal recessive gene
Diabetes mellitus ("Sugar diabetes")	Autosomal recessive gene
Down's syndrome	Extra autosomal chromosome
Dysautonomia	Autosomal recessive gene
Dystrophic epidermolysis bullosa(DEB)	Dominant autosomal or recessive autosomal gene
Huntington's disease (HD)	Autosomal dominant gene
Muscular dystrophy (MD)	Sex-linked recessive gene
Osteogenesis imperfecta (OI)	Dominant autosomal or recessive autosomal gene
Phenylketonuria (PKU)	Autosomal recessive gene
Retinitis pigmentosa (RP)	Autosomal recessive gene
Sickle cell anemia (SCA)	Autosomal recessive gene
Spina bifida (SB)	Autosomal recessive gene
Tay-Sachs disease (TS)	Autosomal recessive gene
Tourette syndrome	Autosomal dominant gene
Turner's syndrome	Sex-linked gene in a missing or distorted X chromosome of females only

Note. From "Genetic Disorders" by H. K. Fink in *Encyclopedia of Psychology* (p. 57–61) by R. J. Corsini, 1994, New York: Wiley. Copyright © 1994 by Wiley. Reprinted by permission.

Strands of DNA serve as templates (models) for the synthesis of ribonucleic acid (RNA) molecules. Each cell in the human body contains the same DNA sequences, thereby storing identical information and commands. Once formed, RNA molecules migrate to various parts of the cell, transporting amino acids to the ribosomes in the case of transfer RNA (tRNA) or serving as templates for protein formation in the case of messenger RNA (mRNA). The resulting proteins are then responsible for the development of the various characteristics of the organism.

Heredity and Psychology

Awareness of the importance of genetic factors in behavior is not new. For generations, farmers and hunters have been breeding animals for specific physical and behavioral characteristics. Geneticists, psychologists, and other professional researchers have also bred animals for numerous traits. For example, psychologists have bred rats for maze-learning ability and emotionality (e.g., Hall, 1938; Tryon, 1940). Studies of family trees have underscored the significance of heredity as a determinant of behavior, but the results of such studies are usually confounded by a failure to control for and take into account environmental differences. Finally, observational and correlational studies of children have revealed a great deal of consistency in abilities and personality from the cradle to adolescence and even into old age (McCrae & Costa, 1982; Thomas, Chess, & Birch, 1968).

The most impressive evidence of a genetic basis for specific cognitive, affective, and psychomotor characteristics has come from studies of twins and other individuals with various degrees of kinship. Comparisons of monozygotic (mz) twins reared together with mz twins reared apart have been particularly intriguing, in that they control for differences in heredity. Illustrative of the results of correlational comparisons of selected physiological characteristics by Thomas Bouchard and his associates are the data in Fig. 3.1. Many of the correlations for both mz and dz (dizygotic) twin pairs are fairly high and the correlations for the dz pairs are, for the most part, not appreciably lower than those for the mz pairs. As is seen in later chapters, the corresponding correlations for cognitive and personality variables are lower than those for these physical and physiological variables. Furthermore, in many situations, the dz correlations are substantially lower than the mz correlations.

The correlation coefficient (Pearson r) is not the only index of genetic relationship computed in studies of the relative influences of heredity and environment on human characteristics. Another numerical index of the degree of inheritance of a trait is the *heritability coefficient* (h^2); this is the proportion of variance in a measure of a trait in a group of people that is attributable to genetic influences. A heritability coefficient may be computed as

$$h^2 = 2(r_{mz} - r_{dz}),$$

where r_{mz} is the correlation between measures of the trait in monozygotic twins reared together and r_{dz} is the correlation between measures of the

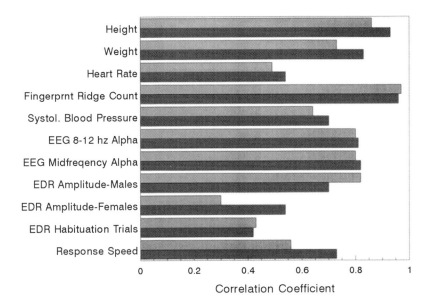

FIG. 3.1.   Correlations for monozygotic twins reared apart and together for 11
physical variables. EEG designates electroencephalograph, and EDR designates
electrodermal response (Based on data in Bouchard, Lykken, McGue, Segal, &
Tellengen, 1990).

trait in dizygotic twins reared together.[3] Thus, if r_{mz} = .85 and r_{dz} = .58, h^2 =
2(.85 − .58) = .54. This indicates that 54% of the group variance in a measure of this trait is attributable to heredity. The reader should be cautioned
that the proportion of variance specified by a heritability coefficient refers
to a group of people and not a single individual. Actually, because every
trait is a result of the interaction between heredity and environment, the
proportion of a trait in a particular individual that is due to heredity alone is
zero. Furthermore, heritability coefficients are not fixed, invariant numbers. Rather, they vary with the characteristics of the group and the time and
place at which measurements are made.

---

[3]Another formula for h^2 is $(r_{mz} - r_{dz})/(1 - r_{dz})$, which is based on different assumptions than
the formula given earlier.

The heritability coefficient (h^2) for a psychological trait is an estimate of the proportion of that trait's variance in the population that can be attributed to heredity. Consequently, subtracting h^2 from 1 yields an estimate of the proportion of the trait variance that can be attributed to a combination of environmental factors and errors of measurement. The environmental variance consists of two parts: one part due to experiences that the individuals have in common (shared environmental variance) and the remaining part due to experiences that they do not have in common (unshared environmental variance). The proportion of total trait variance due to shared and unshared environmental factors is known as the *environmentality coefficient*. It is equal to the difference between the correlations for identical twins reared together and apart. However, approximations to the total, shared, and unshared environmentality coefficient can be determined as follows. An estimate of the total trait variance due to both shared (common) and unshared (specific) environmental factors can be computed as $v_{su} = 1 - h^2$, an estimate of the total trait variance due to shared factors as $v_s = 2r_{dz} - r_{mz}$, and an estimate of the proportion of total trait variance due to unshared environmental factors as $v_u = 1 - r_{mz}$. These formulas assume that the error of measurement is zero—a tenuous assumption at best. As discussed in chapter 8, the shared and unshared environments have different effects on the development of personality at different ages.

When dealing with nonmeasured, dichotomous variables, the concordance rate is the preferred measure of heritability. The *concordance rate* is the proportion of individuals having a specific characteristic or condition who are genetically related to other persons who also have the characteristic or condition (index cases or probands). For example, if the concordance rate for depression in mz twins is found to be .40, it can be estimated that if one member of an mz twin pair has the disorder then the probability is .40 that the other member of the pair will also have it (Allen, 1976). Once the concordance rate between probands and their relatives has been computed, it can be compared with the proportion of people in the general population (the *base rate*) having the condition.

A more accurate measure of the influence of heredity on a dichotomous trait is the *probandwise concordance rate*. This statistic is computed by dividing twice the number of concordant pairs (both members have the trait) in the sample by the sum of the number of concordant and discordant pairs (only one member has the trait). For example, suppose that, in a sample of 50 twin pairs, both members of 30 twin pairs have a specified trait or disorder but only one member of each of the remaining 20 twin pairs has the trait. Then the probandwise concordance rate is $2(30)/[2(30) + 1(20)] = .75$. This rate can then be compared with the proportion of people in the general population who have the trait.

Other statistical procedures have also been employed in developmental investigations of cognitive and affective variables, two of which are structural equation modeling and multiple abstract variance analysis. *Structural equation modeling* may be applied, among other ways, to determine the best-fitting equation to estimate the correlations among trait scores of people having different degrees of genetic relationships (see Ferguson, 1997). *Multiple abstract variance analysis* (MAVA) is a statistical procedure for estimating the degree to which various measures are related to the amount of genetic overlap between individuals with varying genetic relationships who are reared together in the same family or reared apart in different families (Cattell, 1982). It should be emphasized, however, that the results of all of these statistical procedures only apply to groups and not to specific individuals. Furthermore, the magnitude of specific measures of hereditary effects can vary substantially from one sample of persons to another. The reader should also bear in mind that, rather than being independent or additive in their effects, heredity and environment have a joint or multiplicative influence. It is not a matter of one or the other, or even how much or how little of each, with respect to a specific person. Rather, it is a question of the ways heredity and environment interact and cooperate to create various human qualities and behaviors.

As useful as statistical methods may be, research on behavioral genetics is not limited to the computation of correlations, heritability coefficients, and related population genetics statistics. Progress in molecular genetics promises to make even greater contributions to our understanding of genetic influences on cognitive abilities, personality characteristics, and behavior (Saudino & Plomin, 1996). The techniques of molecular genetics of relevance to behavioral science consist of using DNA markers to identify the multiple genes that contribute to quantitatively measured traits. Two of these techniques—*linkage* and *allelic association*—and related research findings are especially important. The technique of linkage consists of tracing the transmission of both a DNA marker and a characteristic of disorder in a family. Of particular interest is sib-pair QTL linkage analysis, which was used to discover a linkage between reading disability and chromosome 6 (Fulker & Cardon, 1994). Also useful in determining whether a DNA marker occurs more frequently among individuals with a particular trait or disorder and those without it is allelic association (Lander & Schork, 1994). When a DNA marker is so close to a trait-relevant gene that its alleles are correlated with the trait in genetically unrelated individuals, the alleles are said to be associated (see Plomin & Saudino, 1994).

SUMMARY

Most modern biologists and psychologists adhere to a monistic philosophy in which the mental and physical, the mind and the body, are viewed as interacting and interdependent rather than separate entities. According to this philosophy, the mind is a function of the body and cannot exist without it. Studies in psychosomatic medicine, and in particular the effects of stress on the body, have employed a number of physiological variables and measuring instruments.

Individual differences are found in all systems of the body. However, because of its close connection with behavior, cognition, and personality, the functioning of the nervous system has been of special interest to psychologists and other behavioral scientists. The human nervous system may be divided for convenience into two parts: central (brain and spinal cord) and peripheral (outside the brain and spinal cord)—or, alternatively, into somatic and autonomic nervous systems. Various neurotransmitters and drugs can affect the transmission of electrochemical impulses in nerve cells (neurons). Sensory neurons carry these impulses from sensory receptors to the spinal cord and brain, motor neurons carry impulses from the central nervous system to the muscles and glands, and association neurons carry impulses between neurons.

A vertical conception of the brain pictures it in terms of five ascending levels: myelencephalon, metencephalon, mesencephalon, diencephalon, and telencephalon. Each of these levels consists of a group of neural structures or areas that contribute to the sensory, motor, and other functions of the nervous system. The crowning jewel of the human nervous system is the cerebral cortex, which consists of two cerebral hemispheres with four lobes each: frontal, parietal, occipital, and temporal. Each lobe has both unique functions and collaborative functions with other areas of the brain. Although specific areas subserving sensory, motor, and language functions have been discovered in the cerebral cortex, the higher order processes in most areas develop and cooperate with those of other areas of the brain.

The ANS is primarily a motor system that controls the smooth and cardiac muscles of blood vessels and visceral organs and the secretions of various glands. The parasympathetic division of the ANS is concerned with digestion and other vegetative functions, and the sympathetic division prepares the organism to meet emergency (fight or flight) situations.

Hormones secreted by the endocrine glands regulate growth, control the rates of body activities, and integrate body functions. Pituitary hormones control the rate of growth and the secretions of the other endocrine glands. Thyroid hormones regulate metabolic rate and affect growth, and the parathyroid hormone assists in control of the body's calcium–potassium balance. Hormones secreted by the adrenal medulla enable the body to meet emergency situations, and those secreted by the adrenal cortex help regulate salt excretion, blood sugar level, and protein and fat metabolism. Insulin secreted by the islets of Langerhans helps maintain the blood sugar level while hormones secreted by the male (testes) and female (ovaries) gonads affect sexual development and behavior.

Development of the brain and other body structures to their present states has occurred through a process of evolution from simpler and less adaptive forms to more complex and adaptive forms. The theory of evolution stemming from Darwin's original formulation is more than a hypothesis designed to account for variations among different species, but there is still some debate concerning how evolution takes place. Recombination of genes and gene mutations are both important in the evolutionary process, although the former is considered more important than the latter. Some biologists maintain that evolution can occur suddenly rather than gradually over the geological time span. Also important in evolution are speciation in different environments and adaptation to relatively stable environments.

Because modern genetics arose after his time, Darwin did not have the advantage of this knowledge in propounding his theory of evolution. By the time the DNA double helix was discovered (in the early 1950s), many of the principles of heredity were already established. The concepts of dominant and recessive genes, sex-linked and sex-limited genes, defective genes on autosomes, and sex chromosomes, as well as the notions of penetrance, pleiotropy, and epistasis, had been formulated. However, the double-helix model extended research on the biochemistry of genetics and increased knowledge concerning the biology of inheritance and genetic disorders. It also led to experimental manipulation of genetic structures and genetic fingerprinting to establish identity in criminal and authenticity cases.

Research on population genetics has led to advances in understanding the influences of heredity on more complex physiological and psychological characteristics. Statistical indexes, such as the correlation coefficient, the heritability index, and the concordance rate, are now computed routinely to assess and document the relative influences of heredity and environment on abilities and personality. Behavior geneticists continue to emphasize that heredity and environment interact rather than acting independently in determining who and what we are. Two techniques of molecular genetics that are of particular value in identifying genes associated with complex behaviors are linkage and allelic association.

SUGGESTED READINGS

Bouchard, T. J., Jr. (1994). Genes, environment, and personality. *Science, 264,* 1700–1701.

Calvin, W. H., & Ojemann, G. A. (1994). *Conversations with Neil's brain.* Reading, MA: Addison-Wesley.

Carlson, N. R. (1998). *Physiology of behavior.* Needham Heights, MA: Allyn & Bacon.

Kalat, J. W. (1998). *Biological psychology* (6th ed.). Pacific Grove, CA: Brooks/Cole.

Plomin, R. (1994). *Genetics and experience: The interplay between nature and nurture.* Thousand Oaks, CA: Sage.

Plomin, R., & McClearn, G. E. (Eds.). (1993). *Nature, nurture & psychology.* Washington, DC: American Psychological Association.

Rose, R. J. (1995). Genes and human behavior. *Annual Review of Psychology, 46,* 625–654.

Steen, R. G. (1996). *DNA and destiny: Nature and nurture in human behavior.* New York: Plenum.

Stemmler, G. (1992). *Differential psychophysiology: Persons in situations.* New York: Springer-Verlag.

Vernon, P. A. (Ed.). (1994). *The neuropsychology of individual differences.* San Diego, CA: Academic Press.

Zuckerman, M. (1995). Good and bad humans: Biochemical bases of personality and its disorders. *Psychological Science, 6,* 325–332.

CHAPTER FOUR

Sociocultural Foundations

Unlike many other mammalian species, most human beings are generally not born in litters. Nevertheless, every blessed event is a social one as well. The newborn becomes a social animal at birth—a member of a family, tribe, social class, and cultural or nationality group. As such, he or she is expected to conform to the expectations and ways of the group, learn appropriate patterns of behavior, and eventually contribute to the welfare of fellow members. Together with biological inheritance and the physical environment, social groups play a crucial role in determining what kind of person an individual becomes. These behaviors represent adaptations to the physical and social environments and enable people to satisfy their biological and social needs more effectively than by acting alone without concern for others.

The process of socialization typically begins at home in a family setting. In their role as socializers and educators of the young, families provide care and support, communicate social norms and values, and provide a place where the first social norms and roles are learned. *Social norms* are enforced standards of behavior that are expected of people in particular situations. Most children eventually learn to behave in accordance with the norms of their group(s), but sometimes they choose to deviate from those norms, at least temporarily. Certain norms are traditions or mores handed down from generation to generation, and deviation from them is often severely censured or punished. The punishment for violation may be especially severe in the case of taboos, such as the prohibition against marriage between brother and sister. Norms need not be explicitly taught, and children typically fail to realize that the norms of their social or cultural group are not necessarily universal. Consequently, most people grow up accepting the norms they have learned as their own personal convictions rather than social conventions that are relative to a particular group.

Roles are patterns of behavior that individuals are expected to display under certain conditions or in specific situations. Thus, the concept of role implies a degree of transitoriness or situation-specificity that may not be representative of the individual's more general, typical behavior. Most people play multiple roles (e.g., that of wife, mother, teacher, friend, confidante, or volunteer) depending on the situation and the task to be performed. Acceptable role behaviors are usually not as punitively reinforced as norms, but too much deviation from assigned role behaviors can get a person into trouble almost as quickly. Both roles and norms vary with gender, age, social class, ethnicity, nationality, and other demographic characteristics.

This chapter is concerned with sociocultural influences on individual development. It deals with the effects of parenting, physical maturation, gender, ethnicity, and culture on individuals and some of the associated problems. The treatment of these topics is brief, but hopefully sufficient to stimulate interest in further reading in the voluminous research literature on each topic. Furthermore, chapters 4 and 10 are a pair—dealing with many of the same topics from different perspectives. Consequently, immediately after reading this chapter, you may wish to peruse chapter 10 rather than waiting until you have studied the material in chapters 5 to 9.

ATTACHMENT AND PARENTING

Only slightly less remarkable than the miracle of birth is human development during the first year of life. A typical newborn has been characterized as "an alimentary canal with a loud noise at one end and no sense of responsibility at the other," but by the end of the first year he or she is distinctively human. The infant has become an active, curious explorer who recognizes people and things, smiles, laughs (and cries), babbles, crawls, and shows fear of strangers. Finally, the first halting steps are taken and imitative noises that sound something like words are made. The process of development is, of course, not uniform for all children: Some children walk and talk earlier than others; some are more alert, more perceptive, and learn faster; and some are more socially conscious.

What accounts for the miraculous transformation in a single year to a real person? Psychological theorists and researchers have studied and written about it for decades, but so far with only middling success. Heredity, environment, experience—all are recognizably important, but precisely how and when they exert their effects are not clear. Pioneer child development researchers such as Arnold Gesell focused on maturation and readiness and collected norms for the appearance of specific perceptual, motor, cognitive, social, and emotional behaviors. However, these norms are only averages, and there is a great deal of individual variation around them. Appearance of the first steps and the first words, for example, can vary extensively with the sex, nationality, and physical characteristics of the child. Developmental norms and theories are still important to child psychologists. However, rather than embracing more general theories of development, emphasis in recent years has been on the analysis of single processes. One process that has occasioned a great deal of interest and appears to be especially important to social development is attachment.

Attachment

The strong affectional tie that binds a person to an intimate companion was designated by Bowlby (1982/1969) as *attachment*. Associated with feelings of attachment is a need for body contact, observable in most mammals, and deprivation of which can have profound physiological and psychological consequences. Both psychoanalytic and learning theorists have viewed attachment to and love of an infant for its mother as associated with the feeding situation. Research by Harry Harlow and his associates (Harlow, 1958; Harlow & Zimmerman, 1959) showed that, when given a choice, young rhesus monkeys chose to spend more time on a terry cloth-covered monkey model than on a wire-covered model, although they received food from the latter. The fact that contact with the cloth-covered monkey mother decreased the fears and increased the feelings of security of young monkeys was revealed when the monkeys were placed in a strange situation or exposed to a fear stimulus. Furthermore, monkeys reared without body contact with other monkeys or exclusively with a cloth-covered mother revealed abnormal behaviors of various kinds.

Studies of the effects of mothering deprivation in humans began with Margaret Ribble (1944), who referred to the physical and psychological *wasting away* observed in infants deprived of mothering as *marasmus*. Subsequent investigations (e.g., Dennis & Najarian, 1957; Goldfarb, 1955; R. R. Spitz, 1946) underscored the destructive effects of such deprivation on the social, emotional, and cognitive development of young children.

Evidence for a three-stage sequence in the development of attachment has been found in both Western and non-Western societies (Ainsworth, 1967; Kermoian & Leiderman, 1986; Schaffer & Emerson, 1964; Takahashi, 1986). In the first stage, the infant shows a preference for people over other objects. Next is a preference for familiar people over unfamiliar ones, progressing in the third stage to a preference for certain people—usually the mother or primary caregiver. An expanded form of this stage conception of attachment (Ainsworth, Blehar, Waters, & Wall, 1978; Bowlby, 1982/1969) describes four phases in the development of close ties with caregivers: (a) undiscriminating social responses (birth to 2–3 months)—responsiveness to voices, faces, and other social stimuli, and particularly humans, but no clear preference for one person over another; (b) discriminating social responsiveness (2–3 months to 7 months)—friendly with familiar as well as unfamiliar people, but more enthusiasm shown for the former; (c) active proximity seeking/true attachment (6–7 months to 3 years)—clear attachments formed; (d) goal-corrected partnership (3 years and older)—children take parents' goals and plans into consideration and adjust their behavior accordingly.

The most extensive research on mother–child attachment has been conducted by Mary Ainsworth and her associates (Ainsworth, Blehar, Waters & Wall, 1978; Sroufe, 1985). These researchers have employed a special technique—the *strange-situation procedure*—to study the relationship between attachment and stranger anxiety. The procedure involves both stranger anxiety and separation anxiety. A strange-situation experiment typically begins with the mother and baby entering an unfamiliar room. The mother sits down and the baby is free to explore. Then an unfamiliar adult enters the room and the mother leaves the baby alone with him or her. The mother returns after a time and then the stranger leaves. After a few more minutes, the stranger returns and the mother leaves again. The mother eventually returns and then the stranger leaves for good.

The individual reactions of 1-year-old infants to the strange-situation procedure were classified by Ainsworth into three categories. Sixty-six percent of the babies were designated in terms of their reactions as *securely attached*; they readily endured separation from their mothers and explored their surroundings. Another 20% of the babies were classified as *avoidant*; they rarely cried when separated from the mother and avoided her when she returned. Although securely attached infants were usually cooperative and free of anger in the situation, avoidant infants did not reach out in time of need, disliked being held, disliked being put down even more, and tended to be very angry. In a third category were the 12% of infants, characterized as *resistant* or *ambivalent*, who became anxious even before their mothers left the room. Despite that they were extremely upset when she left, they behaved ambivalently by simultaneously seeking and resisting contact by kicking and squirming when she returned.

Other investigators have found that less securely attached infants are more easily frustrated, more dependent on adults, and more socially withdrawn (Matas, Arend, & Sroufe, 1978; Sroufe, Fox, & Pancake, 1983; Waters, Wippman, & Sroufe, 1979). Such children also experience greater difficulty in problem solving at ages 2 to 3. Furthermore, failure to form secure attachments in the early years contributes to problems in establishing close relationships with siblings, friends, and marital partners (Ainsworth, 1989; Bowlby, 1973; Rutter, 1979). Be that as it may, an inability to achieve close attachments in infancy does not irreparably damage a person for life. Subsequent childhood experiences can help overcome the damage to socioemotional relationships that might result if they remained unchecked or were not compensated for in some way.

Not only does attachment vary with the individual, but evidence from cross-national comparisons has revealed distinct patterns of attachment in infancy in different groups. From a meta-analysis of international studies of attachment, Van Ijzendoorn and Kroonenberg (1988) concluded that most infants could be characterized as *secure.* However, an *insecure* rather than an *avoidant* pattern was more common in West European countries, whereas the opposite was true in Japan and Israel. A greater percentage of American infants were classified as *insecure* rather than *avoidant,* but the difference between the percentages of infants falling into the two categories was less for infants in the United States than in West European countries.

Parenting Styles

The behavior, personality, and overall life satisfaction of children are determined in some measure by the way in which children are treated by their caregivers. A child's feelings of self-acceptance or rejection, security or insecurity, and competence or incompetence are all affected by the attitudes of these caregivers and the sanctions and reinforcements imposed by them. If parents view their children as worthwhile individuals and provide them with an encouraging and supportive environment, the children are likely to feel capable of mastering the required developmental tasks and applying themselves to accomplish the goals set for and by them.

Parents are the major caregivers in most families, although grandparents and other family members, day care personnel, teachers, and other parental surrogates may also serve that function part of the time. Numerous theories of parenting styles and their effects on children's behavior have been proposed, one of the best known being Baumrind's (1971, 1978) four-category classification. Baumrind grouped parenting styles into four major categories or types: authoritarian, permissive, authoritative, and uninvolved. Each of these styles presumably leads to certain behaviors on the part of children. *Authoritarian* parents are restrictive, rule-emphasizing individuals who expect children to be obedient and who punish behavior that deviates from their rules. In contrast, *permissive* parents are nondemand- ing people who permit their children to establish their own standards of conduct. *Authoritative* parents set behavioral limits and standards and enforce them with a combination of power and reasoning. They encourage their children to conform to these limits, but the children are also permitted to contribute their own reasoning about those limits. Finally, *uninvolved* parents provide only minimal attention and care, failing to set rules and expectations concerning social behavior and school work. Parents of this type are so involved in their own lives that they have little time to teach and guide their children.

Baumrind (1972) found children of authoritarian parents to be anxious, withdrawn, and unhappy as preschoolers. The boys tended to be angry and defiant, whereas the girls were more dependent and lacked self-confidence. Although they did well in school and were not likely to engage in antisocial behavior on the whole, the children of authoritarian parents were not as mature or well-adjusted as the children of authoritative parents. Children of permissive parents tended to be immature, had problems with impulse control, and had a tendency to be dependent and underachieving. They did poorly in school and were more likely to become involved with drugs. Children of uninvolved parents were, as a group, impaired in many aspects of child development—attachment, cognition, play, and socioemotional skills. Delinquency, lack of long-term goals, poor school work, and lack of emotional control were associated with the older children of uninvolved parents. Most mature of all were the children of authoritative parents: The majority displayed higher confidence, better mood, and better self-control. Older children in this group tended to have higher self-esteem and to be more involved with school and academic achievement.

A modification of Baumrind's (1972) theory proposed by Maccoby and Martin (1983) consists of two dimensions: demandingness and responsiveness. Combinations of high and low ratings on each of these dimensions yield four types of parents: *authoritative parents,* who are high in both demandingness and responsiveness; *authoritarian parents,* who are high on demandingness but low on control; *indulgent parents,* who are high on responsiveness but low on demandingness; and *neglecting parents,* who are low on both dimensions.

Authoritarian parents assert their power without warmth, nurturance, or reciprocal communication between parents and children. These parents value obedience, respect for authority, work, tradition, and the preservation of order, and they attempt to control and evaluate the child's behavior according to a set of absolute standards. Children of authoritarian parents are, on the average, moderately competent and responsible, but they are socially withdrawn and lack spontaneity. Daughters of these parents tend to be dependent and lower in achievement motivation; sons tend to be higher in aggressiveness but lower in self-esteem than other boys their age.

Indulgent parents make few demands on their children. The children of these parents tend to be more positive in their moods and have greater vitality than the children of authoritarian parents. However, they also tend to be immature, impulsive, socially irresponsible, and low in self-reliance, and to have difficulty handling aggressive impulses.

Neglecting parents ignore their children and are indifferent to or uninvolved with them. These parents do not necessarily abuse their children, but their behavior is self-centered rather than child-centered. They engage in little social interaction with their children and usually do not know where they are or what they are doing. The children of neglecting parents tend to be impulsive, moody, unable to concentrate, and low in frustration tolerance. They also have problems handling aggression, lack emotional attachments to other people, and are often truant.

Authoritative parents are accepting, responsive, and child-centered, but also controlling. They expect their children to behave according to their abilities and ages, but solicit the children's opinions and feelings in family decision making. Although warm and nurturing, authoritative parents are not averse to imposing punitive and restrictive measures. However, when they do so they provide reasons and explanations to the children. Maccoby and Martin (1983) found that the children of authoritative parents were, for the most part, independent, self-assertive, friendly, and cooperative.

PHYSICAL DEVELOPMENT AND SOCIAL ACCEPTANCE

Mothers and fathers are supposed to love their children, regardless of the children's physical appearance and temperament. However, not all people are so "forgiving," and a child's physical characteristics and behavior are often evaluated unmercifully. These evaluations affect the child's feelings of worth and shape his or her social and antisocial behavior throughout life.

Rate of Maturation

The rate of physical maturation can affect a person's feelings of self-adequacy and self-confidence—feelings that persist into adulthood. Early-maturing boys and girls tend to have more friends and to assume leadership roles, particularly in sports and related physical activities. In contrast, late matura- tion can lead to personal and social difficulties for both sexes, and particu- larly for boys (e.g., Livson & Peskin, 1980). Like late-maturing boys, late- maturing girls tend to be less relaxed and self-confident in social situations, although not to the same extent as the former. Late-maturing boys are more likely than early maturers to be rejected and censured by their age mates, and they often attempt to compensate for their physical inadequacies by en- gaging in attention-seeking behaviors such as clowning. Late-maturing boys may also respond to rejection by their age/sex mates by seeking younger male friends or even nonsexual companionships with groups of girls of their age.

Age Differences

Physical and psychological development do not stop at the end of adoles- cence or early adulthood. Most people continue to change physically, so- cially, emotionally, and cognitively throughout life. However, these changes are not uniform and they are not the same for all people. The average age for vocational preparation and entry, for marriage and having children, and for other socially expected mature behaviors vary extensively from person to person and group to group.

There is a great deal of continuity in behavior and personality across the life span, although marked variations both within and between individuals at each age level also occur. Physical differences among people of different ages are most obvious, but abilities, interests, and temperament also change to some extent with age. As shown in Fig. 4.1, the average heights of men and women remain fairly stable until their 60s and then decrease. The average weights of both sexes increase until the 60s, after which they also decline. As might be expected, weight, which is more affected by environment, shows greater variation than height across successive age groups. Also noteworthy is that the patterns of age-related changes in height and weight are similar for men and women.

The lines in Fig. 4.1 are based on cross-sectional data from different age groups of people, rather than longitudinal data on the same group at differ- ent ages. As illustrated in Fig. 4.2, the number of adults in each age group in- creases up through the 35- to 44-year range and then declines abruptly. Consequently, the mean heights and weights of different age groups are based on different numbers of observations. However, longitudinal mea- surements of height and weight are not greatly different from cross-sec- tional ones.

Of course, age-related changes are not limited to height, weight, and other physical variables that are clearly manifested in appearance. Age changes occur in heart rate, kidney functioning, digestion, sensory acuity, muscle strength, lung capacity, nervous system functioning, and the struc- ture and functioning of other internal organs and systems. Reaction time and other motor skills decline with aging, as does sexual behavior and social rela- tionships. As with physical characteristics, behavior varies extensively with

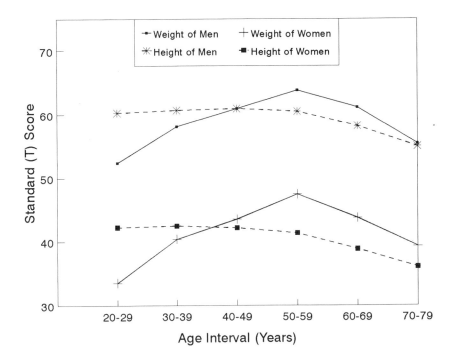

FIG. 4.1. Average heights and weights of American men and women in six age groups. (Based on data in the *Statistical Abstracts of the United States 1997.*)

age and the particular person. For example, the reported frequency of sexual activity for both sexes reaches a peak in the late 20s and then declines in later years (see Fig. 4.3). Prior to age 30, it is slightly higher for women than men but is the opposite in middle and adulthood. The data summarized in Fig. 4.3 do not include sexual activity during later life, and many people continue to engage in frequent sexual activities well into their 80s.

Age differences in physical characteristics and behavior often lead to *ageism*—the process of stereotyping and discriminating against people simply because they are old (Butler, 1974). Ageism is sometimes seen in television programs, as well as other media, employment, and other walks of life. It is more common in youth-oriented cultures such as ours and, like racism and sexism, has prompted legal intervention to combat it.

SEX AND GENDER

The sex of an individual is supposedly determined at the moment of fertilization, depending on whether an X-bearing or Y-bearing sperm penetrates the egg. However, the matter of sex and gender is not quite that simple. For example, there may be two X chromosomes and one Y chromosome (Klinefelter's syndrome), one X and two Y chromosomes (supermale), or only one X chromosome (Turner's syndrome) in the 23rd chromosome-pair position of a fertilized human egg cell. These conditions affect both the sexual appearance and behavior of the individual. In addition, the concentration of sex hormones (testosterone, estrogens) in the intrauterine environment can have an effect on the sexual physiology and psychology of the person (see chap. 3). Finally, sexual physique is not a completely accurate predictor of sexual behavior: Anatomy is not destiny.

Gender Identity and Schemas

Psychologists make a distinction among biological sex, gender role, and gender identity. *Gender role* refers to a specific behavior pattern that is considered appropriate in a given culture for individuals of a particular sex. *Gender identity* refers to the individual's internalized view of him or herself with regard to gender. A number of theories have been proposed to account for the development of gender identity and gender role. Psychoana-

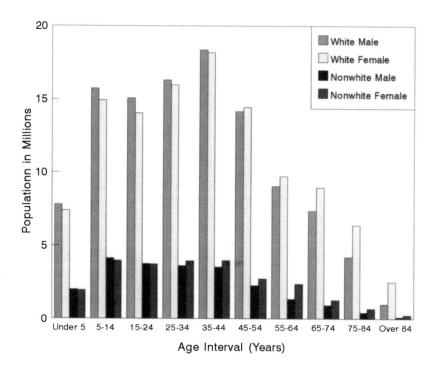

FIG. 4.2.   U.S. population by age, sex, and race in 1997. (Based on data in the *Statistical Abstracts of the United States 1998*.)

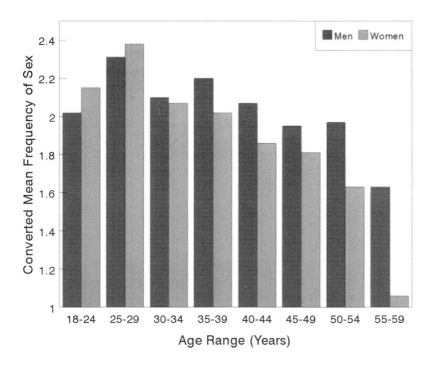

FIG. 4.3.   Converted mean frequency of reported sexual activity by men and women in eight age groups. (Based on data from Laumann, Gagnon, Michael, & Michaels, 1994.)

lytic theory emphasizes the process of identification of the child with the same-sex parent. Behavioral theory stresses the importance of differential familial and cultural reinforcement for and modeling of sex-appropriate behavior. Cognitive theorists emphasize the development of gender schemas in the growing child. A *gender schema* is an internalized process or map by which a person's knowledge and beliefs about people are organized and evaluated in terms of gender-based categories. *Gender schema theory* views gender as a category used by people to cognitively organize information about themselves. By attending to the behavior of other people, the child makes gender-linked associations. These associations, or schemas, serve as guides that motivate and regulate behavior according to cultural definitions of maleness and femaleness.

The process of acquiring gender schemas begins quite early. For example, it has been found that children as young as 9 months can distinguish male from female faces (Leinbach & Fagot, 1993). By 3 years of age, children identify themselves as boys or girls, and soon afterward they begin to group objects and events into masculine and feminine categories (Biernat, 1991; Martin, Wood, & Little, 1990). The acquisition of gender identity continues throughout the preschool and early school years. According to Kohlberg (1966), it takes place in three stages: (a) learning to label the self and others accurately (gender identity), (b) learning that boys become men and girls become women (gender stability), and (c) learning that being male or female is permanent and not changed by cultural gender cues (gender constancy). An alternative four-stage theory of gender identity development was proposed by Eaton and Von Bargen (1981): (a) identifying the self and others (labeling), (b) understanding that identity continues over time (stability), (c) realizing that identity is not changed by wishes (motive), and (d) recognizing the permanence of identity despite changes in hairstyle, clothing, or other superficial features.

Table 4.1 is a composite of research findings pertaining to stages in the development of gender identity. The relationship of these stages to Piaget's (1952) stages of cognitive development in childhood (sensorimotor, preoperational, concrete operational) is evident from the descriptions.

Sex and Gender Differences

As illustrated in Fig. 4.2, until age 44 there are more males than females in the U.S. population. At birth, there are approximately 105 males to every 100 females, but this ratio becomes dramatically reversed in old age. On the average, American women live approximately 5 years longer than American men, resulting in the problems of old age being primarily the problems of women.

Throughout the life span, there are many physical and psychological differences between the sexes; some of the physical differences are listed in Table 4.2. As described in chapters 6 and 8, many significant sex differences in cognitive abilities and personality characteristics have also been found. Many of the reported sex differences are based on stereotypes of masculine and feminine behaviors and personality traits and are not truly representative of all males and females. For example, men are seen as adventurous, strong, dominant, assertive, task-oriented, aggressive, enterprising, and independent, whereas women are said to be sensitive, gentle, emotional, sentimental, weak, submissive, and people-oriented (Best & Williams, 1993; Williams & Best, 1982). Such stereotypes need not wait until adulthood to make their appearance; they are held by children as well. Furthermore, sex stereotypes serve not only as the bases for discrimination in education and employment, but may also contribute to a self-fulfilling prophecy in which people accept the labels applied to their sex and become what they are believed to be.

Geary (1998) argued, however, that gender stereotypes, such as the idea that women gossip more and men help less with the housework, are generally true and are the results of strategies adopted by males and females over the course of evolution to attract mates. Integrating findings from several disciplines, Geary maintains that these sexual strategies are the causes of

TABLE 4.1
Stages in the Development of Gender Identity

Prenatal Period	The fetus develops the morphological characteristics of a male or a female, which others will react to once the child is born.
Birth to 3 Years	Parents and other companions label the child as a boy or a girl, frequently remind the child of his or her gender, and begin to encourage gender-consistent behavior while discouraging cross-sex activities. As a result of these social experiences and the development of basic classification skills, the young child acquires some sex-typed behavioral preferences and the knowledge that he or she is a boy or a girl (basic gender identity).
3 to 6 Years	Once children acquire a basic gender identity, they begin to seek information about sex differences, form gender schemata, and become intrinsically motivated to perform acts that are viewed as appropriate for their own sex. When acquiring gender schemata, children attend to both male and female models. Once their own sex schemata are well established, these youngsters are likely to imitate behaviors considered appropriate for their sex, regardless of the gender of the model who displays them.
Ages 6 to 7 and Beyond	Children finally acquire a sense of gender consistency—a firm, future-oriented image of themselves as boys who must necessarily become men or girls who will obviously become women. At this point, they begin to rely less exclusively on gender schemata and more on the behavior of same-sex models to acquire those mannerisms and attributes that are consistent with their firm categorization of self as a male or female.

Source. From *Social and Personality Development* (2nd ed., p. 384) by D. R. Shaffer, 1988, Pacific Grove, CA: Brooks/Cole. Copyright © 1988 by Brooks/Cole. Adapted with permission.

male–female differences in patterns of play, social behavior, parenting, emotional expression, and cognitive abilities. Males compete for social dominance and cultural success, and those who achieve it usually have more opportunities to mate and procreate. The drive to succeed also results in males spending more time away from home. For their part, females compete for culturally successful males, and therefore tend to gossip and spread rumors concerning their competitors and/or shun them. As children, females also engage in parenting play more often than males, and as adults they spend more time in child care.

TABLE 4.2

Some Physical Differences Between the Sexes

1. The expected life span of females at birth is 78 years, compared with 71 years for males

2. Sexual maturation is brought on by rising levels of estrogen and progesterone in females and by rising levels of testosterone in males.

3. On the average, girls reach puberty at age 11 and boys at age 13.

4. On the average, boys have faster and more coordinated body movements than girls.

5. On the average, the tactile sensitivity, finger dexterity, and smell sensitivity of boys is poorer than that of girls.

6. On the average, men are 5 inches taller and 20 to 30 pounds heavier than women.

7. On the average, men have 40% more muscle and 12% less fat than women.

8. On the average, men sweat more than women.

9. On the average, men can arm-curl nearly twice as much weight and bench-press nearly three times as much weight as women.

10. On the average, men have a million more red blood cells in each drop of blood, absorb 30% less alcohol into the bloodstream, and have 10% more lung volume than women of equivalent size.

11. Men are more likely than women to be left-handed, have deficient color vision, snore in their sleep, have facial hair, and become bald as they age.

12. Women are more likely than men to become rearoused shortly after experiencing orgasm.

13. Women are more likely than men to develop physical problems and chronic disorders (with the exception of hearing problems) in later life.

14. On the average, women pay more visits to physicians and therapists and take more drugs for physical and psychiatric disorders than men.

15. Men are more susceptible than women to cardiovascular and other life-threatening illnesses.

Note. Adapted from Weiss, D. E. (1991). *The Great Divide.* New York: Simon & Schuster.

Friendships. Women of all ages have more friends than men, and those friendships tend to be deeper and longer lasting (Wright, 1989). Women's friendships are characterized by shared feelings and concerns and giving and receiving emotional support and suggestions (Fox, Gibbs, & Auerbach, 1985). In contrast, men's friendships are based more on mutual interests and shared activities. Women explore relationships in their social interactions, whereas men are more likely to focus on doing things and solving problems (Tannen, 1990). Perhaps fearing that it will be construed as a sign of weakness, men are less likely than women to discuss their feelings and concerns with each other. As a consequence, women may find it hard to understand why men constantly feel the need to be strong and brave, whereas men have difficulty understanding why women always want to talk about their problems (Tannen, 1990). Be that as it may, both men and women describe their companionate relationships with women as more intimate, enjoyable, and nurturing than those with men (L. Rubin, 1985; Sapadin, 1988).

Love. Men tend to fall in love faster, fall out of love more slowly, and suffer more from breaking up than women do (Rubin, Hill, Peplau, & Dunkel-Schetter, 1980). Men are also, on the whole, less practical and more romantic in their love relationships—more likely than women to believe in love at first sight, that there is one true love for them, and that love is magical and incomprehensible. Women tend to be more cautious and pragmatic in their love relationships, stressing financial security as much as passion, that happiness is possible with many different mates, and that love cannot solve all interpersonal problems (Peplau & Gordon, 1985). Finally, when a relationship *goes sour,* women are more likely than men to *stick it out* (Cowan & Cowan, 1992).

Sexual Orientation and Physiology. On the whole, men are more liberal in their sexual attitudes and practices than women (Oliver & Hyde, 1993). Men tend to masturbate more, have more premarital and extramarital affairs, and experiment with a greater range of sexual techniques (Janus & Janus, 1993). Men are also more likely than women to view a smile as a promise and to interpret a touch, friendly remark, or eye contact by a woman as a sexual come-on (Kowalski, 1993).

Probably no one would deny the importance of social learning in sexual orientation,[1] but evidence of a biological basis for sexual preference is increasing. For example, there is a great deal of evidence concerning the role of testosterone in male sexual behavior and for a connection between this hormone and aggression in both animals and humans (Archer, 1991; Monaghan & Glickman, 1992). A possible connection between testosterone level and homosexuality has been found in studies of gay men whose mothers experienced extreme stress during pregnancy, which lowered their testosterone level (Ellis & Ames, 1987). Other research findings indicate that an area in the hypothalamus—known as the *sexually dimorphic nucleus*—is larger in males than in females and larger in heterosexual than in homosexual males (Allen, Hines, Shyne, & Gorski, 1989; LeVay, 1991). In addition, certain regions of the corpus callosum, the sheath of nerve fibers connecting the two cerebral hemispheres, is thinner and less bulbous in men's than in women's brains (Clarke, Krafsik, Van der Loos, & Innocenti, 1989). Additional evidence for a biological basis for male and female homosexuality has been obtained from studies of identical and fraternal twins (e.g., Whitam, Diamond, & Martin, 1993). These investigations have shown that a significantly greater percentage of the identical than fraternal twins of gays and lesbians are also homosexual (also see LeVay & Mamer, 1994).

---

[1]*Sexual orientation* refers to a person's sexual preference for members of the same sex (homosexuality), the opposite sex (heterosexuality), or both sexes (bisexuality).

ETHNICITY AND CULTURE

The United States of America has traditionally prided itself on being a *melting pot* of different nationalities, races, and cultures, but this ideal has not been fully realized in practice. Certainly, the Anglo-European dominance of the political, economic, and social institutions of the United States is gradually giving way to other ethnic and social groups, but the population is still predominantly European-American and is projected to remain so well into the 21st century (U.S. Bureau of the Census, 1997b).

The U.S. population is the third largest of any country in the world, but still far behind that of China and India. According to estimates by the U.S. Bureau of the Census (1997b), the U.S. population of 275 million in the year 2000 will be approximately 82% European-American (White); 13% African American (Black); 1% American Indian, Eskimo, and Aleut; and 4% Asian and Pacific Islander. By the year 2025, these percentages are expected to be 78%, 14%, 1%, and 7%, respectively, in a total U.S. population of 335 million. An even greater change is projected in the Hispanic population, which is expected to rise from an estimated 11.4% in 2000 to 17.6% in 2025 (U.S. Bureau of the Census, 1997b).

The extent to which the various minority groups in the United States will become assimilated into mainstream American culture or retain their own cultural identities in a multiracial and multicultural society remains to be seen. The pattern thus far has been for subsequent generations of immigrants to this country to become more or less acculturated and assimilated into the dominant Anglo-American culture, but the degree of that assimilation has been greater for European-Americans than for those of African and Asian ancestry. Contributing to the failure of the melting pot ideal and a turning to a *mosaic* concept, in which different groups retain their own identities while contributing to a multicultural society, are the pronounced racial and ethnic differences among Americans (see Moghaddam, Taylor, & Wright, 1998).

Race

Scientific interest in the distinctness of human races goes back at least as far as the writings of J. F. Blumenbach (1752–1840), a German professor who is credited with the false conclusion that the people of Europe all stem from one White race that originated in the Caucasus. In addition to the Caucasian (White) race, Blumenbach identified four others: Malaysian (brown), Mongolian (yellow), Negro (black), and American (red).

From an evolutionary viewpoint, different races resulted from natural selection and adaptation to local environmental conditions. For example, skin color, body build, and other physical identifiers that are characteristic of members of different races presumably had survival value in the climates and circumstances in which they developed. From a biological standpoint, skin color is of less importance than morphology (form and structure), physiology, and behavior in differentiating among races.

The distinctions among racial groups, which are still applied in some quarters, subsequently led to the notion of a social hierarchy, with Caucasians at the top and Negroes at the bottom. Anthropological studies during the 20th century, however, have underscored the fallaciousness of the idea of a common racial denominator in the makeup of the various peoples of Europe and those of other continents and countries as well (Davies, 1998). Certainly the differences among races in psychological characteristics are relatively trivial compared with those among individuals of the same race.

Ethnicity

The term *ethnic group* is less specific and more culturally oriented than that of *race*. An ethnic group is composed of people who share the same language and customs, but do not necessarily have the same racial makeup. Thus, the inhabitants of Mexico represent a combination of Spanish, Indian, and African ancestry, sometimes referred to collectively as *la Raza*. As in Mexico, Hispanics in the United States may be of any race or racial mixture. However, whether they or their forebears were from Central America, South America, Puerto Rico, Cuba, or elsewhere, the majority of Hispanic Americans designate their race as White.

Both the physical and cultural differences among the various ethnic groups contribute to a failure to become assimilated into the host culture and to intergroup discrimination and conflict. Such discrimination exists in all countries where there are ethnic differences, but it has been studied most extensively in the United States. Differences in skin color, facial features, body build, and behavior patterns make people of other races and ethnic groups more identifiable and act as supports for discriminatory attitudes and treatment. The prejudice and discrimination encountered by minority groups is seen in various social institutions, but its greatest economic effects stem from the lower educational level and less remunerative employment of many minority group members (see chap. 10). The advantages that a higher income can purchase—better food, clothing, housing, education, medical care, and so on—are also more common among Whites than among Blacks and Hispanics in the United States.

Quality of Life in Different Ethnic Groups[2]

The quality of life for many members of the largest (34 million in 1997) minority group in the United States—African Americans—is fairly poor. Teenage pregnancy, out-of-wedlock births, infant mortality, obesity, hypertension, and certain other diseases are higher, and life expectancy at birth is lower than average. The death rates for HIV infection and homicide and the rates of unemployment and poverty are higher than average, and income

---

[2]Population statistics cited in this section were taken from the *Statistical Abstract of the United States: 1998* (U.S. Bureau of the Census, 1998).

and education are lower than average. Among other indicators of a poorer quality of life among African Americans are the higher rates of substandard housing, single-parent families, and divorce, as well as a lower marriage rate. African Americans have made noteworthy economic and social progress during the past few decades, including a substantial increase in the number of middle-class professional and business persons. Nevertheless, they still have a long way to go to reach parity with the White majority.

People of Hispanic origin constitute the second largest (29 million in 1997), and soon to become the largest (projected 59 million by 2025), ethnic group in the United States. Mexican Americans are the most numerous in this group, followed by Puerto Ricans and Cuban Americans. Reflective of the religious beliefs and practices of all Hispanic subgroups are a higher birth rate and a lower divorce rate than average. However, the per capita income and the educational level are lower and the poverty rate higher than average (Lamison-White, 1997; U.S. Bureau of the Census, 1997a, 1997b). Unlike the technical/professional skills possessed by a large number of Asian Americans, with the possible exception of Cuban Americans, recent Hispanic-American immigrants tend to be poorly educated laborers who cannot speak English well (U.S. Bureau of the Census, 1997a). This, added to the fact that many entered the country illegally, limits their full participation in American society. The centrality of the family in Hispanic culture provides a great deal of economic, emotional, and social support for Hispanic Americans, but the macho ethic and the high rate of crime and violence among Hispanic youth pose serious problems for this group.

The status of the third largest (10 million in 1997) minority group in the United States—Asian/Pacific Islanders—is in marked contrast with that of African Americans. Asian Americans, who may have immigrated from China, Japan, Korea, Vietnam, Cambodia, Thailand, or the Philippines, tend to be more highly educated, economically better off, and healthier than either African or Hispanic Americans. Like these two groups, however, Asian Americans generally maintain close ties with their families (Markides, Liang, & Jackson, 1990). Overall, the status of Asian immigrants to this country supports the belief that the United States is still a land of opportunity for those who are motivated to become educated, work hard, and save diligently.

Like African and Hispanic Americans, as a group Native Americans (2.3 million in 1997) fall in the lower half of the educational and income scales (U.S. Bureau of the Census, 1995). Certain health disorders (e.g., high blood pressure, obesity, diabetes, lactose intolerance, alcoholism, cirrhosis of the liver, tuberculosis) are more common in this group than in Americans as a whole. Added to poor nutrition and substandard living conditions, the result is the shortest life span of all American minorities. The cultural status of Native Americans is marginal in that they are viewed as conquered wards or dependents of the federal government. In addition, the lack of cultural homogeneity (400 tribal groups, 250 different languages) places them in a separate category from other ethnic minorities (Edwards, 1983; Gonzalez, 1993).

Cultural Differences

The term *culture* refers to the behavior patterns, mores, attitudes, institutions, and organizations that are handed down from generation to generation and become characteristic ways of thinking and acting in a large group of people. In other words, a person's culture is that part of his or her environment that has been constructed by other members of the group. The study of culture and its influence is primarily the occupation of cultural anthropologists, although sociologists, psychologists, and other behavioral scientists have also contributed. According to the concept of *cultural determinism*, individual choice or free will in most human actions is a convenient fiction. People may believe that they exert choices in what they buy, where the live, what they consume, with whom they associate, and in general what they do and become, but to a large extent these actions are determined by culture (T. Alexander, 1994).[3]

Environmental change often necessitates cultural change, as when people emigrate to another country. For a time, they may experience *culture shock*—a feeling of strangeness and anxiety occasioned by new people and things. This was almost certainly the case for many of the largest nationality groups of immigrants to the United States from Mexico, the former Soviet Union, the Phillippines, Vietnam, the Dominican Republic, China, India, and Cuba in 1995 (U.S. Bureau of the Census, 1997a). However, rather than finding a homogeneous, highly predictable culture to which they could adapt in this country, the immigrants encountered a society composed of many cultures and subcultures.

Of all cultural groups in the United States, the greatest amount has been written and dramatized about the experiences and behaviors of African Americans. As described by Jones (1988), African-American culture tends to be more present-oriented, improvisational, expressive, spiritual, and emotional than White American culture. R. Jones (1991) described a colorful, conspicuous style of behavior consisting of a low, casual, rhythmic walk, the "high five," "thumb grasp," and "chest-bump" greeting, the "spiking" of footballs or "slam dunking" of basketballs, and gyrating to loud rap music as having been adopted by many young African Americans. Anxious to be accepted and prove that "white men can jump," young Whites may elect to imitate this behavior, to the amusement or consternation of their relatives and friends.

Gender identity is formed in childhood, but establishment of an ethnic identity usually does not begin until adolescence. At first, the individual passively accepts the dominant culture; in early adulthood, interest in one's ethnic roots is awakened, culminating in a more solid ethnic identification later (Phinney, 1990). Unfortunately, formation of a strong ethnic or in-

---

[3]Of course the extent to which one becomes a *captive* of culture varies with the individual. For example, like immigrants to the United States, many Americans who live and work abroad may, as a result of their fear and inability to cope with the demands of a different culture, become encapsulated in their own little American ghetto and consequently develop *cabin fever.* Many other American immigrants, and young males in particular, elect to reside and roam freely in a foreign city or countries and thereby benefit and learn from new experiences.

group identity may be accompanied by the stereotyping of other groups and prejudice against them. A deep-seated form of prejudice is *racism,* in which people of other races are characterized as appearing and behaving in a certain way and as inferior to one's own race.

Stereotyping is, of course, not limited to races. Other nationalities and social groups may also be stereotyped in the media and elsewhere. Usually this stereotyping is done in a friendly manner (see Box 4.1), but it can lead to prejudice and intergroup conflict.

In their studies of non-Western cultures, social anthropologists have sometimes made overgeneralized analyses of the customs and character of different countries and cultures. A number of anthropologists and psychologists have attempted to apply psychological theory in their interpretations of intercultural differences in personality traits (Benedict, 1946; Gorer, 1955, 1964/1948; Gorer & Rickman, 1963/1949; Kardiner, 1946/1939, 1959/1945; Malinowski, 1927; Mead, 1969/1935). The research procedure of participant observation employed by these writers has been extended to the analysis of social class differences within our own culture, but the survey method has generally been preferred by sociologists and other social scientists who study social class differences.

Social Class

Although most Americans probably think of the United States as a classless society, as in other societies a system of social stratification based on economic resources, power, and privilege exists in this country. Rather than *social class,* the term *socioeconomic status* is preferred by most scholars to emphasize the combined roles of social influence and financial resources in determining one's position on the social hierarchy. Even when social class categories such as upper, middle, working, and lower (poor) are employed, researchers and social decision makers are quick to emphasize the fluidity or movement between the various classes. Associated with social class or socioeconomic status (SES) are differences in attitudes and behavior. Because certain racial or ethnic groups are more likely to fit in one social class category than another, one must be careful not to attribute to race/ethnicity something that may be best explained by social class.

With respect to the relationships between social class and behavior, people in the lower social classes are said to be more likely to subscribe to a philosophy of immediate gratification that eschews patience and waiting, whereas the contrasting philosophy of delayed gratification is said to be more typical of the middle and upper social classes. To the extent that this is true, and it does make sense in light of the more meager economic resources of the lower social classes, it can affect attitudes and behavior concerning education, work, leisure, obedience to rules and laws, and a host of other activities and pursuits. For example, people in the lower and working classes tend to hold more liberal political views than those in the middle and upper classes. Violence and mental illness are also more common among people who are lower on the social hierarchy, whereas personal health and happiness are greater among those in the higher classes. Socio-

---

Box 4-1: Cultural Differences Explained

Aussies: Dislike being mistaken for Pommies (Brits) when abroad.

Canadians: Are rather indignant about being mistaken for Americans when abroad.

Americans: Encourage being mistaken for Canadians when abroad.

Brits: Can't possibly be mistaken for anyone else when abroad.

Aussies: Believe you should look out for your mates.

Brits: Believe you should look out for those who belong to your club.

Americans: Believe people should look out for and take care of themselves.

Canadians: Believe that's the government's job.

Aussies: Are extremely patriotic to their beer and would sing the anthem if they knew the words.

Brits: Do not sing at all but prefer a brass band to perform the anthem.

Americans: Are flag-waving, anthem-singing, and obsessively patriotic to the point of blindness.

Canadians: Can't agree on the words to the anthem when they can be bothered to sing it.

Americans: Spend most of their lives glued to the idiot box.

Canadians: Don't, but only because the government won't let them have more American channels.

Brits: Pay a tax to watch four lousy channels.

Aussies: Export all their lousy programs, which no one there watches, to Britain, where everybody loves them.

Americans: Will jabber on incessantly about football, baseball, and basketball.

Brits: Will jabber on incessantly about cricket, soccer, and rugby.

Canadians: Will jabber on incessantly about hockey, hockey, hockey, hockey, and how they beat the Americans twice playing baseball.

Aussies: Will jabber on incessantly about how they beat the Poms in every sport they play them in.

Americans: Spell words differently, but still call it English.

Brits: Pronounce words differently, but still call it English.

Canadians: Spell like the Brits, pronounce like Americans.

Aussies: Add *G'day, mate,* and a heavy accent to everything they say in a futile attempt to impress girls.

Brits: Shop at home and have goods imported because they live on an island.

Aussies: Shop at home and have goods imported because they live on an island.

Americans: Cross the southern border for cheap shopping, gas, and liquor in a backward country.

Canadians: Cross the southern border for cheap shopping, gas, and liquor in a backward country.

Americans: Seem to think that poverty and failure are morally suspect.

Canadians: Seem to believe that wealth and success are morally suspect.

Brits: Seem to believe that wealth, poverty, success, and failure are inherited things.

Aussies: Seem to think that none of this matters after several beers.

Brits: Endure oppressively wet and dreary winters and are proud of it.

Americans: Endure bitterly cold winters and are proud of it.

Canadians: Don't have to do either and couldn't care less.

Aussies: Don't understand what inclement weather means.

Brits: Are obsessed with the Queen and royal family peccadilloes.

Canadians: Would gladly settle for Prince Charles having an affair with a Canadian girl.

Americans: Are obsessed with the president, his family, and even their cat.

Aussies: Would be quite happy if Prince Charles had an affair with an Australian cat.

Aussies: Try to forget the accomplishments of their first citizens.

Brits: Are justifiably proud of the accomplishments of their past citizens.

Americans: Are justifiably proud of the accomplishments of their present citizens.

Canadians: Prattle on about how some of those great Americans were once Canadian.

Heaven is where the police are British, the mechanics are German, the cooks are French, the lovers are Italian, and the whole thing is organized by the Swiss. Hell is where the police are German, the cooks are British, the mechanics are French, the lovers are Swiss, and the whole thing is organized by the Italians.

Source. Web site www.moffatt.demon.co.uk/me/humour/diff.html. Contributor unknown.

economic status is also correlated with cognitive abilities and various measures of personality (Filsinger, 1984).

SUMMARY

Socialization involves learning the social norms and roles of appropriate behavior in various contexts. Children acquire feelings of belonging and security by becoming attached to caregivers. Close ties with caregivers develop in a series of phases, beginning with undiscriminating social responses during the first 3 months of infancy and proceeding to a goal-corrected partnership at age 3 and later. Research on attachment has employed the strange-situation procedure of exposing infants to strangers with and without their mothers present and observing how they react. The responses of most infants to this situation indicate that they are securely attached to their mothers, but sizable percentages show avoidant or resistant/ambivalent behavior.

Another factor that has an important influence on child behavior is parenting style. Maccoby and Martin's modification of Baumrind's model of parenting styles and the relationships of these styles to children's behavior and personality describes two dimensions of parenting style: demandingness and responsiveness. Combinations of these dimensions yield four types of parents: authoritative, authoritarian, indulgent, and neglecting. According to the model, parents who employ an authoritative style of being responsive, child-centered, and yet controlling tend to produce independent, self-assertive, friendly, and cooperative children.

Many other factors affect physical and psychological development during childhood and adolescence. For example, early maturing boys tend to be more secure and self-assured than late-maturing boys, but the difference is not so clear cut for girls. Rate of maturity also has an effect on sexual behavior, friendships, love, and other interpersonal behaviors.

Biology and experience combine to yield differences between males and females and the differential treatments accorded them by other people. The child develops a sense of gender identity quite early in life and, for the most part, accepts the differences in gender role prescribed by society. Although there is evidence for significant differences between males and females in both cognitive and affective variables, stereotyping boys and girls in terms of behavior and personality is unfair and socially limiting to both sexes.

There are significant differences in the culture and behavior of various racial and ethnic groups, but an overemphasis on and generalization of these differences can lead to prejudice and discrimination. The five major ethnic groups in the United States are, according to size: Caucasian American (Anglo-American, White), African American (Black), Hispanic American, Asian American, and Native American. The economic, educational, and health situations of Native Americans, African Americans, and Hispanic Americans are poorer than that of Caucasian and Asian Americans. Because members of certain race/ethnic groups in the United States tend to be lower on the socioeconomic scale than others, conclusions regarding racial or ethnic-group differences in abilities, attitudes, and behavior should not be drawn without taking SES into account.

SUGGESTED READINGS

Bowlby, J., & Ainsworth, M. (1992). The origins of attachment theory. *Developmental Psychology, 28*(5), 759–775.
Ellis, A. (1997). *Dealing with differences: Taking action on class, race, gender, and disability.* Thousand Oaks, CA: Corwin.

Fable, D. E. S. (1997). Gender, racial, ethnic, sexual, and class identities. *Annual Review of Psychology, 48,* 139–162.

Geary, D. C. (1998). *Male, female: The evolution of human differences.* Washington, DC: American Psychological Association.

Jones, R. L. (Ed.). (1991). *Black psychology* (3rd ed.). Berkeley, CA: Cobb & Henry.

Lalumiere, M. L., Quinsey, V. L., & Craig, W. M. (1996). Why children from the same family are so different from one another: A Darwinian note. *Human Nature,* 7(3), 281–290.

Martin, C. L., & Parker, S. (1995). Folk theories about sex and race differences. *Personality and Social Psychology Bulletin, 21*(1), 45–57.

Plomin, R. (1994). Nature, nurture, and social development. *Social Development,* 3(1), 37–53.

Rutter, M. L. (1997). Nature-nurture integration: The example of antisocial behavior. *American Psychologist, 52,* 390–398.

Stevenson, M. R. (Ed.). (1994). *Gender roles through the life span.* Muncie, IN: Ball State University Press.

CHAPTER FIVE

Physical Appearance, Performance, and Health

Excellent physical condition does not guarantee success and happiness in modern society. Depending on the area of endeavor, physical attractiveness, vitality, strength, and health may be less important than affluence, intelligence, and social skills. However, even in more cerebral, technological occupations, the absence of pain and physical disability, as well as what others perceive as ugliness, can free a person from the need to engage in endless maneuvers to cope with and compensate for a bad hand dealt by nature. Other things being equal, people who are in good health also have more time and energy to devote to pursuits other than self-preoccupation and self-care. Feeling strong and healthy contributes to one's self-confidence, the belief that even difficult goals are attainable, and the motivation, determination, and endurance to make the attempt. Of course, remaining in good health requires time—to exercise appropriately, eat nutritiously without overeating, and follow other regimens that promote physical well-being. Freed of the distractions created by disability and disease, an individual who is in good physical condition can concentrate on the things, ideas, and persons that matter most. Biology is not destiny, but it can widen the range of possibilities on the one hand or place definite restrictions on one's lifestyle on the other, promoting both pleasure and pain, failure and success.

MEASURING AND DESCRIBING THE HUMAN BODY

The most common of all measurements made on the human body are height and weight. From birth until maturity, these physical variables are frequently measured by family members and health personnel to evaluate a child's rate of growth and maturation. Height and weight are often plotted against chronological age to identify possible growth irregularities that may be symptomatic of a health problem or disorder. Even when there is no physical difficulty, children often worry about their height and weight and whether they are normal or abnormal. This concern, especially with regard to weight, continues after maturity and may lead to obsessive dieting, exercising, and other procedures for overcoming any perceived irregularity.

The average adult American male is approximately 5 feet 10 inches tall and weighs 174 pounds; the average adult American female is 5 feet 4 inches tall and weighs just under 130 pounds. There is, however, a substantial degree of variability around these averages. A sizable number of Americans are under 5 feet tall and weigh less than 100 pounds, whereas others are over 6 feet tall and weigh well over 300 pounds (see Box 5.1). Although the shape of the frequency distribution of body heights is fairly normal for American men and women, the distribution of body weights has a marked positive skew for both sexes, especially females. This is reflective of the tendency for both sexes, and particularly females, to control their weight by diet and exercise. Attentiveness to one's weight is realistic if it does not become an obsession.[1] Thus, statistics from the Third National Health and Nutrition Examination Survey indicate that over one third of Americans ages 20 and over are overweight. Even larger percentages (over 50%) of non-Hispanic Black and Mexican-American women are overweight (National Center for Health Statistics, 1996). The results of surveys of American children and adolescents indicate that smaller, but still substantial, percentages of these groups are also overweight (Ogden et al., 1997; Troiano et al., 1995).[2]

The median value and range for height and weight vary with gender as well as with ethnicity, nationality, social class, historical era, and other variables. For example, Nordics tend to be taller than Latins, middle-class people tend to be larger than lower class people, and, as witnessed by the sizes of beds displayed in historical museums, people in the 20th century are, on the whole, larger than their forefathers. In general, taller people are heavier than shorter ones; however, depending on a combination of genetic factors and habits, there are many short/fat and tall/thin individuals. Body build also varies with geographical area and climate. People who live in cold climates tend to be fatter and have a lower ratio of body surface area to body mass than those who live in tropical climates. This difference has survival value, in that the larger the ratio of surface area to body mass, the greater the dissipation of heat. Basal metabolic rate also varies with climate and culture, but there are wide differences in metabolic rate among individuals living under the same climatic or cultural conditions.

---

[1]Two cases of a weight loss of over 900 pounds are listed in the *Guinness Book of World Records 1998*, both of which were associated with initial weights of over 1,200 pounds!

[2]According to the guidelines of the National Heart, Lung, and Blood Institute, anyone with a body mass index (BMI) of 25 or above is overweight and anyone with a BMI of 30 or above is obese. BMI is determined by dividing body weight in kilograms by height in meters squared (1 kilogram = 2.2 pounds, and 1 meter = 3.28 feet or 39 inches). In addition to computing a person's BMI, another predictor of disease—waist circumference, which is closely associated with abdominal fat—should be measured. In persons having a BMI of 25 to 34.9, a waist circumference of over 35 inches in women or 40 inches in men indicates increased risk of disease.

Box 5.1: Physical Records

Tallest man: 8 ft. 11$\frac{1}{10}$ in.

Tallest woman: 8 ft. 1¾ in.

Tallest living man: 7 ft. 8½ in.

Tallest living woman: 7 ft. 7¼ in.

Shortest man: 22½ in.

Shortest woman: 24 in.

Shortest living woman: 25½ in.

Heaviest man: 1400 lbs.

Heaviest woman: 1200 lbs.

Lightest adult person: 4.7 lb.

Heaviest brain: 5 lb. 1.1 oz.

Lightest brain: 1 lb. 8 oz.

Most fingers and toes: 14 fingers and 15 toes

Longest fingernails: 20 ft. 1 in. (combined length of 5 nails on left hand)

Largest shoe size: 37AA (18½ in.)

Longest hair: 13 ft. 10½ in.

Largest waist: 10 ft. 11 in.

Smallest waist: 13 in.

Longest beard: 17½ ft.

Longest mustache: 133½ in.

Most marriages: 28

Longest marriage: 86 years

Most children born to one mother: 69 (including 16 pairs of twins, 7 sets of triplets, and 4 sets of quadruplets)

Most prolific living mother: gave birth to 55 children

Heaviest surviving baby: 22 lb. 3 oz.

Lightest single birth: 9.9 oz.

Most premature baby: 128 days

Highest number of babies at a single birth: 10

Oldest authenticated human life: 122 years

Oldest living person: 118 years

Fastest man alive: Donavan Bailey (ran 100-meter dash in 9.84 secs)

Strongest man: Juraj Barbaric (pulled a 396.8-ton train a distance of 25 ft. 3 in. along a train track on May 25, 1996)

Source. Guinness Book of World Records 1998. Stamford, CT: Guinness Media, Inc.

Body Types

Statistics on the heights and weights of people are useful to clothing manufacturers as well as business persons and social planners. Height and weight are rough indicators of body shape or form, but they are insufficient for sizing and identification purposes. One early proposal for describing body build or shape in terms of a typology was that of Ernest Kretschmer (1925). Kretschmer classified human physiques into four categories: *pyknic*, or plump; *athletic*, or muscular; *asthenic*, or frail and linear; and *dysplastic*, individuals who did not fit into any one of the other three categories. Similar to, but more sophisticated than, Kretschmer's model is the classification system proposed by Sheldon and Stevens (1942; Sheldon, Stevens, & Tucker, 1940). This somatotype system consists of describing a person's body build according to three components: *endomorphy*, or fatness; *mesomorphy*, or muscularity; and *ectomorphy*, or thinness. Each component is rated on a scale of 1 to 7, with 1 being the least amount and 7 the greatest amount of the component. The result is a three-number designation for a particular physique: The first number indicates the degree of endomorphy, the second number the degree of mesomorphy, and the third number the degree of ectomorphy. Thus, 7–1–1 designates extreme

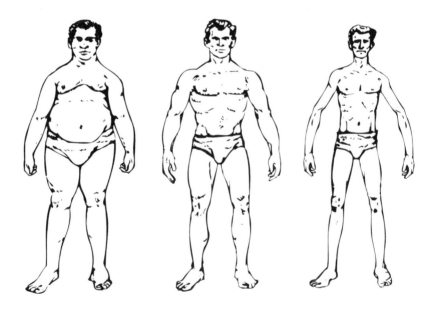

FIG. 5.1.   Sheldon's somatotypes: endomorph, mesomorph, ectomorph. (From *Elements of Psychology [2nd ed.]* by D. Krech, R. Crutchfield, and N. Livson, 1969, New York: Knopf. Copyright © 1969 by Knopf. Reprinted by permission.)

endomorphy, 1–7–1 extreme mesomorphy, and 1–1–7 extreme ectomorphy (see Fig. 5.1).

Both Kretschmer and Sheldon were interested in describing various types of body build as well as relating body build to personality and psychopathology. However, neither Kretschmer's nor Sheldon's systems nor the system proposed by Ceasare Lombroso (1836–1909), was widely accepted as a way to classify different kinds of criminals according to their body builds. For a time, Sheldon's somatotype system found some use in police work, but forensic anthropologists subsequently developed more sophisticated techniques for identifying victims and perpetrators of criminal activity and in determining whether a crime was even committed. With respect to the relationship of physique to abilities and personality, whatever correlations there are probably too small and the exceptions too numerous for body type to be of much value in forecasting behavior.

Anthropometry and Forensic Anthropology

Anthropometry, defined as the measurement of the size and proportions of the human body, has practical application in the science of *ergonomics,* also known as human engineering. Ergonomics is concerned with the design of devices, systems, work spaces, and physical working conditions that are appropriate for the abilities and requirements of the human body. Because thousands of different measurements relevant to the use of tools, workplaces, and even clothing design can be made on the bodies of men and women, a smaller number of choices must be made as to what variables to measure. Among the variables taken into consideration in the design problem are the three measuring planes of the human body: front-on, side-on, and view from above. With respect to these three planes, the concepts of reach and fit are applied in the design of devices and spaces for most efficient operation by people of various shapes and sizes (Kroemer, Kroemer, & Kroemer-Elbert, 1994). The results of analyses and anthropometric measurements of movements in these three planes have been used to determine preferred working zones of the hands and feet and the best shapes of work stations at which operators stand or sit. One area in which anthropometric measurements have been extensively used is in the design of space capsules for astronauts with different physical dimensions.

Another applied area in which anthropometric measurements are made is *forensic anthropology*—a branch of physical anthropology that can contribute to decision making in legal proceedings. The questions that forensic anthropologists attempt to answer are concerned with such matters as the age, sex, ethnicity, stature, or parentage of skeletal or biological materials. To that end, measurements may be taken of the cranium and face (for identification of ethnic group and sex), depth and shape of the pelvis, extent of maturation of the pubic symphysis (for age estimates, especially in females), and sternal rib metamorphosis (for age estimates in males and females; Bennett, 1993).

One useful measure of head shape is the *cephalic index,* computed as 100 times the ratio of the greatest breadth of the head to its greatest length, from front to back. Heads with cephalic indexes of 75 and under are referred to as *dolichocephalic,* those with indexes of 81 to 85.4 are *brachycephalic,* whereas heads with indexes between 76 and 80 are *mesocephalic.* People of European or African descent tend to have longer (dolichocephalic) heads, whereas people of Asian descent tend to have rounder (brachycephalic) heads. Other measures that contribute to ethnic identification are made on the nasal orifice (narrow in Europeans, intermediate in Asians, wide in Africans), incisors shape (shovel-shaped in Asians, blade-shaped in Africans, rarely shovel-shaped in Europeans), zygomatic bone (retreating in Europeans, projecting in Asians, medium in Africans), and face shape (medium in Europeans, wide and flat in Asians, narrow and with protruding jaw in Africans).

Sex differentiation can also be made on the basis of cranial measurements. In females, the skull tends to be smooth, the chin rounded, the brow ridges poorly developed, the mastoid process small, the forehead bulging, and the jaw angle obtuse. In males the skull tends to be rougher where the muscles are attached, the external occipital protuberance (on the back of the skull) larger than in females, the chin square, the brow ridges developed, the mastoid process large, the forehead receding, and the jaw angle nearly 90 degrees.[3] There are, of course, exceptions to these generalizations, and the identification of sex in this manner is far from foolproof.

Other techniques employed in forensic anthropology include (a) dental examination to determine level of development, (b) histological analysis, (c) spinal changes and cranial suture closure to estimate age at death, (d) analyses of fractures and other injuries, and (e) molar and microscopic dismemberment analyses (Reichs, 1998).

Despite the usefulness of the techniques and principles applied by anthropometry and forensic anthropology, care must be exercised in characterizing different race/ethnic groups as having particular physical features such as a particular skull shape or skin color. As noted by Davies (1998),

> Racial and kinship differences have not been discounted (*by science*). But the field has been cleared for a greater emphasis on cultural, religious, and socio-economic factors, for sophisticated genetic analysis based on proven scientific principles, and for the final dismissal of the old obsession with skins and skulls. (p. 735)

PHYSICAL ATTRACTIVENESS

Appearance and behavior are easily obtainable types of information for evaluating people, at least superficially. With patience and perceptiveness,

---

[3]Consult web site nemo.educ.ttu.edu/anderson/race.html for more details.

a better indication of the character and personality of the inner man or inner woman can be obtained, but most social encounters are fairly brief ones and provide little opportunity to figure out what a person is really like under his or her public persona. Nevertheless, first impressions are important in determining a person's acceptability and attractiveness to other people—his or her social stimulus value. Because of its significance as a social variable and its relationship to success in many different arenas, a great deal of attention has been devoted by social psychologists and other behavioral scientists to the study of physical and behavioral attractiveness.

Physical attractiveness plays an important role in determining the *self-concept*—how a person feels about him or herself. According to Cooley's (1922) looking-glass theory of the self, a person's self-concept is the result of reflected appraisals. This implies that people come to see themselves according to their perceptions of how they are seen by other people. Consequently, most people do everything they can, within reason, to make positive impressions on others so they will be favorably evaluated and thereby feel good about themselves. They realize that in most interpersonal contexts—familial, educational, employment, recreational, and romantic—physical appearance is at least as important as ability and personality in determining acceptability and approval (e.g., Collins & Zebrowitz, 1995).

Gender Similarities and Differences

Appearance is quite important to most White females, but they are not the only ones who pay attention to their looks. Men, as well as women of other racial or ethnic groups, spend a substantial amount of time inspecting themselves in mirrors, grooming, and doing other things to make themselves more socially attractive. As seen in their preoccupation with their hair, skin, and other body parts, and with being taller and heavier, many more men than might be expected have body-image problems.

Both gender and sexual orientation are related to body image. For example, the results of an investigation by Siever (1994) provide support for the hypothesis that, because of a desire to attract and please men, gays and heterosexual women tend to be more dissatisfied than heterosexual men and lesbians with their bodies and more vulnerable to eating disorders. Lesbians and heterosexual men were found to be less concerned with their own physical attractiveness and therefore not as dissatisfied with their bodies or vulnerable to eating disorders. However, in a study by Gettelman and Thompson (1993), the respondents tended to overestimate the degree to which gays and lesbians suffered from body-image problems. As seen in the results of this study and others (e.g., Brand, Rothblum, & Solomon, 1992), gender is of greater significance than sexual orientation in determining expressed concerns over physical appearance. More women than men are still ruled by social conventions with respect to physical attractiveness and, consequently, a greater number of women than men have body-image problems and eating disorders (Brand, Rothblum, & Solomon, 1992; Muth & Cash, 1997).

Advertising

Marketers of body-improvement products are aware of the concerns that people have about their weight, and they target young women and men in particular for those products. Women's magazines have many more advertisements and articles on weight loss than men's magazines, but magazines aimed primarily at a male readership contain many more articles and ads than previously concerning such matters as ways to build the upper body and trim the abdomen (the so-called V-*shaped* body). Furthermore, fashion and cologne companies have begun to target men as an expanding market for their ads and products (A. E. Anderson & DiDomenico, 1992).

Because the socially perceived relationship between beauty and sexual attractiveness is generally greater for women than for men, women typically spend more time and effort than men in enhancing and improving their physical appearance. The marketing orientation, according to which people appraise their personal assets and emphasize those for which there is a greater social and economic demand, undoubtedly plays a role in this gender difference.

Analyses of advertisements appearing in the personal columns of newspapers and magazines underscore the belief that "women tend to offer beauty and seek wealth, whereas men tend to seek beauty and offer wealth" (Harrison & Saeed, 1977; Rajecki, Bledsoe, & Rasmussen, 1991). Support for this idea was obtained in a cross-cultural study by D. Buss (1989): *Good looks* was rated more highly by men, whereas *good financial prospect* was rated more highly by women. A man's physical appearance can certainly affect a woman's behavior, but his wealth, status, or social competence can compensate for what he lacks in good looks (Feingold, 1990; Sprecher, 1989; Woll, 1986). Consequently, it is not uncommon for attractive young women to marry older, ordinary looking men of high social or financial status (Elder, 1969).

Social Stimulus Value of Attractiveness

Efforts to make oneself physically attractive are generally not wasted in any society. Parents tend to react more positively to more attractive babies, teachers evaluate attractive children more positively, personnel managers are more likely to hire better looking applicants, verdicts reached by attractive jurors are more likely to be accepted, and sentences given to attractive criminals tend to be less severe (Hatfield & Sprecher, 1986). Compared with less physically attractive people, those with good looks have more friends, better social skills, and a more active sex life (Feingold, 1992a). Both men and women react more positively to physically attractive people of the same and the opposite sex and are more likely to want to spend time with them—either as a friend, date, or mate.

Although attractive people of all ages are perceived as more popular, successful, socially skilled, and happier, they are not considered to be more compassionate or honest than average (Eagly, Ashmore, Makhijani, & Longo, 1991; Feingold, 1992a; Hatfield & Sprecher, 1986). Furthermore, physical attractiveness has little or no relationship to scores on tests of intelligence or personality, and it appears to be unrelated to self-esteem (Major, Carrington, & Carnevale, 1984). As underscored by the lives of celebrated beauties such as Marilyn Monroe, attractive people are not always happy. They may even be suspicious that favorable evaluations of their performance are due to their physical characteristics rather than their abilities, skills, or personality traits. In contrast, less attractive people are more likely to accept praise for their work as sincere (Berscheid, 1981). Superattractive people may also be viewed by people of average looks with jealousy or as being "out of their league" as potential friends or mates. Be that as it may, attractive people are generally evaluated more favorably by all kinds of people and in all types of situations. These favorable evaluations are not limited to older children and adults. Research has shown that even very young children respond more favorably to attractive than unattractive faces (Langlois et al., 1987).

Physical Determinants and Cultural Differences

Among the determinants of female attractiveness that have been examined by researchers are body size, hip size, waist-to-hip ratio, and breast symmetry. From ratings made by college men of pictures of females, it was found that the following characteristics of the female body were judged most attractive, feminine looking, healthy, and desirable for either short- or long-term relationships: slender bodies, low waist-to-hip ratio, large breasts, symmetrical breasts, and slender hips (Singh, 1995a; Singh & Young, 1995). Large body size, high waist-to-hip ratios, and large hips apparently make female figures look older, less attractive, and less desirable for participating in romantic relationships. Symmetry and size of other body parts are also important determinants of perceived attractiveness: Noses, legs, and physiques that are neither very large nor very small are preferred.

However, physical attractiveness is not a simple matter of body symmetry, cuteness, curvaceousness, or muscularity. There is truth in the aphorisms that "Handsome is as handsome does" and "Beauty is in the eye of the beholder." A person may possess excellent physical attributes and yet not be perceived as beautiful or handsome because he or she does not feel and/or act that way. Perceptions of attractiveness also vary with time and place. The standards of beauty of one culture or in one generation may be seen as unacceptable or even repulsive by another culture or generation (Landau, 1989; however, see Cunningham, Roberts, Berbeen, & Druen, 1995). The hour-glass, Gibson Girl figure of the 1890s and the curvaceousness of the post-World War II era have given way to a boyish, slender look in more recent years. Anglo-American culture has traditionally emphasized a more Anglo-Saxon concept of female beauty—the blond, blue-eyed, busty female—but this concept has also changed to some extent during recent decades. Dark, emaciated women are now viewed by many young Americans as paragons of female beauty.

In contrast to the "thin is in" concept of many Western cultures, culture-conscious people of the Efik clan and other communities in Nigeria's southeastern Cross River region believe that rotundity in a woman is a sign of good health, prosperity, and allure. Consequently, as a rite of passage from maidenhood to womanhood, girls in this region may spend months in a "fattening room," gaining weight and learning customs pertaining to the roles of women in the culture. They eat bowl after bowl of rice, yams, plantains, beans, and a mixture of dried cassava and water called *gari*. Unlike contemporary Anglo-American culture, among the Efik to be called a *slim princess* is an abuse to be avoided at all costs (Simmons, 1998).

Cross-cultural variation in standards of attractiveness is also seen in the results of studies of body-type preferences for members of the opposite sex. For example, Jackson and McGill (1996) found that African-American males tend to prefer larger body types for females and associate more favorable and fewer unfavorable characteristics with obese females than do Anglo-American males. Likewise, African-American females tend to associate fewer unfavorable characteristics with obese males than do Anglo-American females.

Although there is a great deal of consensus between men and women in evaluations of attractiveness, standards of beauty also vary to some extent with gender. For example, Schindler and Holbrook (1993) found that, even when they grew older, men tended to retain the preferences for women's styles that were fashionable when the men were in their early 20s. However, women's preferences for both men's and women's styles, and men's preferences for men's styles, were apparently formed across a broad range of years.

In certain cultures, people have pierced their noses, lengthened their necks or penises, bound their feet, distorted the shapes of their heads, dyed their skin and hair, and overeaten or starved themselves. Not to be outdone, women and men in our own culture have subjected themselves to various surgical procedures designed to improve their appearance. They have had their body fat liposuctioned; their lips, breasts, face, and certain other body parts pierced and filled with silicone; their genital organs implanted or tightened; hair transplanted to their scalps or electrolitically removed from other body areas; and so on. Some of these operations have served functional purposes, but most are undertaken simply to improve one's appearance. However, this does not necessarily mean that they are unrealistic. Studies have shown that, compared with men in general, those with male pattern baldness receive lower ratings on physical attractiveness, are judged as having less desirable personal and interpersonal characteristics, and are seen as older than they actually are (Cash, 1990). Even before middle age, men with pattern baldness may notice their hair floating in the sink or bathtub, and may vow to get a transplant or shave it all off in order to make themselves look younger or at least more virile.

Dress

Even more common than surgery as methods for improving one's appearance are makeup, clothing, and posture. Not surprisingly, studies have shown that people of average facial appearance can significantly improve others' judgments of their attractiveness by the appropriate use of makeup. Good grooming, good posture, and aerobic exercise can also assist in overcoming negative evaluations caused by an imperfect body build (e.g., Osborn, 1996). For people who are less than raving beauties and wish to make a positive first impression, nothing succeeds like the careful selection of clothing. A wise choice of clothing can, at least to some degree, direct the viewer's attention toward one's better physical features and away from one's poorer features. To camouflage certain features, dark, plain, and, in some cases, padded clothing is recommended. To enhance other features, light colors and decorative materials are helpful. In Anglo-American culture, a desire to attain to ideals of slenderness and tallness has been important in the selection of clothing by women in particular. In keeping with this ideal, for people who are short and heavy, vertical stripes or other measures that direct the viewer's eye upward rather than across are suggested (Hurlock, 1994).

Body camouflage and enhancement are, of course, not the only determinants of what to wear. Other motives, such as group conformity, comfort, economy, and artistic expression or decoration, also play a role. The extent to which the operation of these motives is seen in the choice of clothing also varies from person to person. As the author discovered some years ago (Aiken, 1963), the strength of each of these motives is correlated with different personality variables. Everyday observations also show that what a person wears often makes a statement regarding his or her interests, attitudes, and personality. In addition, dress is related to environmental and demographic variables such as education, SES, and culture.

Age also affects the choice of clothing, makeup, and other efforts to make oneself more attractive. Most teenagers, and especially girls, are quite interested in clothing, jewelry, and other methods of self-adornment. Not every teenager goes in for tattoos, body piercing, and brightly colored hair, but these and other fads are influenced by peer pressure and the need for social acceptance and admiration. In this manner, the individual attempts to establish a sense of identity and belongingness in preparation for the challenges of adulthood (Martin, 1997).

Mate Selection

Although attractiveness is to some extent culturally relative, women who have a youthful appearance tend to be judged as more attractive by men in a wide range of cultures (Buss, 1980; Cunningham, 1986). From the viewpoint of evolutionary theory, men are generally more attracted to young, healthy, fertile-appearing women with smooth skin, lustrous hair, and full lips and breasts. Mating with such women is presumed to increase the probability of a man's genes being transmitted to future generations. Of course, sexual attractiveness is not merely in one direction: Men tend to place greater value on physical attractiveness in selecting a mate than women do, but most women also prefer attractive men (Feingold, 1990). According to evolutionary psychologists, women are more attracted to mature, dominant men because they have a greater capacity to support and protect women and their offspring (Buss, 1994). Trivers's (1972, 1985) *parental investment model* contends that women are more likely than men to seek mates who possess nonphysical characteristics that maximize the survival or reproductive prospects of their offspring. Analysis of the data from a questionnaire administered by Feingold (1992b) appear to confirm this hypothesis: Women accorded more weight than men to SES, ambitiousness, character, and intelligence—results that were generally invariant across generations and cultures.

Age Changes in Appearance

No matter how hard they try, few people can live up to the ideal of beauty that is fashionable in their culture for very long. This is especially true after age 30, when greying hair and wrinkles typically begin to appear. Perhaps because cultural expectations of physical beauty are directed more toward women than men, young women tend to be rated as more attractive than young men, but older men are rated as more attractive than older women (Henss, 1987).

A list of age-related changes in physical appearance is given in Table 5.1. These symptoms do not occur at the same time in all people. For example, the hair of Asian men typically does not begin greying as soon as that of European men, and women tend to show facial wrinkling more quickly than men. Still most of these changes are inevitable, and moisturizing creams, cosmetic surgery, exercise, and special diets cannot hold them off forever.

PHYSICAL PERFORMANCE

Perhaps even more aesthetically pleasing and admired than the appearance of an attractive human body is what that body can do. The skill manifested by an expert dancer, ice skater, gymnast, or other athletic performer is often a thing of beauty in itself. Training is important, but insufficient, in attaining a high level of perceptual-motor skill. The ability to move with accuracy and grace is a complex product of genetic endowment, instruction, practice, motivation, and self-control. When all of these ingredients are combined in the proper proportions, the result can be an extraordinary demonstration of the kinesthetic capabilities of the human body.

Age Differences

Most people do not attain the athletic proficiency of elite performers, but everyone can engage in and enjoy sports and other perceptual-motor activities. Performance of such skills, which involves the cooperation of various body systems, entails a certain amount of speed, strength, agility, and endurance—capacities that vary with the individual and his or her chronological age. Muscle mass and strength are at a maximum at age 25, decreasing to

TABLE 5.1
Age-Related Changes in Physical Appearance

The skin wrinkles; is rougher, drier, less elastic, and paler; sags into folds or jowls; bruises and blisters more easily; heals more slowly; develops small growths or spots; is more likely to itch; and reveals dilated blood vessels and varicose veins.

The hair is grayer or whiter, less lustrous, and sparser. There are hairs in the nostrils and ears, but less hair in the armpits and pubic area. The eyebrows are dark, coarse, and long.

The nose gets wider and longer, and there are lines from the nostrils to the sides of the mouth.

The mouth shows wrinkles on the sides, there is a loss of teeth, the gums shrink, and a double chin appears.

The eyes develop crow's feet around them, the eye sockets develop a hollow appearance, and the eyelids thicken and droop. The cornea frequently loses its sparkle, and cloudy or opaque areas (cataracts) develop in the lens.

The ears become longer and the earlobes fatter.

The jaw recedes.

The cheeks sag.

The forehead develops lines.

The head circumference increases.

The height and musculature are reduced.

The hips and waist broaden.

The shoulders become narrower.

The breasts sag.

The posture becomes curved or stooped.

A *widow's hump* may develop.

90% of the maximum by age 45, 75% by age 65, and 55% by age 85 (Whitbourne, 1985). The rate of decline can, however, be compensated for by regular exercise.

The physical changes accompanying the aging process typically result in slower, less vigorous, and less precise movements. As shown in Fig. 5.2, for example, both simple and choice reaction time become longer with age. Because of changes in speed, strength, and endurance, as people age they must make adjustments in their performance expectations and the extent of their participation. However, the effects of aging on the body are a highly individual matter, and the process does not impose the same limitations on everyone.

People who were more physically active during young adulthood and middle age are usually better able to continue a fairly high rate of involvement in sports and other physical activities in old age (McAuley, Lox, & Duncan, 1993). Regular exercise over the life span helps keep the cardiovascular, respiratory, and musculoskeletal systems in good working condition and prepared to engage in golf, shuffleboard, pool, or even tennis and skiing at any age. Athletic participation has beneficial effects not only on one's physical condition but also on the self-concept and emotional health (Hill, Storandt, & Malley, 1993; McAuley, Courneya, & Lettunich, 1991; McNeil, LeBlanc, & Joyner, 1991).

Despite its beneficial effects, the extent to which older adults should continue their involvement in athletic pursuits is a matter of some debate. It is maintained by some people, for example, that those who have worked and played hard throughout their youth and middle age should spend most of their time after age 65 resting and relaxing. When this is presented as a recipe for retirement in general, it becomes another example of ageism—stereotyping people simply because they are old. "Different strokes for different folks" is as true in old age as it is at other times of life.

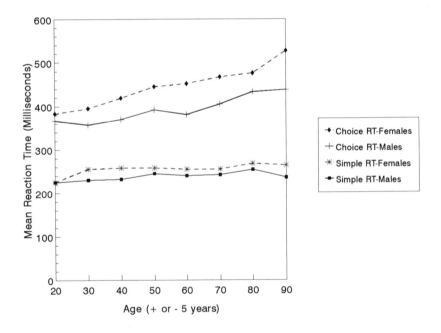

FIG. 5.2.   Age and gender differences in simple and disjunctive (choice) reaction time. (Based on data reported by Fozard, Vercruyssen, Reynolds, Hancock, & Quilter, 1994).

Gender Differences

On the average, females are not as strong as males: They cannot run as fast and, at least in most instances, their physical endurance is not as great. In addition, girls are not socialized to be as athletically competitive as boys; they are expected to concentrate more on developing their social skills rather than their athletic abilities. Girls are culturally conditioned to be co-operative, kind, nurturant, and even passive, whereas boys are expected to be active, competitive, and independent (Oglesby, 1983; Ortner, 1974). As with most stereotypes, there is some truth in these characterizations, but they are by no means inevitable.

Because of the way they are taught to view themselves, coupled with other experiences, girls tend to evaluate their general athletic ability as infe-rior to that of boys. Those who elect to ignore the cultural stereotype and compete in sports may find themselves embroiled in a conflict between the traditional female roles of submissiveness, grace, and beauty, and the male roles of aggressiveness, achievement, and strength. Research has shown, however, that as a group women athletes reportedly experience little such role conflict. Still those who participate intensively in sports that have tradi-tionally been considered inappropriate for women may be labeled as *un-feminine* and *sexually deviant* (Oglesby, 1998; Pedersen & Kono, 1990).

Title IX of the Higher Education Act of 1972 eased the problem of gender discrimination in educational institutions that receive federal funds. This statute, coupled with highly competitive college and professional women's teams in basketball, volleyball, and other sports, helped created a situation of greater opportunity for women and gender equality in sports. Other events, such as the women's movement and the fitness boom, have also en-couraged interest in and the competitiveness of women's sports.

Be that as it may, the older beliefs that participating in strenuous sports causes menstrual difficulties, endangers women's breasts and internal sex-ual organs, and produces unattractive muscles have not been entirely laid to rest. To be sure, women athletes may experience menstrual problems, but the causes of these difficulties are often uncertain and perhaps due to other factors than participation in athletics. In addition, physical injuries are fairly common among women athletes, as they are among men, but with proper training and treatment they can be dealt with effectively.

Homosexual Athletes

The number of lesbians in the general U.S. population is estimated at some-where around 2½% (Diamond, 1993), but the percentage of lesbians in sports is reportedly higher than that (Griffin, 1993–1994). Because they are both female and homosexual, from a social viewpoint lesbian athletes are often in a position of double jeopardy. Also subject to discrimination in sports are two other groups of homosexuals: gays and bisexuals. Male ath-letes tend to be quite macho-oriented as a group, or at least pretend to be, and the presence of gays in their midst can be a source of conflict and divi-sion. Statements made by athletes, coaches, sport psychologists, and others show that homophobia is quite common in the sports world (Rotella & Murray, 1991).

Racial/Ethnic Differences

Approximately 12% of the resident population of the United States is African American, but this group comprises 75% of professional basketball players, 60% of professional football players, and 18% of professional baseball players. Blacks are also found in disproportionate numbers in track and field and boxing ("Blacks in Sports," 1992). Hispanics, who number less than 11% of the U.S. population, are found in much lower percentages in all professional sports except baseball, soccer, and boxing ("The Best," 1993). With the exception of martial arts, even smaller percentages of Asian Americans become professional athletes and, Jim Thorpe notwithstanding, Native Americans are almost unknown in professional sports. Compared with Blacks, White athletes are involved more frequently in swimming, fencing, gymnastics, skiing, skating, and cycling. Even in traditional affluent sports such as tennis and golf, as witnessed by such notables as Althea Gibson, Arthur Ashe, and Tiger Woods, there have been impressive Black champions.

Most of the research that has been conducted on ethnic differences in athletics has compared Whites with Blacks, and traditional explanations of these differences have focused on genetically determined physical characteristics. In stereotypic fashion, Coakley (1982) summarized the findings as indicating that:

> Blacks have longer legs and arms, shorter trunk, less body fat, more slender hips, more tendon and less muscle, a different heel structure, wider calf bones, more slender calf muscles, greater arm circumference and more of the muscle fibers needed for speed and power and fewer of those needed for endurance. Compared to whites, blacks mature more rapidly, their lung capacity is lower, they are more likely to have hyperextensibility ("double-jointedness"), they dissipate heat more efficiently (sweat more), they tend to become chilled more easily in cold weather, and they have superior rhythmic abilities. (p. 265)

As emphasized by LeUnes and Nation (1989), because of the faulty data on which it is based, the prior description should not be taken at face value. To begin, the data were obtained from only a few selected sports and are biased in favor of superior athletes. Furthermore, the data are difficult to interpret because the meaning of the term Black and the relevance of these physical characteristics to superior sports performance are not clear.

The fact that Blacks are superior to Whites in certain sports is undeniable, but sociocultural factors appear to be more important than genetic ones. Racial discrimination and low SES have traditionally kept Blacks out of certain sports, and Black culture has concentrated on those sports that can be played without a great deal of special space or expensive equipment (Coakley, 1990). To an even greater extent than for White children and adolescents, sports stars serve as role models for young Blacks. Even when the

1 individual out of 20,000 high school Black athletes is successful in reaching the professional ranks, racial discrimination may be continued in the form of stacking. *Stacking* is the process of assigning Black players to certain peripheral positions and giving more central positions to White players. This type of discrimination by coaches or managers is not necessarily malevolent: A coach may sincerely believe that the speed, leaping ability, good hands, reckless abandon, and less intense mental activity of Blacks justify relegating them to those positions. However, most such stereotypes can be challenged by pointing to common exceptions. For example, the notion that Blacks are poor long distance runners is contradicted by the Olympic success of African athletes.

Whatever may be the reality of racial discrimination in sports, research indicates that the perception of that reality varies with the race of the beholder. For example, in a survey conducted by *Sports Illustrated* on the relative status of Black and White athletes in professional sports, substantially larger percentages of Blacks than Whites maintained that Blacks in their sport were worse off than Whites with regard to overall treatment, salaries/contracts, support by fans, treatment by coaches, management opportunities, and commercial endorsements (E. Johnson, 1991).

HEALTH AND ILLNESS

Physical attractiveness and participation in sports or other strenuous activities are generally considered to be signs of good health. People who look well, feel well, and behave in an energetic, organized manner are usually viewed as healthy. However, good health is more than the absence of pain, a sickly appearance, and debilitating functional limitations. It is a psychological as well as a physical condition—not merely being disease-free, but existing in a state of positive wellness.

Whether seen from a traditional disease-free viewpoint or from a quality-of-life perspective, health is a highly individual matter. A number of personal and environmental factors can influence a person's health, including chronological age, gender, nationality, race, SES, diet, exercise, a sanitary living environment, and mental well-being.

Age

The relationship between chronological age and health is documented by the results of numerous studies. In a 1994 National Health Interview Survey, for example, 95.6% of adults ages 18 to 24, 92.5% of adults ages 25 to 44, 83.4% of adults ages 45 to 64, and 72.1% of adults ages 65 and over rated their overall health as *good, very good,* or *excellent* (Adams & Marano, 1995).

Physical illness is obviously not just a problem of infancy and old age. Many children and young adults get sick, but the causes are typically acute disorders or accidents rather than chronic, frequently life-threatening illnesses. Young people also tend to recover fairly quickly from diseases such as influenza, which in older adults are more likely to lead to potentially fatal conditions such as pneumonia.

Beginning in the 40s or 50s, the effects of illness on energy, ability, and productivity become more pronounced. The pain and disability caused by illness can have an effect on the individual's sense of well-being, level of social participation, interests, and overall enjoyment of living. Still most middle-aged and older adults describe their health as *good* and may resent the description of older adults as *sick*. Although one's health status is typically poorer in later life than in previous years, not all older adults are hypochondriacs who complain endlessly about their physical condition.

Statistics on the frequency of various diagnoses among patients with short-term hospital stays show that, among the most common diagnostic conditions, circulatory diseases, digestive diseases, respiratory diseases, neoplasms (cancers), musculoskeletal disorders, and endocrine and metabolic disorders all increase with age. Certain other conditions (e.g., injury, poisoning, and genitourinary disease) are related in a curvilinear manner to age: They are most common in the 15 to 44 and 65+ age brackets and least common in the 45 to 64 age group. Finally, admissions for mental conditions are inversely related to age, being most common in the 15- to 44-year group and least common in the 65 and over group. (Graves & Gillum, 1996)

As indicated by more frequent and longer hospital stays and more contacts with physicians, health is typically poorer in later life. However, socioeconomic, sociocultural, and psychological factors also affect the frequency of visits to physicians. Women account for more physician contacts than men, Whites have more physician contacts than Blacks, and people with higher incomes have more physician contacts than those with lower incomes (National Center for Health Statistics, 1995).

Accidents

Pain and disability are caused not only by physical illnesses but also by injuries suffered in accidents. Every year approximately 2.6 million Americans are hospitalized for injuries, 37.2 million are treated in hospital emergency departments, and 60.5 million seek medical treatment or suffer a day or more of restricted activity from an injury. The cost of these injuries can also be assessed in monetary terms, amounting to an estimated $478.3 billion in 1997 alone (National Safety Council, 1998).

Figure 5.3 illustrates the rates of injuries (fractures, sprains and strains, open wounds and lacerations, contusions, and others) leading to restricted activity and/or medical attention in four age groups of males and females. Considering the higher exposure of males and younger adults to potentially more dangerous situations, it is perhaps not surprising that the injury rate is higher for males than females and for younger than older adults (U.S. Bureau of the Census, 1997b). Although the lowest injury rate occurs in older adulthood, the death rate due to accidents follows a different age-related pattern. The rate of deaths caused by motor vehicle accidents rises abruptly during the late teens and early 20s, then drops and stays fairly

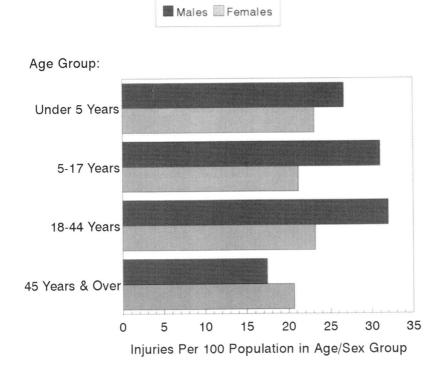

■ Males ▦ Females

Age Group:

Under 5 Years

5-17 Years

18-44 Years

45 Years & Over

0   5   10   15   20   25   30   35

Injuries Per 100 Population in Age/Sex Group

FIG. 5.3.   Rate of injuries by age and sex, 1980–1993. (Based on data from U.S. National Center for Health Statistics, *Vital and Health Statistics*, Series 10, No. 190; early reports; unpublished data.)

constant until the late 60s and 70s, after which it rises again. Deaths due to other types of accidents are quite low during childhood, rise slightly during early adulthood, and remain fairly steady until the late 60s and early 70s. The dramatic rise in accidental deaths during later life is due in large measure to falls and other mishaps caused by declining perceptual-motor and cognitive abilities (R. Anderson, Kochanek, & Murphy, 1997).

Nationality and Culture

Both general health status and the prevalence of specific diseases are related to geographical region, climate, diet, health care, sanitation, pollution, and other factors that vary from country to country and from place to place within the same country. Furthermore, beliefs concerning the causes of specific illnesses and appropriate treatments for them can vary substantially with the culture and subculture. The health beliefs of immigrants to the United States are affected by the length of time the person has been in this country, as well as education and the social pressures for acculturation (Congress & Lyons, 1992).

Gender

In addition to age, nationality, and culture, health status varies with gender, race, SES, and lifestyle. For example, in the 1994 National Health Interview Survey, lower percentages of females than males, of Blacks than Whites, and those with lower than higher incomes, rated their health as *good, very good,* or *excellent* (Adams & Marano, 1995). Women are more likely than men to be afflicted with arthritis, diabetes, and other chronic but less fatal conditions, whereas men are more likely than women to have heart disease and cancer. With respect to health care, older men are also more likely to be cared for at home by their wives. A greater percentage of older women, who are more likely than older men to be widowed, are cared for in nursing homes (Lentzer et al., 1992).

The frequency of accidental injuries also varies with gender. The number of injuries sustained by women between the ages of 18 and 44 is less than that sustained by men in that age range. However, women over age 45 have more accidental injuries than men. This gender difference may be due to the fact that there are more women than men over age 45, but it is also true that older women who sustain falls are more likely than older men to be seriously injured (U.S. Bureau of the Census, 1997b). Because of the decreased density and greater porosity in the bones of older adults, fractures of the the vertebrae, ribs, and hips occur more easily. This fracturing tendency is exacerbated by the long-term loss of bone mass in osteoporosis—a common disorder in later life and especially in older women.

Race

On the whole, Whites and Asian Americans are healthier than Blacks and more likely to view their health as good. The better health status of Whites than Blacks is underscored by statistics on life expectancy. In 1996, the life expectancy of White Americans was 73.8 years for males and 79.6 for females, but it was only 66.1 years for Black males and 74.2 years for Black females (Ventura, Peters, Martin, & Maurer, 1997). These life expectancy figures are all-time highs for White men, Black men, and Black women in this country.

SES and Family Characteristics

Americans of higher socioeconomic status enjoy better health and assign higher ratings to their health than Americans of lower status. Both poorer health and physical disabilities are more common among Americans of lower SES and occur at a younger age than in Americans who are higher on the socioeconomic scale. Self-ratings of health status are also positively correlated with annual income (National Center for Health Statistics, 1991).

Associated with SES are family characteristics such as education, income, marital status, and family size. As documented in a report published by the National Center for Health Statistics (J. Collins & LeClere, 1997), these factors can have an important impact on the health status of family members. This report found that the healthiest people were those who were living with a spouse, children living in two-parent households, and people living in families with higher education and income.

Lifestyle

Among the various lifestyle factors that affect health are smoking, heavy drinking of alcoholic beverages, polluted air and water, drug use, sexual habits, physical exercise, personal cleanliness, and quality of health care. (See Box 5.2 for statistics related to unhealthy lifestyle habits.) Psychosocial factors such as compliance with recommended treatments, social support, emotional stress, and personality characteristics can also affect the severity and duration of an illness. The roles of stress and personality in health and disease are dealt with in some detail in chapter 9.

SUMMARY

Physical appearance and capabilities are important contributors to a person's self-concept and social acceptance. Looking good and feeling strong and healthy increase one's self-confidence and willingness to attempt difficult tasks and receive the approval of other people.

This chapter is principally concerned with the physical structure and functioning of the individual and the ways in which variations in these characteristics influence success and failure. Both individual and group differences in physical characteristics are considered, in addition to their personal and social consequences. The chapter begins with a discussion of methods of measuring and describing the human body, deals next with the determinants of physical attractiveness and performance and their outcomes, and ends with a brief discussion of health and illness.

Measurements of height, weight, and overall body shape are useful in many different fields, including developmental biology, medicine, human engineering, sports, and commercial fields such as clothing manufacturing. Systems of classifying the human body into a small number of categories or types, such as Sheldon's somatotype theory, are interesting but have not proved useful. Of greater practical value in engineering, forensics, and medicine are more detailed measurements of the structure of the head and other bones, examination of body tissues and blood, and an analysis of body chemistry. In ergonomics, body measurements are made to assist in the design of human-operated machines and work spaces. In forensic medicine, measurements made on the body contribute to the identification of victims and an understanding of the circumstances of crimes. These measurements vary with the age, sex, race, and other characteristics of people.

To a large extent, physical attractiveness is "in the eye of the beholder," but there is some consistency both within and between different cultures in what

---

Box 5.2: Statistics Related to Unhealthy Lifestyle Habits

Alcohol

More than 50% of Americans ages 12 years and over drink alcoholic beverages in a given month; 16% of these are binge drinkers who have five or more drinks on a particular occasion.

Illegal Drug Use

Approximately 8% of Americans ages 12 to 17 and 22% of high school seniors smoke marijuana in a given month. Over 2% of high school seniors and 1% of persons ages 18 to 25 use cocaine in a given month. Over 2% of high school seniors use inhalants in a given month.

Exercise

Over 60% of adults do not exercise adequately, and 25% are not active at all. Nearly half of Americans ages 12 to 21 are not vigorously active on a regular basis. In high school, enrollment in daily physical education classes dropped from 42% to 25% from 1991 to 1995. Only 19% of all high school students are physically active for 20 minutes or more in physical education classes every day of the school week. The consequence of inadequate exercise, combined with overeating, is overweight. Over 35% of adults, 12% of adolescents (ages 12 to 17), 14% of children (ages 6 to 11), and 8% of preschoolers are overweight.

Smoking

28% of American men and 23% of American women (ages 18 and over), 38% of high school dropouts ages 25 and over, and 12% of people with 16 or more years of education smoke cigarettes; 20% of adolescents (ages 12 to 17) smoke cigarettes in a given month.

Sexually Transmitted Diseases

In the United States, 68,953 cases of syphilis (26.2 cases per 100,000 population), 477,638 cases of chlamydia (182.2 cases per 100,000 population), and 392,838 cases of gonorrhea (149.5 cases per 100,000 population) were reported in 1995.

Source. Web Site www.cdc.gov/nchswww/fastats.

---

constitutes physical attractiveness. Having a youthful appearance, for example, is a criterion of physical attractiveness in most societies. Both men and women prefer more physically attractive members of the opposite sex, but women in particular also assign high ratings to cognitive and social skills, grooming, and financial status in potential dates or mates (see Singh, 1995b).

A great deal of time, energy, and material wealth is expended by people in an attempt to improve their physical attractiveness, and much of it is probably well spent. Being physically attractive does not guarantee success or happiness, but it has many personal and social advantages. There is an extensive research literature on the measurement of physical attractiveness, particularly in females, and the effects of being attractive. One interesting, but not surprising, finding is that the appropriate use of cosmetics, apparel, and other adornments can go a long way toward compensating for physical defects.

In Western culture, and indeed throughout the world, athletic ability is a highly valued personal and social asset. The heroes and models of a large percentage of people—both young and old—are skilled athletic performers and champions. Ability and success in different sports varies with age, gender, race/ethnicity, and culture. Physical characteristics obviously play an important role in determining athletic success, but sociocultural factors and training methods are at least as important.

The frequency of health problems increases with age after young adulthood, but health status is a highly individual matter and varies with hereditary and environmental factors. In their avoidance of disease and accidents, some people appear to live charmed lives, whereas others are victims of almost every disease or mishap that comes along. General health status and accompanying disease and death vary significantly with nationality and culture, gender, race, SES, and lifestyle. Psychological factors such as anxiety, depression, and the individual's ability to predict and control for potential health risks are also associated with health status.

SUGGESTED READINGS

Adler, N., & Matthews, K. (1994). Health psychology: Why do some people get sick and some stay well? *Annual Review of Psychology, 45,* 229–259.

Buss, A. H. (1994). The strategies of human mating. *American Scientist, 82,* 238–249.

Cogan, K. D., & Petrie, T. A. (1996). Diversity in sport. In J. L. Van Raalte & B. W. Brewer (Eds.), *Exploring sport and exercise psychology* (pp. 355–373). Washington, DC: American Psychological Association.

Congress, E. P., & Lyons, B. P. (1992). Cultural differences in health beliefs: Implications for social work practice in health care settings. *Social Work in Health Care, 17*(3), 81–96.

Friedman, H. S., Tucker, J. S., Schwartz, J. E., Tomlinson-Keasey, C., Martin, L. R., Wingard, D. L., & Criqui, M. H. (1995). Psychosocial and behavioral predictors of longevity. *American Psychologist, 50*(2), 69–78.

Harris, J. R., Pedersen, N. L., Stacey, C., & McClearn, G. E. (1992). Age differences in the etiology of the relationship between life satisfaction and self-rated health. *Journal of Aging and Health, 4,* 349–368.

Janisse, P. (Ed.). (1988). *Individual differences, stress, and health psychology.* New York: Springer-Verlag.

Larsen, R. J., & Kasimatis, M. (1991). Day-to-day physical symptoms: Individual differences in the occurrence, duration, and emotional concomitants of minor daily illnesses. Special Issue: Personality and daily experience. *Journal of Personality, 59*(3), 387–423.

Theories, Concepts,
and Correlates of Cognitive Abilities

Since its beginnings in the research of Francis Galton, J. M. Cattell, William Stern, and other pioneer psychometricians during the late 19th and early 20th centuries, the field of differential psychology has been concerned in large measure with individual differences in cognitive abilities.[1] Although it was preceded by the efforts of Galton and others to measure what they designated as *intelligence,* the first practical test of intelligence, or general mental ability, was constructed by Alfred Binet and Thèodore Simon. Based to some extent on Binet's early speculations concerning the nature of intelligence, the Binet–Simon Intelligence Scale was a kind of hodgepodge of subtests fashioned from observations of the kinds of tasks that children are required to accomplish in school. It was originally designed to identify school children who, because of limited mental ability, could not profit sufficiently from instruction in regular school classrooms. However, the Binet–Simon Intelligence Scale and other early individual- and group-administered tests of cognitive abilities came to serve a wider range of practical and research purposes. In research contexts, these tests provided a means for assessing the cognitive abilities of individuals and for comparing the abilities of different groups of people. Subsequent developments in intelligence testing—including construction of the Wechsler series, tests for the physically handicapped, infant intelligence tests, culture-fair tests, and measures of special abilities—led to extensive research and a voluminous literature on individual and group differences in cognitive abilities. Chronological age, gender, race/ethnicity, nationality, culture, urban/rural residence, education, SES, family size, birth order, and historical era are some of the demographic variables that have been related to scores on tests of intelligence and special cognitive abilities. The influences of biological vari-

---

[1]The terms *mental, intellectual,* and *cognitive* are used somewhat interchangeably in this chapter. From a technical viewpoint, cognitive is perhaps preferred by contemporary psychological researchers.

ables, such as genetics, brain structure and functioning, diet and nutrition, drugs and other chemicals, as well as climate, season of birth, and other environmental factors, have also been studied. The effects of untoward experiences and accidents on cognitive abilities; efforts to change cognitive functioning by special training, exercise, or teaching; and the effects of motivation, mental disorder, and even music on these abilities have also been investigated. However, rather than attempting to describe every research investigation on these topics conducted over the past 100 years, this chapter focuses on a few selected topics that have received fairly extensive coverage in the psychological literature and continue to do so.

THEORIES OF INTELLIGENCE

Ideally research is guided by theory. However, as in attempting to solve any complex problem, the path toward answers to research questions meanders and often goes backward rather than forward. A well thought-out theory, based on meaningful concepts, logic, and prior research findings, can often assist in predicting and understanding behavior, but there is no guarantee that it will actually do so. Furthermore, because they are human, theorists may be reluctant to abandon hypotheses in which they have invested their time, energies, and egos even when their speculations fail to be verified by experience and experiment. For this and other reasons, many of the theories of intelligence that were fashionable during the late 19th and early 20th centuries and have not stood the test of time are still around today in one form or another.

It can be argued that more important than whether a theory is right or wrong is whether it is useful or nonuseful. For example, many conceptions of intelligence as a conglomeration of factors or special abilities (e.g., Cattell, 1963; Guilford, 1967; Spearman, 1927; Thurstone, 1938; P. E. Vernon, 1960) are not absolutely correct in the sense of providing an accurate understanding of the structure of intellect. Nevertheless, they have been heuristic in their role of suggesting ideas and promoting further research. These psychometric theories or models stemmed from empirical/statistical demonstrations that scores on a large number of people on a sizable number of tests could be condensed into a smaller number of factors or traits. Spearman (1927) described *intelligence* in terms of a general factor (g), plus several specific factors. Thurstone (1938) characterized intelligence as a composite of seven primary mental abilities. The final form of Guilford's (1967; Guilford & Hoepfner, 1971) structure-of-intellect model contained 150 different factors (5 operations × 5 contents × 6 products).

For a time, debate raged over the most efficient way of conceptualizing intelligence in terms of factors and in particular the generality of intelligence. This debate has been muted to some extent, ending in acceptance by a majority of psychometricians of a general intelligence factor (g) and a hierarchical model, with a general factor at the apex and major and minor group factors falling below (e.g., P. E. Vernon, 1960). However, differences in interpretation remain. For example, followers of R. B. Cattell opt for dividing the general intelligence factor into fluid ability (g_f) and crystallized ability (g_c). *Fluid ability* is conceptualized as inherent, genetically determined cognitive ability as manifested in problem solving and novel responses. *Crystallized ability*, consisting of knowledge and skills acquired by experience and education, is specific to certain fields and applied to tasks involving fixed habits.

The theory of intellect, or human cognition, embraced by research and practicing psychologists has varied to some extent with nationality and professional interests. For example, British psychologists focused more on a general intelligence factor, whereas American psychologists found models consisting of several group factors of intelligence more acceptable. With regard to specialty, psychometricians were more apt to conduct research along trait-factor lines and construct tests to measure various cognitive factors, whereas developmental psychologists tended to follow Piaget's (1954) theory of cognitive development, school teachers were drawn to Gardner's (1983, 1994) seven frames of mind, and specialists in the newer area of cognitive psychology looked to information-processing models and computer analogies (e.g., R. J. Sternberg, 1985, 1988). The greatest amount of research concerned with intelligence was conducted by specialists in either psychometrics or developmental psychology, although much research on cognitive abilities was purely empirical and not inspired by any theory.

Some theories of intelligence have attempted to be more comprehensive and provide a universal appeal by incorporating findings from research on human development, cultural anthropology, and neuropsychology. For example, Gardner's (1994) conceptualization of intelligence in terms of seven forms—linguistic, logical-mathematical, spatial, musical, bodily kinesthetic, intrapersonal, and interpersonal—draws on findings from cross-cultural research, developmental/educational psychology, and behavioral changes due to brian injury.

An example of another current theory that has attempted to incorporate findings from neuropsychological research is the PASS (Planning, Attention, Simultaneous, and Successive Processes) model (Das, Naglieri, & Kirby, 1994). This model is based on Luria's (1966) conception of cognition in terms of three functional units. According to the PASS model, the first functional unit (brain stem and limbic system) is responsible for arousal, attention, and discrimination among stimuli. The second functional unit (posterior regions of the cerebral cortex, including the occipital, temporal, and parietal areas) is concerned with reception, analysis, and storage of information by means of simultaneous and successive reasoning processes. The third functioning unit (anterior parts of the cerebral hemispheres, particularly the prefrontal region) is concerned with planning, regulating, and verifying mental activity. The three functional units operate on the person's knowledge base, which consists of all the information in long- and short-term memory that is available to the person at processing time. The effectiveness of processing is determined by the integration of this knowledge base with the planning of the third functional unit, the attention of the first functional unit, and the simultaneous and successive reasoning processes of the second functional unit that are required by the particular task. The output of this processing consists of speaking, writing, and other motor actions.

Descriptions of other theories of cognitive abilities, such as R. J. Sternberg's (1985) triarchic theory, are given at various points in this chapter and the next. However, these descriptions are not comprehensive, and the reader is encouraged to consult other sources (e.g., Aiken, 1996a; Flanagan, Genshaft, & Harrison, 1997; R. J. Sternberg & Grigorenko, 1997) for more detailed information.

STABILITY AND CHANGE IN COGNITIVE ABILITIES

Scores on tests of intelligence and other cognitive abilities are not fixed, unvarying measures. Not only are they influenced by errors of measurement, but they rise and fall to some extent over time as the individual gains experience and undergoes biological changes. The reliability of a set of test scores (i.e., their relative freedom from errors of measurement) varies appreciably with the specific test, the individual being tested, and the conditions under which testing takes place. Of all psychological and educational measuring instruments, the highest reliabilities—often in the .90s—have been obtained with tests of cognitive abilities. For traditional individual tests of intelligence, which have total score standard deviations of around 15 or 16 points, a reliability coefficient in the .90s will yield a standard error of measurement of approximately five points. This is the basis for the statement that IQ scores change only around five points on retesting. This figure is, of course, only an average, and an IQ score may occasionally vary by 20 points or more when the physical health, emotional state, or living conditions of the person change significantly.

An IQ score is a measure that takes into account the chronological age of the person being tested. Consequently, it might be expected that a child's IQ will not change appreciably as he or she matures. In scoring the first edition of the Stanford–Binet Intelligence Scale, IQ was defined as the ratio of mental age (MA) to chronological age, both expressed in months, and then multiplied by 100 (IQ = (MA/CA) × 100). An examinee's MA on this test was determined from the pattern of subtests that he or she passed at each age level and then converted to a ratio IQ by this formula. For a person's IQ to remain constant from year to year, the MA had to increase by the same amount as the CA. This was approximately the case during the early school years, but it was realized by early mental testers that the MA stops increasing at some point. Whether a person's maximum MA is attained at 15, 16, 18, or some other chronological age was debated extensively but never resolved. In testing older adolescents and adults with the first two editions of the Stanford–Binet, 16 or 18 years was used as the CA to compensate for the fact that the MA stops increasing at those ages. Later versions of the Stanford–Binet, the Wechsler tests, and many other intelligence tests avoided the question of what to use in the denominator of the ratio IQ formula by converting the raw test scores to deviation IQs. A deviation IQ is computed as IQ = 100 + sz, where s is the standard deviation of the scores and z is the difference between the raw score and the mean divided by the standard deviation. Still the move to deviation IQs did not resolve the issue of how intelligence changes with chronological age.

Age Changes in Intelligence

Early research on age changes in intelligence test scores was based almost entirely on cross-sectional data, consisting of the scores of different chronological age groups (Doppelt & Wallace, 1955; H. E. Jones & Conrad, 1933; Yerkes, 1921). The classic aging pattern obtained in these studies is that of a rise in scores up to the late teens or early 20s, followed by a plateau during young adulthood, and then a decline during middle and late adulthood. As with all cross-sectional data, the fact that the results were based on independent groups of people in different chronological age ranges made it impossible to separate bona fide age changes from cohort differences. Older cohorts generally had less education than younger ones and grew up in a different sociocultural climate. Consequently, it is possible that the apparent age decrement in intelligence was due to cohort differences rather than biopsychological changes with age.

A somewhat different rise-and-fall pattern of changes in intelligence test scores as a function of age was obtained in longitudinal studies in which the same individuals were retested at successive ages. The results of longitudinal investigations conducted by Bayley and Oden (1955), Campbell (1965), Nisbet (1957), and Owens (1953, 1966) indicated that intelligence test scores remain fairly stable or decrease only slightly after early adulthood. The great majority of these studies were conducted on college graduates, but other longitudinal studies with people of average intelligence (Charles & James, 1964; Eisdorfer, 1963; Tuddenham, Blumenkrantz, & Wilkin, 1968) and mentally retarded adults (Baller, Charles, & Miller, 1967; Bell & Zubek, 1960) yielded similar results. Viewed in their entirety, the results of longitudinal studies indicate that intelligence increases slightly during early adulthood, reaches a plateau during the late 20s, and declines slowly after that. However, the magnitude of the decline varies with the individual. People of above-average intelligence, as well as those who continue to use their cognitive abilities, may show no decline at all and even an improvement up to late middle age.

As in cross-sectional studies, there are methodological problems with longitudinal studies. One problem is that of *selective attrition,* which is the fact that people of lower intelligence are less likely to report for repeated testings. Another methodological problem of longitudinal investigations is the *regression effect,* witnessed by the fact that people whose initial scores are very low or very high tend to score closer to the mean on retesting. As discussed in chapter 2, more complex developmental research designs that take the methodological shortcomings of the cross-sectional and longitudinal procedures into account have been devised, but they are expensive and time-consuming. Perhaps even more important in efforts to understand the development and decline of cognitive abilities is the fact that general intelligence tests do not measure only one factor.

In both cross-sectional and longitudinal studies, the specific pattern of variation in test scores with age depends on the particular test. For example, scaled scores on the Information, Vocabulary, and Arithmetic subtests of the Wechsler Adult Intelligence Scale–Revised (WAIS–R) do not show significant age-related changes. However, scaled scores on the Picture Completion, Picture Arrangement, and Digit Symbol subtests decline substantially after young adulthood (Wechsler, 1981).

More extensive studies of the differential patterns of changes in cognitive test scores during adulthood were conducted by Schaie (1990, 1994) and his co-researchers in the Seattle Longitudinal Studies. Among the findings of these studies are those concerned with the relationships of age to scores on five SRA Mental Abilities Tests: Verbal Meaning, Spatial Orientation, Inductive Reasoning, Number, and Word Fluency. Results of both cross-sectional and longitudinal studies of these five abilities are shown in Figs. 6.1a and 6.1b. Note that the relationship between test score and age varies with the specific ability and research methodology employed. During middle adulthood, the rate of decline is greatest for Spatial Orientation and Inductive Reasoning and less for Word Fluency, Verbal Meaning, and Number. The greatest drop during old age is seen in Verbal Meaning, which is a slightly speeded test.

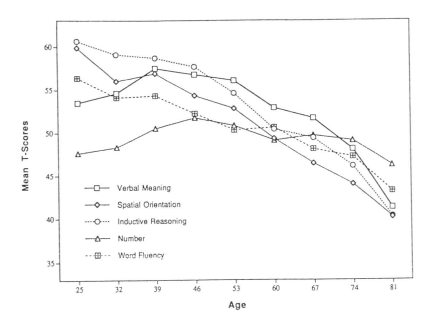

FIG. 6.1a.   Mean scores on five cognitive abilities as a function of age: Cross-sectional data (Schaie, 1994).

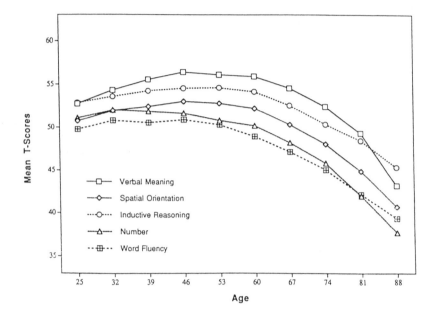

FIG. 6.1b.   Mean scores on five cognitive abilities as a function of age: Longitudinal data (Schaie, 1994).

In general, greater age-related declines are observed on tasks requiring mainly fluid ability than on tasks in which crystallized ability plays a greater role. A number of researchers (Christensen et al., 1994; Horn, 1982; Horn & Hofer, 1992) have also found greater age-related declines in scores on measures of fluid than on measures of crystallized ability.

Acknowledging that cognitive abilities decline somewhat with age, Schaie and his associates (Baltes & Willis, 1982; Schaie & Willis, 1986; Willis, 1990) emphasized the plasticity of these abilities and that their decline can be arrested and even reversed. Environments that provide varied opportunities for intellectual stimulation and a flexible lifestyle are seen as contributing to the maintenance of an optimal level of cognitive functioning in adults. Not only have Schaie and his coworkers encouraged the development of these kinds of environments in later life, but they have also devised a variety of techniques for training older adults to improve their test scores. In addition to instruction in specific cognitive skills, such training may emphasize anxiety reduction and motivation. Older adults can also learn to compensate for decrements in cognitive skills by limiting their involvement in activities in which those deficits are most obvious and concentrating on those in which they are less pronounced.

The success of intervention or special training in improving cognitive abilities underscores the role of environment in shaping those abilities. However, research indicates that at least half the total variance in IQ scores is accounted for by genetic factors (Bouchard, 1997; Loehlin, Horn, & Willerman, 1997; Pedersen, Plomin, Nesselroade, & McClearn, 1992; Plomin, 1997). Heredity appears to be an even more important determinant of intelligence in adults than in children (Plomin, 1997). As people grow older and interact more with their environments, heredity becomes more important and environment less so in the manifestation of intelligence. Older adults typically have had a wider variety of experiences than younger adults, and consequently have been exposed to a greater number of ways in which to express their intelligence. The biological foundations for intelligence that were laid down at the moment of conception become more and more apparent with aging.

Finally, there is some evidence for a so-called *terminal drop*, or a general decline, in cognitive abilities shortly before a person's death (Lieberman, 1965; Reimanis & Green, 1971; Riegel & Riegel, 1972). The terminal drop is reportedly manifested in decrements in IQ, memory, cognitive organization, sensorimotor abilities, and even personality characteristics during the last months or years prior to a person's death (White & Cunningham, 1988). There is some debate over whether the terminal drop is a genuine phenomenon or a methodological artifact. If it is genuine, it is probably due to declines in the functioning efficiency of the cardiovascular system and other vital systems of the body during old age.

Health Status

The average life span for Americans is 72 years for men and 78 years for women, but there is a great deal of variability around these averages. Individual differences are also apparent in health status—not only in old age but at all times of life. Poor health has both physical and psychological effects: it leads to pain, disability, loss of energy, increased depression, and lower motivation to assert oneself intellectually and socially. These factors also take their toll on adaptability and functioning intelligence. Furthermore, the relationship between health and intelligence is bidirectional: Not only can poor health reduce the efficiency of intellectual functioning, but, either through ignorance or inadequate financial resources, people of lower intellectual abilities are less likely to take care of their health.

Among the health disorders that can have pronounced effects on cognitive functioning in later life are Alzheimer's disease and hypertension. The symptoms of Alzheimer's disease, which affects an estimated 20% of Americans between the ages 75 and 84 and 47% of those over age 85 (Evans et al., 1989), include a gradual deterioration of memory and other cognitive abilities, disorientation, and a general disintegration of personality and behavior over time. Mental alertness, adaptability, sociability, and tolerance for new things or changes in routine all gradually decline.

Hypertension is associated with cardiovascular disease and stroke, which, by interfering with the flow of oxygen to the brain, can affect intellectual abilities and other skills (speaking, walking, etc.). Emphysema, acute infection, poor nutrition, injuries, and surgery can also lead to a temporary reduction in the brain's blood supply and consequently interfere with intellectual functioning. The loss of neuronal tissue, changes in metabolic rate, and declines in blood circulation also have depressing effects on cognitive functioning.

Stability of Infant Intelligence

Not many years after the publication of the first edition of the Stanford–Binet Intelligence Scale, tests were designed to measure the intelligence of children below the Stanford–Binet's lower limit of 2 years. Pioneering research by Arnold Gesell during the 1920s paved the way for the assessment of children's physical and mental development. Subsequent research and test development work by other child development specialists resulted in a number of tests (California First-Year Mental Scale, Griffith's Mental Development Scale, Cattell Infant Intelligence Scale, etc.) designed specifically to measure the cognitive abilities of infants and young children. These tests were employed in research on child development for diagnosing mental retardation and other developmental delays and for practical purposes such as adoptive placement decisions. For the most part, these early infant tests were replaced by instruments such as the Bayley Scales of Infant Development (BSID). The BSID is appropriate for testing individuals between 1 month and 36 months, but the Neonatal Behavioral Assessment Scale (NBAS) has an even lower range (from 3 days to 4 weeks).

Despite extensive, repetitive efforts to construct intelligence tests for infants and toddlers that can forecast later intellectual abilities, these efforts have not met with great success. As illustrated in Fig. 6.2, scores on tests administered to children under 2½ years have low correlations with their scores on tests administered after age 3 (also see Humphreys & Davey, 1988). One explanation for these low correlations is the difference in the nature of the tasks on intelligence tests for infants and tests appropriate for older children. Infant intelligence tests are primarily measures of sensorimotor development (e.g., lifting and turning the head, following a moving object with the eyes, reaching for and grasping an object). The tasks on intelligence tests administered after infancy are more linguistic or verbal in nature. The low reliabilities of infant intelligence tests resulting from the greater distractibility or inattentiveness of infants in the testing situation, in addition to qualitative and quantitative changes in cognitive abilities occurring during infancy and early childhood, also contribute to the low predictive validities of these tests.

Observations of age of talking, walking, or other cognitive and perceptual-motor skills have proved no better than infant intelligence tests in predicting later cognitive development. For example, 1½-year-olds who talk in sentences more typical of 3-year olds are not especially likely to be able to read by age 4½ (Crain-Thoreson & Dale, 1992). By the time children enter kindergarten, however, their intelligence test scores have improved significantly as predictors of their scholastic achievement (Tramontana, Hooper,

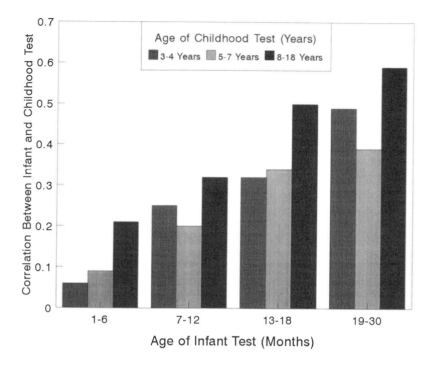

FIG. 6.2.   Median correlations between infant test scores and childhood IQs
(McCall, 1979).

& Selzer, 1988). Scores on intelligence tests administered at age 7 and beyond are even more stable and continue to gain in stability and validity during childhood.

Changes in Scholastic Assessment Test Scores

For the most part, research concerned with the reliability and validity of
scores on tests of intelligence and other cognitive abilities in infants and
young children have involved longitudinal comparisons of scores of the
same individuals over time. Also of interest to researchers are
cross-sectional studies in which comparisons are made between the scores
of comparable age groups tested at different times. Illustrative of the second type of research are studies of changes in Scholastic Assessment Test
(SAT) scores from one year to another.

The SAT is certainly one of the most reliable and widely administered of
all tests of cognitive abilities. Used for student admission to colleges and
universities throughout the United States, the SAT is administered to hundreds of thousands of high school students annually. The first section of the

SAT, consisting of Verbal Reasoning and Mathematical Reasoning sections, is a test of academic aptitude. The items on this section of the test are changed every year, but the scores are expressed on a common scale that makes it possible to compare mean scores from year to year.

A plot of mean scores on the Verbal and Mathematical sections of the SAT from 1972 to 1997 is shown in Fig. 6.3. Note that the mean scores on both sections of the test decreased during the 1970s but leveled off and even rose slightly during the early 1990s. A similar decline during the 1970s was observed in mean scores on other standardized measures of cognitive abilities (American College Tests, Minnesota Scholastic Aptitude Test, the Iowa Tests of Educational Development, and the Comprehensive Test of Basic Skills). Furthermore, the decline occurred in both males and females, all ethnic groups, and in students of high and low ability.

Clearly the declines in college admissions test scores during the 1970s and 1980s became a cause of concern in American education. Many explanations for the decline were proposed, including lower parental education, less concern for and supervision of children, lack of motivation on the part of students, too much television, increased permissiveness of society, and reduced attention paid to students by teachers (Elam, 1978). Additional ex-

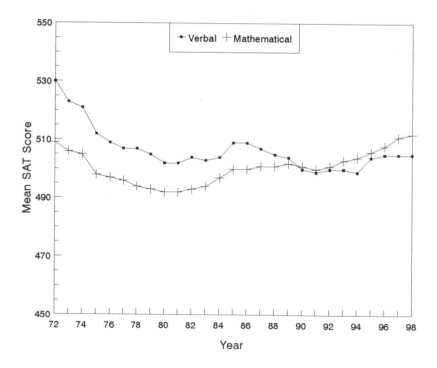

FIG. 6.3.   Changes in SAT scores from 1972 to 1998 (Based on data from College Entrance Examination Board).

planations included drugs, sex, lack of economic incentives for acquiring a good education, and spacing of children within families (Zajonc, 1986). In a review published by Austin and Garber (1982) during the early 1980s, it was concluded that approximately half the decline in SAT scores during the late 1960s and early 1970s was caused by changes in the socio-economic, ethnic, and gender composition of the group of students who took the test. Because these changes had presumably exerted their effects by 1970, further declines in scores during the 1970s were attributed to pervasive social forces. Included among these forces were such things as less intellectually demanding high school curricula, diminishing educational standards, lower teacher abilities, changes in the role and social structure of American families, television, sociopolitical disruption during the early 1970s, and lower student motivation. More recently, Williams and Ceci (1997) noted that the pool of high school seniors who took the SAT became less selective in the 1960s and 1970s and that the number of institutions requiring it increased. They speculated that if the SAT had been taken by all high school seniors rather than by a self-selected sample in the 1950s and early 1960s, the observed decline in scores during the late 1960s and early 1970s would have been substantially less (see Berliner & Biddle, 1995).

Lake Wobegon Effect

In contrast to the annual decline in SAT scores, during the 1980s it was noted that a large majority of students in elementary school districts throughout the United States were scoring above the national norms on annually administered achievement tests (Cannell, 1989). One explanation for this phenomenon, which was dubbed the *Lake Wobegon effect* after Garrison Keilor's fictional Minnesota community "where all children are above average," was that the tests were not being restandardized as often as they should. Among the other factors that allegedly contributed to the increasing scores were that teachers were coaching students on the test questions, allowing them more than the scheduled time to finish the test, and even altering completed answer sheets to make them more accurate.

The Lake Wobegon Effect prompted recognition of the need for more frequent renorming of standardized achievement tests and concern over the professional and ethical responsibilities of teachers with respect to standardized testing. It has been known for many years that scores on standardized achievement test batteries tend to creep upward when the same battery is administered year after year in particular schools. These increases are undoubtedly due in some measure to the fact that teachers are teaching to the test. Although it is certainly the teacher's responsibility to provide instruction to students on materials in the same subject and of the same type as those on the tests, students should not be coached on items identical to those on the test. Sympathy for students and second-guessing of what they actually know or should have known are understandable, but the administration of standardized tests requires adherence to standard procedures if the scores are to be meaningful. Teachers should work to improve students' knowledge in areas of the test on which they make low scores, but not rehearse them on the test items themselves.

Flynn Effect

Also in contrast to the decline and leveling off of SAT scores, there is evidence that IQ scores in developed countries have actually increased during the past three generations (see Fig. 6.4). Political scientist James Flynn (1987), after whom this effect was named, concluded that the mean IQ score of an average 20-year-old today is 15 points higher than that of a person of the same age in 1940 and is still increasing at an estimated .33 IQ points per year in the general population. The IQ increase is greater for tests like the Raven Progressive Matrices, which is primarily a measure of visuospatial ability, than for tests such as the Wechsler and Stanford–Binet, which measure not only visuospatial ability but also vocabulary, general information, arithmetic, and other acquired knowledge. The fact that the effect is larger on measures of fluid ability than on crystallized ability and appears to be due to environmental rather than genetic factors indicates that improvements in formal schooling are not the only responsible factor (J. R. Flynn, 1998). Rather, the Flynn effect has been attributed to a combination of better schooling, greater educational attainment of parents, greater parental attention to children, improved SES, better nutrition, fewer childhood diseases, and a more technologically complex society. Greenfield (1998) credited much of the increase to the special visual effects provided by television, computers, video games, and other technological devices. Regarding other possible explanations for this phenomenon, it has been noted that severe malnutrition and deficiencies in iodine, iron, and other nutrients associated with lower IQS as well as shorter stature have declined markedly during this century. Some psychologists (e.g., Lynn, 1998; Sigman & Whaley, 1998) have concluded that there is compelling evidence linking rises in intelli-

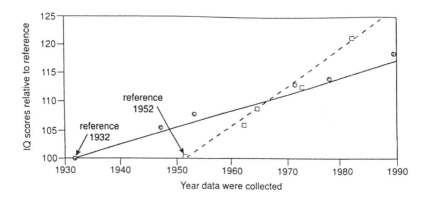

FIG. 6.4.   Increases in intelligence test scores since 1932. The solid line is a plot of the adjusted mean scores of Americans on the Wechsler and Stanford–Binet tests. The dashed line is a plot of the mean scores of 18-year-old Dutchmen on the Raven Progressive Matrices (Neisser, 1998).

gence to improved nutrition, but others (e.g., Martorell, 1998) maintain that it is unlikely that better nutrition is responsible for the Flynn effect.

GENDER AND ETHNICITY

There are no more controversial topics in the study of individual and group differences, and probably in all of psychology, than the nature and extent of differences in the cognitive abilities of the sexes and the various racial and ethnic groups. Research findings and debates in these areas strike at the heart of the democratic ideals of equality by birth and opportunity. During the past half-century, increasing efforts have been made by government and other social institutions to redress the wrongs inflicted on minority groups and women in our society and indeed throughout the world. These efforts in education, employment, and other areas where discrimination existed and there was no real equality of opportunity have been based on the principle of justice as well as the belief that, given a chance to learn and work in a level playing field, all people will pursue their hopes and dreams to the best of their abilities. Consequently, the idea that individual achievement and other indicators of socioeconomic success are limited by restriction of opportunity *and* unchangeable mental abilities affects both the motivation and identity of those who have been told that, at long last, they have a chance to prosper.

Research on intelligence, which was one of the first psychological topics to be studied, has been pursued for over 100 years. Unfortunately, particularly during the early years of the 20th century, the findings of such research were used to justify certain race-centered social engineering proposals. Politicians and other social leaders who were concerned with such issues as restricted immigration, sterilization of the unfit, educational classification and segregation, and employee selection or rejection have sometimes used intelligence test results to justify their proposals and practices. In light of this history lesson, it is not surprising that IQ testing has become a negative term to many individuals.

Because of its profound social implications, some social scientists believe that a moratorium should be placed on research concerned with racial differences in intelligence and other cognitive abilities. It is alleged that no matter how well intentioned they may be, researchers do more harm than good when their activities and findings threaten the fundamental principles and beliefs on which democratic society is founded. With reference to the activities of Nazi scientists during the 1930s and 1940s, it is argued that when science leads to the erosion and abandonment of the values on which a culture is based, it is time to call a halt to this kind of science. With respect to research on gender and race differences in cognitive abilities, however, that time has certainly not yet arrived. As long as critical, dissenting voices are permitted to publicly react to such research—to question not only the accuracy of its findings but also how they are interpreted and the extent to which they contribute to the broader aims of society—then those who wish to do so should be permitted to continue with their efforts if those efforts are pursued with social sensitivity and an awareness of human values and beliefs. Progress in society as well as science is rarely achieved in an atmosphere in which everyone agrees with everyone else, but rather one in which there is lively, informed debate and a willingness to play by socially accepted rules.

Gender Differences

Analyses of sex differences in total scores on tests of general intelligence have, with some exceptions (e.g., Dai, Ryan, Paolo, & Harrington; 1991; Lynn, 1994), indicated that the mean scores of males and females are not significantly different. Be that as it may, Reilly and Mulhern (1995) found that, on the average, undergraduate males' self-estimates of IQ were higher than those of females and higher than their actual IQs. Not only were females' self-estimated IQs lower than those of males, but they were also lower than their measured IQs. The finding that males tend to rate their own IQs higher than females rate their own IQs was confirmed in a study by Furnham and Rawles (1995). These researchers also found that both males and females rated their fathers' IQs as higher than their mothers' IQs and their grandfathers' IQs as higher than their grandmothers' IQs. As seen in the results of a study by Hamid and Loh (1995), belief in the intellectual superiority of males is not restricted to Western culture. These researchers found that a sample of Chinese women estimated their own IQs as lower than a sample of Chinese men estimated their own IQs. In addition, both sexes estimated their fathers' IQs as higher than their mothers' IQs. These findings may indicate that the socially encouraged submissive, inferior roles for women and the dominant, superior roles for males are internalized and generalizable across cultures.

Intelligence tests are constructed so that sex differences in overall scores are small or nonexistent, but reviews of sex differences in specific cognitive abilities (e.g., Brody, 1992; Halpern, 1994, 1997) have concluded that males and females differ in their performance on tests of certain specific abilities. Halpern (1997) listed two dozen tests on which women have obtained higher average scores than men and a dozen tests on which men have obtained higher average scores than women. In general, Halpern concluded that women do better on tasks requiring rapid access to and use of phonological, semantic, and other information in long-term memory; literature and foreign languages; production and comprehension of complex prose; tasks requiring fine motor dexterity; perceptual speed; and decoding nonverbal communications. Women also make higher grades in school, have better speech articulation, and have lower perceptual thresholds (for touch, taste, odor, etc.) than men. In contrast, men perform better than women on tasks requiring transformations in visual working memory; tasks involving moving objects; motor tasks involving aiming; tests of knowledge in general and knowledge of geography, mathematics, and science in particular; and tasks demanding fluid reasoning.

Three areas that have occasioned the greatest amount of research on sex differences are verbal, quantitative, and visuospatial abilities. The largest samples in which the first two abilities have been measured consist of the thousands of high school students who take the SAT every year. The mean scores given in Table 6.1 are typical of recent results on the SAT–Verbal and SAT–Mathematical tests. In 1998, the mean SAT–Mathematical score of males was 35 points higher than that of females, and the mean SAT–Verbal score of males was 7 points higher than that of females. The causes of these sex differences are not clear, but sex differences in mathematical ability and spatial reasoning appear to have declined somewhat in recent years (Linn & Hyde, 1989; Shea, 1994; see also Hedges & Nowell, 1995). Although sex differences in mean scores on tests of quantitative abilities are not pronounced until the high school years (Hyde, Fennema, & Lamon, 1990), even at the junior high level the number of mathematically talented boys far exceeds the number of girls in that category (Stanley, 1990).

TABLE 6.1

Mean SAT and ACT Scores in 1998 by Ethnic Group and Gender

Group	SAT–Verbal	SAT–Math	ACT
Composite			
Males	509	531	21.2
Females	502	496	20.9
Both sexes	505	512	21
American Indian or Alaskan Native	480	483	19
Asian, Asian American, or Pacific Islander	498	562	21.8
Black or African American	434	426	17.1
Mexican or Mexican American/ Chicano	453	460	18.5
Puerto Rican	452	447	
Other Hispanic origin	461	466	19.6
White	526	528	21.7
Other ethnic groups/ Multiracial	511	514	21.3

Source. Data provided by Educational Testing Service and American College Testing Program.

In addition to sex differences in mean scores on certain tests, the variance of scores on tests of mathematical, spatial, and certain verbal abilities, and even in overall scores on intelligence tests, have been reported as greater for males than for females (Cahan & Ganor, 1993; Feingold, 1992c, 1994; Hedges & Nowell, 1995). Various linguistic problems (stuttering, dyslexia, etc.) and other learning disorders are more common in males than in females, but a larger percentage of males are also found at the higher end of the mental ability continuum (Hedges & Nowell, 1995).

With respect to spatial ability, males score significantly higher than females on mental rotation, space perception, and spatiotemporal tasks, all of which involve manipulations in short-term memory (Halpern, 1994; Law, Pellegrino, & Hunt, 1993). The largest differences favoring females are found on measures of vocabulary and word fluency (ability to generate words).

A number of biological and psychosocial hypotheses have been proposed as explanations for sex differences in cognitive abilities. One set of neuropsychological theories is based on the sexual dimorphism of structures such as the hypothalamus, the amygdala, and the cerebral cortex. For example, the average female brain is smaller than that of the average male, but the language areas in the brains of females are proportionally larger than those of males (Harasty, Double, Halliday, Kril, & McRitchie, 1997). In addition, the density of neurons per volume within the language area of the left temporal lobe is higher in females than in males (Witelson, Glezer, & Kigar, 1995). Another interesting hypothesis that has some empirical support is that female brains are more bilaterally organized than male brains (i.e., that cognitive functions in females are less specific to a particular cerebral hemisphere). For example, the corpus callosum, a band of nerve fibers connecting the two cerebral hemispheres, is thicker and proportionally larger relative to total brain size in females than in males.[2] The fact that this difference permits better conductivity between the hemispheres of females than of males is cited in support of the hypothesis of greater bilateral organization in female than in male brains (Innocenti, 1994; Jancke & Steinmetz, 1994; Johnson, Pinkston, Bigler, & Blatter, 1996). The idea that different brain areas are involved in the functioning of male and female brains while performing specific cognitive tasks is also supported by positron emission tomography (PET) scan data (Shaywitz, Shaywitz, Pugh, & Constable, 1995).

With regard to task specificity and cerebral localization of function, males tend to perform better on tasks that depend on the orbital prefrontal area of the frontal cortex, whereas females perform better on tasks that depend on the inferior temporal cortex (Overman, Bachevalier, Schuhmann, & Ryan, 1996). The results of a number of studies of sex differences in performance on specific tasks also point to the temporal variability of sex hormones in males and females. Women tend to perform better on tests of mo-

---

[2]Also of interest is the fact that the *corpus callosum* is approximately 11% thicker in left-handed than in right-handed people, facilitating cross-hemisphere transfer of information and greater bilateral representation of cognitive and other psychological functions in left-handers (Driesen & Raz, 1995; Habib et al., 1991).

tor coordination and verbal facility but poorer on tests of spatial reasoning during times of the month when estrogen levels in their blood are highest (Hampson, 1990; Kimura & Hampson, 1994). The performance of males on spatial skills tests also fluctuates with their testosterone levels, which are higher early in the morning than later in the day and higher in autumn than in spring (Kimura & Hampson, 1994; Moffat & Hampson, 1996). Furthermore, giving testosterone to older men to enhance their sexual functioning improves their performance on visuospatial tests (Janowsky, Oviatt, & Orwoll, 1994). Viewed as a whole, these findings suggest that cognitive performance is significantly associated with the level of sex hormones in the blood.

Despite the fact that some of the smallest brains on record have been those of recognized geniuses (e.g., Walt Whitman and Anatole France) and some of the largest brains have been those of severely retarded persons, overall research findings point to a modest positive correlation between brain size and intelligence (see Jensen & Sinha, 1991; Willerman, Schultz, Rutledge, & Bigler, 1991). In the Willerman et al. (1991) investigation, the brains of 20 male and 20 female college students, half with IQs of 103 or below and half with IQs of 130 or above, were measured by magnetic resonance imaging. The results showed that higher IQ students had significantly larger brains than lower IQ students, leading to an estimated correlation between IQ and brain-to-body size ratio of approximately .35. In light of these findings, it may seem contradictory that the large difference in brain size between males and females is not reflected in the mean IQ difference between the sexes. As an explanation, Jensen and Johnson (1994) suggest that female brains may have a greater density of neurons or other structural, organizational, or hormonal differences that permit more efficient neural processing than male brains. Jensen and Johnson also maintained that the correlation between brain size and IQ is of approximately the same magnitude in males and females, but this was not found to be the case in a study conducted by Willerman et al. (1991). The correlation between brain size and WAIS–R IQs, after controlling for differences in body size, was .65 in men, .35 in women, and .51 for both sexes combined. Willerman and his coworkers also found that a larger left than right cerebral hemisphere was associated with higher nonverbal ability in males but with higher verbal ability in females (Willerman, Schultz, Rutledge, & Bigler, 1992).

Psychosocial explanations of sex differences in cognitive abilities have focused on differential sociocultural reinforcement of sex-typed behaviors and the stereotyping of male and female roles. Girls are expected to be more accomplished in linguistic and social skills, whereas boys are expected to be better at mathematical, mechanical, and problem-solving tasks. Consequently, girls often perceive themselves as inferior in these areas and tend to avoid courses and careers involving them. Even if sex differences in these abilities are biologically-determined, appropriate training, combined with a nondiscriminatory educational, employment, and social system, can undoubtedly reduce the magnitude of those differences.

Nationality and Culture

Influenced by Francis Galton's interest in individual and group differences in intelligence and the eugenics movement of improving humanity through selective breeding, early mental testers such as Henry Goddard, Lewis Terman, and Robert Yerkes showed a concern with racial and nationality differences in intelligence test scores and with methods of controlling what they saw as the intellectual deterioration of the American population. Analyses of scores on the Army Alpha and Beta tests administered to American soldiers during World War I (Yerkes, 1921) and subsequent studies of immigrants (Brigham, 1923; Hirsch, 1926) appeared to support the belief that immigrants from Southern and Eastern Europe had lower average intelligence than those from Northern and Western Europe. These findings were later repudiated (Brigham, 1930), and subsequent studies demonstrated that scores on American intelligence tests varied with the similarity between the examinees' native culture and the dominant American culture. Public and professional interest in genetics and anthropology, in particular, combined with prejudice triggered by ethnocentrism and the perceived economic and social threat of foreigners, provided a supportive climate for continuing research on ethnic and cultural differences in intelligence.

One factor that has presumably contributed to the lower intelligence test scores of people of different nationalities, cultures, and SES is the speededness of many of these tests. People in preliterate societies, for example, may not share the Western cultural emphasis on speed, on attaining a solution in the smallest number of steps, on the superiority of mental to physical manipulations, and that originality or creativity is superior to imitation or conformity (Gill & Keats, 1980). Unlike the time- and self-centeredness of contemporary Western culture, people in more traditional societies are more likely to associate intelligence with gradualness and patience and to stress the importance of cooperation, sociability, and a sense of honor (Wober, 1974). From a Confucian perspective, intelligence consists of benevolence and doing what is right; the Taoist tradition emphasizes humility, freedom from conventional standards of judgment, and knowledge of oneself and external conditions (Yang & Sternberg, 1997). Furthermore, intelligence test materials may be perceived differently by children in different societies. For example, Ortar (1963) found that, when shown a picture of a head having no mouth, Oriental immigrant children to Israel were more likely than native Israeli children to say that the body was missing. Among people in the New Guinea highlands, a block design test was found to be useless because the examinees tried to use both the tops and sides of the blocks when instructed to copy a two-dimensional model (Ord, 1971).

Race and Ethnicity

Much of the research on racial/ethnic groups has centered on Black–White differences, but other ethnic groups (e.g., Hispanics, Asians, and Native Americans, in particular) have also been studied. A general result of analyses of the mean intelligence test scores of various racial/ethnic groups in the United States is that Asian Americans usually score at least as high as White Americans, but that the mean scores of African Americans, Hispanic Americans, and Native Americans are lower than those of Whites. Figure 6.5 is a somewhat idealized representation of the results of a number of early investigations comparing the distributions of intelligence test scores of three ethnic groups. As illustrated by this figure, all three distributions have the same normal shape and variance, but the mean for Whites is 15 points higher than the mean of Blacks and 3 points lower than the mean of East Asians (Flynn, 1991). However, there is a substantial amount of overlap among the three distributions, and the differences in scores among individuals in each group are significantly larger than the mean differences between groups.

As witnessed by statistics from the national standardization of the Wechsler and Stanford–Binet tests (Reynolds, Chastain, Kaufman, & McLean, 1987; Thorndike, Hagen, & Sattler, 1986), a gap of one standard deviation in the mean IQs of Blacks and Whites has persisted. Nevertheless, the gap in the mean scores of Whites and Blacks on tests of intelligence and academic

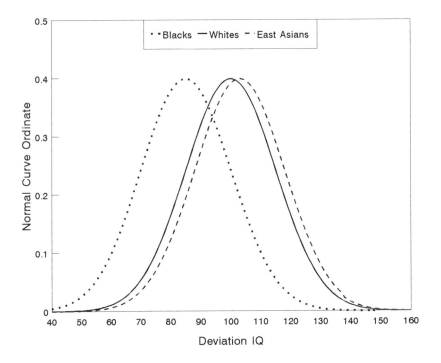

FIG. 6.5.   Traditional comparison of IQ distributions for Whites and Blacks.

achievement narrowed by almost half from 1970 to 1990. Explanations for the reduction in the Black–White gap point to increased spending on education and increased parental education, particularly among minorities, in recent years (Williams & Ceci, 1997).

Higher mean scores for Whites than for Blacks have also been found on nationally administered tests such as the SAT and the ACT (see Table 6.1). The mean SAT–Verbal and SAT–Mathematical scores for other ethnic groups shown in this table are also in approximately the same order as those found in comparisons of intelligence test scores for the various groups. Note that on the SAT–Verbal, the mean of Whites is at the top, followed by Asian Americans, Native Americans, Hispanic Americans, and Blacks. On SAT–Mathematical, the mean is highest for Asian Americans, followed by Whites, Native Americans, Hispanic Americans, and Blacks.

In addition to ethnic differences in overall mean scores on intelligence tests, analyses of subtest scores indicate that the various ethnic groups have different cognitive strengths and weaknesses. Native Americans and Hispanics score higher in visual reasoning than in verbal reasoning (Suzuki & Gutkin, 1993; R. L. Taylor & Richards, 1991), Asian Americans score higher on visual reasoning and numerical reasoning than on verbal subtests (Lynn & Hampson, 1986), and Blacks are better in verbal than in visual reasoning (Taylor & Richards, 1991). Hispanic Americans also tend to score higher on performance tests than on verbal tests of intelligence. Explanations for the differential ability patterns of ethnic groups are speculative and probably more environmental–cultural than genetic in origin. For example, the high visuospatial abilities evinced by many Inuits and other Arctic peoples are presumably the result of experience, although evolutionary (survival of the fittest) interpretations cannot be discounted.[3]

Within-group differences in abilities may be intriguing, but greater professional and political interest has been shown in racial differences in cognitive abilities and the extent to which they are determined by genetics and experience. Probably few psychologists fail to recognize the important role of heredity in determining cognitive abilities. Estimates of the proportion of variance in intelligence test scores that can be attributed to heredity range from 50% to 90%. Still many psychologists have stressed what they consider the more important question of how education and other experiences can be directed toward the optimization of genetic potential.

Although not denying the significance of environment, certain psychologists (Jensen, 1985; Lynn, 1987; Rushton & Osborne, 1995) have focused on genetically based differences in brain functioning and have stressed the limited effectiveness of environmental intervention. One neurophysiological variable of interest to these psychologists is response speed. E. M. Miller (1994) concluded that people with greater intelligence have faster and less variable response times than average, that response time becomes longer with aging, and that it increases more rapidly with increased task complexity

---

[3]*Smilla's Sense of Snow*, a novel by Peter Høag (1995) that was made into a motion picture, capitalized on the uncanny ability displayed by many Arctic men and women in orienting and navigating in what appears to an outsider as a barren, homogeneous white landscape.

in older than in younger adults. Furthermore, he maintained that people with large brains (relative to their body sizes) are more intelligent, that more intelligent brains use less energy, and that individual and group differences in intelligence may reflect differences in myelination of neural axons.

Intelligence Test Bias

Reminiscent of killing the messenger who brings bad news, over the years intelligence tests have repeatedly been attacked as biased against minority groups. Although it is possible to construct an intelligence test on which Blacks do not score lower than Whites, for example, by including many items to measure memory ability and few items to measure spatial ability, such tests would probably be of no more practical value than the so-called *culture-free* tests of yesteryear. In terms of the traditional definition of *test bias*, intelligence tests are not biased against either group in that they are equally predictive of the educational and occupational performances of Blacks and Whites (e.g., Hunter, Schmidt, & Hunter, 1979).

An environmental explanation of racial differences in intelligence test scores is perhaps more consistent with democratic ideals, and such an explanation is certainly plausible. School integration, Head Start, and many other educational programs have been based on the assumption that racial differences in cognitive abilities are the result of discrimination and can be reduced by educational intervention, affirmative action, and racial integration. One research approach designed to determine the effects of environmental intervention on intelligence consists of comparing adopted children with natural children in families. For example, the results of a study by Scarr and Weinberg (1976) showed that the IQs of Black children adopted into White families were higher than those of their natural parents. A subsequent study conducted by Scarr, Weinberg, and Waldman (1993) on Black children who were adopted by White families also found substantial gains in the IQs of these children. However, the results of other studies of adopted children (e.g., Scarr & Weinberg, 1978) indicate that such IQ increases diminish significantly as children become adolescents and young adults.

Despite the arguments of Herrnstein and Murray (1994) concerning racial differences in intelligence test scores, the reasons for these differences remain unclear. Actually, from 1973 to 1988, Blacks' scores on nationally administered tests of cognitive ability and educational achievement improved but Whites' mean score remained unchanged. It now appears, however, that the Black–White gap has stabilized and is no longer decreasing (National Center for Educational Statistics, 1996). Whatever the future may hold, the fact that the gap between the mean scores of Blacks and Whites became smaller rather than larger during the 1970s and 1980s is inconsistent with Herrnstein and Murray's (1994) *dysgenic hypothesis* that low-IQ parents are outbreeding high-IQ parents and thus lowering the overall intelligence of the population.

HOME, SCHOOL, AND WORK

Cognitive abilities are complex products of heredity and environment—the results of genetics combined with prenatal and postnatal events. These events consist of biological, psychoeducational, and sociocultural factors acting in concert to shape the physiological and behavioral functioning of individuals. Not only do heredity and environment act jointly in influencing behavior, but the range of environmental stimuli to which a person is sensitive is limited by his or her genetic endowment. Still even if it is not possible to make a silk purse out of a sow's ear, some kind of serviceable container can usually be fashioned.

Recognizing that heredity places limits on what the individual is capable of doing and achieving, it is a fact that most people never reach the upper limit of their capabilities. To a large extent, this is the fault of the environmental influences to which a person is exposed after, and perhaps even before, birth. Home and family are where it starts for most people, but school, work, and other social and nonsocial contexts are also important. The effects of these human and nonhuman environments on an individual's cognitive abilities are interactive and reciprocal. For example, the influences of home and school are stronger when they are mutually supportive—for better or worse. Furthermore, not only does environment influence cognitive abilities, but those abilities also help to shape and select the individual's environment. To some extent, people perceive, create, and choose environments or features of environments that are congruent with their own needs and abilities.

Because of the complexity of environments and their effects on cognitive abilities, it may seem pointless and unproductive to isolate single, specific environmental factors for study. However, attempting to investigate the effects of multivariate environments on multidimensional abilities poses innumerable problems of control and yields results that may defy clear interpretation. As a kind of compromise, investigations of environmental influences on behavior are usually limited to a few selected variables. This is the strategy employed in most of the following studies of the relationships of home, school, and work on cognitive abilities. Because researchers can rarely move people around like chess pieces, most of these studies are correlational in nature. The results indicate that measures of intelligence are related to a host of variables: structure and dynamics of home life, schooling, job performance, criminal behavior, and a wide range of achievements (see Sternberg, 1994a).

Homes and Families

Most children in our society grow up in families, although a sizable percentage of these are one-parent families and/or families with surrogate parents. A family is a kind of miniature society, in which the rules and expectations of the larger sociocultural groups are communicated to children. By means of informal instruction and example, and by showing approval or disapproval of the child's efforts and performances, parents and other family members exert a powerful influence on the socialization of children. In part because of their primacy, these *first lessons* are important ones, but they are usually modified and extended by the influence of the peer group, school, church, and other encounters and social institutions.

The influence of families in shaping the abilities and personalities of children varies with family structure and dynamics. An important structural variable is the number of people in the family—a variable that affects the amount of individual attention given to each child. The tendency for larger families to consist of intellectually duller individuals has been documented for over a century in the United States and other countries (e.g., Lancer & Rim, 1984; Steelman & Doby, 1983; M. E. Wagner, Schubert, & Schubert, 1985). This inverse relationship between family size and intelligence is undoubtedly multicausal and multidirectional. Not only is less attention usually given to the cognitive development of children in larger families, but adults of lower intelligence tend to have larger numbers of children. In addition, the birth order and spacing of children within families is related to the intellectual abilities and achievements of the former. When children are born closely together, the family resources allocated to each child—not only parental attention and time but also educational materials and opportunities—are reduced (Lancer & Rim, 1984; Zajonc, 1976). A related factor is birth order, in that first-born children tend to score higher on tests of intelligence than later borns (Altus, 1966; Lewis & Jaskir, 1983; MacPhee, Ramey, & Yeates, 1984). First-borns also talk earlier and more clearly, learn to read earlier, and are better at problem-solving and perceptual tasks than later borns. In both smaller families and with first-borns, parents have more time to interact with children and provide greater encouragement and assistance to them in mastering various developmental tasks (Kilbride, Johnson, & Streissguth, 1977). Consistent with the parental emphasis on language development in the child is the finding that the relationship among family size, birth order, and intellectual abilities is more pronounced on verbal than on nonverbal measures (Lancer & Rim, 1984).

Family size and birth order are, of course, not independent in their effects on cognitive abilities. They are related to and interact with other variables such as parents' education, SES, ethnicity, and culture. One of the most consistent findings of research on individual differences is that SES, defined as a composite of parental income, education, and occupation, is positively correlated with IQ. SES also interacts with race in the relationships of these two demographic variables to intelligence test scores. This is demonstrated by the finding that the relationship of SES to IQ scores is stronger for Whites than for Blacks and Mexican Americans ("Mainstream Science," 1994). Furthermore, adjustments for socioeconomic differences between White and Black children significantly reduce IQ differences between the two groups (Brooks-Gunn, Klebanov, & Duncan, 1996).

In addition to their associations with ethnic and cultural differences, SES and education were found in previous generations to be associated with urban/rural place of residence. Because of improved transportation and communication facilities, the IQ superiority of urban over rural children dropped from an average of six IQ points a generation ago to around two points (Reynolds, Chastain, Kaufman, & McLean, 1987). Television, better schools, farming technology, and other sources of information and stimulation have provided today's rural children with opportunities for cognitive growth that their parents and grandparents did not have. Consequently, the vocabularies, level of knowledge, and general cognitive abilities of children living on farms today are on a par with those of city dwellers.

Family size, birth order, SES, ethnicity and culture, and, through them, such influential biological variables as nutrition, sanitation, and health care are all related to the intelligence of children. However, the dynamics of the home environment go beyond these variables. Home environment, including parenting style, the provision of a supportive home environment, and other measures of the within-home treatment of children, are even more important than SES and biomedical risk factors as predictors of the intelligence test scores of young children (Hunt, 1961; Molfese, DiLalla, & Bunce, 1997; Skodak & Skeels, 1949). Be that as it may, in recent years the extent to which moderate differences between the family environments of children result in differences in their performance on intelligence tests has been questioned. The results of various studies indicate that, although the effects of sharing the same home and parents are significant in early childhood, by late adolescence the effects of those experiences on intelligence test scores have become quite small (Baumrind, 1993; J. F. Jackson, 1993; Scarr, 1992, 1993). In other words, it can be argued that differences in the lifestyles of families may, over the long term, have little influence on the abilities measured by intelligence tests.

School and Education

Education is even more highly related than home environment and SES to the performance of children on intelligence tests. Traditionally, education has been emphasized as the way in which those who are not born to wealth and status can achieve those things. In the United States, younger adults tend to have had more formal education than older adults, males more than females, Whites more than Blacks, Non-Hispanics more than Hispanics, individuals residing in the West and Northeast more than those residing in the Midwest and South, and those living in metropolitan areas more than those living in nonmetropolitan areas (Day & Curry, 1995). The intelligence test scores of children are related to both their own education and that of their parents (Grissmer, Kirby, Berends, & Williamson, 1994; Luster & McAdoo, 1994). This tends to be true not only for Whites, but also for Blacks, Asian Americans, and other cultural groups.

Academic achievement depends on persistence, interest in school work, study skills, teaching practices, and family or cultural values regarding educational achievement and scholarship (see Flynn, 1991). However, the variable that usually has the highest correlation with intelligence test scores is school grades (Neisser et al., 1996). The intelligence–grade correlation tends to be higher with the more heterogeneous populations of students in elementary and junior high school, but even at the high school and college levels measures of intelligence are significant predictors of educational achievement. That the positive relationship between intelligence and educational achievement is not due primarily to differences in social class background is demonstrated by the finding that the relationship between these two variables remains significant even when SES and parental education are statistically controlled (Thomas, Alexander, & Eckland, 1979)

As with other environmental variables related to intelligence, there is a bidirectionality or reciprocality in the relationship between intelligence and schooling. To begin with, children with higher IQs are more likely to be rewarded for their efforts with high grades and promotions and to attend college than children with lower IQs. For example, Kaufman (1990) reported that the mean IQ of college graduates was 33 points higher than that of individuals with 7 years or less of formal schooling. Not only are children with higher intelligence more likely to perform better in school and attend longer, but formal education also improves performance on intelligence tests (Ceci & Williams, 1997).

As noted previously in this chapter, research has shown that the IQs of children from cognitively poor backgrounds can be increased by adoption into cognitively rich homes (e.g., Scarr, Weinberg, & Waldman, 1993). In addition, educational programs such as Headstart and television programs such as the Electric Company have been associated with gains in IQ scores (Zigler & Berman, 1983). Unfortunately, the initial boost given to IQ by both adoption and Headstart typically fades with time (Haskins, 1989; Scarr & Weinberg, 1978). The Abecedarian Project (Ramey & Campbell, 1991) found gains of four to five IQ points as a result of intensive educational treatment, but these results, like those of other educational intervention projects, were not considered to be long term (Spitz, 1986). In addition to difficulties in demonstrating lasting effects of educational intervention on mean IQ scores, such interventions have failed to produce any change in the variance of the scores (Detterman & Thompson, 1997).

Cognitive Ability and Occupation

Intellectual (cognitive) ability and educational level are associated with each other, and both variables are related to occupational status and income (see Fig. 6.6). Scores on intelligence tests are reasonably good predictors of performance in a variety of occupations (Morris & Levinson, 1995). This is illustrated by Harrell and Harrell's (1945) classic study of the mean scores on the Army General Classification Test (AGCT) obtained by thousands of World War II military recruits who later entered various civilian occupations. Comparisons of the mean AGCT scores of individuals in over 70 occupations revealed that accountants, lawyers, and engineers were at the top; teamsters, miners, and farmers were at the bottom; and other occupational groups were arranged in between in order of decreasing mean AGCT score. There was, however, a wide range of scores within each occupational group. For example, some truck drivers had higher scores than some teachers. Furthermore, individuals with the same AGCT scores differed markedly in occupation and income.

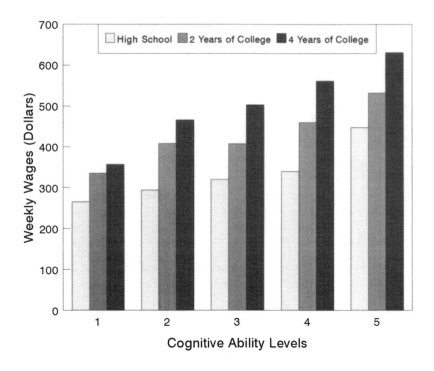

FIG. 6.6.   Average weekly wages in 1992 by levels of schooling and cognitive ability (Ceci & Williams, 1997, p. 1057).

Correlations between scores on intelligence tests and measures of job performance (supervisor ratings, work samples, earnings, etc.) typically range between .30 and .50 (Neisser et al., 1996; R. K. Wagner, 1997). Intelligence and education are, of course, only two of many variables related to occupational status and income. For example, the importance of gender differences is seen in the fact that women comprise 55% of the U.S. population 18 years and older and 46% of management, but only a small percentage are on corporate boards of directors, in the U.S. senate, or in state governors' chairs (Morrison & Von Glinow, 1990). With respect to the occupational status of minorities, Blacks and Hispanic Americans tend to have lower occupational status and lower incomes than Whites. For Asian Americans, the situation is different. In comparison with Whites, significantly larger percentages of the Chinese- and Japanese-American populations are employed in managerial, professional, or technical occupations (U.S. Bureau of the Census, 1997b).

Rather than intelligence being a direct cause of occupational level, it is likely that the relationship between the two variables is due to the fact that they are both related to social class background and education. Children of middle- and upper class backgrounds are more likely to have been prepared to perform well on intelligence tests and in school, thereby paving the way for them to enter higher status occupations. High scores on measures of intelligence or scholastic aptitude are required for admission to good colleges and universities, and graduation from such institutions and acceptable performance on other (professional) examinations are required for entry into more prestigious occupations. However, Hunter and Schmidt (1996) argued that the major reason that intelligence test scores predict job performance so well is because individuals of higher intelligence learn relevant job knowledge more quickly and learn more of it. Consequently, Hunter and Schmidt maintained that the current social policy of discouraging the use of tests of mental ability in hiring is counterproductive.

Whatever the pattern of causation among intelligence, education, SES, and occupation may be, it is not simple and direct. All four of these variables are positively related, but the effects of one variable on another also depend on the remaining variables. For example, Thomas, Alexander, and Eckland (1979) found that the positive correlation between IQ and educational attainment remained significant even when SES was statistically controlled. However, when IQ was statistically controlled, the correlation between SES and educational attainment was slightly negative. The authors concluded that the correlation between IQ and school marks is not due primarily to differences in socioeconomic background, but rather to the fact that both SES and educational level are affected by intellectual ability. Therefore, it can be argued that the higher grades made by upper and middle-class students are the results of their higher cognitive abilities.

SUMMARY

The largest amount of research in differential psychology has been conducted on cognitive abilities and on general cognitive ability (intelligence) in particular. Studies of group differences in intelligence have focused on demographic variables such as chronological age, gender, nationality and culture, race/ethnicity, home and family environment, education, and occupation. Numerous investigations have also been conducted on biological correlates and causes of individual differences in abilities, including heredity, drugs, and brain structures and dynamics. Research and reflection with respect to the nature of intelligence, its neuropsychological foundations, and the relative roles of heredity and environment in shaping it have so far failed to provide a comprehensive picture of what intelligence consists of, where it comes from, and how it works. Be that as it may, many older conceptual oversimplifications and biases pertaining to intelligence have been disposed of, and progress in science and technology promises to provide a much better understanding of this important construct in the future.

Scores on intelligence tests administered during infancy and early childhood are not highly correlated with scores on intelligence tests administered at school age and are not good predictors of academic achievement.

However, the reliability of the intelligence tests scores of school-age children is quite respectable.

The positive correlations among measures of cognitive abilities support the concept of a general cognitive factor (g), which typically shows some decline after early adulthood. However, the magnitude of the age-related decline in intelligence varies with the research methodology employed and the individuals who are examined. Intellectually brighter individuals and those who continue throughout life to exercise their cognitive abilities show less decline than other people. Furthermore, the pattern of age-related changes is not the same for all abilities. The results of both cross-sectional and longitudinal studies indicate that most cognitive abilities decline somewhat after middle age and the rate of decline is greater for fluid than for crystallized abilities. Results from the Seattle Longitudinal Studies indicate that spatial orientation and inductive reasoning begin declining sooner than word fluency, verbal reasoning, and numerical ability.

As suggested by annual changes in SAT scores, the Lake Wobegon effect, and the Flynn effect, changes in scores on tests of intelligence, scholastic ability, and scholastic achievement can be attributed to a combination of environmental and methodological factors.

The difference between the mean scores of males and females on general intelligence tests is inconsequential, but the variance of IQ scores is usually greater for males than females. Thus, the numbers of intellectually very bright and very dull males appear to be larger than the corresponding numbers of females. In addition, the sexes differ in various specific abilities. In general, women attain higher scores than men on measures of long-term memory, verbal ability, fine motor dexterity, and perceptual speed. In contrast, men perform better than women on tests requiring visual memory, moving objects, aiming, and a knowledge of geography, mathematics, and science. A great deal of research has been conducted on differences between the scores of males and females on tests of spatial abilities: Males typically perform better than females on these tests.

Neuropsychological explanations of sex differences in cognitive abilities have focused on the dimorphic nature of brain structures such as the corpus callosum and the hypothesis that female brains are more bilaterally organized than male brains. A substantial amount of research has also been conducted on the differential effects of male and female hormones on cognitive abilities. Psychosocial explanations of sex differences emphasize the role of differential reinforcement for gender-appropriate behavior, sex-role modeling, and sexual stereotyping.

On the average, Blacks, Hispanic Americans, and Native Americans score lower than Whites on tests of general intelligence, but Asian Americans typically score at least as high as Whites on these tests. Differences between ethnic groups in the pattern of specific abilities have also been noted. Although it has been argued, and research appears to support the argument, that genetic factors play a significant role in determining Black–White IQ differences in intelligence, it appears that the gap narrowed during the 1970s and 1980s.

SES, parental education, parenting style, family size, birth order, occupational status, and certain other environmental factors are interrelated and interactive in their effects on children's intelligence. Many of these variables are also reciprocal in their effects. For example, intelligence affects education and education affects intelligence. Intelligence and educational level are also positively related to occupational status and income. Despite its relationship to other predictors of life success, intelligence makes an independent contribution to the prediction of such criteria. In fact, measures of intelligence are the most versatile or general of all predictors of performance in academic and occupational contexts.

SUGGESTED READINGS

Carroll, J. B. (1997). Psychometrics, intelligence, and public perception. *Intelligence, 24*(10), 25–52.

Daniel, M. H. (1997). Intelligence testing: Status and trends. *American Psychologist, 52,* 1038–1045.

Gustafsson, J. E., & Undheim, J. O. (1996). Individual differences in cognitive functions. In D. C. Berliner & R. C. Calfee (Eds.), *Handbook of educational psychology* (pp. 186–242). London: Prentice-Hall International.

Halpern, D. F. (1997). Sex differences in intelligence: Implications for education. *American Psychologist, 52,* 1091–1101.

Hedges, L. V., & Nowell, A. (1995). Sex differences in mental test scores, variability, and numbers of high-scoring individuals. *Science, 269*(5220), 41–45.

Schaie, K. W. (1996). Intellectual development in adulthood. In J. E. Birren, K. W. Schaie, R. P. Abeles, M. Gatz, & T. A. Salthouse (Eds.), *Handbook of the psychology of aging* (4th ed., pp. 266–285). San Diego: Academic Press.

Sternberg, R. J., & Kaufman, J. C. (1998). Human abilities. *Annual Review of Psychology, 49,* 479–502.

Suzuki, L. A., & Valencia, R. R. (1997). Race-ethnicity and measured intelligence: Educational implications. *American Psychologist, 52,* 1103–1114.

Wagner, R. K. (1997). Intelligence, training, and employment. *American Psychologist, 52,* 1059–1069.

Williams, W. M., & Ceci, S. J. (1997). Are Americans becoming more or less alike? Trends in race, class, and ability differences in intelligence. *American Psychologist, 52,* 1226–1235.

Exceptional and Special Cognitive Abilities

A major use of intelligence tests and other measures of cognitive abilities in both applied and research contexts has been the diagnosis and classification of individuals according to their functioning abilities. When administered by well-trained, perceptive psychometrists, these tests continue to serve the traditional goals of identifying mentally retarded, gifted, and learning disabled (LD) persons. In addition, tests of intelligence and special abilities are widely used in educational, employment, military, and other organizations or institutions for selecting people who are capable of performing certain specified tasks. The broader bandwidths (Cronbach, 1970) of general intelligence tests make them effective predictors of a wide range of criteria. However, the narrower bandwidths of measures of special abilities often give them greater fidelity as predictors of more delimited criterion measures. Be that as it may, Vernon (1960) maintained that general intelligence is more important than special abilities in determining academic and occupational success.

Although differences in the mean scores of different groups on tests of general and special cognitive abilities are often statistically significant, variations among such scores within groups are extensive. Almost everyone performs significantly better on some types of tests than on others, so the correlations among tests of special abilities are typically rather modest. In any event, both kinds of ability measures—general and specific—are widely administered for a variety of purposes. Like the relationship between test batteries and single-subject tests of achievement, tests of general intelligence and special abilities often serve complementary functions in applied contexts. A general intelligence test may be administered first as a screening device and then followed up with one or more tests of special abilities for purposes of specific classification and placement.

This chapter continues the discussion of general and special cognitive abilities that was begun in the last chapter. The primary concern of that chapter was with research and theory pertaining to demographic differences in cognitive abilities, and general intelligence in particular. The present chapter has a more applied, diagnostic orientation. It begins with a discussion of exceptionally low or high cognitive abilities. After that, measurement and research on special abilities and what these efforts may contribute to our understanding of human cognitive functioning are considered.

GENERAL AND SPECIFIC COGNITIVE DISABILITIES

Developmental delays and deficiencies in general intelligence and specific cognitive abilities are not independent of other disorders. In fact, until the 19th century a clear distinction between mental retardation (*idiocy*) and mental disorders (*insanity*) was not made in medicine or law. In addition to clarifying the difference between these two conditions, Esquirol (1945/1838) observed that there are different degrees of mental retardation. He also maintained that the best way to determine the degree of retardation is to assess the person's facility in language usage. Additional tests and assessment procedures were subsequently devised by Seguin (1907/1866) and other French psychologists for diagnosing mental retardation—efforts that culminated in the Binet–Simon Intelligence Scale of 1905.

Unlike mental retardation, which affects the ability to learn in many different areas, a specific learning disability involves a more delimited learning difficulty, such as reading, mathematics, spelling, or writing. Even this distinction is not clear cut. Thus, a child who has been diagnosed as mentally retarded is likely to have a greater deficiency in one area than another or he or she may be gifted in a particular area. In addition, a child with a specific learning disability may be highly talented or gifted in another area. For example, a child may be unable to read and yet be adept at playing music "by ear."

In the process of diagnosing a child as having a specific learning disability, mental retardation is first eliminated as a cause, as are physical handicaps and emotional disturbances. Furthermore, a physical handicap or emotional disorder, as well as fatigue or lack of motivation, a drug overdose, or various other states, can have a temporary or relatively permanent depressing effect on specific cognitive functions. Problems of learning associated with such conditions are not always apparent until the child enters school and is subjected to formal learning experiences and adult expectations. Then teachers, counselors, and health personnel must cooperate closely with parents to determine the specific causes of the problem and plan appropriate educational, psychological, and/or medical methods of treating it.

Mental Retardation

A variety of systems have been employed in classifying the level of severity of mental retardation. In the early years of the 20th century, the terms *moron, imbecile,* and *idiot* were used to designate high, middle, and low grades of "feeblemindedness."[1] Because of their derogatory connotations,[2] these labels were subsequently abandoned and the following IQ-based categories were adopted by the American Association of Mental Deficiency (AAMD):

Mild mental retardation: IQ = 50–55 to 70

Moderate mental retardation: IQ = 35–40 to 50–55

Severe mental retardation: IQ = 20–25 to 35–40

Profound mental retardation: IQ = below 20 or 25

As employed by the AAMD, the term *mental retardation* is defined as "significantly subaverage general intelligence functioning, resulting in or associated with concurrent impairments in adaptive behavior and manifested during the developmental period" (Kidd, 1983, pp. 243–244). The AAMD classification system was not uniformly adhered to from state to state. In most cases and states, the upper limit of 70 (two standard deviations below the mean IQ) was extended to 75, but it was still possible to be mentally retarded in one state and not in another (Frankenberger, 1984).

A different system of classifying the degree of retardation was proposed by the National Association for Retarded Children (NARC) and the American Psychiatric Association. The categories and corresponding IQ intervals in this system are:

Marginally independent: IQ = 50 to 75

Semidependent: IQ = 25 to 50

Dependent: IQ = 0 to 25

The fourth edition of the *Diagnostic and Statistical Manual of Mental Disorders [DSM–IV]* (American Psychiatric Association, 1994) also listed the following as necessary for a diagnosis of mental retardation:

Significantly subaverage intellectual functioning: an IQ of approximately 70 or below on an individually administered IQ test (for infants, a clinical judgment of significantly subaverage intellectual functioning).

Concurrent deficits or impairments in present adaptive functioning (i.e., the person's effectiveness in meeting the standards expected for his or her age by

---

[1]Several years ago the American Association of Mental Deficiency changed its name to the American Association of Mental Retardation. Even the term *mental retardation* has been objected to by some professionals, who advocate replacing it with the presumably less socially stigmatizing label of *mental impairment* or *developmental disability.*

[2]In the 19th and early 20th centuries, people who are now referred to as "mentally retarded" were sometimes exhibited for amusement and profit by P. T. Barnum and other "freak show" impresarios. These exhibits undoubtedly contributed to the development and perpetuation of the association of human differences with "danger, inferiority, subhuman characteristics, and animal traits," and to popular characterizations of disability and mental retardation in horror and gangster movies and in the comics (e.g., cone head, pinhead, etc.; Bogdan, 1986; Lindfors, 1984).

his or her cultural group) in at least two of the following areas: communication, self-care, home living, social/interpersonal skills, use of community resources, self-direction, functional academic skills, work, leisure, health, and safety.

The onset is below age 18. (p. 50)

The inclusion of adaptive behavior in the AAMD and NARC classification systems, required by Public Law 94-142, represented a recognition of the importance of academic and vocational attainments, motor skills, socioemotional maturity, and other indicators of independent functioning and maintenance and the ability to meet cultural demands for personal and social responsibility. Adaptive behavior can be assessed by an informal analysis of a person's history and current behavior or by a standardized rating scale (Vineland Adaptive Behavior Scale, Adaptive Behavior Inventory for Children, etc.) that covers a wide range of personal and social behaviors; this scale is completed by a parent, teacher, or other caregiver who has observed the person carefully. Table 7.1 lists the adaptive behaviors that are typical of mildly, moderately, severely, and profoundly mentally retarded individuals during preschool age, school age, and adulthood.

An even more recent definition of *mental retardation,* which relies less on the concept of IQ than prior definitions, was proposed by the American Association of Mental Retardation (1992). According to this definition, *mental retardation* refers to substantial limitations in present functioning characterized by significantly subaverage intellectual functioning, manifested before age 18, and existing concurrently with related limitations in two or more of the following adaptive skill areas: communication, home living, community use, health and safety, leisure, self-care, social skills, self-direction, functional academics, and work. In applying this definition, it is assumed that:

Valid assessment considers cultural and linguistic diversity as well as differences in communications and behavioral factors.

The existence of limitations in adaptive skills occur within the context of community environments typical of the individual's age peers and is indexed to the person's individualized needs for supports.

Specific adaptive limitations often co-exist with strengths in other adaptive skills or other personal capabilities.

With appropriate support over a sustained period, the life functioning of the person with mental retardation will generally improve.

The AAMR definition was criticized by Jacobson and Mullick (1992) and a number of other professionals and has not been widely employed. Be that as it may, almost all programs for diagnosing and treating mentally retarded children take into consideration the individual's ability to communicate and otherwise socially interact and to engage in instrumental activities of daily living.

TABLE 7.1

Characteristic Behaviors at Three Age Levels
and Four Levels of Mental Retardation

Age	Behavior
Mild Mental Retardation (IQ = 50–70)	
Preschool Age (0–5)	Slower than average to walk, feed self, and talk, but casual observer may not notice retardation.
School Age (6–21)	Learns perceptual-motor and cognitive skills (reading and arithmetic) on third- to sixth-grade level by late teens; can learn to conform socially.
Adult (21 and over)	Usually achieves social and vocational skills needed for maintaining self; requires guidance and help when under unusual economic or social stress.
Moderate Mental Retardation (IQ = 35–49)	
Preschool Age (0–5)	Most development noticeably delayed, particularly in speech; can be trained in variety of self-help activities.
School Age (6–21)	Learns to communicate and take care of elementary health and safety needs; learns simple manual skills, but makes little or no progress in reading and arithmetic.
Adult (21 and over)	Performs simple unskilled or semiskilled tasks under supervised conditions; participates in simple games and travels alone in familiar places; incapable of self-maintenance.
Severe Mental Retardation (IQ = 20–34)	
Preschool Age (0–5)	Pronounced delay in motor development; little or no speech; benefits from self-help (e.g., self-feeding) training.
School Age (6–21)	Usually walks unless locomotor disability present; can understand and respond to speech; can profit from training in health and other acceptable habits.
Adult (21 and over)	Follows daily routines and contributes to self-maintenance; needs direction and close supervision in controlled environment.

(continued on next page)

Profound Mental Retardation (IQ below 20)

Preschool Age (0–5)	Extreme retardation in all areas; minimal sensorimotor abilities; requires nursing care.
School Age (6–21)	Obviously delayed in all areas of development; responds with basic emotions and may benefit from training in use of limbs and mouth; must be closely supervised.
Adult (21 and over)	May be able to walk and talk in a primitive way; benefits from regular physical activity; cannot take care of self, but requires nursing care.

Note. From "A Rationale for Degrees of Retardation," 1955, *American Journal of Mental Deficiency, 60,* p. 262.

Another system of classification has been employed for purposes of special class placement and instruction in school situations. The term *educable mentally impaired* is used for children who are mildly retarded, *trainable mentally impaired* for those who are moderately retarded, *trainable (dependent)* for children who are severely retarded, and *custodial (life support)* for those who are profoundly retarded (Sattler, 1988). An estimated 2% to 2.5% of the U.S. population is mentally retarded, but less than 1.5% of public school students are diagnosed as retarded. In 1994, over 600,000 children in U.S. public schools were identified as retarded, a larger percentage being boys than girls. Although Whites outnumber all other ethnic groups in the total number of retarded children, as shown in Fig. 7.1, the percentage within each racial/ethnic group diagnosed as mentally retarded varies from group to group (U.S. Department of Education, 1997). Blacks rank first among all ethnic groups in the percent of children in the group diagnosed as retarded, followed in order by American Indians, Whites, Hispanics, and Asian/Pacific Islanders.

In only about 25% of the cases of mental retardation are the causes of the disorder known (Zigler & Hodapp, 1986). These 364 or more organic disorders, which are associated primarily with severe or profound retardation, encompass a variety of conditions that damage the central nervous system. Included among them are: major gene problems such as galactosemia, gargoylism, phenylketonuria, and Tay-Sachs disease; genetic-dependent conditions such as cretinism, hydrocephaly, and microcephaly; chromosomal abnormalities such as Down's syndrome and Klinefelter's syndrome; and intrauterine infections, birth trauma (head injury, oxygen deprivation or oversupply), and diseases contracted during infancy (meningitis, encephalitis, lead poisoning, etc.). In more developed countries, these conditions are responsible for relatively small percentages of retarded persons, but disorders associated with malnutrition, in particular, account for a fairly high percentage of retarded persons in less developed countries.

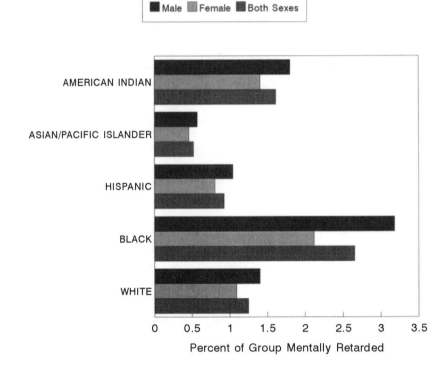

FIG. 7.1.   Percentages of mentally retarded children in U.S. public schools by sex and ethnicity. (Based on unpublished data from "1994 Elementary and Secondary School Civil Rights Compliance Report," projected values for the nation. U.S. Department of Education, Office for Civil Rights, July 22, 1997.)

In the great majority of cases, most of which are moderately or mildly retarded, the cause of mental retardation is uncertain or unknown. Genetic (familial) factors, combined with an environment characterized by neglect, poor stimulation, and a lack of formal learning experiences, are thought to be determinative factors in many instances. However, many of these disorders may be due to undiscovered organic factors that time and medical science will reveal. An example is fragile-X syndrome, which, after Down's syndrome, is the second most common genetic cause of mental retardation. During the late 1960s and 1970s, it was discovered that approximately 10% of mentally retarded males for whom there was thought to be no organic basis for their condition had fragile-X syndrome (Dykens, Hodapp, & Leckman, 1994).

Mild mental retardation is by far the most common type of retardation and is associated with many of the same demographic variables as borderline and dull-normal intelligence (IQ = 70–89): low parental education, minority group membership, unemployment or low-level employment, poor nutrition and health, and substandard living conditions in general. Heredity is thought to be a significant factor in mild retardation, but the unstructured and unpredictable environments of children in this category undoubtedly contribute to their retardation. The home environments of many mildly retarded children are characterized by inadequate language models, lack of intellectual simulation, and less concern for their welfare in general.

Somehow mental retardation can be treated when the cause is identified early enough. In the vast majority of cases, however, the condition is incurable, and training and education rather than physical treatments are emphasized. With appropriate supports over a sustained period, the life functioning of a mentally retarded person generally improves. Most of this care is given in the home, but both private and state-operated residential facilities are also available. In 1993, approximately 230,000 retarded Americans were living in some 58,000 private facilities and approximately 70,000 retarded persons were living in some 1,800 state-operated facilities. Such residential care is not cheap: Daily maintenance expenses in a state-operated facility for retarded persons averaged $225 per resident in 1993 (U.S. Bureau of the Census, 1997b).

The term *special education* has traditionally referred to classes for educable and, to a lesser extent trainable, mentally retarded children in schools. Detterman and Thompson (1997) maintained, however, that the methods employed by special educators are in no sense "special," but rather are merely standard instructional procedures with some slight attention paid to the special needs of the students who are served. They argued that effective special educational methods that take into account individual differences in cognitive abilities have yet to be developed. Consequently, the *one size fits all* philosophy still generally prevails in American schools. Special education is not truly special because the nature and development of cognitive abilities are not understood well enough to design appropriate educational methods for special children.

Specific Learning Disabilities

Children who score at or above the mean on a general intelligence test do not necessarily do well in all school subjects. They may have pronounced physical handicaps, emotional disturbances, low motivation, or a home environment that is not conducive to study and learning. Some children of average or above-average intelligence have none of these problems, but still experience difficulties in learning to read, making arithmetic calculations, spelling, writing, or the performance of other scholastic tasks. At one time, such children were incorrectly diagnosed as mentally retarded. However, for the past few decades, the term *learning disability* (LD) or *specific learning disability* has been applied to these kinds of problems. According to Public Law 101-476, the Individuals with Disabilities Education Act (IDEA) of 1990:

The term "children with specific learning disabilities" means those children who have a disorder in one or more of the basic psychological processes involved in understanding or in using language, spoken or written, which disorder may manifest itself in imperfect ability to listen, think, speak, read, write, spell, or to do mathematical calculations. Such disorders include such conditions as perceptual handicaps, brain injury, minimal brain dysfunction, dyslexia, and developmental aphasia. Such term does not include children who have learning problems which are primarily the result of visual, hearing or motor handicaps, of mental retardation, of emotional disturbance, or of environmental, cultural, or economic disadvantage.

As indicated by this definition, LDs are not limited to problems with reading, language, memory, thinking, or other cognitive skills. Impairments in perception and motor coordination, as well as behavioral problems such as distractibility, hyperactivity, impulsivity, and perseveration, are also included.

Parents and classroom teachers are usually the first to detect that something is wrong with a child who has a learning disability, but too often it is assumed that the child is simply not trying hard enough. Diagnosis of a learning disorder requires careful observation of the child and administration of tests designed to determine the nature and severity of the problem. It is important to eliminate other possible physical and psychological problems in the diagnosis, especially sensorimotor handicaps and low general intelligence. Ideally, the diagnostic process involves the efforts of a multidisciplinary team consisting of a teacher or other specialist who is knowledgeable in the area in which the disability is manifest, the child's regular teacher, and one or more persons qualified to administer and score relevant psychometric instruments and interpret the results.

Procedures for identifying LDs vary from state to state; the number of children who are identified as LD in one state may be five times as great as in another state (Reynolds, 1990). Consequently, estimates of the percentage of LD children range from 5 to 20 or 30. As mandated by federal law, the basic criterion for a diagnosis of *specific learning disability* is a discrepancy between the child's ability and achievement in one or more of the following areas: oral expression, listening comprehension, written expression, basic reading skill, reading comprehension, mathematics calculation, or mathematical reasoning.

Difficulty in learning to read and spell (*dyslexia*) is the most common form of LD. Dyslexic children experience reading difficulties because of problems with phonological coding (i.e., decoding printed letters into blended sounds). When asked to read out loud, a dyslexic child reads slowly, haltingly, and laboriously. The left cerebral hemisphere apparently functions differently in dyslexics, who are three to four times more likely to be boys than girls, than in nondyslexics (Forster, 1994).

Less common than verbal learning problems are nonverbal disabilities in mathematics, handwriting, and spatial cognition (Rourke, 1989). These problems, which occur in an estimated 1% to 10% of LD persons and in .1% to 1% percent of the general population, are thought to be caused by abnormal functioning of the right cerebral hemisphere (Pennington, 1991). Non-verbal learning problems are observed most often in mathematics, particularly in concept formation and spatial cognition. On intelligence tests such as the WISC–III, children with nonverbal LDs typically do better on verbal subtests, which measure language skills, than on performance subtests, which require visuospatial and visuomotor skills. The reverse is true of children with verbal disabilities.

Following diagnosis of an LD, an *individualized educational plan* (IEP), consisting of short- and long-term objectives and procedures for achieving them, is prepared. In addition to the school-related deficits to be remedied by an IEP, some provision must be made for treating accompanying emotional or behavioral problems. These problems are more frequent in LD children than in other children. However, whether they are causes or effects of LDs or whether both the psychological problems and the LD are due to some common organic factor are not known.

In 1994, an estimated 2,368,283 American school children, 7.37% of whom were boys and 3.44% girls, were diagnosed as having specific LDs (U.S. Department of Education, 1997). As shown in Fig. 7.2, the percentage of children in a particular ethnic group with an LD varied with the group: American Indians had the largest and Asian/Pacific Islanders the smallest percentages of LDs of any ethnic group.[3]

Eligibility criteria for providing services to LD persons are not the same from state to state. In most cases, an assessment is made to determine whether there is a significant discrepancy between the level of achievement expected from a child's score on a standardized intelligence test and his or her score on a conormed achievement test. In California, the score on a general intelligence test must be at least 1½ standard deviations above the score on an appropriate standardized achievement test for a child to be eligible for such services. Other states have mandated a 1 standard deviation discrepancy and/or other criteria and procedures for determining whether a child's actual achievement is keeping pace with his or her expected achievement.

The etiology of most learning disorders is complex and unclear, and there is considerable debate as to whether these disorders are caused by neurological, developmental, or experiential factors, or a combination of these. There is evidence that LDs run in families (Oliver, Cole, & Hollingsworth, 1991). In other cases, teratogens—viruses, drugs, chemicals, radiation, and other external agents that cross the placental barrier and harm the embryo or fetus—are involved. Postnatal factors, such as convulsions caused by high fevers or from inhaling leaded contaminants, are other possible causes (Needleman et al., 1990). In most cases, there is nothing ostensibly wrong with the brain or other body organs, but something is obviously not functioning properly.

---

[3]Of the 5.03 million U.S. children and youth with disabilities who were served by state and federally operated programs in 1996, 51.3% had specific learning disabilities, 20.3% had speech or language impairments, 11.3% were mentally retarded, and 8.6% were seriously emotionally disturbed (Data from U.S. Department of Education, Office of Special Programs).

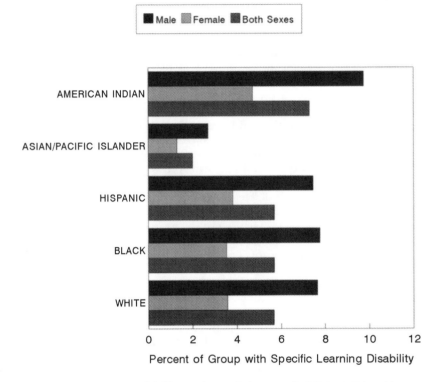

FIG. 7.2. Percentages of children with specific learning disabilities in U.S. public schools by sex and ethnicity. (Based on unpublished data from "1994 Elementary and Secondary School Civil Rights Compliance Report," Projected values for the nation. U.S. Department of Education, Office for Civil Rights, July 22, 1997.)

Most children diagnosed with specific LDs do not appear to have damaged brains, but there is no doubt that brain dynamics are involved in such disorders. Recent research concerned with cerebral correlates of these conditions has centered on the planum temporale—an area on both sides of the brain that is known to play a role in language development. In dyslexics, this structure is the same size on one side of the brain as on the other, whereas in nondyslexic individuals, the left planum temporale is noticeably larger than the right. According to the researchers, certain reading problems are related to this difference (Leonard et al., 1996).

Whatever the origin of an LD may be, it causes problems for the afflicted individuals and those who deal with them. In fact, the short attention span, poor concentration, and excessive motor activity of children with attention deficit hyperactivity disorder (ADHD) may prompt parents and teachers to seek help not only for the child but for themselves as well. Three medications—methylphenidate (Ritalin), dextroamphetamine (Dexedrine or Dextrostat), and pemoline (Cylert)—are effective in the treatment of both children and adults with ADHD. Although these are stimulants, and may consequently seem contraindicated in the treatment of hyperactivity, they have the paradoxical effect of reducing restlessness and improving concentration. Various types of individual and group counseling may also be of help to LD persons. In the case of school children, tutoring by and social interaction with teachers, parents, and other caring persons who can assist the child in coping with the disorder are recommended.

Sensory, Motor, and Emotional Disorders

In addition to mentally retarded or LD children, children who have disorders of vision, hearing, and other sensory, neuromuscular, and orthopedic problems fall in the category of *special children.* Children with serious emotional disturbances are also *special* in the sense that they require instructional techniques other than those used with *normal* children. Although not strictly learning disabilities in the sense of representing cognitive deficiencies, these conditions can have pronounced effects on the learning process.

Physical disorders and handicaps occur more frequently than average in mentally retarded individuals, but they are obviously not limited to persons with below-average IQs. A handicap is, of course, not the same as a disability, the extent of which varies with both the nature of the handicap and the personality and compensatory ability of the afflicted individual. A handicap that is disabling for one person may act as a challenge to another, promoting even greater achievement than would otherwise have occurred. The extent to which this is possible and the manner in which it is accomplished vary with the severity of the handicap. For example, total blindness is more severe than partial sightedness, and consequently is more likely to affect the development and measurement of one's cognitive abilities. The same is true of total deafness as opposed to being hard-of-hearing. Both seeing and hearing are obviously important in shaping cognitive abilities. However, because of the critical role of language in cognitive development, intelligence appears to be affected more by loss of hearing than by loss of sight (Ackerman, 1991). In any event, various special tests have been designed to measure the intelligence and other abilities of people who have visual or auditory defects.

The development and assessment of cognitive abilities are also affected by cerebral palsy and other severe motor disabilities. Individuals with severe neuromuscular or orthopedic handicaps typically respond more slowly and laboriously than average, so time becomes a critical factor in learning and assessment tasks that require muscular movements. Such children may have particular difficulty in speaking and otherwise making themselves understood, leading to an improper diagnosis of mental retardation and an incorrect educational strategy.

Special classes within the public schools are rarely provided for children who have sensory, neuromuscular, or orthopedic handicaps, although special private schools are available. Structural or physical adaptations are, as mandated by law, provided for these children, but the emphasis is on integrating them into the regular classroom. This is also true of seriously emotionally disturbed children, although the disruptiveness caused by these children often necessitates segregating them in special classes or providing individual instruction. Such is the case with children who are diagnosed as having ADHD, conduct or behavioral disorder, or autism. ADHD, which is characterized by inattention, impulsivity, and hyperactivity, affects an estimated 3% to 5% of the school-age population (Dinklage & Barkley, 1992). Conduct disorders are also quite common, but autism less so. Other emotional problems that occur in children and require special attention if not special classes include anxiety, depression, and phobias.

Children classified as having serious emotional disturbances constitute less than 1% of the school population. There are substantially more boys than girls in this group, and in fact boys have more behavioral problems in general than girls. As illustrated in Fig. 7.3, serious emotional disturbances are more common among Blacks and American Indians than in other ethnic groups of public school students, and least common of all among Asian/Pacific Islanders (U.S. Department of Education, 1997).

INTELLECTUAL GIFTEDNESS AND CREATIVITY

Gifted, talented, creative, and *genius* are just a few of the terms referring to very high cognitive abilities, either in general or in a specific area. Galton, Terman, and other pioneers in mental testing applied the term *genius* to individuals with exceptionally high mental ability, but for most people *genius* refers not to potentiality alone but to creative productivity as well. Of course, genius is not restricted to a particular field: There are scientific geniuses, mathematical geniuses, literary geniuses, musical geniuses, artistic geniuses, and political geniuses. In addition, in popular parlance, a person may be said to have a genius for getting into trouble, for figuring people out, or for almost anything.

Characteristics of the Mentally Gifted

Beginning with the research and writings of Galton (1962/1869), for more than a century scientific investigations of the characteristics, causes, and correlates of mental giftedness have been conducted and reported. The earliest studies were biographical and anecdotal, and the first systematic longitudinal study of mental giftedness was begun by Lewis Terman and his associates in 1922. In the Terman study, 1,528 California school children with IQs of 135 and above were followed up and questioned every 5 years or so throughout their lives to determine how they had fared. The findings exploded several popular myths concerning gifted individuals (e.g., "early ripe, early rot," "bright children are sickly," and "genius is akin to insanity"). These *termites* (Terman + mites), as they have somewhat affectionately been dubbed, were heavier at birth and remained heavier than average; they walked and talked earlier and matured at an earlier age than average;

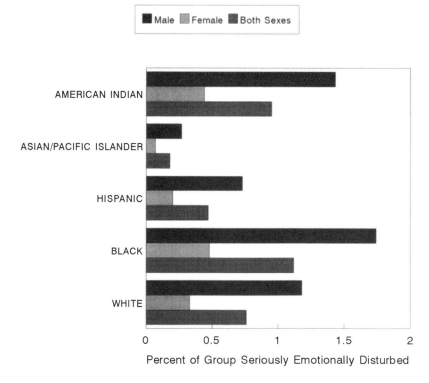

FIG. 7.3.   Percentages of seriously emotionally disturbed children in public schools by sex and ethnicity. (Based on unpublished data from "1994 Elementary and Secondary School Civil Rights Compliance Report," Projected values for the nation. U.S. Department of Education, Office for Civil Rights, July 22, 1997.)

and their general health was better. Their mental and physical superiority was retained in adulthood: They earned more educational degrees, attained higher occupational success and salaries, were no worse in personal and social adjustment, achieved greater marital success, and were physically healthier than the average adult (Terman & Oden, 1947, 1959). However, the fact that, when educational level was statistically controlled, the IQ scores of these individuals had no relationship to their occupational achievement suggests that their occupational success was due to educational attainment rather than intelligence per se. It is also noteworthy that none of the *termites* became a famous composer, artist, or poet or achieved the same level of renown as a Mozart, Einstein, Hemingway, or Churchill. Intelligence, as measured by the Stanford–Binet, obviously has its limits and is by no means the sole determinant of stellar achievement and prestige. Furthermore, many of the *termites* admittedly failed to live up to their potential and expressed regrets at not having done so (see Gardner, 1997).

Winner (1997) distinguished between *moderately gifted* children with IQs between 130 and 150, who may be one or two grades ahead of their school classmates, and *profoundly gifted* children who have IQs above 150. Unlike the moderately gifted children, who constituted the largest portion of Terman's sample, all of the children studied by Hollingworth (1942) were profoundly gifted. Hollingworth's subjects tended to have more adjustment problems than Terman's—a distinction between the moderately and profoundly gifted that has also been noted by other investigators (Eysenck, 1995; Janos & Robinson, 1985). Profoundly gifted children frequently demonstrate astounding accomplishments at a very early age, such as memorizing an entire musical score, figuring out how to identify all prime numbers, and discovering algebraic rules on their own (Feldman & Goldsmith, 1991; Winner, 1996). Typically they can read before entering kindergarten and are superior in problem solving and other forms of abstract thinking. Many are fascinated with numerical and musical patterns and with creating new approaches and solutions (Jackson, 1992).

Like other children, intellectually gifted children are not without problems. For example, they may be gifted in one area (e.g., spatial ability), but have an LD in another area (e.g., dyslexia). Furthermore, highly gifted children are more likely than others to be introverts and loners (Ochse, 1991). They also have a higher rate of socioemotional problems and tend to be independent and nonconforming. They generally have high intrinsic motivation to attain mastery, derive great pleasure from work, and are quite egocentric about their abilities (Janos & Robinson, 1985).

Education of the Gifted and Talented

The term *gifted and talented* is employed by educators to designate children who demonstrate high intellectual or other cognitive abilities. Typically children assigned to this category are required to have IQs of approximately 130 and above, but teachers' ratings and recommendations, as well as other criteria, may also be applied. According to Public Law 95-561,

> Gifted and talented children means children, and whenever applicable, youth, who are identified at the preschool, elementary, or secondary level as possessing demonstrated or potential abilities that give evidence of high performance capability in areas such as intellectual, creative, specific academic, or leadership ability, or in the performing and visual arts and who by reason thereof require services or activities not ordinarily provided by the school.[4]

Data published by the Office for Civil Rights of the U.S. Department of Education (1997) indicate that approximately 6% of American school children fall in the *gifted and talented* category. Figure 7.4 is a descriptive breakdown of this group of children by race and sex. Slightly larger percentages of females than males and larger percentages of Asian/Pacific Islanders and Whites than American Indians, Hispanics, and Blacks are classified as

---

[4]Congressional Record, October 10, 1978. Educational Amendments of 1978, 20 USC 2701 (1978); 92 STAT.2143.

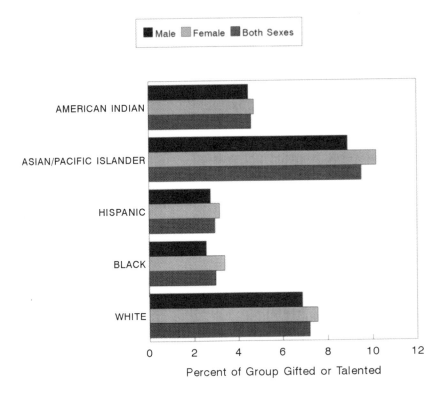

FIG. 7.4. Percentages of gifted and talented children in U.S. public schools by sex and ethnicity. (Based on unpublished data from "1994 Elementary and Secondary School Civil Rights Compliance Report," Projected values for the nation. U.S. Department of Education, Office for Civil Rights, July 22, 1997.)

mentally gifted and talented. Some of these children are exceptional in mathematics, others in verbal reasoning, others in music or art, and still others in social leadership. They may show generally accelerated mental development, early intellectual specialization, or unusual aptitudes (in memory, imagination, observation, etc.; Leites, 1990).

Strategies for educating gifted and talented students include early school admission, acceleration and grade skipping, advanced study, independent study, mentoring, and special resource rooms. The number of school districts and programs for these students has increased dramatically in recent years. In fact, almost all school systems in the United States now have some sort of special instructional program for gifted children.

Students in these programs spend the majority of their school time in regular classrooms, but they are taken out for several hours each week to participate in special activities for the gifted. Regional centers for gifted and talented children and other institutions devoted to students with superior abilities have also been established throughout the United States. In general, gifted students fare quite well—intellectually, socially, and emotionally—in these programs. However, critics often characterize special programs for the gifted as elitist or undemocratic and recommend that they be discontinued. In particular, ability tracking in the schools has come under fire as "one of the most divisive and damaging school practices in existence" (Carnegie Council on Adolescent Development, 1989, p. 49). It has also been alleged that ability tracking lowers children's self-esteem and creates a self-fulfilling prophecy, in which children who are labeled as nongifted live up to the label (Lipsey & Wilson, 1993; Slavin & Braddock, 1993).

In a real sense, all school children—not just those who are mentally retarded, LD, or gifted—are *special* and should be treated as such. To date, however, the promise of adapting instruction to individual differences has not been realized. Rather, schools have too often settled on a pedagogical practice of adjusting the curriculum and teaching so everyone passes and very little real learning takes place. Educational standards in American schools need to be raised, and the failure to do so has resulted in the distressingly low level of performance of even our brightest students (Winner, 1997). The fear that the elevation of educational standards would result in a large percentage of children falling by the wayside is simply not substantiated by research. On the contrary, as emphasized by Edmonds (1982), Levin (1987), and Winner (1997), most students, and not merely the best students, rise to meet the challenge when classroom standards are raised.

Creativity

The single most valid assessment procedure for identifying intellectually gifted children is an individually administered test of intelligence such as the Stanford–Binet Intelligence Scale or the Wechsler Intelligence Scale for Children. These tests also do a fair job of predicting scholastic achievement, but they were not designed to measure the expertise, imaginative thinking skills, venturesomeness, and high intrinsic motivation that are viewed as essential to creative performance (Sternberg & Lubart, 1991, 1992). The first of these four essential characteristics of creative performance—expertise—consists of a well-developed store of knowledge. The second essential—imaginative thinking—consists of the ability to see things in new ways; to recognize patterns and connections. The third essential—a venturesome personality—is one that tolerates ambiguity and risk, persevering in overcoming obstacles and seeking new experiences. The fourth essential for creative performance—high intrinsic motivation—consists of being motivated primarily by interest, enjoyment, satisfaction, and challenge rather than by external pressures (see Amabile & Hennessey, 1992).

Other cognitive and affective traits that are said to be characteristic of creative people are ideational fluency, flexibility, unconventionalism, social sensitivity, nondefensiveness, a greater willingness to concede faults, and close ties with parents (MacKinnon, 1962). However, these characteristics are not sufficient to ensure creative performance. Creativity cannot flourish in a highly structured, demanding environment in which one is constantly concerned with winning social approval (Amabile & Hennessey, 1992). The environment must stimulate and support creativity and the taking of chances, as well as encourage intrinsic and delayed rewards for effort. Furthermore, truly creative people are their own severest critics. They do not settle for satisfactory or second best; even when products on which an enormous amount of time has been spent fail to pass their personal tests, creative people usually have the courage to put them aside and search for a new approach.

Creative thinking is more a matter of divergent thinking about open-ended problems that have a number of possible solutions, rather than convergent thinking about problems with a single solution. Unlike the convergent items on intelligence tests, the items on measures of divergent or creative thinking are scored in terms of fluency (number of responses) and novelty (originality or uncommonness). Examples of creativity tests are the Christensen–Guilford Fluency Tests and the Torrance Tests of Creative Thinking.

Not all creative people do well in school; like highly gifted children, they are no strangers to unhappiness and adjustment problems. Webb and Meckstroth (1982) noted that intellectually gifted children who are also highly creative are often troublesome to their parents and feel troubled themselves. Realizing that they are different from other children, they are presumably aware of the envy of their classmates and burdened by high expectations. Those who are particularly sensitive and under great stress to perform publicly may become depressed, use drugs, fail to perform up to their capacity, and occasionally drop out of society altogether. Regarding adjustment problems in creative adults, Jamison (1989, 1993) found that a group of British artists (novelists, painters, playwrights, poets, sculptors) whom she studied were much more likely than less creative people to have been treated for mania and depression. In another study, Andreasen (1987) found that 80% of the 30 faculty members in a writers' workshop exhibited depression or some other form of mood disorder, and 43% were diagnosed as manic–depressive. Excitement, if not mania, is not uncharacteristic of those who feel they are on the verge of a great discovery or achievement. And depression is a natural and understandable reaction of those who aspire to great accomplishments but fail to attain them. However, extreme excitement or depression would not seem to be conducive to productivity.

SOME OTHER INTELLIGENCES

As recognized by Charles Spearman over three quarters of a century ago (Spearman, 1927), intelligence tests such as the Stanford–Binet and the Wechsler series measure both general and specific factors. In addition, they are fairly good predictors of certain criteria, but not others. Finally, general intelligence tests do not measure all the abilities that are worth measuring or even all that have been proposed.

Practical Intelligence

Although Binet-type tests arguably represent one of the best available ways of forecasting performance in school-type situations, they are substantially less effective as predictors of behavior in more real-world, out-of-school contexts. However, the fact that the validity of conventional tests of intelligence varies with the situation and the criterion of successful performance does not mean that they are not useful or impractical. Rather, their practicality is limited by the characteristics of the persons being tested, the criteria being predicted, and the situation and cultural context. For example, Binet-type tests do not effectively distinguish between people who reportedly possess a great deal of know-how, common sense, street smarts, or implicit intelligence and those who do not. Of course, this has been known for about as long as intelligence tests have been available, but recently there has been a renewed interest in understanding and measuring so-called *practical intelligence.*

The process of understanding and measuring practical intelligence should ideally begin with a definition. Unfortunately, as with the concept of *intelligence* in general, the definition of *practical intelligence* varies with the definer. One working definition was provided by Sternberg (1994b): "Practical intelligence is the ability to solve the ill-defined problems that arise in daily life for which there may be no clear-cut answers" (p. 822). Note that the open-endedness of the problems to which practical intelligence is applied make them similar in some ways to the items on measures of creative thinking.

A theoretical foundation for the construct of practical intelligence was provided by Sternberg (1986, 1997). At its broadest level, Sternberg's theory is concerned with *successful intelligence,* defined as the ability to achieve a balance between adaptation to changing environmental conditions, shaping the environment in such a way that one's strengths are maximized and one's weaknesses are compensated for, and selecting completely new environments in which to achieve one's goals and those of one's society and culture. Successful intelligence depends on three broad abilities: analytical, creative, and practical. *Analytical abilities* involve identifying a problem, defining its nature, devising a solution strategy, and monitoring the solution. *Creative abilities* are needed to generate various options for solving the problem, and *practical abilities* are needed to implement the options and make them work.

Various measures of practical intelligence, some of which are similar in structure to conventional intelligence tests (with a practical twist), have been devised. These tests reportedly do a better job than Binet-type tests of identifying people with practical skills, such as assembling milk cases in a milk-processing plant, being an expert racetrack handicapper, shopping in grocery stores, serving as a city manager, or applying a sophisticated, nonacademic mathematical strategy to calculate the cost of a purchase (Sternberg, 1997). However, most tests of practical intelligence have not been adequately standardized or validated and show no immediate signs of replacing conventional intelligence tests.

Emotional Intelligence

An alternative definition of *practical intelligence* proposed by Ford (1986) involves transactional goals that are social in nature. Included among these goals are establishing good relations with other people, treating them fairly, and showing concern for their rights. These behaviors are also characteristic of social intelligence—an extremely practical ability in our highly populated, service-centered world.[5] Related to social intelligence is the understanding of nonverbal behavior and feelings (Rosenthal, Hall, DiMatteo, Rogers, & Archer, 1979). Many of these feelings are emotional, and the extent to which they are perceptible to the experiencer and other people also varies from person to person.

The concept of *emotional intelligence* has much in common with the two kinds of personal intelligence—interpersonal and intrapersonal—delineated by Gardner (1983). Gardner described *interpersonal intelligence* as the ability to detect the moods of other people and to lead them and *intrapersonal intelligence* as involving knowledge of one's own feelings and understanding how to use that self-knowledge productively. According to Gardner, interpersonal intelligence is more valued in apprenticeship systems, whereas intrapersonal intelligence was more esteemed in old-fashioned religious schools.

Mayer and Salovey (1993, 1995) theorized and conducted research on emotional intelligence. They began by defining *emotional intelligence* as a type of social intelligence that involves the ability to monitor one's own and others' emotions, discriminate among them, and use the information to guide one's own thinking (Mayer & Salovey, 1993). They viewed emotionality as contributing to specific abilities and emotional management or regulation as influencing information channels and problem solving. Mayer and Geher (1996) conducted a study on the ability to regulate one's emotions and its relationship to measures of empathy and emotional defensiveness, as well as SAT scores. The results demonstrate that some forms of emotional problem solving require both emotional openness and general intelligence.

SPECIAL ABILITIES

Measures of intelligence, or general mental ability, are a kind of hodgepodge of cognitive tasks having different interrelationships. Tests of intelligence designed to measure scholastic aptitude contain verbal (vocabulary, anagrams, rhyming, etc.), mathematical (computations, problems), and other school-type tasks. Individual and group intelligence tests may also contain items designed to measure perceptual speed and accuracy, memory, inductive and deductive reasoning, and other cognitive skills. The statistical procedures of factor analysis, pioneered by Spearman (1927), reveal that underlying the multiple tasks constituting individual and group tests of

---

[5]*Social intelligence* has been defined as "people's effectiveness in accomplishing valued social goals within a particular context or cultural setting" (Ford, 1994, p. 974). The cultural relativism of this definition is seen in the fact that whether a particular pattern of behavior is intelligent depends on whether the social group or culture in which the behavior takes place views the behavior as appropriate and valuable. Cultural relativism is also emphasized by Gardner (1994) in his definition of *intelligence*: "the ability to solve problems or fashion products that are appreciated in at least one culture or community" (p. 740).

intelligence is a general intellective factor or g. The versatility of g as a predictor of performance on a wide range of criteria has been repeatedly demonstrated over the years. Most educational programs and jobs demand some degree of g for effective performance. However, other, more specialized abilities are also important. Among these special abilities, linguistic, quantitative, and memory are perhaps the closest to general intelligence, but measures of sensory/perceptual, psychomotor, spatial, mechanical, and clerical abilities also contribute to performance on certain kinds of jobs. Other special abilities, such as artistic and musical ability, have also been measured and investigated, but with somewhat less success than more vocationally oriented abilities.

Memory

Intelligent behavior requires memory, both primary (short term) and secondary (long term). On intelligence tests, primary memory may be measured by the accuracy with which a series of numerical digits can be repeated forward or backward after hearing the series for the first time. People of average intelligence can recall approximately 7 digits forward and 5 digits backward, whereas mentally retarded individuals can recall only about 5 digits forward and 3 digits backward. Secondary memory is measured by tests that necessitate recalling verbal or nonverbal materials to which the person was exposed at some time in the past. Defining a series of words, solving a set of arithmetic problems, and responding correctly to other verbal items are examples of tasks on intelligence tests that require good secondary memory. These tasks also necessitate the exercise of good working memory—that part of the long-term store of facts or events being thought about or attended to at a particular time.

The transfer of information into long-term storage normally occurs by means of verbal (practice or repetition) and visuospatial (mental picturing) codes and by associating the information to be memorized with something that is already known. Mnemonic strategies such as the peg-word method and the method of loci are also employed by memory experts for coding purposes. The *peg-word method* begins by learning a list of peg words—say words that rhyme with the numbers 1 to 20—and then imagining each of 20 items to be memorized as interacting with the peg word of the same number. In the *method of loci*, a series of distinct locations along a familiar route is selected and each object to be remembered is imagined as being placed at a particular spot along the route. To recall the objects, the individual simply takes a mental trip along the route and retrieves the objects that were placed there.

Aging has an effect on memory. On almost every kind of memory task, older adults perform less well than younger adults. However, the effects of age are usually more noticeable on secondary than on primary memory. Although it varies from person to person, older adults are typically less adept at organizing, associating, and integrating material so it can get into long-term storage. They experience greater difficulties than their younger contemporaries in forming associations and using visual images to encode and retrieve information (Hoyer & Plude, 1980). The effects of age on memory are more apparent on factual knowledge and rules for manipulating knowledge about the world than on skilled, automatic actions or procedures (Hultsch & Dixon, 1990). In addition, the memory deficit is greater on tasks requiring that the learned material be recalled rather than merely recognized (Craik & McDowd, 1987).

Regardless of age, individuals with good working memories have a definite advantage. They can read, follow directions, perform arithmetic computations, learn vocabulary, take notes, write, solve problems, and learn complex materials better than individuals with poor working memories. In addition to the capacity of working memory, people differ in the strategies they employ in learning, using, and retrieving information, as well as in their store of information that is relevant to what is to be learned (Engle, 1994). The ready availability of a body of knowledge with which unlearned material can be associated obviously facilitates the task of learning that material.

Of special interest to memory researchers are people with exceptional memories in some area, such as family trees, the Bible, mathematics, or music. Certain individuals appear to possess *eidetic imagery*, in which a mental picture of a scene, a page of text, or a chessboard arrangement is retained. However, even exceptional memory has its limits. For example, research findings indicate that the exceptional memory is usually limited to a single type of information, such as numerical digits. On other types of material, the individual's memory is average or sometimes even below average. Furthermore, rather than being a genetically based gift, it seems likely that exceptional memory is acquired primarily through experience (Ericsson, 1985).

As illustrated by the savant syndrome, exceptional memory can occur in the absence of high or even average intelligence. *Savants,* formerly called *idiot savants,* are individuals who are moderately to mildly retarded, and usually have some degree of autism, but who demonstrate exceptional abilities in mathematical calculations, musical performance, or artistic production. An example is calendar calculating, in which the individual can, when given a specific date in the past or future, name the day of the week on which the date has or will fall and perform other calculations with respect to the calendar. Some savants are capable of remarkable feats involving memory in the arts (music, drawing, sculpture, etc.; L. Miller, 1989; Selfe, 1977). Whatever the area of outstanding performance may be, in almost all cases it stems from an exceptional memory in that area. The remarkable memories of savants are typically quite restricted and cannot be adapted or extended to new tasks and different situations (Howe, 1989; Treffert, 1989).

Vocational Aptitudes

Tests of special abilities, or aptitudes, are available as measures of a single ability or as a battery of multiple aptitude tests. Among single-aptitude tests, both performance (hands-on) and paper-and-pencil tests are available. There are sensory/perceptual abilities tests, psychomotor skills tests, spatial abilities tests, mechanical abilities tests, and clerical abilities tests. In addition, there are batteries of aptitude tests, such as the Differential Aptitude Tests (DAT), the General Aptitude Test Battery (GATB), and the Armed Services Vocational Aptitude Battery (ASVAB). The DAT has been used extensively for academic and vocational counseling in junior and senior high school, and the GATB has been used for the occupational planning and placement of adults. As might be expected, scores on the more verbally oriented subtests of the DAT have higher correlations with grades in more verbal school subjects, whereas scores on more quantitatively oriented subtests have higher correlations with grades in scientific and technical courses. As a group, males score higher than females on the Mechanical Reasoning and Space Relations subtests of the DAT, whereas females score higher than males on Perceptual Speed & Accuracy and Language Usage. Because of these sex differences, both separate and combined norms for the sexes are provided.

Administered to more people than any other aptitude test battery is the ASVAB. The ASVAB is the uniform selection and classification test battery in all the armed forces of the United States; it is also used in the vocational counseling of high school students. The ASVAB consists of the 10 tests listed in Fig. 7.5. Many of these are achievement tests rather than aptitude tests in the traditional sense of the term. In any event, there is a wide range of individual differences in the scores on each test. The mean scores also vary with age, education, and sex. As illustrated in Fig. 7.5, males score higher than females on all tests except Paragraph Comprehension, Numerical Operations, and Coding Speed. These sex differences are especially pronounced on Auto and Shop Information, Mechanical Comprehension, and Electronics Information, performance on which would seem to be greatly influenced by specific experience. Sex differences in ASVAB scores are consistent with those obtained with single tests of ability: Males score higher than females on measures of mechanical and spatial ability, whereas females typically score higher than males on tests of clerical ability. As suggested in Fig. 7.5 by the higher mean scores of postsecondary than 12th-grade students, scores on the DAT improve with experience and training.

None of the various tests of spatial, mechanical, or clerical abilities measures a single factor. For example, Carroll (1993) identified five factors on tests of spatial ability: visualization, speeded rotation, closure speed, closure flexibility, and perceptual speed. The results of factor analyses also indicate that performance on tests of mechanical ability is a function of spatial ability, general reasoning ability, and mechanical knowledge and experience (Alderton, 1994). Manual dexterity and speed of perceiving similarities and differences are required for clerical work, but verbal and quantitative abilities are also important. Consequently, in addition to items designed to measure perceptual speed and accuracy, clerical tests contain items similar to those found on intelligence tests. Finally, the abilities measured by spatial, mechanical, and clerical abilities tests are important not only in areas that are obviously concerned with engineering, mechanics, or office work, but also in fields such as dentistry and art.

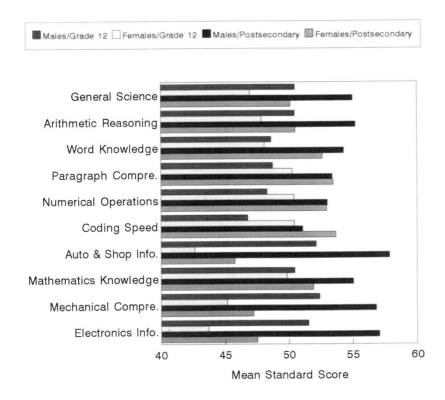

FIG. 7.5.   Mean scores of 12th-grade and postgraduate males and females on the 10 tests on the Armed Services Vocational Aptitude Battery. (Based on data in *ASVAB 18/19 Technical Manual* [U.S. Department of Defense, 1993].)

Other Special Abilities

Less widely administered than tests of mechanical ability, clerical ability, and aptitude test batteries are measures of artistic and musical abilities. Of course, painting and sculpture require more than a single ability: Spatial ability, judgment, manual dexterity, creative imagination, and other factors are involved. One may appreciate art and be a good judge of artistic accomplishment but be unable to produce an acceptable piece of art. Consequently, measures of art judgment and aesthetic perception, as well as performance tests of art ability, have been devised. None of these tests, however, has been extensively employed for selection or classification purposes.

Two areas in which child prodigies typically demonstrate high ability are mathematics and music. To some extent, these abilities develop without formal instruction, although most famous mathematicians and musicians had the benefit of good teachers and mentors in childhood. Perhaps the foremost example of a musical prodigy is Wolfgang Amadeus Mozart, who had a very close relationship with his father. The inner drive that propelled Mozart, who composed 609 pieces of music during his relatively short life, was also evident in the three Bs of musical composers—Bach, Beethoven, and Brahms.

As with most exceptionalities, the relative importance of innate ability, motivation, and instruction in musical talent is not clear. There is some evidence of a weak general factor of musical ability, but most investigations have shown that several abilities contribute to musical accomplishment. One such factor is the ability to discriminate among different pitches—the perfect pitch that has presumably characterized many famous musicians. Biological differences and their interaction with experience are undoubtedly important. For example, recent research findings indicate that the auditory cortex is significantly larger in musicians than in nonmusicians and early musical training can increase the size of this brain area (Schlaug, Jaencke, Huang, & Steinmetz, 1995; also see Maugh, 1997).

SUMMARY

Children with extremely high or low intelligence, in addition to those with special learning, physical, or emotional disabilities, are designated as *exceptional* or *special* in schools. Of course, all children are special or exceptional in some way, in the sense that they are individuals with special characteristics and educational needs. However, the mentally retarded, physically disabled, learning disabled, mentally gifted, and those with serious emotional problems have received particular attention by school and public officials.

The mentally retarded constitute approximately 1.5% (1.6% of males, 1.2% of females) of the population of American school children, children with specific learning disabilities constitute another 5.5% (7.5% of males, 3.5% of females), the gifted and talented nearly 6% (5.7% of males, 6.3% of females), and the seriously emotionally disturbed approximately .8% (1.2% of males, .3% of females). A large majority of mentally retarded children and adults are in the mildly retarded category, and therefore can benefit from academic skills training and special classes. Children diagnosed as having a learning disability are not mentally retarded, but they experience problems with specific school subjects such as reading, spelling, or arithmetic. Both mentally retarded and LD children require special treatment and educational intervention to compensate or cope with their deficits and thus function adequately in school and society.

The traditional stereotype of mentally gifted children being physically weak, unhealthy, and emotionally disturbed does not hold for the majority of these children, and especially those who are moderately gifted (IQs under 150). However, because of their obvious differences, highly gifted children are more likely to experience socioemotional problems. Various educational procedures, including acceleration, mentoring, enrichment, special classes, and special schools, have been employed in the education of the gifted.

Children with artistic, musical, or other creative talents also require special attention to develop their abilities. Creative performance is a function of relatively high intelligence, high motivation, special training, and a supportive environment. Research findings suggest that highly creative individuals have a greater than average susceptibility to mood disorders.

General intelligence, as measured by Binet-type tests, is more highly correlated with success in school-type tasks than with performance in out-of-school situations. Sternberg and others have emphasized the importance of practical or tacit intelligence (know-how, street smarts) for success in real life. Other intelligences that have been identified and studied are social intelligence, emotional intelligence, intrapersonal intelligence, and interpersonal intelligence. Measures of these intelligences, however, show no signs of replacing conventional intelligence tests.

Binet-type tests are measures of a general intelligence factor (g), scores on which are significantly related to a wide range of performance criteria. In addition to being influenced by g, as well as motivation and habits, learning and performance in a particular domain are a function of special abilities. Among the special abilities that have been measured and researched are memory, psychomotor abilities, spatial ability, mechanical ability, clerical ability, artistic ability, and musical ability. Memory, which is basic to cognitive performance in general, has been studied extensively by experimental and physiological psychologists. These researchers have differentiated among primary, secondary, tertiary, working, and other types of memory, as well as the effects of various coding methods on the storage and retrieval of information. Memory ability declines with age, but the extent of the decrement varies with the individual and can be compensated for. In addition, some people who do not possess unusually high abilities in other areas have exceptional memories. For example, savants are mentally retarded and usually autistic, but they have exceptional memory in mathematical, musical, or artistic areas.

Of all measures of special abilities, tests of psychomotor, spatial, mechanical, and clerical abilities have been used most extensively in vocational contexts. Males generally score higher than females on tests of spatial and mechanical abilities, whereas females score higher on tests of clerical abilities. Tests of musical ability and art judgment and production are also available, but they have not been widely used.

SUGGESTED READINGS

Brody, L. E., & Mills, C. J. (1997). Gifted children with learning disabilities. *Journal of Learning Disabilities, 30*(3), 282–296.
Buss, W. G. (1996). Intelligence testing and judicial policy making for special education. *Psychology, Public Policy & Law, 2*(3–4), 584–602.
Cheatham, S. K., Rucker, H. N., Polloway, E. A., & Smith, J. D. (1995). Savant syndrome: Case studies, hypotheses, and implications for special education. *Education & Training in Mental Retardation & Developmental Disabilities, 30*(3), 243–253.

Detterman, D. K., & Thompson, L. A. (1997). What is so special about special education? *American Psychologist, 52,* 1082—1090.

Palmer, C. (1997). Musical performance. *Annual Review of Psychology, 48,* 115–138.

Polloway, E. A., Patton, J. R., Smith, T. E. C., & Buck, G. H. (1997). Mental retardation and learning disabilities: Conceptual and applied issues. *Journal of Learning Disabilities, 30*(3), 297–308.

Robinson, A., & Clinkenbeard, P. R. (1998). Giftedness: An exceptionality examined. *Annual Review of Psychology, 49,* 117—139.

Stanley, J. C. (1997). Varieties of intellectual talent. *Journal of Creative Behavior, 31*(2), 93–119.

Sternberg, R. J., & Kaufman, J. C. (1998). Human abilities. *Annual Review of Psychology, 49,* 479–502.

Winner, E. (1997). Exceptionally high intelligence and schooling. *American Psychologist, 57,* 1070–1081.

CHAPTER EIGHT

Personality Theories, Concepts, and Correlates

As implied by its definition as the sum total of the qualities, traits, and behaviors of a person and by which, together with his or her physical attributes, the person is recognized as unique, *personality* is perhaps the most individual of all human differences. Despite a century of research, human personality remains one of the most elusive and profound of all mysteries. Even our descriptions of personality are, in a very real sense, rudimentary. When it comes to understanding how it develops and changes as a result of biological, social, and other influences, we are just beginning to attain some insights. Nevertheless, there is an abundance of research data on the subject, and anyone who wishes to understand the origins and dynamics of personality should become acquainted with this information.

THEORIES OF PERSONALITY

Research on personality, as in other areas, depends on theory, measurement, methodology, and resources. A variety of theories have been proposed to explain how personality develops and changes, what factors influence it and how they do so, what role personality plays in determining behavior and influencing social acceptance and success, how and why it becomes disordered, and what sorts of treatments or interventions are effective with personality disorders.

Occasionally, in a fit of frustration, one may conclude that people are incomprehensible and that there is no sense in trying to understand them. However, most of us are not quite ready to go that far, and we entertain various notions or hypotheses as to why people do this or that. Apparently, these commonsense theories work fairly well in practice or we would have to resign ourselves to living in a completely chaotic, unpredictable social universe. In the main, we are able to understand other people well enough most of the time to cope with them and satisfy our own needs.

Historically, commonsense theories of personality have classified people according to types or traits. Typologies are less popular today than they

167

once were, but at least one—Carl Jung's theory of four bipolar types: extraversion/introversion, sensing/intuiting, thinking/feeling, and judging/perceiving—has retained its position as a result of the Myers–Briggs Type Indicator inventory.

In both primitive and advanced societies, members of particular groups are readily construed as different in their physical abilities, mental abilities, temperament, and a host of other traits. In general, members of various social groups experience little difficulty in categorizing others in terms of their wisdom, strength, bravery, honesty, comicalness, and so on. This seeming naturalness of the trait approach undoubtedly accounts for its continuing popularity among laymen and professionals alike. Among the most prominent trait/factor, or dispositional, theorists of personality have been Gordon Allport, Henry Murray, Raymond Cattell, and Hans Eysenck. Eysenck's model of three personality supertraits and the Big Five traits conception of Costa and McCrae (1986) are described herein.

Theories based on traits, factors, or types focus on what has been called the *structure* of personality, whereas other theorists have taken a less static, more dynamic, approach. Such is the case with the most ambitious of all conceptions of personality—psychoanalytic theory. The classical psychoanalytic theories of Sigmund Freud, Carl Jung, and Alfred Adler, as well as the subsequent neoanalytic approaches of Karen Horney, Harry Sullivan, Erik Erikson, and Erich Fromm depict human personality as being dynamically fashioned from the interactions between certain basic instincts (sex, aggression, etc.) and societal controls over their expression during progressive stages of development. Psychoanalytic theories differ in the emphasis placed on the importance of these instincts, and on unconscious as opposed to conscious events, in the development of personality and disorders. Yet all take a psychodynamic viewpoint in conceiving of personality as a vehicle for the channeling and expression of motives.

Phenomenological, or self, theorists such as Carl Rogers and Abraham Maslow also recognize the centrality of motives of various kinds in the formation of personality. Rogers in particular was more concerned with the individual's perception of him or herself (the self-concept) and the psychological environment. Classical psychoanalytic theory views personality development as being arrested or distorted, and consequently psychological abnormalities appearing, as a result of the repression and damming up of basic instincts. But Rogers saw these problems as stemming from a failure of the person's positive regard for him or herself. To Rogers, a person comes to lack positive self-regard as a consequence of parents and significant other people placing conditions on their acceptance of him or her as a worthwhile individual. According to classical psychoanalysis, treatment of a psychological disorder can only be effective when the patient has insight into the repressed motives and conflicts that are presumed to be at the root of the problem. In contrast, Rogers and other self-theorists maintain that psychotherapy is successful only when the individual restructures his or her self-concept in an interpersonal atmosphere characterized by acceptance and unconditional positive regard.

Psychodynamic theories of personality are concerned primarily with motivation and conflict and phenomenological (self) theories are concerned with perception, whereas the social learning theories of Julian Rotter, Albert Bandura, and Walter Mischel emphasize the importance of learning in a social context. To social learning theorists, personality and behavior—both adaptive and maladaptive—are learned by modeling the behaviors of other people and receiving reinforcement for socially acceptable behavior. The smiles, pats on the back, and expressions of approval given by others are, of course, not the only factor in the person's development of a sense of self-efficacy. The person must also be at least somewhat successful in mastering the various tasks that society expects him or her to accomplish.

Trait-factor, psychoanalytic, self, and social learning theories of personality have all had their advocates and have stimulated a great deal of debate, research, and some applications. However, none of the various theories that fall into these four categories is sufficiently comprehensive and precise to provide an unambiguous portrait of personality development, functioning, stability, and disorders.

Despite the large number of hypotheses concerning personality that have been generated over the years, on one test of their validity—the ability to make accurate behavioral predictions—they have not fared very well. For the most part, what we have in psychology, and in the psychology of personality in particular, is a collection of interrelated assertions concerning human behavior, cognitions, and feelings, but far less than a systematic structure from which unerring predictions and explanations can be made.

Much contemporary theorizing about personality consists of fairly simple hypotheses or theories concerning relationships between variables rather than comprehensive, grandiose conceptions pertaining to the causes and effects of human behavior. Most often these theories consist of a few interrelated concepts from which predictions and explanations of certain bits of behavior are made.

Furthermore, no contemporary theory of personality provides a clear picture of the dynamic interactions of heredity and environment in shaping personality or the relative contributions of organic and experiential factors in its determination. However, it is certainly true that giving undivided attention to the role of experience while neglecting biology and chemistry is counterproductive. Personality theorists of the future will have to be much more knowledgeable in genetics, neurophysiology, and biochemistry and their influences on human structure and functioning if they hope to understand the different styles and idiosyncracies that constitute personality.

VARIABLES, MEASURES, AND METHODOLOGY

Good theories are important but not sufficient for effective science-making in the field of personality psychology. The variables that are selected as the basic constructs of theories must be defined and measured. As with the number of hypotheses or ideas relating to human personality, there is no shortage of variables or concepts. Table 8.1 is a list of 20 personality variables that were cited most frequently in the psychological research litera-

TABLE 8.1

The 20 Most Frequently Cited Personality-Related Terms
in the Psychological Research Literature between 1995 and 1998

Achievement motivation

Aggression

Anxiety

Attributions

Compulsivity

Conformity

Dependency

Depression

Hostility

Impulsivity

Introversion/extraversion

Locus of control

Openness to experience

Risk taking

Self-actualization

Self-concept

Self-efficacy

Self-monitoring

Type B (behavior or personality)

Type A (behavior or personality)

ture from 1995 to 1998. Typically these variables are measured by paper-and-pencil questionnaires and scales, although in many cases projective techniques and other instruments have also been administered.

Several of the variables listed in Table 8.1 have been the subjects of continuing, long-term research studies conducted in various contexts. Such is
the case with achievement motivation, anxiety, introversion–extraversion,
and the self. Research on the self (self-actualization, self-concept,
self-efficacy, etc.) has been especially popular among psychologists with a
more humanistic or phenomenological orientation. Investigations of other
variables (e.g., field dependence/independence, locus of control, repression–sensitization) was pursued extensively for several years but gradually
declined in popularity.

Many personality variables are interconnected. Consequently, scores on
measures of them are related. For example, measures of affiliation motivation, agreeableness, considerateness, and sociability are positively correlated with each other but negatively correlated with egocentricity, selfish-
ness, and shyness. Anxiety, depression, and neuroticism are also interrelated variables, as are attributions and locus of control, openness to experi-

ence, and sensation seeking. Consequently, it is not surprising that descriptive explanations of personality in terms of a few broad factors have substantial support.

Eysenck (1982) maintained that three factors or supertraits—introversion/extraversion, emotional stability/instability (neuroticism), and psychoticism—provide an adequate description of personality. Eysenck and Eysenck (1975) characterized a typical introvert and extrovert as follows:

> The typical introvert is quiet, retiring sort of person, introspective, fond of books rather than people; he is reserved and distant except to intimate friends. He tends to plan ahead, "looks before he leaps," and mistrusts the impulse of the moment. He does not like excitement, takes matters of everyday life with proper seriousness, and likes a well-ordered mode of life. He keeps his feelings under close control, seldom behaves in an aggressive manner, and does not lose his temper easily. He is reliable, somewhat pessimistic, and places greater value on ethical standards.

> The typical extrovert is sociable, likes parties, has many friends, needs to have people to talk to, and does not like reading or studying by himself. He craves excitement, takes chances, often sticks his neck out, acts on the spur of the moment, and is generally an impulsive individual. He is fond of practical jokes, always has a ready answer, and generally likes changes; he is carefree, easygoing, optimistic, and "likes to laugh and be merry." He prefers to keep moving and doing things, tends to be aggressive and loses his temper quickly; altogether his feelings are not kept under control, and he is not always a reliable person. (p. 5)

Regarding Eysenck's second dimension of personality, emotionally unstable (neurotic) individuals are described as anxious, moody, restless, touchy, emotionally responsive individuals who have difficulty returning to a normal state after a stressful experience. At the other extreme of this dimension are emotionally stable individuals, who are described as calm, careful, and even-tempered. High scorers on Eysenck's third dimension of personality—psychoticism—are described as "egocentric, aggressive, impulsive, impersonal, cold, lacking in empathy and concern for others, and generally unconcerned about the rights and welfare of other people" (Eysenck, 1982, p. 11). Eysenck and others have conducted a great deal of research on these three dimensions, particularly on perceptual and physiological correlates of introversion/extraversion.

Other psychologists (e.g., Costa & McCrae, 1986) maintain that five factors—neuroticism, extraversion, openness to experience, agreeableness, and conscientiousness—are necessary and sufficient to account for differences among personalities (see Table 8.2). The five-factor model of personality has stimulated a great deal of empirical research, and some studies have found the factors to be highly consistent across different cultures and nationalities (Goldberg, 1994; McCrae & Costa, 1987; Ostendorf & Angleitner, 1994). Ostendorf and Angleitner's (1994) review is supportive with respect to the structural validity of the model across several languages and cultures. They maintain that the model provides a robust description of

TABLE 8.2

The Big Five Personality Factors

Neuroticism:	High scorers on measures of this factor are described as anxious, insecure, self-conscious, self-pitying, worrying, and vulnerable; low scorers are described as calm, comfortable, even tempered, secure, self-satisfied, and unemotional.
Extraversion:	High scorers on measures of this factor are described as active, affectionate, fun-loving, sociable, passionate, and talkative; lower scorers are described as passive, quiet, reserved, retiring, sober, and unfeeling.
Openness to Experience:	High scorers on measures of this factor are described as creative, curious, imaginative, independent, liberal, and original; low scorers are described as conforming, conservative, conventional, down-to-earth, uncreative, and uncurious.
Agreeableness:	High scorers on measures of this factor are described as acquiescent, generous, good-natured, helpful, soft-hearted, and trusting; low scorers are described as antagonistic, critical, ruthless, stingy, suspicious, and uncooperative.
Conscientious:	High scorers on measures of this factor are described as careful, conscientious, hardworking, persevering, punctual, and well organized; low scorers are described as careless, disorganized, late, lazy, negligent, and weak-willed.

personality that proves to be highly replicable. However, Block (1995) questioned the conceptual and methodological assumptions of the five-factor model and concluded that there are serious uncertainties concerning it and the substantive meanings of the factors. Butcher and Rouse (1996) also criticized the five-factor model on a number of points, in particular as a description of psychopathology.

Measuring Instruments

Numerous psychometric instruments have been designed to measure the variables under consideration in research and applications in personality psychology (Table 8.3). One indicator of the extensiveness of research on a particular variable or construct is the frequency with which the variable and measures of it are cited in the psychological literature. As indicated by the large number of citations for the Beck Depression Inventory (BDI), the Hamilton Depression Scale, and the State–Trait Anxiety Inventory (STAI), depression and anxiety have been especially popular research topics. This is hardly surprising when one realizes that these are two of the most prominent symptoms of mental disorder and that clinical psychology is the most popular area of psychology. Although paper-and-pencil instruments such as the Minnesota Multiphasic Personality Inventory–2 (MMPI–2) and the Child Behavior Checklist (CBCL) tend to be used more often in research than projective techniques, the Rorschach Inkblot Test continues to be employed extensively in both research and practical applications. Among paper-and-pencil inventories, briefer, trait-oriented instruments such as the Eysenck Personality Questionnaire and the Eysenck Personality Inventory remain quite popular.

TABLE 8.3

The 20 Most Frequently Cited Personality Assessment Instruments in the Psychological Research Literature Between 1995 and 1998

Rank	Instrument
1	Hamilton Depression Scale
2	Beck Depression Inventory
3	Child Behavior Checklist
4	State–Trait Anxiety Inventory
5	Eysenck Personality Questionnaire
6	Dementia Rating Scale
7	SCL–90
8	Minnesota Multiphasic Personality Inventory–2
9	Eysenck Personality Inventory
10	Rorschach Inkblot Test
11	Brief Symptom Inventory
12	NEO Personality Inventory
13	Adjective Check List
14	Children's Depression Inventory
15	16 Personality Factor Questionnaire
16	Millon Clinical Multiaxial Inventory (all forms)
17	Bem Sex-Role Inventory
18	Thematic Apperception Test
19	California Psychological Inventory
20	Maslach Burnout Inventory

Inventories such as the MMPI were originally designed for diagnostic purposes in clinical contexts, but many personality assessment instruments have been developed for research on specific psychological concepts and questions. Examples are the Omnibus Personality Inventory, which was designed in connection with research on creativity (MacKinnon, 1962), the *F* scale for research on the authoritarian personality (Adorno et al., 1950), and the Sensation Seeking Scale for research on sensation seeking (Zuckerman, 1994). Special psychometric instruments have also been constructed for research on the hereditary bases of personality, the continuity of personality across the life span, and the relationships of personality to gender, ethnicity, social class, culture, and other demographic variables.

Research Methodology

In addition to hypothetical or theoretical conceptions concerning the relationships and operations of selected variables, and valid measures of them, research on personality requires the application of a methodology for determining the relationships and influences of those variables, hence confirming or disconfirming predictions and other hypotheses stemming from them. To a large extent, different assessment procedures and methodologies have been associated with different theoretical persuasions. Researchers in the psychoanalytic tradition have preferred observations, verbal reports, and projective techniques for assessing personality and more subjective clinical methodologies for analyzing the operations of conscious and unconscious motives and conflicts. In contrast, trait-factor theories have relied more on questionnaires and rating scales, the results of which are analyzed by correlational, factor analytic, and other statistical procedures. Researchers in the behavioristic tradition have also employed observations, interviews, and paper-and-pencil assessments, but they have preferred experimentation and other methods that permit better control over extraneous variables. Cognitive psychologists, who have a more mixed heritage, apply objective, behavioral methods whenever possible, but they also collect data by means of less objective self-report and introspection.

Personality variables may be viewed as independent (causal), dependent (effect), or intervening (moderator) variables. As illustrated in Fig. 8.1 by the multiple connections among background variables, personality variables, and behavior outcome variables, all three factors can influence each other. In studies concerned with the causes, development, or modification of personality characteristics, background factors such as heredity, child- rearing practices, age, gender, race/ethnicity, culture, diet and drugs, and physical (external and internal) characteristics are typical independent variables (Path A in Fig. 8.1). In studies concerned with the influences or causal contributions of personality to behavior, various types of behavioral outcomes may be of interest (Path B in Fig. 8.1). Included among these outcomes are criminal behavior, academic success, occupational success, athletic performance, physical health and disease, mental disorders, marital happiness, consumer behavior, and addictions. In multivariate investigations, the effects of multiple independent variables on several personality variables, or the effects of multiple personality variables on several behavioral outcomes variables, are investigated. Selected personality variables may also combine with genetic and environmental variables to determine their effects on behavior (Path C in Fig. 8.1). The seven research pathways in Fig. 8.1 are a recognition that behavior has multiple determinants and personality characteristics interact in many different ways with other factors to influence behavior. However, there are problems with these multivariate research designs, including difficulties in measuring and controlling many different variables simultaneously and meeting the more stringent assumptions underlying the statistical models on which multivariate designs are based.

The remainder of this chapter consists primarily of illustrative examples of the research plans diagrammed in Fig. 8.1. Most of the studies in these examples are basically correlational in nature, with little attempt to control extraneous variables and thereby establish causal relationships. It is tempting, and perhaps even reasonable, in many cases to employ cause–effect terminology in describing the outcomes of such studies. However, it should always be kept in mind that correlation implies prediction but not causation. If two variables are significantly related, one variable can be predicted from the other at a better than chance level, but still not be able to tell which variable, if either, is the cause and which is the effect.

BIOLOGICAL FACTORS

The realization that animals can be bred for different temperaments goes back thousands of years, and the fact that humans can inherit personality

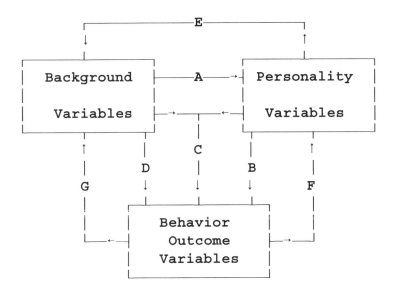

FIG. 8.1.   Types of personality research.

traits from their progenitors has probably been known at least as long. Philosophers, poets, playwrights, and other observers of human similarities and differences have described individual differences in personality characteristics for hundreds of years. However, scientific study of the inheritance of personality is much more recent. Despite an abundance of data on the biological bases of personality obtained from studies in experimental and population genetics, diseases, accidents, and other investigations, knowledge of the ways in which heredity influences personality is far from complete.

Heritability of Personality Traits

Figure 8.2 is a graphical comparison of the correlations of monozygotic (mz) and dizygotic (dz) twins on three personality variables: emotionality, activity, and sociability (Buss & Plomin, 1984, 1986). The higher correlations for mz than for dz twin pairs supports the conclusion of a hereditary basis for these variables. Among the other personality characteristics that have been found to have significantly higher mz than dz correlations are introversion and extraversion (Floderus-Myrhed, Pederson, & Rasmuson, 1980; Rose et al., 1988), altruism and aggressiveness (Rushton et al., 1986), and shyness (Kagan, Reznick, & Snidman, 1988; Robinson, Kagan, Reznick, & Corley, 1992). For example, the results of studies by Robinson et al. (1992) and Plomin and McClearn (1993) indicate that approximately 57% of the variance in the shyness scores of a large group of children was attributable to heredity. There is also evidence of a genetic basis for anxiety, fears, obsessions, and other emotional problems (Breier, Charney, & Heninger, 1984; Ohman, 1986; Rose & Ditto, 1983; Weissman et al., 1984) and in mental disorders such as alcoholism, bipolar disorder, and schizophrenia (Caldwell & Gottesman, 1991; Gottesman, 1991; McGue & Lykken, 1992).

As described in chapter 3, another statistical measure of the influence of heredity on a characteristic is the heritability coefficient (h^2). Heritability coefficients for personality characteristics vary with the particular characteristic, but are lower than those for general intelligence. Bouchard (1994) estimated that approximately 50% of the variance in measures of personality characteristics is attributable to heredity. However, the reader should be cautioned that this percentage applies only to populations and not to individuals.

Efforts to determine the relative contributions of heredity and environment to individual characteristics have often yielded confusing results. Pundits from Ignatius Loyola, founder of the Society of Jesus, to Sigmund Freud, the founder of psychoanalysis, have emphasized the importance of early experiences in shaping character. However, research indicates that common rearing environments enhance familial resemblance during adulthood only slightly and on only a few behavioral dimensions. Within the same family, there may be wide individual differences in personality among siblings exposed to the same environmental influences. Research has found that the effects on personality of environmental experiences shared among members of the same family are generally smaller than those of nonshared

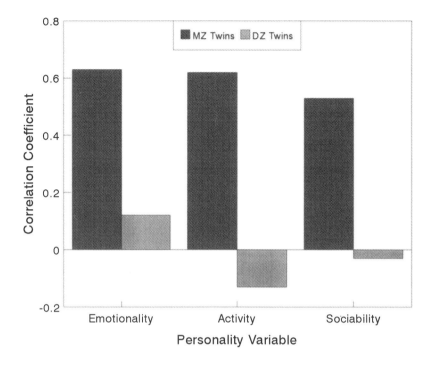

FIG. 8.2. Average correlations of parental ratings of identical and fraternal twins on three personality variables (Adapted from Buss & Plomin, 1984).

experiences unique to the individual (Bouchard, 1994; Saudino & Plomin, 1996). Among the possible nonshared experiences that influence personality are differential parental treatment; differential extrafamilial relationships with friends, peers, and teachers; and nonsystematic factors such as accidents or illness (Plomin, Chipuer, & Neiderhiser, 1994). The fact that nonshared events and experiences increase with age may account for their growing importance as the child matures. Apparent exceptions to the rule that the effects of shared family environments are relatively insignificant in shaping differences in personality are seen in the results of research on juvenile delinquency (Edelbrock, Rende, Plomin, & Thompson, 1995) and in observational measures of shyness, activity, and aggressiveness during early childhood (Cherny et al., 1994; Plomin et al., 1993; Saudino & Eaton, 1995).

In every culture, and particularly when extensive freedom of choice is permitted, children tend to elicit and select experiences that are congruent with their genetic endowment. They pursue activities that permit expression of and rewards for their genetically based talents and temperaments. They make different choices regarding what to attend to and what to ignore than children who possess other genes. Temperamentally active or emotionally labile babies elicit different responses from their caregiver than do calm, docile babies. Well-behaved, attractive youngsters are likely to stimulate greater adult affection and interest than difficult, unattractive children. In addition, parental characteristics and behaviors interact with the dispositions of children. Highly emotional parents are likely to create unstable environments that have greater negative effects on children with certain genetically based dispositions. The child's reactions, in turn, further exacerbate parents' problems and so on in a reciprocal, interactive fashion.

Physiological Correlates of Personality

Heart and respiration rates, pressure and volume of the blood, indicators of brain activity, muscle tension, body temperature, the galvanic skin response, and other physiological measures have been recorded in psychological research investigations for several decades. Results of twin studies show that many of these measures of emotional arousal or activation have a genetic basis (Bouchard et al., 1990). However, attempts to find patterns of such physiological responses that differentiate between various emotions or personality traits have not been particularly encouraging. Among the positive research findings are that depression is associated with lower heart rate (Henriques & Davidson, 1989), more rapid acquisition of conditioned fears is associated with higher heart rate (Hodes, Cook, & Lang, 1985), and the galvanic skin response is habituated more slowly in anxious and neurotic individuals (O'Gorman, 1983).

With respect to brain localization and emotion, studies have found a relationship between depression and damage to the left anterior region of the brain. Other findings point to a relationship between more negative emotions (fear, nervousness, avoidance, depression) and selective activation of the right anterior region of the brain. In contrast, positive emotions (interest, joy, enthusiasm) are associated with activity in the left anterior region of the brain (Ahern & Schwartz, 1985; Davidson, 1991, 1993; Tomarken, Davidson, Wheeler, & Doss, 1992). A simple test of hemisphericity, or individual differences in the level of activation of the two cerebral hemispheres, is to observe the direction of a person's eye movements when he or she is presented with a pleasant or unpleasant task or problem. In a right-handed person, eye movements to the left indicate relatively greater activity in the right hemisphere, whereas eye movements to the right indicate relatively greater activity in the left hemisphere (Gur & Reivich, 1980; see Box 8.1). The pattern of hemispheric activation is more complex in left-handed people and cannot be determined without additional testing.

Jerome Kagan and his coworkers (Kagan, 1994; Kagan, Reznick, & Snidman, 1988) found greater pulse rates, more widely dilated pupils, and increased muscle tension in shy children than in outgoing children who were confronted with new situations or people. Kagan also found significantly higher blood levels of monamine oxidase (MAO) in shy than in outgoing children (Kagan, 1994; Kagan et al., 1988). The production of this enzyme, which regulates the concentration of two neurotransmitters that are

---

Box 8.1. A Test of Hemisphericity

Read each of the following statements to a friend or fellow student who is right-handed and observe the direction of his or her eye movements after each problem is presented:

a. Tell me how you feel when you are anxious.

b. Visualize and describe the most upsetting photograph you have ever seen.

c. Imagine that you are relaxing on the beach looking westward over the Pacific Ocean on a clear, sunny day. Your friend is resting peacefully with his back toward your right side and looking straight ahead. In what direction is he looking?

d. Make up a sentence using the words *shock* and *anger.*

e. Try to visualize your mother's face and tell me what feeling or emotion you experience.

f. Tell me how you feel when you are frustrated.

g. Picture and describe the most joyous scene you have recently viewed.

h. Imagine that you are a veterinarian and must make a long and deep incision on a dog. You must cut a straight line from the dog's left eye to his right shoulder. Visualize making the incision and tell me what parts of the dog's face you would cut through.

i. Make up a sentence using the words *rhapsody* and *pleasure.*

j. Visualize and describe the most beautiful photograph you have recently seen.

If the eyes of the examinee to whom you gave this test moved to the right on seven or more of the items, he or she showed activation of the left hemisphere. If the examinee's eyes moved to the left on seven or more items, he or she showed right activation. This test has been adapted from a study by Schwartz, Davidson, and Maer (1975) and is not a conclusive measure of hemisphericity. However, research findings suggest that people who consistently move their eyes to the left are affected more by negative emotional content, whereas individuals who consistently move their eyes to the right are affected more by positive emotional content. Was this true of your examinee, considering that Items a, b, d, f, and h contain negative emotional content and Items c, e, g, i, and j contain positive emotional content?

---

important in emotion and motivation, is thought to be genetically directed. Because high scorers on Zuckerman's (1994) Disinhibition Scale, a measure of sensation seeking, tend to have lower blood levels of MAO than low scorers, this variable is considered to have a hereditary basis. Finally, the level of testosterone in the blood is also related to sensation seeking, as well as to extraversion, dominance, and heterosexual activity (Zuckerman, 1995).

The multiplicity of neurotransmitters and associated receptor sites has stimulated research on the relationships between neurotransmitter receptors and personality. A working hypothesis of these investigations is that people differ in the number and sensitivity of receptors and that variations in personality may be attributable in some measure to these differences (, 1995). Research in behavioral genetics has employed DNA markers to discover genes that contribute to complex behaviors. Illustrative of this type of research are studies of genes that control the development of dopamine type 2 (D2) and dopamine type 4 (D4) receptors. According to the *reward deficiency syndrome* concept, people with the D2 form of the receptor fail to obtain a normal amount of reinforcement in everyday life and are therefore likely to seek more adventurous, pleasurable methods of stimulating their D2 receptors. This is presumably the case in alcoholism, drug abuse, obesity, and habitual gambling (Blum, Cull, Braverman, & Comings, 1996). In contrast, people who inherit a gene that controls development of the D4 receptor are more likely to exhibit a so-called *novelty-seeking* behavioral syndrome, characterized as impulsive, exploratory, and quick-tempered (Benjamin et al., 1996; Ebstein et al., 1996). Whether or not these and other findings linking neurophysiology to personality are confirmed, biological variables (health, nutrition, other genes, etc.) as well as individual experiences undoubtedly play significant roles in the behavioral manifestations of personality.

Perhaps the most extensive research concerned with the relationships of personality characteristics to physiological states has stemmed from Eysenck's (1967) hypotheses concerning introversion and extraversion. According to Eysenck, people seek a moderate, comfortable level of central nervous system arousal. Because their cortical excitation levels are lower and their sensory thresholds are higher, extraverts are internally underaroused and hence more likely to seek external stimulation and condition less rapidly than introverts. Support for this hypothesis has been obtained in various investigations (Bullock & Gilliland, 1993; Davis & Cowles, 1988; Eysenck, 1990; Geen, 1984; Howard, Cunningham, & Rechnitzer, 1987; Nichols & Newman, 1986; Pearce-McCall & Newman, 1986).

One of the simplest confirmations of Eysenck's hypothesis that introverts are internally overaroused and therefore tend to avoid external sources of arousal involves the lemon juice test. When drops of natural lemon juice are placed on their tongues, introverts tend to salivate more than extraverts (Deary, Ramsey, Wilson, & Riad, 1988). Other studies have shown that introverts are also affected more than extraverts by stimulants such as caffeine and affected less by depressants such as alcohol (Stelmack, 1990). Introverts also show greater cortical arousal to simple auditory and visual stimuli (De Pascalis & Montirosso, 1988; Stelmack & Michaud-Achorn, 1985; Stenberg, Rosen, & Risberg, 1988, 1990).

Eysenck maintained that the cortical excitation levels of normal and neurotic persons are different for introverts and extraverts. Neurotic introverts (anxiety, phobic, and obsessive–compulsive neurotics) presumably have higher cortical excitation levels than normal introverts. Neurotic extraverts (psychopathic or antisocial personalities) have higher cortical excitation levels than normal extraverts, but lower levels than normal introverts. Consequently, neurotic extraverts, who have frequent encounters with the law, are thought to possess insufficient fear to inhibit the expression of their impulses.

Introversion and are related to other personality variables, such as shyness, sociability, and sensation seeking. For example, extraverts score higher than introverts on Zuckerman's Disinhibition Scale. Introversion and extraversion are also related to the P300 wave and other measures of cortical arousal. P300 is an electrically positive brain wave appearing about 300 milliseconds after a momentary stimulus that is particularly meaningful to the observer. Larger P300 waves in response to novel stimuli have been observed in introverts than in extraverts (Polich & Martin, 1992; Wilson & Languis, 1990). Furthermore, the P300 waves of psychotics have been found to be of lower amplitude than those of normals (Stelmack, Houlihan, & McGarry-Roberts, 1993), and the latencies of the P300 waves of neurotics are shorter than in normals when the groups are matched on extraversion (Pritchard, 1989). Evidence for shorter latencies in brainstem-evoked auditory potentials for introverts than for extraverts has also been reported (Stelmack & Houlihan, 1995).

PERCEPTUAL AND COGNITIVE STYLES

The notion that personality is reflected in perception is at the heart of projective techniques such as the Rorschach Inkblot Test and the Thematic Apperception Test. Although not all assumptions regarding the determinative influence of personality on perception have been verified, a significant amount of research has found moderate, but significant, relationships between personality characteristics and certain aspects of perception. For example, it has been demonstrated that, compared with extraverts, introverts are more vigilant, more sensitive to pain, and more disrupted by overstimulation (G. Wilson, 1978). Speed of responding on several perceptual and learning tasks (e.g., word recognition, identification of incomplete figures, dark adaptation, and conditioning) is also related to personality (Eysenck, 1962; Eysenck & Rachman, 1965). However, the majority of these tasks are rather crude measures and show no immediate signs of replacing traditional personality assessment devices.

Field Independence/Dependence

One of the most systematic series of investigations of the relationships between personality and perception was conducted by Herman Witkin and his colleagues (Witkin & Goodenough, 1977; Witkin et al., 1973). Three tests (Body Adjustment Test, Rod and Frame Test, and Embedded Figures Test) were used in these studies to classify individuals as field independent or field dependent. On the Body Adjustment Test, the subject (person) is seated in a chair located in a tilted room and directed to adjust the chair to a true vertical position. On the Rod and Frame Test, the person is seated before a luminous rod situated in a luminous square frame in a darkened room and instructed to adjust the rod to the true vertical position when the rod and frame are tilted in opposite directions. On the Embedded Figures Test, the speed with which simple figures can be found in a series of complex forms is determined (Fig. 8.3). According to Witkin, these three tests measure much the same thing: the ability to differentiate aspects or parts of a complex, confusing whole. People who are able to find the upright position accurately and the embedded figures quickly are field independents, whereas those who have difficulty finding the upright position and locating the embedded figures are field dependents.

Of particular interest is that field independents and field dependents tend to have different personalities. Witkin's description of a typical field-independent person is that of a secure, independent, more psychologically mature, self-accepting individual who is active in dealing with the environment, tends to use intellectualization as a defense mechanism, and is more aware of his or her inner experiences. In contrast, a typical

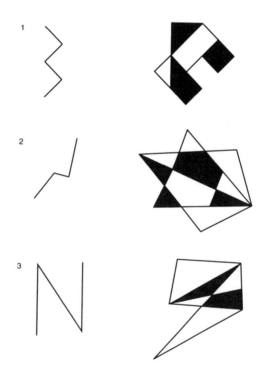

FIG. 8.3.   Sample item on the Embedded Figures Test. People who have difficulty locating the figures at the left in the complex patterns at the right may be characterized as field dependent. (From Witkin, Moore, Goodenough, & Cox, 1977. Adapted by permission of the publisher.)

field-dependent person is less secure, psychologically immature, passive, less attuned to inner experiences, and more likely to use repression and denial as defenses. Gender and sociocultural differences in these two perceptual styles have also been found. Males are typically more field independent than females, and members of hunting and foraging cultures are more field independent than those living in sedentary, agricultural societies (Witkin & Berry, 1975). In terms of childrearing practices, the parents of field independents are usually less restrictive and less authoritarian than those of field-dependent children.

Cognitive Styles

Field independence and field dependence have been referred to as *perceptual styles,* but the way in which people come to know and understand the world also involves cognition. For this reason, perhaps a more appropriate term for designating the various strategies or approaches that people employ in their efforts to understand their experiences and deal with them more effectively is *cognitive styles.* Although they involve mental processing, cognitive styles may also be construed as characteristics of personality. Research has been conducted on various cognitive styles, including: reflectivity/impulsivity, broad/narrow categorizing, intolerance for ambiguity (for incongruous or unrealistic experiences), cognitive complexity/simplicity, and automatization/restructuring (Bostic & Tallent-Runnels, 1991). Several of these styles are related to strategies or modes of thinking and problem solving (analytic vs. synthetic, abstract vs. concrete, etc.) that were investigated long before the term *cognitive styles* became fashionable. In addition, the various styles are not independent of one another. Finally, it may be that preference for a particular cognitive style varies not only with the person but with the situation or problem.

Other than field independence/dependence, the greatest amount of research has been conducted on the *reflective/impulsive style.* Reflectives are slow and accurate in solving problems, whereas impulsives are quick and inaccurate. Kagan's (1966) Matching Familiar Figures Test, an illustrative item that is shown in Fig. 8.4, is a popular measure of the reflective versus impulsive style. On each of the items on this test, the child's time and accuracy in correctly determining which of several response figures matches the stimulus figure are recorded. Reflective children tend to respond more slowly and more accurately than impulsive children.

Various theories or models of cognitive styles have been proposed, one example being McKenney and Keen's (1974) two-dimensional information-assimilation model. At the two poles of the first dimension in this model are the preceptive and receptive planning modes; the two poles of the second dimension are the systematic and intuitive modes. Preceptives assimilate information by "chunking" it into their own concepts or categories, whereas receptives assimilate information in a raw form, thereby storing it as new data rather than concepts. Systematics create orderly, sequential plans or strategies, whereas intuitives, who prefer ideas rather than

FIG. 8.4. Sample item from the Matching Familiar Figures test. The examinee is told to select the picture in the second or third row that is identical to the picture in the first row. (From Kagan, 1966. Copyright © 1966 by the American Psychological Association. Reprinted with permission.)

plans, skip the part analysis of a problem and move immediately to a whole analysis. Scores on each pole of the model are determined by different tests: the preceptive mode by an elaboration test, the receptive mode by an identical pictures test, the systematic mode by a paper-folding test, and the intuitive mode by a scrambled-words test.

Although many of the references to research on cognitive styles are several decades old, interest in their assessment and applications continues in the United States, Great Britain, and other countries (e.g., Epstein, Pacini, Denes-Raj, & Heier, 1996; A. Jones, 1997; Riding & Read, 1996; Sorrentino, Holmes, Lhanna, & Sharp, 1995; Wooten, Barner, & Silver, 1994). After reviewing the literature on cognitive styles and presenting their own theory and research, Sternberg and Grigorenko (1997) concluded that cognitive styles are still in style and potentially as useful as tests of cognitive abilities in predicting performance in school and occupational contexts.

DEMOGRAPHIC CORRELATES

As with scores on tests of cognitive abilities, scores on measures of personality vary with gender, birth order, ethnicity, culture, and other demographic variables. This has led designers of standardized rating scales, inventories, and other personality assessment devices to provide different norms for different demographic groups.

Gender

Women make significantly higher scores on the Depression scale of the MMPI–2 (Hathaway & McKinley, 1989); on the Hypochondriasis and Anxiety scales of the Basic Personality Inventory; on the Empathy, Anxiety, Cooperativeness, Organization, Traditional Values, and Responsibility scales of the Jackson Personality Inventory–Revised; and on the Affiliation, Harmavoidance, Nurturance, Play, Sentience, Social Recognition, and Succorance scales of the Personality Research Form. In contrast, men score higher than women on the Denial, Interpersonal Problems, Alienation, and Social Introversion scales of the Basic Personality Inventory; on the Innovation, Energy Level, and Risk Taking scale of the Jackson Personality Inventory–Revised; and on the Achievement, Aggression, Autonomy, Change, Dominance, Endurance, and Understanding scales of the Personality Research Form (D. Jackson, 1989a, 1989b, 1994). Whether these gender differences in personality test scores are fundamental or due simply to a greater willingness by women than men to admit certain behaviors but not others is debatable. However, gender differences in temperament and personality are observable from early childhood and would appear to be influenced substantially by heredity. This is particularly true of traits such as aggressiveness and dominance (Plomin, 1994).

Chronological Age

One fairly consistent finding concerning the relationship of personality to chronological age is that the incidence of depression is higher in older than in younger adults (Olin et al., 1992). On the average, older adults are also more conforming (Lanyon, 1973, 1978), less active, less hostile, and less impulsive than their younger contemporaries (Rubin, 1981). The stereotype of older adults as rigid and traditional is descriptive of some people, but many other older adults are quite flexible and open-minded (Helson & Moane, 1987).

The general pattern of an individual's personality traits is established fairly early in life, becoming more pronounced but not changing appreciably with age. Introversion/extraversion, openness to experience, neuroticism, and sociability are relatively stable from childhood through early and even later adulthood (Costa & McCrae, 1994; McCrae & Costa, 1984). Although men tend to grow somewhat more introverted with aging, extraverted young men tend to remain that way in middle and old age. However, the degree of continuity of personality across the life span varies with the individual. The personalities of some people are highly consistent, whereas others continue to develop and change. Changes in personality can be precipitated by dramatic or traumatic life events, such as severe losses or frustrations, but such events may have a positive, negative, or no effect whatsoever.

To some extent, continuity of personality across the life span can be attributed to the fact that people are attracted to environments that fit their personalities and consequently necessitate little change on their part to adapt (Ahammer, 1973). Furthermore, people tend to create their own environments and even their own personalities as they interact with the world and learn what is possible and what is not, what is rewarded and what is not. A human being is not a mere automaton cast this way and that by an impersonal environment, but rather a thinking, planning creature with ideas, aspirations, and dreams concerning what he or she wants to become and obtain. Consequently, the observed stability of personality may be determined more by the individual than the environment in which he or she lives (Lerner & Busch-Rossnagel, 1981).

Evidence pertaining to the stability of personality has also been obtained in research on another demographic variable: marital status. Not only are men and women more likely to marry individuals with personalities that are similar to their own, but husbands and wives who are temperamentally similar mutually reinforce each others' characteristics. In contrast, spouses who are dissimilar in certain respects influence each other to change and become more alike (Caspi, Herbener, & Ozer, 1992).

Birth Order

As noted in chapter 6, family size, birth order, socioeconomic status (SES), nationality, and culture are all related to cognitive abilities. Not surprisingly, these same demographic variables influence personality. For example, research has revealed a tendency for first-born children to be more serious, responsible, studious, and competitive, whereas later-born children are more outgoing, relaxed, imaginative, and athletic (Altus, 1966; Eisenman, 1992; Kilbride, Johnson, & Streissguth, 1977). These personality differences have been attributed to the fact that parents are usually more anxious and restrictive with first-borns and spend a greater amount of time with them than with later-borns. This is particularly true when the first-born child is a girl. An interaction between birth order and gender is also seen in the fact that first-born males are more creative than later-born males, but the reverse is truer of females (Eisenman, 1992).

Ethnicity

Because ethnic background is related to scores on many psychological tests, separate norms for Whites, Blacks, and other racial/ethnic groups have been provided on some tests. Gynther (1981) noted that Blacks typically make higher scores that Whites on MMPI scales measuring nonconformity, alienation, and impulsivity. Dahlstrom and Gynther (1986) concluded that these findings were valid and not caused by any ethnic group bias in the MMPI items. However, they recommended that research on the adequacy of the MMPI for different ethnic groups be continued. In a subsequent study of the scores of Black and White men who took the MMPI–2 as a part of their court-ordered forensic psychological evaluation, men in the former group scored higher than those in the latter group on two content scales: Cynicism and Antisocial Practices (Ben-Porath, Shondrick, & Stafford, 1995). And in a sample of combat veterans examined by Frueh, Smith, and Libet (1996), Black veterans showed greater elevations than White veterans on the F–K index and Scales 6 (Paranoia) and 8 (Schizophrenia) of the MMPI–2.

Culture

The notion that people of different nationalities or cultures have distinctive, enduring patterns of behavior and/or personality characteristics has occupied scholars, statesmen, and even marketers for many years (see T. Clark, 1990). Scientific investigations of the relationships of culture and personality date back at least to the cross-cultural research of Bronislaw Malinowski, Ruth Benedict, and Margaret Mead. These cultural anthropologists maintained that individual and cultural differences in personality and behavior are due largely to differences in socialization. With respect to Western, and particularly American, culture, Whiting and his colleagues (C. Edwards & Whiting, 1980; Whiting & Edwards, 1988) contrasted the emphasis on independence, self-assertiveness, and achievement in Western culture with the social interdependence and cooperativeness stressed by many non-Western cultures. Such culture-specific personality characteristics are interpreted as the results of differential reinforcement of certain behaviors. For example, in certain cultures, *bad* behaviors are punished but *good* behaviors are not rewarded. Some cultures reinforce shyness and formality in new situations, whereas other cultures emphasize boldness and risk taking.

Personality characteristics that typify a given culture depend to some extent on traditions, the nature of the economy, and what characteristics are considered important to survival. In traditional agricultural societies, for example, group cooperation is considered essential for planting, tending, harvesting, and storing crops, so responsibility, reliability, and obedience are more likely to be emphasized. In traditional hunting/gathering societies individual ability, initiative, and bravery are deemed more important. Consequently, these societies place a greater premium on achievement, self-reliance, and independence (Barry, Child, & Bacon, 1959). Even so, a particular society is rarely successful in fostering culturally desirable characteristics in all its members, and individual differences in personality persist despite social pressures to conform.

OTHER CORRELATES OF PERSONALITY

In research designs based on Path B in Fig. 8.1, studies are conducted to determine the effectiveness of measures of personality as predictors for purposes of selection, classification, and diagnosis. The extent to which these measures can make accurate distinctions is determined by validity studies (see chap. 2). The results of these studies are expressed as correlation coefficients, regression coefficients, percentages of criterion variance accounted for by the personality variables, and other indexes of predictive validity.

Vocational Interests and Personality

The prediction of occupational choice and performance is primarily a statistical matter, but efforts have been made to supply it with a theoretical foundation. An illustration is J. L. Holland's (1985) theory of vocational personalities, which is based on the premise that people seek and remain in environments that are congruent with their personalities. People are happier, more satisfied, and more productive in such environments than in those that are incongruent with their personalities. Because the theory maintains that congruence between an individual's personality and particular occupations is the primary factor in occupational selection, stability, and satisfaction, when the personality and environment are incompatible, either the environment must change or the person must find a more compatible environment.

Holland's RIASEC (Realistic, Investigative, Artistic, Social, Enterprising, Conventional) model of vocational choice consists of the six vocational personalities symbolized in Fig. 8.5 and six corresponding work environmental themes. Both the work environments and the personalities are idealizations, and any individual personality is a composite of two or more ideal types. The consistency of an interest pattern is determined by the extent to which the person's scores on the six personality variables are close to each other in the hexagonal model in Fig. 8.5. Patterns in which only one or two of the six scores are high are said to be more differentiated than those with a larger number of high scores. A person who has only a few vocational goals is said to have a keen sense of personal identity, whereas environmental identity is present when the goals, tasks, and rewards in a particular environment are stable over time. Another condition, that of congruence, is said to exist when the personality types match the environmental types.

Holland's vocational personalities model has served as a stimulus for research on career interests and choices for many years. When complemented by measures of vocational aspiration, it has achieved notable successes. In addition, the variables in the RIASEC model have been shown to be closely related to four of the Big Five personality variables (Tokar & Swanson, 1995). However, Holland (1996) has argued that the model should be revised to include the idea that different belief systems are characteristic of different personality types and are promoted by different environments. He maintained that the explanatory power of the model should be improved by selectively incorporating the concepts of career beliefs and strategies into it.

Personality Assessment in Employment Contexts

Personality assessment instruments may be administered in (a) the workplace to forecast productivity, accidents, and other aspects of on-the-job

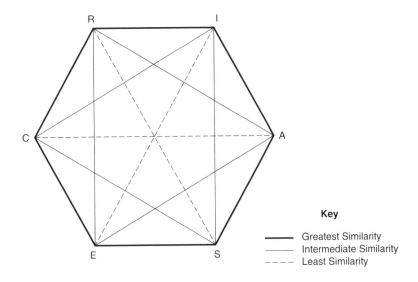

Key

— Greatest Similarity
—— Intermediate Similarity
- - - - Least Similarity

FIG. 8.5. Holland's hexagonal (RIASEC) model of vocational personalities. A corresponding set of six themes is used to describe work environments. R= Realistic, I = Investigative, A = Artistic, S = Social, E = Enterprising, C = Conventional.

behavior; (b) schools and colleges to predict course grades, adaptability, and other indexes of academic and nonacademic performance; and (c) government and military situations to predict many of these same criteria. Personality tests may also be administered in clinical and counseling contexts to analyze and diagnose personal problems and disorders. Hundreds of research investigations designed to evaluate the effectiveness of personality assessment instruments and procedures in the prior situations have been conducted over the years, but the results have been interpreted in various ways.

Although the use of personality tests in educational and employment situations has been criticized as invalid and intrusive (e.g., Furnham, 1992), these instruments have sometimes contributed to the selection of applicants for jobs and programs. An example of one such success was the application of the MMPI to the selection of Peace Corps candidates (Hobbs, 1963; Wiggins, 1973). More recently, Barrick and Mount (1991) found that measures of conscientiousness were reliable predictors of job proficiency and turnover in five occupational groups.

A review of the research literature on personality assessment in business and industry concluded that the findings provide some grounds for optimism concerning the use of personality measures in employee selection, particularly when the tests are selected on the basis of job analyses and when job-tenured employees are studied (Tett, Jackson, & Rothstein, 1991). Various writers (e.g., Furnham, 1992; Hogan, Hogan, & Roberts, 1996) have concluded that there is sufficient evidence to justify the continued use of personality testing in the workplace. Hogan, Hogan, and Roberts (1996) maintained that well-constructed personality measures are reliable and valid forecasters of on-the-job performance, nondiscriminatory, and have fewer shortcomings than alternative methods of assessment (assessment center, interview, honesty/integrity tests, biographical data, cognitive tests, etc.).

Personality Traits as Moderator Variables

As illustrated by Path D in Fig. 8.1, background factors can have a direct effect on behavior without the intervention of personality. For example, many reflexes and other automatic or conditioned behaviors are not dependent on or influenced by personality. Another example is a strong situation or environment in which the vast majority of people conform and behave alike regardless of their individual penchants or idiosyncracies. However, as illustrated by Path C in Fig. 8.1, personality variables usually combine with background variables to influence behavior outcomes. Personality and background variables may combine in a simple additive manner or the pairing may be an interactive one in which the effects of a specified background variable depend on the state of a particular personality variable. For example, the relationship between parenting behavior and child behavior may be different for introverted and extroverted children. The possible results of another situation, in which the personality variable of compulsivity interacts with cognitive ability (a background variable) to affect academic performance, is depicted in Fig. 8.6. In this hypothetical case, the slope of the line relating grade point average (GPA) to cognitive ability is higher and steeper for compulsive than for noncompulsive students.

Perhaps less common than the ordinal interaction pictured in Fig. 8.6 is a disordinal interaction, in which the two prediction lines cross. For example, Stacy et al. (1992) found a modest disordinal interaction in the effects of social influence on adolescent smoking. The smoking tendencies of both low and high self-efficacy adolescents increased as their friends' social influence became stronger. However, there was a disordinal interaction between the personality variable (self-efficacy) and the independent variable (social influence) in the effects of these two variables on the dependent variable (smoking tendency). When the social influence of friends was weak, smoking tendency was lower for adolescents with low self-efficacy than for those with high self-efficacy. However, when the social influence of friends was strong, smoking tendency was higher for adolescents with low self-efficacy than for those with high self-efficacy (see Fig. 8.7).

Personality variables, such as those in the two examples described earlier, are sometimes referred to as *moderator variables,* in that they affect the correlation between background and behavioral outcome variables. Consider the results of an investigation on predicting the job performance

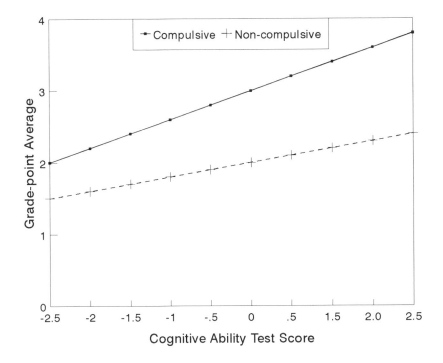

FIG. 8.6.   Moderating effect of level of compulsivity on the relationship between grade point average and ability test score.

of warehousers from scores on tests of personality and ability (Wright, Kacmar, McMahon, & Deleeuw, 1995). As shown in Fig. 8.8, the personality variable—achievement need—was positively related to performance among high-ability workers but negatively related to performance among low-ability workers. In this investigation, ability was the moderator variable and a personality characteristic (achievement need) was the independent variable. In most instances, it makes little difference whether the personality variable is thought of as moderating the effects of background variables or the background variables as moderating the effects of personality. In a study conducted on a group of British employees, for example, gender was the moderator variable; anxiety was found to be negatively correlated with height for men but not for women (Melamed, 1994).

Comparison between correlation coefficients is not the only statistical procedure by which the effects of moderator variables may be determined. Mixed-designs analysis of variance (ANOVA), analysis of covariance (ANCOVA), and multiple-regression analyses may all be appropriate for analyzing the independent and joint effects of background and intervening personality variables on behavior. Unfortunately, the moderator variable approach to behavior prediction has not been a resounding success. Following Zedeck's (1971) review of relevant studies of moderator variables up to 1970, interest in adapting this approach to employee selection waned. More recently, a number of measures of personality (locus of control, hardiness, Type A, optimism, neuroticism) and coping have served as moderator variables in investigations of stress/strain relations at work. The theory and methodology of these investigations is more sophisticated than those of earlier studies, and further research is encouraged (Parkes, 1994).

SUMMARY

Research on personality is guided by psychological theories, logic, and previous empirical findings from research and practice. Psychodynamic, phenomenological, trait-factor, behavioral, and cognitive theories all pro-

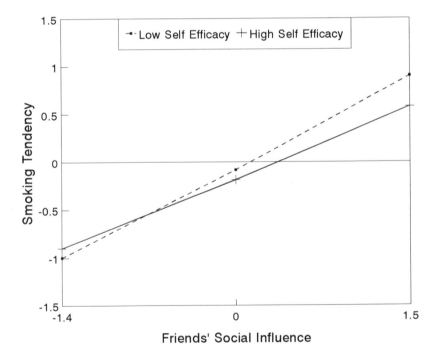

FIG. 8.7.   Moderating effect of self-efficacy on the relationship between friends' social influence and smoking tendency. The broken line depicts the results for the low self-efficacy group; the unbroken line depicts the results for the high self-efficacy group (Adapted from data in Stacy et al., 1992).

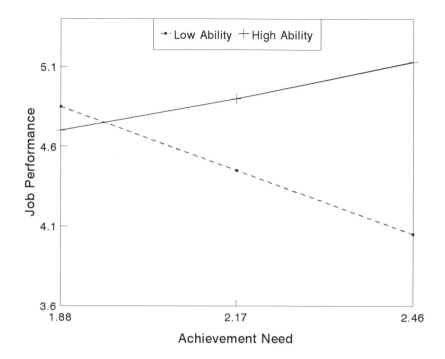

FIG. 8.8.   Moderating effect of ability on the relationships between achievement
need and job performance. The broken line is a plot of the results for the low-ability
group; the unbroken line is a plot of the results for the high-ability group (Adapted
from Wright et al., 1995).

vide explanations and predictions for human behavior and are better than
no theories at all in the business of science making. In addition to serving as
models for research and practice, personality theories (trait-factor theories
in particular) have served to stimulate the construction of various psychometric instruments. However, the rating scales, inventories, projectives,
and other personality assessment devices prompted by a particular theoretical persuasion have not been limited in their use to testing the propositions or verifying the predictions of that theory. Such instruments have often been administered in empirical studies prompted by other hypotheses
and for psychodiagnostic purposes. However, theories of personality are
much less precise than theories in the natural sciences, and the tests and
techniques for assessing individual differences in personality are less reliable and valid than in physics, chemistry, and biology. For these reasons,
the science of personality consists mainly of heuristic principles rather than
definitive conclusions or laws.

Depending on the particular purposes and design of a research investigation, personality variables may serve as background variables, outcome variables, or intervening (moderator) variables. Most research studies with personality variables have used them as predictor or background variables for forecasting behavioral outcomes.

Substantial evidence obtained from studies of twins and other relatives point to a strong genetic component in various personality traits. Among these traits are introversion/extraversion, altruism, aggressiveness, emotionality, activity level, and shyness. Heredity also plays an important role in various personality problems and mental disorders, including anxiety, fears, obsessions, alcoholism, bipolar disorder, and schizophrenia. Statistical indexes or measures for representing the contribution of heredity to personality characteristics are correlation and regression coefficients, proportions of variance accounted for, and heritability coefficients.

Various neurophysiological indicators of autonomic and brain functioning are related to personality characteristics, but efforts to find specific patterns of physiological responses that are indicative of specific emotional states or personality characteristics have not been successful. Research concerning the relationships of neurotransmitters and receptor sites to personality characteristics appears promising.

Personality characteristics vary with gender, age, birth order, ethnicity, culture, and parental behavior. The effects of these variables on personality are, however, far from uniform across different individuals.

Holland's RIASEC model linking vocational interests and career choices to personality traits has had some notable successes, but further revisions of the model, incorporating into it the concepts of vocational aspirations and career beliefs and strategies, are needed. Efforts to use personality traits as intervening or moderator variables in predicting employee and student performance from ability and other background variables have also met with some success. However, enthusiasm for the moderator variable approach to prediction—in employment as well as academic and clinical situations—has waned in the past two or three decades.

SUGGESTED READINGS

Bouchard, T. J. (1994). Genes, environment, and personality. *Science, 264,* 1700–1701.

Butcher, J. N., & Rouse, S. V. (1996). Personality: Individual differences and clinical assessment. *Annual Review of Psychology, 47,* 87–111.

Epstein, S. (1997). This I have learned from over 40 years of personality research. *Journal of Personality, 65*(1), 3–32.

Feist, J. (1994). *Theories of personality* (3rd ed.). Ft Worth, TX: Harcourt Brace.

Holland, J. L. (1996). Exploring careers with a typology. *American Psychologist, 51,* 397–406.

Pervin, L. A. (1996). Personality: A view of the future based on a look at the past. *Journal of Research in Personality, 30,* 309–318.

Pervin, L. A. (1996). *The science of personality.* New York: Wiley.

Plomin, R., Owen, M. J., & McGuffin, P. (1994). The genetic basis of complex human behaviors. *Science, 264,* 1733–1739.

Rose, R. J. (1995). Genes and human behavior. *Annual Review of Psychology, 46,* 625–654.

Ruth, J.-E., & Coleman, P. (1996). Personality and aging: Coping and management of the self in later life. In J. E. Birren, K. W. Schaie, R. P. Abeles, M. Gatz, & T. A. Salthouse (Eds.), *Handbook of the psychology of aging* (4th ed., pp. 308–322). San Diego, CA: Academic Press.

Saudino, K. J., & Plomin, R. (1996). Personality and behavior genetics: Where have we been and where are we going? *Journal of Research in Personality, 30,* 335–347.

Stelmack, R. M., & Houlihan, M. (1995). Event-related potentials, personality, and intelligence: Concepts, issues, and evidence. In D. H. Saklofske & M. Zeidner (Eds.), *International handbook of personality and intelligence* (pp. 349–365). New York: Plenum.

CHAPTER NINE

Personality Problems
and Disorders

Like news reporters, behavioral scientists have often been criticized for focusing more on the negative than the positive features of human experience—on illness rather than health, tragedy rather than triumph, and conflict rather than community. If this is so, there is good reason for it. Success and happiness are rarely viewed as problems requiring solutions, but failure and sadness are. When things go well, people seldom ask for help and none is needed, but when things go wrong in either a personal or societal sense, the human community must be informed so it can direct its resources toward solutions and assistance. Among the difficulties that confront almost everyone at one time or another are those concerned with human relationships, illness and accidents, injury and loss, and how to use one's abilities to obtain what is needed and desired in the time that is available. This chapter is concerned with the personal and social misfortunes that confront people. It focuses on three topics in which personality characteristics play a role: illness and accidents, mental disorders, and crime. These are social as well as personal matters, but personality is shaped by social interactions.

STRESS AND ILLNESS

We live in a constantly changing world, subject to events that are often unpredictable and uncontrollable. Even when we think that we are ready for everything and can handle anything, life has a tendency to surprise and confront us with something that was not anticipated. Furthermore, even when we have planned and prepared for a particular event, we may become so excited and wound up that we have difficulty dealing with it in a rational manner. In any case, whether the event is rewarding or punishing, pleasant or unpleasant, it produces a certain amount of stress that must be dealt with in some manner.

Stress may be physical or psychological, and specific or general. Selye's (1976) *general adaptation syndrome* (GAS) theory is concerned with

196

nonspecific stress—a reaction of the body to any stressor. The stress produced by a stressor prompts a physiological reaction sequence that leads to an expenditure of a greater amount of energy than usual. The first stage, or alarm reaction, consists of the mobilization of the body's resources through increased activity of the autonomic nervous system (ANS). During this stage, corticosteroid hormones are secreted by the adrenal glands and the immune system becomes more active. Following the initial alarm reaction is a second stage of the GAS: a stage of resistance. At this stage, the signs of the alarm reaction diminish and the body settles in for a long-term siege. If the body's resources become depleted, the third and final stage of the syndrome—exhaustion—occurs. In this stage, the body's capacity to withstand stressors declines, and the individual may become permanently incapacitated.

Stressors include physical conditions such as injuries to the body, lack of sleep, and inadequate or improper nourishment, as well as psychological events such as frustration, conflict, and loss. Disasters and catastrophes (plane crashes, tornadoes, etc.), in which more than one person is involved, are obviously stress provoking, but so are everyday hassles (getting to school or work on time, getting caught in traffic) and disruptions or changes in one's life. Hassles, which are frequently referred to as background or secondary stressors, are usually dealt with fairly easily. However, personal problems, such as a serious illness, academic failure, loss of a job, death of a loved one, or other primary stressors can produce a much higher level of stress.

Stress may be accompanied by physical symptoms and disorders involving the gastrointestinal, musculoskeletal, respiratory, circulatory, and other body organs and systems. Peptic ulcers, migraine headaches, chronic backache, bronchial asthma, and neurodermatitis are among the most common reactions to emotional stress. According to many medical practitioners, all illness is psychosomatic, in the sense that it is the joint product of physical and psychological factors—of the body and the mind.

Research evidence shows that, by suppressing the response of the immune system, stress increases one's susceptibility to a wide range of disorders (Cohen & Williamson, 1991; Kiecolt-Glaser & Glaser, 1992, 1993). Depression and other negative emotions, in particular, act as sources of stress that suppress the immune system and increase the likelihood of life-threatening illness (Herbert & Cohen, 1993; Weisse, 1992). However, patients who are able to verbalize their problems and feelings about their illness tend to have a greater chance of survival than those who keep their feelings bottled up inside (O'Leary, 1990; Temoshuk, 1992).

Burnout, Bereavement, and Posttraumatic Stress Disorder

Among the stress-related conditions that have received particular attention by psychologists are burnout, bereavement, and posttraumatic stress disorder (PTSD). The symptoms of burnout are headaches, backaches, emotional exhaustion, lessened productivity, social withdrawal, and feelings of depersonalization. Burnout is more common in compulsive, insecure workaholics whose jobs no longer provide them with a sense of self-fulfillment. Such individuals generally experience low self-esteem in their activities outside the workplace, and they attempt to compensate by becoming workaholics. As a result, burnout victims receive recognition and rewards on the job, but overwork finally catches up with them.

Symptoms of psychosomatic disorder (headaches, depression, gastrointestinal disorder, oversleeping, irritability, loss of interest, lack of energy, increased alcoholic intake, reduced efficiency) are also found in some recently retired workers (Butler & Lewis, 1982) and in bereavement (see chap. 10).

Called by different names in previous wars and times, but still the same syndrome, is *posttraumatic stress disorder* (PTSD)—a condition precipitated by any traumatic event (combat, natural disasters, accidents, rape, etc.). Attacks of anxiety, insomnia, nightmares, social interaction difficulties, substance abuse, and in some cases a reexperiencing of the stressful event (flashbacks) are among the symptoms of PTSD. The individual may avoid important activities, become emotionally numb, have difficulty sleeping, be hyperalert, and experience other signs of excessive arousal. PTSD can also lead to severe depression, marital problems, and divorce, which are understandably more common among victims of combat (E. Hunter, 1981). Such symptoms are also seen in civilians who have experienced earthquakes, airplane crashes, shipwrecks, and other highly stressful events (see Box 9.1).

Personality Variables

As schematized in Fig. 9.1, the appraisal and reaction to a stressful situation depend not only on its severity but also on the cognitions and personality of the individual. Cognitions that influence the perception of a stressor consist of the individual's beliefs and feelings about disease and the cognitive and behavioral strategies (e.g., denial, submission, aggression, reasoning, etc.) that have proved effective in coping with similar events or situations in the past. The particular strategies that are employed in dealing with stressors also vary with the temperament, self-concept, and other personality characteristics of the individual. In general, a person's cognitive and personality styles are fashioned fairly early in life. The associated behavioral patterns that develop in childhood and young adulthood are harbingers of what will happen to the person and what he or she will become later in life.

The findings of numerous research studies underscore the fact that personality adjustment in childhood and young adulthood influences physical and mental health in middle and older adulthood. For example, Vaillant

FIG. 9.1.   Determinants of stress.

Box 9.1: Clinical Case: Posttraumatic Stress Disorder

Frank is a 42-year-old long-distance truck driver. Four months ago on a trip from Kansas City just after sundown there was a light rain. A motorcyclist going well over 80 mph without a helmet passed his truck. The motorcyclist moved over into his lane, hit a patch of slick road, and started to slide. Frank attempted to turn his truck to avoid the motorcyclist but still hit him with his left tire. The quick turn also caused Frank to lose control of his rig; he went off the side the road and his truck rolled over. Frank sustained severe injuries to his back and a piece of glass struck and severely damaged his left eye.

During the past 3 months, Frank has been having nightmares in which he relives the accident. He is also having trouble sleeping and wakes up if there is the slightest noise. He has been unable to drive since the accident, although his doctor has released him. Frank has also been unable to travel (even as a passenger) on a freeway since his accident. Frank's wife drives back streets when she takes him to his physician appointments. Frank's wife has been very supportive, but she is concerned that the accident has changed him, and she cannot quite understand why he cannot drive. If Frank sees a motorcycle, he becomes very distressed: His heart starts to race, he becomes light headed, and he starts to sweat. He has also been unable to even visit his former employer because the sight of large trucks also makes him distressed.

Source. Case study reprinted with permission of Drake University.

(1979) found that male college students who were diagnosed as *poorly adjusted* were much more likely than those who had been diagnosed as *well adjusted* to become seriously ill and die in middle adulthood. Vaillant interpreted these findings as indicating that good adjustment and positive mental health have a beneficial effect on physical well-being in midlife, whereas poor adjustment has the opposite effect.

Among the personality variables that have been examined for their relationships to stress reactions are hardiness (Funk, 1992; Kobasa, 1979; Kobasa, Maddi & Kahn, 1982), optimism (Scheier & Carver, 1992; Wengler & Rosen, 1995), Type A personality (Cooper, Kirkcaldy, & Brown, 1994), neuroticism (Larsen & Kasimatis, 1991; Bolger & Zuckerman, 1995), self-identity (J. Brown & McGill, 1989), self-efficacy (Bandura, 1989; Kempen, Jelicic, & Ormel, 1997), and self-healing (Friedman, 1991). Perhaps most extensively studied of all these variables is the so-called *Type A personality,* described as aggressive, competitive, hostile, quick-acting, and constantly striving. Research on the Type A personality led Friedman (1990; Friedman & Booth-Kewley, 1987) to conclude that a personality characterized by depression, anger/hostility, and anxiety is an important factor in coronary heart disease (CHD). In fact, these three variables are associated with a range of bodily complaints (Watson & Pennebaker, 1989).

Another series of studies in health psychology has been concerned with *hardiness*—the ability to withstand stress and remain healthy (Kobasa, 1979). Hardiness consists of the following three characteristics:

commitment—a clear sense of purpose, involvement with other people, and the ability to recognize one's goals, priorities, and values;

control—the ability to select a course of action, incorporate external events into a dynamic life plan, and be motivated to achieve; and

challenge—a feeling that change is positive and one has an opportunity to integrate his or her life goals into new situations.

Compared with people who have a high incidence of physical illness, those with a low incidence of physical illness score higher on measures of hardiness. Of course, this does not prove that hardiness acts as a buffer against illness: Physical illness may decrease feelings of hardiness or both variables may be caused by something else (e.g., heredity). However, research findings indicate that a sense of control is the key ingredient in the role of hardiness in coping with the effects of stressful conditions such as noise and crowding (Funk, 1992).

The predictability of a stressor and the ability to control it have been emphasized by other investigators as important factors in coping with stress. The concept of control is also inherent in the perceptual style of *locus of control* (Rotter, 1966). People who have an internal locus of control believe that they can control their own lives, whereas those with an external locus of control believe that their lives are controlled by fate, luck, or other external forces.

Hardiness is only one of the variables comprising what Friedman (1991) called a *self-healing personality*—a personality consisting of characteristics that promote good health. A second trait in the self-healing personality is optimism—a generalized tendency to expect positive rather than negative outcomes to a situation. Optimists report having fewer symptoms of physical illness, take an active, problem-focused approach in coping with stress, and recover more quickly from illness and surgery (Scheier & Carver, 1985, 1992). Seligman (1991) described optimism and pessimism as attributional or explanatory styles. In contrast to pessimists, optimists are more likely to blame their failures on external, temporary, and specific factors and credit their successes to internal, permanent, and global factors. This approach fosters hope, effort, and a high regard for oneself. Optimists have also been found to have stronger immune responses than pessimists, which may help account for the fact that people who are optimistic in their youth tend to be healthier in later life than those who are pessimists (Kamen-Siegel et al., 1991; Peterson, Seligman, & Vaillant, 1988). In addition, optimism can be instilled by self-training in making more optimistic interpretations of one's experiences (Seligman, 1991).

Coping Styles

A related cognitive model of coping is the distinction made by Folkman and Lazarus (1980) between *problem-focused* and *emotion-focused* strategies. The former consists of obtaining additional information to actively alter a stressful situation, whereas the latter consists of employing behavioral or cognitive techniques to manage the emotional tension produced by the situation. In general, research has shown that young adults prefer more problem-focused forms of coping, as in confrontation, planning, and seeking social support. In contrast, older adults prefer more emotion-focused forms of coping, as in distancing, accepting responsibility, and positive reappraisal (Folkman, Lazarus, Pimley, & Novacek, 1987). As people grow older, they are less likely to employ confrontation and aggression and more likely to cope by using denial, detachment, humor, and other passive strategies (Felton & Revenson, 1987; Folkman et al., 1987).

Not all factors that are instrumental in coping with stress and illness are personal: Social support is also important. Social support from interested, caring people in times of stress has both a cognitive and an emotional component. Not only does it provide emotional assistance, but information is obtained on what is to be expected and what actions should be taken to deal with the situation. As documented by the classic Alameda County Studies (Berkman & Syme, 1979) and other research on the role of social support in illness (Baron et al., 1990; Case et al., 1992; L. Clark, 1993; S. Taylor, 1990), social interaction is positively associated with both physical and mental health.

Personality and Disease Specificity

Stimulated to some extent by psychoanalytic theories of personality, for many years medical researchers attempted to discover links between personality characteristics and specific physical illnesses. Dunbar (1943) maintained that underlying every psychosomatic disorder is a predisposing personality pattern or conflict. The target organ or system associated with the disorder was believed to be symbolically connected to a mental conflict of some sort. Reflective of this hypothesis is Dunbar's assertion that it is "more important to know what kind of patient has the disease than what kind of disease the patient has" (p. 23). The quest was taken up by F. Alexander and French (1948), who maintained that bronchial asthma, essential hypertension, peptic ulcers, and many other physical disorders are related to intrapsychic conflicts (oral, anal, maternal, etc.). Environmental events were thought to trigger particular conflicts, producing emotional reactions and giving rise to specific physical disorders. For example, acne was said to be caused by guilt over exhibitionism, colitis by an inability to fulfill obligations, diabetes by frustrated dependency needs, and hyperthyroidism by psychic trauma stemming from loss of the mother during childhood. A list of personality variables associated by these researchers with certain other disorders is given in Table 9.1.

TABLE 9.1
Hypothesized Relationships Between Personality
and Specific Illnesses

Illness	Associated Personality Characteristics
Arthritis	Perfectionism, excessive interest in athletics, competitiveness
Cancer	Passivity, hopelessness in the face of stress, tendency to suppress resentment, marked inability to forgive
Diabetes	Chronic anxiety and depression
Gastric ulcers	Passivity, dependency
Hypertension	Hostility, competitiveness
Migraine headaches	Perfectionism, rigidity, resentment, unconscious hostility, preoccupation with success
Tension headaches	Dependency, depression, worry, sexual conflicts

Note. Most of these relationships between personality characteristics and specific illnesses have not been confirmed by research.

Mothers, in particular, were believed by psychoanalytic theorists to play a critical role in the determination of health problems. Concepts such as *asthmatogenic mother,* described as an overprotective, rigid individual who blurs the boundaries between parent and child roles, were fashionable during this period. However, in recent years it has become clear that the relationships between personality characteristics and physical illness described by these researchers are, for the most part, nonexistent. Even when there is a connection, the personality variables are more likely to be the results of the illness rather than vice versa (Ezrin, 1977). For example, there is little or no support for specific personality characteristics or intrapsychic conflicts being causal agents in diabetes, asthma, or rheumatoid arthritis (Creer & Kotses, 1983; Dunn & Tuttle, 1981; Spergel, Ehrlich, & Glass, 1978).

There is some evidence of a relationship between psychological problems and headaches (Blanchard, Andrasik & Arena, 1984). In addition, anger and hostility appear to be contributing factors in cardiovascular disease. However, there is no evidence of a particular personality syndrome being a determinant of a specific illness. The existence of an *alcoholic personality,* a *headache personality,* an *ulcer personality,* or an *AIDS personality* are not supported by research.

Anorexia

A possible exception to this generalization is *anorexia nervosa*, which is an eating disorder characterized by a pathological fear of being fat and consequent excessive dieting and emaciation. Anorexia and bulimia are approximately nine times as common in females as in males (Hartung & Widiger, 1998). Most anorexics are young White women from upwardly mobile, achievement-oriented families. They are characterized as dissatisfied with their bodies, afraid of losing self-control, driven, hardworking, and perfectionistic. These characteristics are similar to those found in obsessive–compulsive disorder (Davis et al., 1995). Many anorexics are interpersonally distrustful, describing their mothers as domineering, ambivalent, intrusive, and overbearing and their fathers as "emotional absentees" (Carson & Butcher, 1996).

Psychodynamic explanations of anorexia view it as a way of exerting control or denying one's sexuality. Another factor that undoubtedly contributes to anorexia in young women is the societal emphasis on thinness. Biological factors, such as a malfunctioning hypothalamus, have also been explored as possible causes of anorexia and accompanying menstrual irregularities (Licinio, Wong, & Gold, 1996).

Accidents and Personality

Every year over 90,000 lives are lost and hundreds of thousands of disabling injuries are sustained from accidents in the United States. Accidents involving motor vehicles are the most common cause of accidental death, but falls, poisoning, drowning, fires, suffocation, and firearms also take their toll in the home, at work, in motor vehicles, and in public places. These accidents, which are more likely to occur at night, on weekends, during holidays, and during the summer and fall than at other times, are caused by a combination of unsafe conditions and unsafe acts (National Safety Council, 1998).

Among the individual difference variables that are related to accidents are age, physical condition, intelligence, and personality. Teenage and elderly drivers have higher rates of automobile accidents than other age groups, and the death rate for accidents other than those involving motor vehicles is substantially higher in old age than at other times of life. Sensory defects and loss of motor coordination contribute to the higher accident rate for older people, who are less likely to perceive potentially dangerous situations (small objects on the floor, open doors or other projecting objects, something burning, etc.). Although it is clear that health and fatigue influence the accident rate, the results of studies of the relationship of cognitive abilities to accidents are unclear. Inexperience with a task increases the likelihood of an accident, but lower than average intelligence appears to be a factor only on jobs requiring frequent judgments (Schultz & Schultz, 1993). Even less conclusive are the findings of studies of the relationships of personality characteristics to accidents.

At one time, a great deal of attention was focused on the so-called *accident-prone personality*. It was maintained that, because of temperament or habit pattern, people with this type of personality are more likely to have accidents. The observation that in job situations a small number of workers seemed to have a large percentage of the accidents appeared to give credence to this notion, but later research failed to show that accident proneness is a consistent personality characteristic. This does not mean, of course, that temporary emotional states such as anger or depression cannot increase the likelihood of an accident. Any emotional or cognitive state that distracts a person or induces him or her to take unwarranted risks can increase the chance of an accident and consequent injury.

The results of a number of investigations offer support for a connection between specific personality characteristics and accidents. For example, Shaw and Sichel (1971) found that accident repeaters were less emotionally stable, more hostile toward authority, higher in anxiety, and had more problems getting along with other people and less stable work histories than nonrepeaters. Another early study found that individuals characterized as excessively ambitious and harboring revengeful attitudes had a higher than average accident rate (McGuire, 1976). More recently, Niemcryk, Jenkins, Rose, and Hurst (1987) found that air-traffic controllers who displayed Type A behavior were more likely than those showing Type B behavior to experience injuries on the job. Even more comprehensive was a study conducted by Hansen (1989) on the relationships of biodata, personality, and cognitive variables to accidents in a large sample of industrial chemical workers. Hansen found that a social maladjustment scale constructed from the MMPI and a measure of neurotic distractibility were both significantly and independently related to the rate of accidents.

Hansen's study and those conducted by other researchers (e.g., Arnett, 1990; Montag & Comrey, 1987; Perry, 1986) led Furnham (1992) to conclude that there is good evidence that personality variables are related to all kinds of accidents in all sorts of populations. For example, with regard to traffic accidents the results of recent research indicate that drivers with higher levels of arousal take more risks, are more likely to engage in thrill and adventure-seeking behavior, and are less inhibited in socially stimulating situations than drivers with lower levels of arousal (Trimpop & Kirkcaldy, 1997). The results of other studies indicate that an aggressive–competitive personality (Magnavita et al., 1997), alcoholism, or a personality disorder of some kind (McDonald & Davey, 1996), and a low level of conscientiousness (Arthur & Graziano, 1996) are more common among people who have a greater number of automobile accidents. Furthermore, Caspi et al. (1997) found that many of the personality characteristics that are related to dangerous driving habits in early adulthood could be identified in early childhood and were also associated with other risky behaviors (alcohol dependence, violent crime, unsafe sex) engaged in at age 21.

MENTAL DISORDERS[1]

The diathesis stress model sees the occurrence of a mental disorder as a consequence of stress acting on a biopsychosocial predisposition toward the condition. According to this viewpoint, stress alone does not usually lead to severe mental disorders. Rather, when combined with predisposing factors such as cerebral trauma, neurochemical imbalance, or developmental difficulties, stress acts as a precipitating stimulus. As shown in Table 9.2, a variety of demographic variables are also associated with frequent mental distress. The statistics listed in this table were obtained from a telephone survey of a large random sample (436,107) of adults in the United States between 1993 and 1996. The percentages of respondents who reported frequent mental distress were higher among women than men, 18- to 24-year-olds than other age groups, Native American/Alaska Natives than other race/ethnicity groups, separated or widowed adults than those of other marital status, persons who had not graduated from high school than those with more education, the unemployed than the employed, and those with annual incomes of less than $15,000 than those with larger incomes (Center for Disease Control, 1998).

Statistics on Mental Disorders

Approximately 1 in 10 Americans experiences some disability because of schizophrenia, depression, panic disorder, obsessive–compulsive disorder, or another mental disorder at any given time, and 1 in 4 has a serious mental disorder during his or her lifetime (see Fig. 9.2). Each year over 30 million people who are suffering from mental disorders make office visits to physicians in the United States. Over 16% of these consultations are for depression, 4.5% are for schizophrenia, and 11% are for anxiety disorders. Drugs are the most popular treatments for these mental disorders, and approximately 80 million prescriptions are written for psychopharmacological drugs. The total annual cost of all kinds of treatments for mental illness in this country surpasses $150 billion, with treatments for schizophrenia alone amounting to $30 billion (National Institute of Mental Health, 1998).

Schizophrenia

The most chronic and disabling of all mental disorders is schizophrenia, which affects more than 2 million Americans each year. Schizophrenia is more common in lower than in middle and upper socioeconomic areas and more common in children born in the winter months. Both infectious agents and obstetric complications, or factors closely associated with them, are the most plausible explanation for the winter excess of schizophrenia (Bradbury & Miller, 1985).

---

[1]Serious emotional disturbances in children, which can have a pronounced influence on cognitive abilities and learning, are discussed briefly in chapter 7. However, children and adolescents, as well as adults, may also develop many of the disorders described in the present chapter.

TABLE 9.2

Percentages of a National U.S. Sample of Respondents Reporting Frequent Mental Distress

Variable	%
Sex	
Male	10.1
Female	6.9
Age	
18–24	10.0
25–34	8.7
35–44	9.4
45–54	9.1
55–64	7.8
65–74	6.1
75+	6.8
Race/Ethnicity	
White, non-Hispanic	8.3
Black, non-Hispanic	9.7
Hispanic	10.3
Asian/Pacific Islander	6.1
Native American/Alaskan Native	12.9
Other	10.7
Marital Status	
Married	7.3
Divorced	13.4
Widowed	15.9
Separated	18.5

(continued on next page)

Never married	9.3
Unmarried couple	12.0

Education Level	
Less than high school graduate	12.9
High school graduate	9.0
Some college or technical school	8.6
College graduate	5.9

Employment Status	
Employed for wages	6.7
Self-employed	7.0
Unemployed 1 year or less	14.7
Employed more than 1 year	17.8
Homemaker	9.4
Student	9.6
Retired	11.9
Unable to work	33.2

Annual Household Income	
Less than $15,000	15.5
$15,000–$24,999	10.0
$25,000–$49,999	7.2
$50,000 or over	5.7

Source. Self-reported Frequent Mental Distress Among Adults—United States, 1993–1996. (May 1, 1998). *Morbidity and Mortality Weekly Report,* Vol. 47, No. 16. Washington, DC: Center for Disease Control.

The onset of schizophrenia is typically in the late teens or early 20s, and on the average it develops earlier in males than in females (Kalat, 1998). Like cancer, schizophrenia is not a single disease entity, and the symptoms vary from person to person (Heinrichs, 1993). Overt symptoms may include auditory (hearing voices) and visual (seeing visions) hallucinations, delusions (false beliefs), and disordered thought processes. In addition to

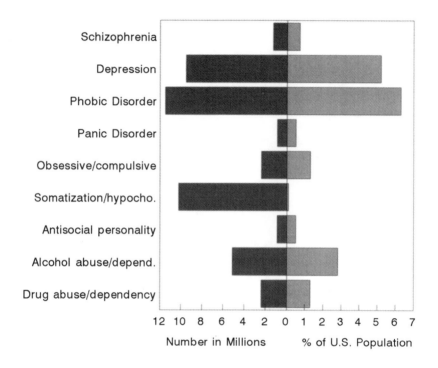

FIG. 9.2.   Statistics on mental disorders in the United States. (Source: National Institute of Mental Health).

these so-called *positive symptoms* are *negative symptoms,* such as social withdrawal, blunted emotional reactivity, and inadequate self-care and motivation (Andreasen et al., 1995). Most chronic schizophrenics are meek and mild individuals who are not dangerous and often prefer to spend their lives in the less stressful environment of a mental hospital. However, the legal requirement that patients who are not considered dangerous to themselves or other people must be eventually released from an institution results in many schizophrenics wandering and living in the streets of large cities. Separated from the routine and structure of institutional life, they often fail to take their prescribed medications or care for their physical needs properly and thus are frequently a source of annoyance to other people.

Schizophrenia is generally believed to have a biological basis, and there is substantial evidence that the condition runs in families (Gottesman, 1991). One theory is that early onset schizophrenia is due to a failure of cerebral neurons to form appropriate connections during fetal development—a structural error that is not expressed until puberty (Weinberger, 1996). According to this neurodevelopmental hypothesis, stressful experiences can aggravate the symptoms but do not by themselves cause the disorder.

Various antipsychotic drugs, including Thorazine, Mellaril, Clozaril, and Haldol, often have dramatic effects on the remission of symptoms in schizophrenia. Unfortunately, many of these drugs, which block dopamine or stimulate glutamate synapses, have side effects such as drowsiness, nausea, dry mouth, photosensitivity, dizziness, and tremors, which often increase in frequency and severity as the patient continues taking the drug.

Affective Disorders

Even more common than schizophrenia are affective (mood) disorders, which affect approximately 18 million American adults annually. The fourth edition of the *Diagnostic and Statistical Manual of Mental Disorders (DSM–IV)* (American Psychiatric Association, 1994) describes two major types of affective disorders: major depression and bipolar disorder. The symptoms of major depression are persistent depression in thought and mood, sleep disturbance, reduced appetite, and low energy. The ability to concentrate, remember, and think are affected, and feelings of pessimism and worthlessness are also present.

The biological basis of depression is unclear. In most depressed patients, the level of activity in the right prefrontal cortex is greater than that in the left and the level of cortisol released by the adrenal cortex is elevated (Licinio, Wong, & Gold, 1996; Starkstein & Robinson, 1986). A genetic basis for the disorder is suggested by the fact that depression tends to run in families (Weissman et al., 1984). Treatments for depression include medications such as Wellbutrin capsules, Prozac, Zoloft, and Tofranil, and, in certain cases, electroconvulsive shock therapy (ECT).

The symptoms of bipolar disorder are mixed, consisting of the alternation of depressive and manic episodes. During the manic phase, energy and mood are heightened, thinking is sharpened and creative, and the patient is self-confident but irritable. In extreme mania, the patient has grandiose delusions and his or her behavior becomes psychotic and disruptive. The evidence of genetic causation is even stronger for bipolar disorder than for schizophrenia (Blackwood et al., 1996; Freimer et al., 1996; Ginns et al., 1996). Lithium is effective in reducing the severity of symptoms in both the manic and depressive episodes of bipolar disorder, but other medications may also be prescribed (Schou, 1997). As with other psychotropic medications, lithium can have side effects (tremors, headaches, memory impairment, fatigue, lethargy, nausea, excessive urination, diarrhea), and is contraindicated for patients with cardiovascular or kidney disease.

Pronounced mood swings also occur in *seasonal affective disorder* (SAD), particularly among residents of regions close to the North Pole where there are many more hours of daylight in the summer than in the winter. Patients with SAD are depressed in winter but feel happier and more active during the summer (Madden, Heath, Rosenthal, & Martin, 1996). The condition is often treated by having the patient sit in front of very bright lights for an hour or more before the sun rises or after it sets or even in the middle of the day (Penev, Zee, & Turek, 1997).

Anxiety Disorders

Several different types of anxiety disorders have been identified, five of the most serious being generalized anxiety disorder, panic disorder, phobias, obsessive–compulsive disorder, and PTSD. The primary symptom of all five conditions is intense anxiety, but in the last four it is accompanied by other symptoms. In *panic disorder*, the person has repeated attacks of terror or fear that strikes suddenly and without warning. There are feelings of impending doom and various physical symptoms (accelerated heartbeat, gasping, sweating, muscle weakness, dizziness, and feelings of unreality). In *phobias* (claustrophobia, agoraphobia, etc.), anxiety is directed toward a particular object or situation that the person is desperate to avoid. Characteristic of *obsessive–compulsive disorder* (OCD) are recurrent, unwanted thoughts (obsessions) and ritualized, seemingly purposeless acts. The fourth type of anxiety disorder—PTSD—was discussed earlier in the chapter. Most anxiety disorders are treatable with a combination of behavioral therapy and medication. Among the behavioral therapies that have been successfully applied to the treatment of anxiety are systematic desensitization, counterconditioning, and extinction (Wolpe, 1982). Cognitive therapies of the sort described by Beck (1993) are also useful in treating anxiety disorders. Included among the medications for anxiety are Valium, Xanax (for panic disorder), BuSpar tablets, Vistaril capsules, and Prozac (for obsessive–compulsive disorder).

Suicide

Suicide is not a disorder in itself, but rather an ever-present threat in certain stressful conditions or mental disorders. For example, an estimated 1 in 10 persons with schizophrenia dies of suicide. Suicide is an even greater risk in cases of severe depression and is more common in older White males than in any other demographic group. However, depression is not the only factor in suicide. Personality traits such as impulsivity and aggressivity, as well as factors such as addiction, suicide or attempted suicide in close relatives, divorce, separation, and parental discord are all possible contributors to attempted suicide (Bronisch, 1996; Maltsberger, 1997).

The rate of suicide varies with age, sex, and race/ethnicity. A typical suicidal patient is a White, male, Protestant over 45 years and probably addicted to alcohol and/or drugs. Living alone, isolated, with limited support, and either separated, divorced, widowed, or never married are also red flags for suicide.

Various antianxiety and antidepressant drugs are prescribed in the treatment of suicide, but counseling is also important in enabling the individual to get control over his or her life.

DIAGNOSIS

Table 9.3 is a list of the major categories of the fourth edition of the *DSM–IV* (American Psychiatric Association, 1994). The diagnostic system of *DSM–IV* is multiaxial, in that the patient is classified on the following five different axes: I. Clinical Disorders, II. Personality Disorder & Mental Retardation, III. General Medical Conditions, IV. Psychosocial and Environmental Problems, and V. Global Assessment of Functioning. Each patient's condition is labeled with a five-digit code on Axis I and Axis II and rated in severity as *mild, moderate,* or *severe.* Physical disorders accompanying the diagnosed mental disorder(s) are classified on Axis III, and the severity of the accompanying psychosocial stressors is classified on Axis IV. Finally, a global assessment of the patient's functioning (GAF) is made on Axis V.

Once a diagnosis has been made, inpatient treatment may be provided in a state or county mental hospital, a private psychiatric hospital, a

TABLE 9.3

Major Diagnostic Categories in *DSM–IV*

Disorders Usually First Diagnosed in Infancy, Childhood, or Adolescence: Mental retardation, learning disorders, motor skills disorder, communication disorders, pervasive developmental disorders, attention deficit and disruptive behavior disorders, feeding and eating disorders of infancy or early childhood, tic disorders, elimination disorders, other disorders of infancy, childhood, or adolescence

Delirium, Dementia, Amnestic, and Other Cognitive Disorders Due to a General Medical Condition Not Elsewhere Classified

Substance-Related Disorders: Alcohol-related disorders, amphetamine-related disorders, caffeine-related disorders, cannabis-related disorders, cocaine-related disorders, hallucinogen-related disorders, inhalant-related disorders, nicotine-related disorders, opioid-related disorders, phencyclidine-related disorders, sedative-, hypnotic-, or anxiolytic-induced disorders, polysubstance-related disorder, other substance-related disorder

Schizophrenia and Other Psychotic Disorders

Mood Disorders: Depressive disorders, Bipolar disorders

Anxiety Disorders

Somatoform Disorders

Factitious Disorders

Dissociative Disorders

Sexual and Gender Identity Disorders: Sexual dysfunctions, Paraphilias, Gender identity disorders

Eating Disorders

Sleep Disorders: Primary sleep disorders, sleep disorders related to another mental disorder, other sleep disorders

Impulse-Control Disorders Not Elsewhere Classified

Adjustment Disorders

Personality Disorders

Other Conditions That May Be a Focus of Clinical Attention

Source. American Psychiatric Association, 1994.

nonfederal general hospital psychiatric service, a Department of Veterans Affairs psychiatric service, a residential treatment center for emotionally disturbed children, or a free-standing psychiatric outpatient clinic. Patients are treated in these facilities on an inpatient, outpatient, or partial care treatment basis. The most common psychiatric diagnosis among all age groups is affective disorder, but schizophrenia is the second-most common diagnosis in young and middle-aged adults. Alcohol-related disorder increases in frequency up through young adulthood and then declines; organic disorders increase gradually up through older adulthood (National Center for Health Statistics, 1995). Many older adults with organic disorders (Alzheimer's, multi-infarct dementia, Parkinsonism, Korsakoff's syndrome, Creutzfeldt–Jakob disease, etc.) are cared for in nursing homes and other long-term care institutions.

Gender Differences

Anxiety disorders (panic, phobias, separation anxiety, etc.) and depression are approximately twice as common in women as in men (Culbertson, 1997), but men are four times as likely as women to commit suicide (R. Anderson, Kochanek, & Murphy, 1997). The incidence of schizophrenia is approximately the same in both sexes, as are delusional disorder, bipolar I disorder, cyclothymic disorder, obsessive–compulsive disorder, and hypochondriasis. Attention deficit hyperactivity disorder (ADHD), conduct disorder, and eliminative disorders (enuresis, encopresis) are more common in boys than girls, and antisocial personality, substance-related disorders, and sexual disorders are more common in men than in women. Schizoaffective disorder, bipolar II disorder, conversion disorder, and somatoform disorder are more common in women than men. Of the various sleep disorders, insomnia and nightmares are more common in females and breathing-related sleep disorder is more common in males, but sex differences in the incidence of narcolepsy, sleep terrors, and sleepwaking disorders are not significant. Among the various personality disorders (see next section), paranoid, schizoid, schizotypal, antisocial, and compulsive personality disorders occur more often in males; borderline, histrionic, and dependent personalities disorders are more common in females; and the two sexes are about equal in narcissistic and avoidant personality disorders (Hartung & Widiger, 1998).[2]

Personality Disorders

The vast majority of individuals who come to the attention of psychiatrists, clinical psychologists, and other mental health professionals are suffering from anxiety reactions, depression, or psychotic symptoms (withdrawal from reality, distorted thought processes and perception, etc.). However, there is another group of psychopathological conditions that are not classified as psy-

---

[2]It is advisable to exercise caution in interpreting these gender differences in mental disorders. As pointed out by Hartung and Widiger (1998), sampling bias and problems with the diagnostic criteria are potential sources of error in the results of investigations concerned with gender differences.

choneuroses or psychoses in which the individual does not feel anxious or disturbed, yet the personality is so different from normal that he or she is unable to be a productive, contributing member of society. In such individuals, cognition, affectivity, interpersonal functioning, or impulse control may all deviate markedly from what is expected of people in a particular culture. These *personality disorders,* as they are labeled, are stable, pervasive patterns of experience and behavior that have developed by adulthood, are expressed across a variety of situations, and are resistant to change.

Ten of the most common personality disorders are listed in Table 9.4. The three disorders in Cluster A (paranoid, schizoid, schizotypal) are characterized by odd or eccentric behavior. People diagnosed as having disorders in this cluster have abnormal cognitions or ideas, speak or act in strange ways, and experience difficulties in relating to others. The four disorders in Cluster B (antisocial, borderline, histrionic, narcissistic) are characterized by dramatic, emotional, or erratic behavior. People diagnosed as having disorders in this cluster tend to be impulsive, often violate social norms, act out, and can be self-abusive and hostile toward others. The three disorders in Cluster C (avoidant, dependent, obsessive–compulsive) are marked by frequent anxiety and fearfulness. People diagnosed as having disorders in this cluster are excessively afraid of social relations and have feelings of being out of control. Other problems such as substance abuse, unemployment, divorce and family problems, and criminality are also associated with many of these disorders. Personality disorders may not be clearly manifested in behavior until early adulthood, but childhood conditions such as problems with conduct, social interactions, or self-identity are often forerunners of them. A sample case of a disorder in each of the three clusters is described in Box 9.2.

Of the various types of personality disorders, antisocial personality, also known as psychopathic or sociopathic personality, is the most socially destructive and therefore has stimulated the greatest amount of research. Not all antisocial personalities are criminals; in fact, some become quite prominent businessmen, politicians, and other influencers of people. However, the irresponsible, unpredictable, unreliable, and aggressive attitudes of antisocial personalities frequently lead to lying and deception, alcohol and drug abuse, stealing, vandalism, and violence—all with no apparent sense of guilt. Many of these individuals are superficially charming, have good verbal skills, and are average or above average in intelligence. These characteristics, when combined with an adventurous, thrill-seeking attitude, make such persons successful manipulators, con men, and swindlers who prey on unsuspecting, trusting people.

CRIMINAL BEHAVIOR

Given an exact reckoning, and not just a count of those apprehended and charged, the number of Americans who have committed a prosecutable criminal offense at one time or another would surely amount to a substantial majority of the population. Statistics on the types of criminal offenses and their relationships to various demographic variables are discussed in

TABLE 9.4

Personality Disorders

Personality Disorder	Characterized by a Pervasive Pattern of
Paranoid	Distrust and suspiciousness of others such that their motives are interpreted as malevolent
Schizoid	Detachment form of social relationships and a restricted range of expression of emotions in interpersonal settings
Schizotypal	Social and interpersonal deficits marked by acute discomfort with and reduced capacity for close relationships, as well as by cognitive or perceptual distortions and eccentricities of behavior
Antisocial	Disregard for and violation of the rights of others
Borderline	Unstable interpersonal relationships, self-image, and affects; marked impulsivity
Histrionic	Excessive emotionality and attention seeking
Narcissistic	Grandiosity in fantasy or behavior, need for admiration, and lack of empathy
Avoidant	Social inhibition, feelings of inadequacy, and hypersensitivity to negative evaluation
Dependent	Excessive need to be taken care of that leads to submissive and clinging behavior and fears of separation
Obsessive– Compulsive	Preoccupation with orderliness, perfectionism, and mental and interpersonal control at the expense of flexibility, openness, and efficiency

Source. Adapted from descriptions in the *Diagnostic and Statistical Manual of Mental Disorders* (4th ed.) by the American Psychiatric Association (1994).

chapter 10. This section is not concerned with the incidence of particular crimes, but rather with theories and research on the sociopsychological causes of criminal behavior and violent offenses in particular.

Theories of Criminal Behavior

What causes people to commit crimes? Is it anger, material deprivation, a need for excitement, self-esteem, compulsion, or impulsiveness? Surely all of these things, and many others as well, are immediate stimuli for certain crimes. Still, as in the case of mental illness and human behavior in general,

Box 9.2:   Three Cases of Personality Disorders

Schizotypal Personality Disorder.   Fred is a 29-year-old unemployed man. He states that he can often read people's minds and finds it disturbing to be in crowds. He thinks other people know that he is reading their minds, and resent him. He often feels he is leaving his body, but can concentrate on not *slipping away.* He states he does not have hallucinations, but he does think that he can help his family if he concentrates real hard on their safety when, for example, they take a trip on an airplane. He had a girlfriend for about a year when he was in college. He said that "she got tired of my reading her mind." She also wanted to go out and do more, but Fred stated that he was just too uncomfortable in social situations.

Fred has held a number of relatively unskilled jobs, such as dishwasher, parks maintenance, and book store clerk. He often had difficulty getting to work on time and felt that his boss was always watching him. He has trouble with schedules, and some days he feels "too spacy" to be around anyone. He has neither been in the hospital nor received any medications. He applied for rehabilitation services because he thinks he needs some help finding and keeping a good job.

Borderline Personality Disorder.   Becky is 25 years old. She was recently released from the hospital after she drove her car into Ben's (her boyfriend's) office. He sells real estate and has an office on the first floor of a strip mall. She said she wanted to kill herself and him because he split up with her and she is "devastated" with pain.

Becky has had seven live-in boyfriends since she left her parents' home at the age of 15. She usually meets someone, falls "madly in love," and moves in with him within weeks. After a few months, she discovers that he is not as wonderful as she first thought. She starts to see the man as mean, withholding, selfish, and lazy. They often have numerous fights with separations and reunions. After a year or so, Becky usually finds a new man and begins the cycle again. Becky had been living with Ben for about 3 months prior to the accident.

Becky has held "about a hundred" jobs. She is often enthusiastic and a great worker for the first few weeks. She then starts to complain about the coworkers and begins to have conflicts with her supervisor. She often quits or is fired after an angry shouting match with her supervisor.

Becky is requesting rehabilitation services because she is so "depressed" and hurt; she is not sure she will ever feel happy again. She still thinks about killing herself but not as much. She wants help finding a job where the people will appreciate her and they do not all turn out to be mean and selfish.

Avoidant Personality Disorder.   Todd is a 23-year-old man who was brought to ACME Rehabilitation by his mother. His mother says she is sure there is something wrong with him and she would like ACME's help getting him a job. Todd graduated from high school 5 years ago, but has never worked. He stays at home all day. He has no friends, although he "chats" with strangers over the Internet. Todd's grades in school were average. He did not like PE in school because he was afraid of being hurt. He likes to read and orders books and magazines through the mail. He does not like to go out and does not like to talk to strangers because they are often "abrubt" with him. If family or friends come to the house, he will speak to them, but he reports that it makes him feel awkward and uncomfortable.

Source. Case studies reprinted with permission of Drake University.

criminal acts have both predisposing and precipitating causes. Biological, sociological, and psychological theories of crime deal more with the predisposing or background factors that increase the probability of committing crimes. However, it is recognized that even people who do not show a predisposition for crime may become criminals if the situation is sufficiently provocative or appealing.

Biological Theories. Among the biological factors that have been examined for their contributions to criminal behavior are a genetic predisposition toward criminality, a particular body build, a damaged brain, and an excess or deficit of certain hormones or other biochemicals. With respect to genetics, Rushton and Erdle (1987) estimated that 40% of the population variance in the trait of aggressiveness, which appears to play a role in violent crime in particular, can be accounted for by heredity. The incidence of head injuries and other types of neurological aberrations or problems has also been found to be greater in people who commit violent crimes (Goleman, 1987a, 1987b; Jutai, Hare, & Connolly, 1987; D. Lewis, Pincus, Bard, & Richardson, 1988).

Another series of investigations focused on chromosomal abnormalities such as the XYY pattern (Court-Brown, 1968). One of the most thorough studies found an above-average frequency of police records among the small percentage of men with the XYY pattern (42% of the .3% with XYY had police records), but the difference was attributed to the below-average IQs of the XYY men (Witkin et al., 1976). In addition, a mesomorphic body build has also been found to be more common in delinquents than in nondelinquents (Glueck & Glueck, 1950, 1956).

More recent research on biological factors in criminality has concentrated on testosterone (e.g., Dabbs, Carr, Frady, Riad, 1995) and lower platelet monoamine oxidase (MAO) activity (af-Klinteberg, 1996; Alm, af-Klinteberg, Humble, & Leppert, 1996; Kristiansson, 1995) in criminals and noncriminals. For example, Dabbs et al. (1995) found that prison inmates who had committed personal crimes of sex and violence had higher testosterone levels than prisoners who had committed property crimes.

The high-testosterone prisoners also violated more prison rules, especially those involving overt confrontation. In another series of research investigations, af-Klinteberg (1996, 1997) and his co-researchers found evidence for a negative relationship between platelet MAO activity with hyperactivity in adolescents and violent criminal behavior in adults. This research is intriguing, but so far it has failed to provide conclusive proof of the role of biological factors as causes and predictors of criminal behavior.

Sociological Theories.   Sociological explanations of criminal behavior stress the importance of sociocultural factors such as inequality of opportunity to attain socially defined personal and material goals (Cloward & Ohlin, 1960). Conflicts between the norms of the dominant culture and those of various subcultures are also considered to be important (W. Miller, 1958). For example, Miller viewed adherence to the "trouble, toughness, smartness, excitement, fate, and autonomy" traditions of the lower class as incongruent with the dominant middle-class values in the United States, and consequently a serious cause of social problems. The concept of *differential association*, which asserts that criminal behavior results from socialization of the individual into a value system that supports such behavior, has also been emphasized by certain sociologists and criminologists (Sutherland, 1939). From another sociological perspective, criminal behavior is viewed as a consequence of society's labeling certain acts as deviant. According to this proposition, the criminal's behavior as well as the reactions to that behavior and the labels placed on it by society contribute to the view of the behavior as deviant (Gove, 1980; Lemert, 1972).

Psychological Theories.   One of the oldest psychological theories of criminal behavior is Freud's interpretation of it as a reaction to a com- pulsive need for punishment resulting from feelings of guilt associated with the Oedipus complex (Wrightsman, 1994). Other psychoanalysts have viewed criminality as more characteristic of immature personalities, who lack control over id impulses, or as the manifestation of a failure to internalize the reality principle and thereby control impulses for immediate gratification (Nietzel, 1979). Behavioral and social learning theorists have stressed the role of interpersonal interaction, reinforcement, and modeling as determinants of criminal behavior (Bandura, 1977; Conger, 1980). To a great extent, their viewpoint that antisocial behavior stems from inadequate control of the individual by external social pressures is in keeping with traditional childrearing lore. Finally, cognitive dispositional theorists such as Yochelson and Samenow (1976; see also Samenow, 1984, 1996) maintained that criminals perceive and think about the world in different ways than noncriminals. For this reason, Samenow (1996) argued that criminal behavior is altered not by rehabilitation but by changing the way the criminal thinks.

Correlates and Predictors of Criminal Violence

Certain crimes of violence such as serial murder, sadistic rape, and child molestation are viewed by society as so horrendous that it is often assumed that the perpetrators are mentally ill. Only a minority of people who commit crimes suffer from severe mental disorders, but the probability of violent crime is higher than average among those with antisocial personalities, borderline personality disorder, schizophrenia, major depressive disorders, manic disorder, paranoid disorders, and mental retardation (Crocker & Hodgins, 1997; Eronen, 1995; Eronen, Hakola, & Tiihonen, 1996; Hodgins et al., 1998; Holden, Pakula, & Mooney, 1997; Kreutzer, Marwitz, & Witol, 1995; Rice, 1997; P. Taylor et al., 1998; Tiihonen, Hakola, & Eronen, 1995). Accompanying many cases of mental disorder associated with violent crime, as well as violent crime in general, are alcohol and substance abuse (Eronen, 1995; Eronen, Hakola, & Tiihonen, 1996; McKenzie, 1995; Tiihonen, Hakola, & Eronen, 1995; Vuckovic, Misic-Pavkov, & Doroski, 1997).

Considering the importance of being able to forecast violent criminal acts as early as possible, and particularly whether persons who have already committed such acts will do so again, it is not surprising that dozens of research studies have been conducted with violent offenders of all ages (see Monahan, 1996). Under the assumption that the seeds of violence are sown in childhood and adolescence, particular attention has been paid to the behaviors and personalities of juvenile delinquents. The results of many of these studies confirm the ordinary observations that the best predictor of future behavior is past behavior and the best predictor of future violence is past violence. Even so, many false-positive and false-negative cases are observed when the frequency of previous violence is used to predict violent behavior.[3]

Some of the other background variables associated with criminal violence and related offenses are listed in Table 9.5. A number of personality inventories have also been administered in research on violent behavior. Foremost among these are the Multidimensional Personality Questionnaire (Caspi et al., 1997; Krueger et al., 1994), the Psychopathy Checklist (Alm, af-Klinteberg, Humble, & Leppert, 1996; Hill, Rogers, & Bickford, 1996; Hodgins, 1997; Rice, 1997; Serin & Amos, 1995), and the Eysenck Personality Questionnaire (Sigurdsson & Gudjonsson, 1996). A number of studies have found high scores on psychopathy-related scales of these inventories, indicating high impulsivity, exploitativeness, low conformity, and sensation seeking, in violent offenders (Daderman & af-Klinteberg, 1997; Quinsey, 1995).

SUMMARY

The events and circumstances to which people are exposed contribute to their personality characteristics. Those characteristics, in turn, affect the selection and modification of their living environments. Thus, personality influences and is influenced by fortune and misfortune. This chapter deals primarily with the misfortune side of the coin—in particular, the role of personality as correlate, cause, and effect in stress, physical illness, accidents, mental disorders, and criminal behavior.

---

[3]A *false-positive error* occurs when violence is predicted but does not occur; a *false-negative error* occurs when violence is not predicted but does occur.

TABLE 9.5
Background Variables Linked by Research to Violent Crime

* Low reading ability, deviant mother–child interactions, frequent changes of residence before age 9, several changes of parents during childhood, a single parent, criminal convictions by age 18 (Henry, Caspi, Moffitt, & Silva, 1996).

* Maladjustment in elementary school; separation from parents before age 16; criminal history; single, separated, or divorced; history of alcohol abuse (Quinsey, 1995; Rice, 1997).

* Hyperactivity–impulsivity–attention problems, conduct problems (af-Klinteberg, 1997; Lynam, 1996).

* High number of school, social, personal, and family problems; gang membership; arrests (Cox, 1996).

* Aggressive and antisocial behaviors in childhood (Geberth & Turco, 1997).

* Alcohol abuse (Kreutzer, Marwitz, & Witol, 1995).

Stress—the physical and psychological response to an emergency situation or other stressor—ranges from everyday hassles to fatal accidents or illnesses. Selye's GAS is a three-stage (alarm reaction, resistance, exhaustion) physiological response of the organism to any stressor. A variety of physical symptoms and disorders may be caused or exacerbated by prolonged stress. Among these are psychosomatic conditions such as chronic headaches, backaches, or gastrointestinal disorders. Burnout, bereavement, and PTSD are three psychological syndromes that are characterized by reactions to stressful situations.

Personality variables found by research to be related to stress reactions include hardiness, optimism, Type A personality, locus of control (internal/external), neuroticism, self-identity, and self-efficacy. The concept of self-healing personality includes the traits of hardiness and optimism. The ability to predict and control stress, which is obviously important in reducing its effects, is possessed to a greater degree by people with certain personality characteristics.

Ways of coping with stress vary not only with personality, but with age, sex, race/ethnicity, and culture. For example, young adults prefer problem-focused forms of coping (confrontation, planning, seeking social support), whereas older adults prefer emotional-focused forms of coping (distancing, accepting responsibility, positive reappraisal). Social support is also important in providing both emotional and cognitive assistance in times of stress.

The results of research on connections between specific personality characteristics or intrapsychic conflicts and specific illnesses have not been very positive. For example, there does not appear to be any such entity as an alcoholic personality or an ulcer personality. However, there is evidence for significant relationships between psychological characteristics or problems and certain conditions (e.g., chronic headaches, anorexia).

Depression and anxiety are two major symptoms of mental disorder, but a variety of other affective, cognitive, and perceptual symptoms may also be present. The diathesis stress model of mental disorder views abnormal behavior as the consequence of a precipitating stressful situation acting on a predisposing biopsychosocial substrate.

Although the organic bases for schizophrenia, severe depression, and bipolar disorder have not been clearly identified, there is sound evidence for the role of genetic factors in each of these conditions. Pharmacological and other treatments can help control the symptoms of these disorders, but they cannot cure them. When combined with psychotherapy, drugs are also helpful in treating anxiety disorders (generalized anxiety disorder, panic disorder, phobias, obsessive–compulsive disorder, PTSD) and other psychiatric conditions.

Personality disorders, which are pervasive, persistent, maladaptive patterns of behavior that are highly resistant to change, are grouped by *DSM–IV* into three clusters: A (paranoid, schizoid, schizotypal), B (antisocial, borderline, histrionic, narcissistic), and C (avoidant, dependent, obsessive-compulsive). Of these 10 personality disorders, antisocial personality—characterized by extreme self-centeredness, hostile and hurtful actions, lack of guilt feelings, difficulty in forming close personal relationships, manipulative and dishonest behavior, and a seeming inability to profit from experience—has been the subject of the greatest amount of research and writing.

Various background factors of a biological, psychological, or sociological nature have been proposed as predisposing causes of crime. Among the biological factors are heredity, chromosomal abnormalities, head injuries or other neurological disorders, body type, and chemical imbalances. Sociological theories of crime point to factors such as inequality of economic and social resources and opportunities, conflict with group norms, differential association, and the social labeling of certain acts as deviant. Psychological theorists have viewed criminal behavior as the consequence of a compulsive need for punishment, a lack of control due to immaturity, social reinforcement and modeling, and different perceptions and cognitions concerning the world.

Regarding the relationships between crime and mental disorders, the frequency of violent crime is higher than average among people with antisocial personalities, borderline personality disorder, schizophrenia, major depressive disorder, manic disorder, paranoid disorders, and mental retardation. Alcohol and substance abuse are also associated with a higher than average rate of criminal behavior.

The best predictor of violent behavior is a record of past violence, as noted in interviews, observations, and other case history material. However, personality ratings and inventories can also contribute to the prediction of violence. Scores on measures of the characteristics of psychopathic personality (high impulsivity, exploitativeness, low conformity, sensation seeking, etc.) are particularly useful.

SUGGESTED READINGS

Adler, N., & Matthews, K. (1994). Health psychology: Why do some people get sick and some stay well? *Annual Review of Psychology, 45,* 229–259.

Avashalom, C., Begg, D., Dickson, N., Harrington, H., Langley, J., Moffitt, T. E., & Silva, P. A. (1997). Personality differences predict health-risk behaviors in young adulthood: Evidence from a longitudinal study. *Journal of Personality and Social Psychology, 73,* 1052–1063.

Brannon, L., & Feist, J. (1997). *Health psychology: An introduction to behavior and health* (3rd ed.). Pacific Grove, CA: Brooks/Cole.

Butcher, J. N., & Rouse, S. V. (1996). Personality: Individual differences and clinical assessment. *Annual Review of Psychology, 47,* 87–111.

Cooper, C. L., Kilcaldy, B. D., & Brown, J. (1994). A model of job stress and physical health: The role of individual differences. *Personality and Individual Differences, 16,* 653–655.

Harkness, A. R., & Lilienfeld, S. O. (1997). Individual differences science for treatment planning personality traits. *Psychological Assessment, 9,* 349–360.

Heston, L. L. (1992). *Mending minds.* New York: W. H. Freeman.

Krueger, R. F., Caspi, A., Moffitt, T. E., Silva, P. A., & McGee, R. (1996). Personality traits are differentially linked to mental disorders: A multitrait-multidiagnosis study of an adolescent birth cohort. *Journal of Abnormal Psychology, 105,* 299–312.

Strack, S., & Lorr, M. (Eds.). (1994). *Differentiating normal and abnormal personality.* New York: Springer.

Wrightsman, L. S. (1994). *Psychology and the legal system* (3rd ed.). Pacific Grove, CA: Brooks/Cole.

Differences Across the Life Span

Biological and psychological differences among individuals are apparent from birth. Newborns already possess physical and behavioral characteristics that set them apart from each other: They vary in weight, length, Apgar rating,[1] and a host of other measurements. Baby and child care books may provide helpful information that applies to children in general, but distinctions must still be made between the capabilities and other characteristics of different children.

As children mature and develop into social creatures, most learn to ascertain the expectations and wishes of other people and try to please them. The family and the wider society into which a child is born provide encouragement and approval of acceptable behavior and contributions to the welfare of the social groups of which they are a part. Although other people accept and reward a certain amount of individuality, there are strong sanctions against extreme nonconformity to group norms and rules. Appropriate and inappropriate behavior vary with culture, gender, age, and other demographic characteristics, but everyone is expected to show respect for and allegiance to certain social groups to be accepted and supported by them.

A certain amount of obedience is required in all cultures, but the emphasis on conformity is greater in the more collectivist cultures of Asia, Africa, and Central and South America than in the highly individualistic cultures of mainstream America, Australia, and Northern Europe. In collectivist cultures, people see themselves as part of a larger social network. Priority is given to the goals of the family, clan, or other social groups, and a person's identity is defined with respect to those goals. In individualistic cultures, priority is given to individual goals, and a person's identity is defined in terms of his or her personal characteristics (Markus & Kitayama, 1991). The emphasis in individualistic cultures on independence and in collectivist cultures on interdependence is stressed and fostered in the child from the

---

[1]The *Apgar rating* is a composite of ratings on a scale of 0 to 2 of heart rate, respiration, muscle tone, reflexes, and color assigned to newborns 1 minute and 5 minutes after birth. An Apgar rating of 7 to 10 is normal.

moment of birth. Consequently, by the time children have become adults, in most cases they have internalized the cultural norms and have come to identify with the customs, aspirations, and expectations of the culture.

The extent to which individualism and collectivism are espoused by a particular country or region depends on such factors as the homogeneity, complexity, and affluence of the corresponding society (Triandis, 1989). For example, Japanese society is highly collectivist in orientation and homogeneous in its ethnic characteristics. The United States is very heterogeneous in ethnic makeup and also highly individualistic. Members of all ethnic groups in the United States adhere to the precepts of mainstream American culture to some extent, but the beliefs and practices of a particular ethnic subculture in this country may be quite different from those of mainstream America. For example, the dominant Anglo-American culture has been described as "future-oriented, reserved, rationalistic, and achievement-driven," whereas the Black subculture is characterized as "present-oriented, improvisational, expressive, spiritual, and emotional" (R. Jones, 1991). These descriptions are somewhat stereotyped or over-generalized because the differences in behavior and beliefs within each subcultural or racial group are greater than those between groups.

Regardless of gender, race, religion, or other characteristics, when a member of one cultural group is exposed to another culture, a certain amount of culture shock takes place. This is merely another illustration of the shock of the new or unfamiliar for which the individual may have no readily accessible coping mechanisms. A natural reaction to culture shock is to withdraw or become ghettoized by restricting one's social interactions to people who share one's own customs and values. However, when a person lives and works in a different culture for an extended period of time, a certain amount of acculturation or change in habits and perspective is typical. Various acculturation strategies may be employed by the newcomer, ranging from complete separation from the host culture on the one hand to assimilation into it and abandonment of the old culture on the other hand. Most people opt for a compromise or integration strategy, in which the old culture is retained to some extent while adapting to the host culture. However, some unfortunate souls are unable to identify with either culture and consequently become marginalized.

In contrast to the biological and psychological emphases of previous chapters, the present chapter is more sociological in its orientation. The stress is on human beings as social creatures who, from the cradle to the grave, become temporary or permanent members of certain groups and institutions and identify themselves accordingly. As described by sociologists and social psychologists, the passage through life is punctuated by certain developmental tasks: acquisition of both a general and specific education; training and experience in becoming an effective worker or professional and a wise consumer; loving, marrying, becoming a parent, and maintaining familial and nonfamilial relationships; serving as a responsible citizen who is interested in social problems, laws, and politics; pursuing spiritual and philosophical reflections and practices; and preparing for the end of life and one's legacy. Birth, schooling, work, marriage, family, leisure, religion, and death are all life events and processes that are confronted in both similar and various ways by different people. This chapter is concerned with the diversity of ways in which people navigate the passage through life and how these passages are both expressions and determinants of attitudes, beliefs, values, and overall perspective on the meaning of life and how it should be lived.

EDUCATION, EMPLOYMENT, AND EXPENDITURES

From the moment of birth, and perhaps even before, to be alive is to learn. Much of this learning is informal or incidental, especially during the early years, but even formal instruction does not wait until the first day of school. By the time they are in first grade, the majority of children have attained at least some of the basics of reading and arithmetic and in many cases a bit of competence in writing and a few elements of science, geography, and current events. The acquisition of this fundamental educational knowledge and skills, together with the learning of cooperative and considerate behavior and discipline, continues throughout the school years. One of my school teachers was fond of saying that "Education is for everyone, but school is for scholars." By this he presumably meant that children acquire a certain amount of education out of school, but obtaining optimum benefit from instruction requires attention, ability, and persistence. As important as formal schooling may be, a great deal can be learned out of school at any age. As indicated in chapter 6, people who continue to explore the world through observation, reading, conversation, and hobbies tend to experience less decline in their cognitive abilities as they grow older.

The Pursuit of Formal Education

In almost every time and place, knowledge has been respected and its pursuit has been viewed as important in achieving success and avoiding trouble. Hopefully by the time they have graduated from high school, adolescents have a fairly good general understanding of how the human and nonhuman aspects of their world function, and they possess the abilities to make their way in that world. In recognition of the value of a good education, coupled with parental and social pressure, over 80% of Americans stick it out through high school and 24% or more graduate from college (see Fig. 10.1).

Approximately equal percentages of men and women, but a greater percentage of younger than older adults, are high school graduates. With respect to ethnic group, a greater percentage of Asian Americans than Whites, and a greater percentage of Whites than Blacks, American Indians, or Hispanic Americans are high school graduates. On the average, residents of Southeastern states have less formal education than those living in the Northeastern, Midwestern, or Western states, and people who live in nonmetropolitan areas have less formal education on the average than those in metropolitan areas (Day & Curry, 1997).

Highest Educational Level:

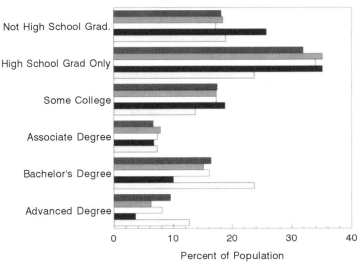

FIG. 10.1.   Highest educational level of Americans 25 years and older by sex, March 1997. (Based on data from U.S. Census Bureau, Annual Demographic Survey, March CPS Supplement, 1997 Data Table Topic List.)

Both high schools and colleges play the dual roles of attempting to equip students with the basic knowledge and skills to function adequately in human society and providing them with the specialized information and training needed to pursue particular occupations or professions. Specialized training is also made available by technical and business schools, graduate schools, and professional schools.

Enrollments in U.S. colleges and universities have risen dramatically during the past half century. Today over 15 million Americans are enrolled in higher education programs, and over 6 million of these students are at least 25 years of age. The rise in the number of students at all levels of formal education is not merely a result of the increased size and affluence of the general population. Equally important is the fact that an increasing number of the available jobs, and particularly those with high salaries, require more formal, specialized, highly technical education than in previous times. The greatest rewards—in terms of salary, benefits, prestige, and interesting, self-fulfilling work—go to those individuals who stay in school and continue to pursue further education even after becoming high school graduates (see Fig. 10.2).

Employment and Earnings

By the time they have graduated from high school or college, most young Americans have had some work experience, either part or full time. In 1995, nearly 17 million individuals between the ages of 16 and 24 were enrolled in high schools and colleges in the United States. Forty-four percent of these students—48% of whom were male, 52% female, 86% White, and 9% Black—were also employees (U.S. Bureau of Labor Statistics, 1997).

Work experience is a requirement of some educational programs, but students also take outside jobs to obtain extra spending money to meet their material needs and desires and to pay some of their educational expenses. Research has found that a moderate amount of part-time work experience is beneficial, but that 15 + hours a week increases the likelihood of drug and alcohol abuse, smoking, delinquency, and lower education at-

Highest Educational Attainment:

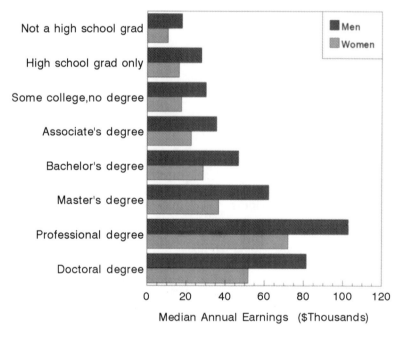

FIG. 10.2.   Median annual income of year-round, full-time U.S. workers by sex and level of education—1997. (Based on data from U.S. Bureau of the Census, Current Population Reports, p. 20–505)

tainment among teenagers (National Research Council, 1998). On the other hand, out-of-school jobs can make students feel valued and appreciated, provide an opportunity to learn financial- and self-management skills and may serve as preliminary training and experience for postgraduate employment. However, many low-level jobs typically do not pay very well, yield few if any fringe benefits, and may result in getting stuck in dead-end occupations. In general, research has found that a moderate amount of part-time work experience is beneficial, but that 15 hours of work a week increases the likelihood of drug and alcohol abuse, smoking, delinquency, and lower educational attainment among teenagers (National Research Council, 1998).

The number of Americans in the labor force during any given year varies with gender, race/ethnicity, age, education, marital status, geographical region, urban/nonurban residence, and other demographic variables. Of course, these relationships are not independent of each other. For example, race, education, age, and geographical region are all interrelated.

There are elements of both sexism and racism in the fact that the rate of employment is generally higher for men than for women and for Whites than for Blacks and Hispanics. As shown in Table 10.1, larger percentages of women are employed in technical, sales, and administrative support and in service occupations. Among Blacks, larger percentages are in service occupations and in the operators, fabricators, and laborers categories. Among Hispanics, larger percentages are in farming, forestry, and fishing and in the operators, fabricators, and laborers categories. Furthermore, the unemployment rate tends to be higher for Black than for White or Hispanic men and higher for Black and Hispanic women than for White women (U.S. Bureau of Labor Statistics, 1997).

Concerning the relationships of employment to chronological age and education, the employment rate is higher for people in their late 30s and early 40s than for other age groups and for high school and college graduates than those with less formal education. The two occupational categories containing the largest numbers of college graduates are (a) managerial & professional speciality, and (b) technical, sales, and administrative support. The two occupational categories with the largest numbers of high school graduates are (a) technical, sales, and administrative support, and (b) service occupations. The two occupational categories containing the largest numbers of non-high school graduates are (a) service occupations, and (b) operators, fabricators, and laborers (U.S. Bureau of Labor Statistics, unpublished data).

The rate of employment is higher for married men with spouse present than for single, divorced, widowed, or married men with spouse absent. However, the employment rate is higher for single women than for married, widowed, or divorced women. With respect to geographical region, the employment rate tends to be lower in highly populated cities such as Los Angeles and New York City and in more populous states such as California.

During the past few decades, the incomes of almost all demographic groups in the United States—men and women, Blacks, Whites, and Hispanics, and people of all ages and in all sections of the United States—have risen, but the median income still varies substantially with demographic

TABLE 10.1
Percentages of Females, Blacks, and Hispanics in Six Occupational Groups in 1997

Occupational Group	Percentage of Employees in Group		
	Female	Black	Hispanic
Management and professional specialty	48.9	7.3	5.0
Technical, sales, and administrative support	64.1	10.5	7.9
Service occupations	59.4	17.6	14.6
Precision production, craft, and repair	8.9	8.1	12.1
Operators, fabricators, and laborers	24.7	15.1	15.4

Source. U.S. Bureau of Labor Statistics, *Employment and Earnings*, monthly, January issues; and unpublished data.

group. In addition to being greater for people with more education, median annual income is higher for males than for females and for Whites than for Blacks and Hispanics. Median income also varies with chronological age, rising sharply from young adulthood to middle age and then declining markedly in old age. It is also somewhat different in different parts of the United States: It is higher in the Northeast and Midwest than in the South and West. Earnings tend to be greatest in large cities such as New York City, San Francisco, and the District of Columbia and in highly industrialized states such as Connecticut, New Jersey, and New York than in less industrialized states such as Idaho, Montana, North Dakota, South Dakota, and Mississippi. Not surprisingly, median incomes are highest for executives, administrators, managers, and professional people than for other occupations (U.S. Bureau of the Census, 1997a).

Poverty

The official U.S. government definition of *poverty* includes a set of money income thresholds that vary with the size and composition of the family. According to this definition, which is based on money income alone, in 1996 an estimated 13.7% of the total U.S. population was living in poverty (i.e., poor). Because of the substantially greater number of Whites in the total population, two thirds of all poor Americans are White. Of the remainder, the percentage of the group designated as poor was highest for Hispanics and Blacks, next highest for Asian/Pacific Islanders, and lowest for non-Hispanic

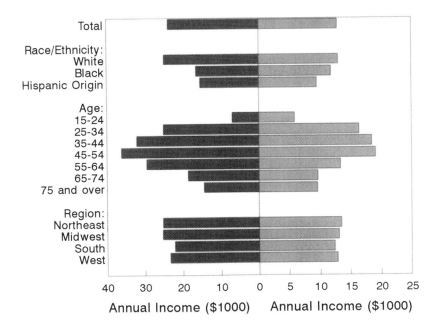

FIG. 10.3.   Median annual income of U.S. workers by sex, race and Hispanic origin, age, and geographical region. (Based on data from U.S. Bureau of the Census, 1997a.)

Whites. The poverty rate also varies with chronological age, geographical region, and place of birth: It is higher for children than for other age groups, higher in the South than in other regions of the country, higher in central cities than in suburbs or nonmetropolitan areas, and higher for foreign-born than for native-born individuals (Lamison-White, 1997).

Expenditures

In addition to the types of occupations held, the number of hours worked, and the wages and benefits obtained for that work, people differ in how they spend their money. In a credit-driven economy, people frequently spend money they do not have, but generally speaking expenditures are dependent on income. Average annual expenditures in the United States are lower for Blacks than for the combined Whites and other ethnic categories and greater for middle-aged adults than other age groups. Expenditures are also higher for non-Hispanics than for Hispanics, higher for individuals with more than those with less education, higher in urban than in rural areas, higher for home owners than for nonhome owners, and higher in the West and Northeast than in the Midwest and South (U.S. Department of Labor, 1998).

Types of expenditures also vary with race and ethnicity. For example, compared with Whites, on the average Blacks spend a slightly larger percentage on housing but a lower percentage on personal insurance and pensions. Blacks also spend more than average on fish and seafood, fresh fruit juices, and telephone services. Hispanics spend more than average on meats, fruits and vegetables, baby food, and hair care products (Russell, 1996). For both Blacks and Whites, the percentage of annual expenditures is greatest for housing, followed by transportation and food. Personal insurance and pensions, apparel and services, health care, and entertainment are also high on the list of expenditures for most Americans.

The rank order of these expenditures also varies with chronological age. For example, despite their Medicare and Medicaid benefits, in comparison with other age groups, a larger percentage of the expenditures of people age 65 and over is for health care and food and a smaller percentage is for apparel and services and personal insurance and pensions.

MATES AND FAMILIES

Human beings are social creatures whose physical and psychological well-being depends greatly on their relationships with other people. Most of those relationships are nonsexual, although the popularity of aphrodisiacs attests to the high interest in being capable sexual performers. For most people, the sex drive is expressed primarily toward persons of the opposite gender, but homosexual relationships, masturbation, and sexual deviations or disorders such as voyeurism, exhibitionism, pedophilia, and sadomasochism are not rare.

Love

When most people speak of love, they are referring to romantic love. However, there are types of love other than the desire to form a physical and psychological union with another person. A person may love him or herself, God, humanity, conversation, philosophy, life, animals, or almost anything. Love may also be expressed in different ways: through passion, intimacy, decision commitment, or, more commonly, as a combination of all three of these factors (Sternberg, 1986).

Fundamental to all kinds of love is attraction. Counter to the popular notion that opposites attract, most people are attracted to those who are like themselves in physical, cognitive, and personality characteristics and interests. Also incorrect is the notion that for everyone there is one true love out there waiting if only he or she can be found. Rather, in most cases, there are many different people with whom one could be equally happy (or unhappy), but the opportunity to meet most of them never arises. Consequently, together with similarity and physical attractiveness, proximity is an important determinant of love (Byrne, 1971). In today's highly mobile society, people seldom limit their choices to the girl or boy who lives next door or down the street, but the physical space in which we move and live—our residential neighborhood, the place where we work, and so on—provides many of the candidates for our affections.

Like most other human needs, the expression of the need for love varies with age, gender, and culture. Of course, there are certain similarities between younger and older adults in what they look for in love relationships. For example, Reedy, Birren, and Schaie (1981) found that adults of all ages ranked emotional security first, and respect, community, help and play behaviors, sexual intimacy, and loyalty next in order. However, the standings of young, middle-aged, and older adults on these variables changed with age: Communication scores were higher for young adults, sexual intimacy was higher for younger and middle-aged adults, and emotional security and loyalty were higher for older adults. The results of other studies indicate that passion and sexual intimacy are usually more important to younger adults, whereas older adults place greater emphasis on affection and faithfulness. An interaction between age and gender is seen in the finding that the desire for emotional closeness is stronger in younger than in older women, but greater in older than in younger men (Huyck, 1982).

Attitudes and behavior with respect to love and mating also vary with culture. Mating and associated expectations are generally more traditional or conservative in Mediterranean countries and more modern or liberal in Scandinavian countries. Buss, Abbott, Angleitner, & Asherian (1990) found that the greatest variability among different countries was in attitudes toward premarital chastity.[2] Be that as it may, throughout the world women tend to place a higher value on a man's earning potential, but men place greater value on a women's physical attractiveness (Buss et al., 1990).

Marriage and Divorce

Over 90% of Americans marry one or more times—a figure that is higher for Whites than for Hispanics and higher for Hispanics than for Blacks (see Table 10.2). The median age for the first marriage has increased in recent years and is greater for Asian Americans than for Whites and greater for Whites than for Blacks and Hispanics (Saluter & Lugaila, 1998).

Approximately half of all American couples who are living together are not married, but a sizable percentage of these cohabitants eventually marry. *Traditional marriage*, in which the husband is the dominant partner and decision maker and the wife the primary housekeeper and child rearer, has been declining in popularity, but it remains the most common type. *Companionate mar-*

---

[2]An emphasis on chastity has also varied widely with historical era. P. Brown (1988) observed that "To modern persons, whatever their religious beliefs, the Early Christian themes of sexual renunciation, of continence, celibacy, and the virgin life have come to carry with them icy overtones" (p. 446).

riage, in which no distinction is made between male and female roles, has increased in popularity in recent years, especially with more highly educated, affluent couples. Even more liberal are *open marriages*, in which the partners also have sexual relationships with other people, and *group marriages*, in which couples are legally married to each other but share living quarters, duties, and sexual partners (Duberman, 1974).

Kurdek and Schmitt (1986) described a series of phases—blending, nesting, maintaining—through which most marriages progress, including periods of cooperation and conflict. To an increasing extent, couples are apparently unable to resolve their conflicts and problems and therefore opt for divorce. The divorce rate, which is higher in the United States than in any other country, is higher among Blacks than Whites and among non-Hispanics than Hispanics. Among Hispanics, the rate of divorce is highest for Puerto Ricans and lowest for Cuban Americans (Bean & Tienda, 1987). Divorce is also more common when a child is born before marriage (particularly to a teenager), in lower educational and lower income groups, and among those who attend religious services less frequently (Glenn & Supancic, 1984; U.S. Bureau of the Census, 1992). The fact that the divorce rate has increased but the average number of years of marriage before divorcing has declined in recent years has been attributed to a number of social factors. Among these are the increased financial and social independence of women, availability of welfare, and changes in public attitudes and laws (e.g., no-fault divorce) regarding divorce.

Of course, divorce is not necessarily the end of marriage for all people. An estimated 4 out of 10 marriages in the United States are remarriages for

TABLE 10.2

Marital Status by Sex, Race, and Hispanic Origin

	White		Black		Hispanic	
	Male	*Female*	*Male*	*Female*	*Male*	*Female*
Martial Status	*Percent*					
Never married	24.8	21.2	46.8	41.0	40.8	29.6
Married, spouse present	56.7	55.1	34.9	27.7	46.0	48.4
Married, spouse absent	2.9	3.2	6.4	9.5	6.1	7.6
Widowed	6.7	10.7	2.5	10.0	1.3	5.9
Divorced	8.9	9.8	9.3	11.8	5.9	8.4

Source. Saluter and Lugaila (1998).

one or more of the partners. Remarriage is more common for men than for women, for young adults than for middle-aged and older adults, for Whites than for Blacks or Hispanics, and for less educated than for more educated women. The stability of remarriages varies with the age of the partners and the circumstances under which the first marriage was terminated. Remarriage between older couples whose prior marriages were terminated by death rather than divorce from their partners are more likely to be enduring than those of younger couples who remarry after divorce (U.S. Bureau of the Census, 1992).

The number of Americans who are married or divorced reaches a peak in the 40s, whereas the number and percentage of widowed persons are highest in old age. There are more widows than widowers, the percentage of widows being greatest among White females and second highest among Black females. Due in large measure to the fact that residents of the northeastern region of the United States tend to be older and those in the western United States younger than in other parts of the country, the percentage of widowed persons is highest in the Northeast and lowest in the West (Saluter, 1996).

Homosexuality

Much less common and less enduring than heterosexual relationships are homosexual unions. Efforts to legitimize homosexual unions in the sense of establishing similar legal rights and responsibilities as for heterosexual marriages have met with only token success. Homosexual unions of either sex can be close coupled (enduring) or open coupled. In open-coupled relationships, which are more common among gays than lesbians, the partners live together but have other lovers as well.

A large number of gay men live alone in what Bell and Weinberg (1978) characterized as *functional, dysfunctional,* or *asexual* relationships. Both functional and dysfunctional gays have active sex lives, but the former are comfortable and the latter troubled or unhappy with their homosexuality. An even larger number of live-alone gays are asexuals who live quiet, withdrawn lives, have little sexual contact, but appear to be untroubled by their sexual orientation.

Birth Rates and Parents

In earlier times, having a large family was viewed as a source of pride and often a necessity for survival. In a world in which the mortality rate was extremely high, only a minority of infants reached maturity. Therefore, a family had to have many children (at least five) for it and the society of which it was a part to endure. In our own world of limited resources, however, overpopulation rather than underpopulation is of greater concern.

Traditionally, one of the major purposes of marital union was to produce children. Throughout the world, however, a large percentage of births occur out of wedlock and, perhaps of greatest concern, to unmarried teenagers who cannot support themselves. As shown in Fig. 10.4, both the birth rate per 1,000 population and the percentage of births to women between the ages of 15 and 19 are highest in the less-developed countries of Western, Eastern, and Middle Africa and lowest in Europe and North America.

Both the *crude birth rate*—the number of births per 1,000 population—and the *fertility rate*—the number of births per 1,000 women ages 15 to 44 years—in the United States have declined in recent years. Nearly 4 million babies were born in this country in 1997, yielding an estimated overall birth rate of 14.6 and a fertility rate of 65.3 (Ventura, Anderson, Martin, & Smith, 1998). Over 99% of these babies were born in hospitals and 7.5% had low birth weights (under 2,500 grams).

As shown in Fig. 10.5, both the birth rate and fertility rate are higher for Hispanics than for any other race/ethnic group, but the total number of births is highest for non-Hispanic Whites.

The peak childbearing years are lower for American Indians, Blacks, and Hispanics (20–24 years) than for Asian/Pacific Islanders and Whites (25–29 years). Furthermore, the birth rate among teenagers is highest for Blacks and next highest for Hispanics. Among the 50 states, the birth rate in 1997 was highest in Utah and lowest in Maine (Ventura et al., 1998).

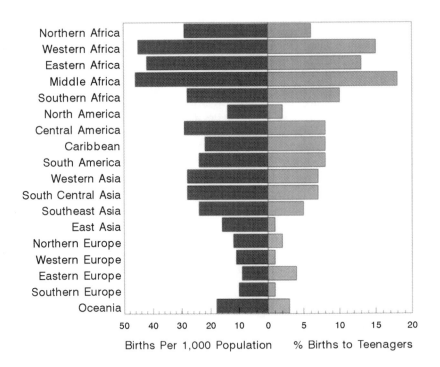

FIG. 10.4.　Births rates and percent of births by mothers 15 to 19 years old in regions throughout the world. (Based on data in Population Reference Bureau, 1998.)

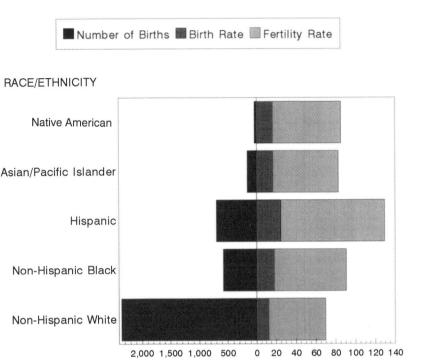

FIG. 10.5.   Births and birthrates for five ethnic groups in the United States. (Based on data in Ventura, Martin, Curtin, & Matthews, 1998.)

The number and rates of birth as well as the types of households into which children born in the United States grow up vary with race/ethnicity. Approximately three fourths of non-Hispanic White children and two thirds of Hispanic children, but only one third of Black children, live in two-parent households. Even in two-parent households, both parents are employed outside the home in approximately 40% of the cases—a percentage that increases as the children grow older. Of course, children not living in two-parent households do not necessarily reside with either of their parents. Millions of children live with their grandparents or other relatives while others live with nonrelatives, in group homes or institutions, or alone (Saluter & Lugaila, 1998).

As middle- and upper class children mature and grow into adulthood, they typically leave home and the size of the household decreases. Lower class households are more likely to be multigenerational and less likely to show a decrease in the number of residents as time goes by. In general, however, the number of people who live with their relatives declines with age and the number who live alone increases. The percentage of householders and the number of people who own their own homes also increase with aging (Saluter & Lugaila, 1998).

FRIENDSHIPS AND ORGANIZATIONAL MEMBERSHIPS

Although the family is the most important socializing force in childhood, as children mature and interact with the wider community, peer groups and other persons outside the home have increasing influences on the behavior, beliefs, and desires of individuals. In some ways, these encounters are even more crucial than those in the family. In general, people can count on their families to accept and nurture them, but in the wider social world the test of social acceptability is more severe.

Friendships

Many people in our society, and older people in particular, live alone. Still all of us are social creatures whose identities depend on interactions with other people. All of us are mutually interdependent beings who attain our greatest joys (and sorrows) from conversing, working, and playing with our fellow humans. Almost from the very beginning, these social interactions are not limited to our families, but also involve neighbors and friends as well.

As discussed in chapter 4, females of all ages are more relationship oriented and therefore tend to have more friends than males. Age is also related to friendships: Young adults have more friends than middle-aged and older adults, and middle-aged adults have more friends than older adults (Aizenberg & Treas, 1985; Antonucci, 1985). Young married adults have more friends than single or widowed adults, but older widows and widowers see their friends more often than older married couples (Antonucci, 1985; Hess, 1971). Among the factors contributing to a decline in the number of friendships with aging are fewer opportunities to meet people, voluntary disengagement from social activities, and health problems. Older adults are much more selective in their social contacts than younger adults. Social contacts in young adulthood are motivated more by information seeking, whereas in older adulthood emotional regulation is more important in establishing such contacts (Carstensen, 1993, 1995).

Friendships also vary with the interrelated variables of race/ethnicity and socioeconomic status (SES). On the average, Whites have more friends than Blacks, and people of higher SES have more friends than those of lower SES. The extent of social relationships outside the home varies, of course, with the closeness of the primary and extended family group. Some cultural groups are more family oriented than others and consequently not as active in extrafamilial society. Furthermore, social relationships need not be friendships but may be business, political, or other goal-oriented associations.

Social Organizations

Many social interactions are direct or indirect encounters with representatives of the various organizations and institutions that make up a society.

These establishments constitute a large part of a culture and play a critical role in shaping interests, abilities, and overall philosophy of life. Awareness of and contact with the service-providing and profit-making organizations within a locality, state, and nation are necessary for peace of mind and often for survival. The food we eat, the clothing we wear, the houses that protect us from the elements and serve as launching pads for our activities, in addition to other necessities and luxuries of modern living, are provided in large measure by people whom we rarely see and do not know. These individuals are employed in the public or private sector by educational, financial, health, insurance, manufacturing, governmental, recreational, entertainment, transportation, utility, law enforcement, and other organizations. Even if we seldom if ever come in contact with them, they possess power over us and affect our material and mental well-being.

In the not-too-distant past, and still to some extent in small, out-of-the-way places, interactions with product and service providers were on a one-to-one basis. Offices, stores, and agencies were smaller then and more personal in their interactions with the public. In the modern era of mergers, conglomerates, and world-wide telecommunications, we are more likely to interact with a recorded voice or words printed on a computer screen than with a living, breathing human being whom we can see and who can see us. In the interest of efficiency and profitability, tasks that once required the human touch are now performed in a standardized, mechanical fashion that is little concerned with individual differences between customers or clients.

Be that as it may, the business of living requires that we attend to and do our best to cope with these impersonalities and try to filter out the information from the standard background noise, the wheat from the chaff. This is seldom easy, especially when our models, heroes, and imitable lifestyles are the make-believe creations of television and motion picture writers and producers. Children growing up with a daily dose of fantasy from the media often find it difficult to tell what is real or true as opposed to preplanned, profit-motivated entertainment. Television characters who are murdered come back to life, so why shouldn't a school mate or storekeeper? Repeated encouragement to "do your own thing," "do it my way," or to "look out for number one first" encourages a negative answer to Cain's famous question. We are encouraged to imitate multimillion-dollar athletes, whose accomplishments can be emulated by less than one in a million viewers, by using products that have nothing to do with their success. Constant exposure to such messages may also result in altruism being viewed with amusement and as a "sucker play." Over a period of time, such a situation results in a perpetual attitude of irresponsibility and instability.

Without the perspective and context provided by concerned adults and other sources of bona fide information, there is no guidance to help the individual distinguish between primary and secondary process thinking—no guarantee that in a crisis he or she will be able to tell the difference between fantasy and reality. Even those institutions—educational, health, religious, governmental—that people could traditionally count on to dispense reasonable propositions and recommendations all too often become callous and subservient to the almighty entertainment dollar.

This description is obviously not typical of all citizens in modern society or even necessarily a majority of them. Despite strong countervalent forces, many individuals of all races, classes, and creeds are able to develop and maintain a deep sense of social justice and philanthropy. Parenting style is important in this regard, but so are the examples provided by peer groups, teachers, and others. The molding of character is complex and not easily understood and in no small measure influenced by heredity as well as environment. Within a democratic society, there is perhaps less that can be done to control for the genetically based "bad seed" than to provide more suitable environments for moral development. Although it is probably never too late to change a person's moral outlook, it is better that it be done sooner rather than later. The future builds on the past, the past can never be undone, and first lessons are the most important ones. The examples of immoral, socially destructive behavior must be removed from the home, neighborhood, and airwaves while children are still impressionable enough to profit from examples of good behavior and not be tempted by the greed and thrill seeking of irresponsible, self-centered individuals.

Religions

Countries on all continents of the world and Oceania contain adherents to a variety of religions. Among these are practitioners of the four major religions, Christians, Muslims, Hindus, and Buddhists, as well as Sikhs, Jews, Bahá'is, members of folk religions, new religions, ethnic religions, and millions of nonreligious people and atheists. Christianity is the dominant religion on all continents except Asia, where one quarter of the population identifies itself as Muslim and less than 9% as Christian. Christianity is particularly dominant in Northern America and Latin America. Over 90% of Latin Americans and over 80% of Northern Americans identify themselves as Christians. One third of the total number of Christians in the world are Roman Catholics, the largest percentage of whom are Latin Americans and Europeans (U.S. Bureau of the Census, 1997b).

Despite the focus of many Americans on self-interest and materialism, in terms of the professed beliefs of its citizenry, the United States is one of the most religious countries in the world. Religious membership is expressed not only in spiritual beliefs, but in many other aspects of behavior and appearance (clothing, food, mannerisms, habits, etc.). Even reportedly nonreligious Americans are influenced by religion in their culture, social interactions, holidays, and other aspects of everyday life. According to a recent Gallup poll, an estimated 67% of Americans are members of a church or synagogue and 60% attend church once a month or more. Regular church attendance is more common among older than younger and middle-aged adults, among women than men, among non-Whites than Whites, among Protestants than Catholics, and among Republicans than Democrats. It is also more common among people with a high school education or less than those who have more than a high school education. Church attendance is also more common among those with below median incomes, and in Southern and Eastern states than in Western and Midwestern states (Newport & Saad, 1997).

With respect to religious identification, 87% of Americans say they are Christians (58% Protestant, 27% Roman Catholic, 1% Mormon, 1% Eastern Orthodox). The remainder are Jews (3%), Muslims (2%), Buddhists, Hindus, or Sikhs, or indicate no religious preference at all (5%). The largest Protestant denominations are Baptist (19%), Methodists (9%), Lutherans (6%), Presbyterians (5%), Church of Christ (3%), and Episcopalians (2%) (Newport & Saad, 1997).

The increasing cultural pluralism of the United States has been accompanied by the growth of evangelical Christian and many non-Christian religions during the past 25 years. However, this growth has been accompanied by a decline in the membership of Presbyterian, Episcopal, Congregational, and other traditional, more doctrinaire denominations. Many former adherents to traditional religious denominations, and young adults making their first religious commitment, have joined nondenominational megachurches or have become involved in hybrid combinations of two or more religions. Theologians and other writers have noted that the expanding religious diversity is redefining the nation and leading to further social and political conflict (M. Rourke, 1998).

As with other social changes produced by expanding cultural diversity, religious intolerance, as manifested in discrimination and religiously motivated hate crimes, demands constant vigilance by peacekeepers. Furthermore, the political power of the Religious Right, as seen in its influence in such issues as abortion, censorship, and more generally *family values,* has undoubtedly polarized the nation and led to an increasing concern as to whether cultural diversity will ever lead to genuine pluralism.

CRIME AND PREJUDICE

Among the problems that extend beyond the individual and encompass entire societies are poverty, malnutrition, disease, crime, war, terrorism, and social discrimination. Advances in scientific medicine, public health, agriculture, and industrial production have contributed substantially to solving the first three of these problems. Modern methods of law enforcement, education, and diplomacy have been instrumental in the reduction of crime, war, and discrimination during recent years, but these problems still plague our planet. An entire book could easily be devoted to any one of these social problems, but here we must make do with just a few pages.

Crime

Like other social problems, the rate and type of crime varies with race/ethnicity, gender, chronological age, education, and SES. For example, the arrest rate for Blacks is five times that of Whites for violent crimes, four times that of Whites for property crimes, and three times that of Whites for all crimes in all age groups (U.S. Department of Justice, Federal Bureau of Investigation, 1997). The number of arrests of both males and females increases steeply up to ages 15 to 19 and then declines gradually from young adulthood to old age. At all ages, and particularly during the teenage years, property crime exceeds violent crime as a cause of arrest.

The number of arrests also varies with the particular offense, the most common being alcohol-related offenses, followed by property crimes and drug abuse and then violent crime and disorderly conduct. However, the rank order of arrests for different crimes varies with age. Individuals under age 18 are more likely to be arrested for motor-vehicle theft, vandalism, and arson, whereas adults between the ages of 25 and 44 constitute a larger percentage of arrests for fraud, prostitution, family violence, driving under the influence, and drunkenness (U.S. Department of Justice, Federal Bureau of Investigation, 1997).

As shown in Fig. 10.6, the rate of victimization for all crimes of violence varies with gender, age, race/ethnicity, and household income. The crime victimization rate is higher for males than for females, is higher for Blacks and Hispanics than for Whites and non-Hispanics, and varies inversely with both chronological age and household income. Not shown in the chart is that the victimization rate for violent crimes is higher for never married persons than for married divorced/separated or widowed persons, higher in the West and Midwest than in the Northeast and South, and higher for urban than for suburban and rural residents (U.S. Department of Justice, Bureau of Justice Statistics, 1997). Thus, the most likely victim of violent crime is a never-married Black or Hispanic teenage male living in a low-income household in an urban area of the West or Midwest.

Although older adults are more afraid of crime, younger adults are more often its victims. A disproportionate number of teenagers are victims of personal crimes—a figure that drops to its lowest level in older age. However, older victims of crime, and older women in particular, are more likely than younger adults to sustain injuries as the result of a violent attack and to require expensive medical care for these injuries (Bachman, Dillaway, & Lachs, 1998). Regardless of age, the rates of victimization for robbery and assault are higher for males than females, higher for Blacks than Whites, and higher for Hispanics than non-Hispanics (Perkins et al., 1996).

Social Prejudice and Discrimination

Social prejudice has existed since time immemorial, contributing to discrimination in employment, education, housing, and social memberships, as well as terrorism, armed conflict, and other forms of violence against persons and property. *Prejudice,* which literally means prejudgment, is often instigated by competition or other events perceived as threats and is sustained by stereotyping. Stereotypes may be based on physical characteristics such as skin color or facial features or on behavioral mannerisms. In any event, stereotypes are overgeneralizations that facilitate identification or recognition of members of the group toward which prejudice is felt. The objects of prejudice are commonly members of another racial, ethnic, or religious group, but prejudice may also be expressed toward females (*sex-*

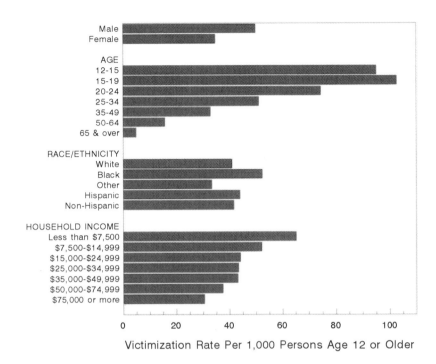

FIG. 10.6.   Victimization rates for violent crimes. (Based on statistics form U.S. Department of Justice, Bureau of Justice Statistics, 1997.)

ism), older adults (*ageism*), people of other sexual orientations (e.g., *homophobia*), disabled persons, or even prochoicers. Whatever the outgroup may be, its members are viewed by the ingroup as inferior, odd, or threatening in some way and hence deserving of harsh treatment.

Racial discrimination has been a continuing social problem in many countries, and in the United States in particular. Despite the Civil War of the 1860s, the civil rights movement of the 1960s, and numerous legislative statutes designed to ensure equality of opportunity and status, Black–White relations in the United States remain a source of concern. Blacks and Whites have different perspectives and attitudes on many social issues, especially the rights and circumstances of each group. For example, data from the General Social Survey conducted by the National Opinion Research Center (Davis & Smith, 1994) show that, although both Blacks and Whites agree that conditions for Blacks have improved in recent years, the two groups differ in their opinions with regard to such issues as why Blacks have not progressed more, affirmative action, and the role of the government. Whites tend to feel that the poorer jobs, hours, and lower incomes of Blacks are due to their lack of motivation, whereas Blacks tend to blame racial discrimination. In addition, whereas only a small percentage of Whites favor preferential hiring and promotion to make up for past discrimination in employment, a majority of Blacks are in favor of such affirmative action procedures. Furthermore, a substantially larger percentage of Whites than Blacks feel that the latter get more attention from government than they deserve.

Sometimes prejudice gets out of hand and leads to hate crimes. The 1990 Hate Crime Statistics Act mandates the collection of data on *hate crimes,* which are defined as crimes motivated by preformed, negative bias against persons, property, or organizations based solely on race, religion, ethnicity/national origin, sexual orientation, or disability. During 1997 in the United States, 8,049 bias-motivated criminal incidents involving 9,861 offenses of this sort were reported to the FBI. Seventy percent of these offenses were crimes against persons, consisting of intimidation, destruction/damage/vandalism of property, simple assault, or aggravated assault. Thirty-nine percent of the offenses were anti-Black and 12% anti-White. Eight offenses were murders, 5 precipitated by racial bias, and 3 by sexual-orientation bias. Sixty-seven percent of the victims were persons; the remainder were businesses, religious organizations, and various other targets. Among the offenders, 63% were White and 19% Black (U.S. Department of Justice, Federal Bureau of Investigation, 1998).

Efforts to reduce prejudice toward ethnic minorities have met with some success, but a few interracial acts of violence and the attendant publicity can undo years of dedicated work. To reach a larger audience, television programs that focus on similarities between ethnic minorities and the majority population expose viewers to many ethnic minorities and provide explicit information have been found useful (e.g., Vrij, Van-Schie, & Cherryman, 1996). Activities requiring cooperation among members of different ethnic groups can also be instrumental in reducing prejudice. Less directly, efforts to reduce frustrations (economic, social, personal, etc.) and enhance the effectiveness of coping mechanisms can minimize the tendency to displace aggressions on other groups. Finally, exposure to and interaction with appropriate minority role models can, especially with children, serve as counterexamples of stereotypes and protect against prejudicial propaganda.

DEATH AND BEREAVEMENT

Dying is an event experienced sooner or later by everyone, but it is an event to which most people do not look forward and for which they are least prepared. However, as reported in a survey by Kalish and Reynolds (1981), as most people grow older their feelings concerning death and dying shift from being afraid or neutral to being unafraid and sometimes even eager. Perhaps contrary to what might be expected, older adults also reported thinking about death less often than younger and middle-aged adults. With regard to preparations that they might make or how they would spend their time if they were terminally ill, younger adults were more apt to indicate that their activities would change markedly and that they would show greater concern for other people. Older adults stated that they would either not change at all or simply withdraw into an inner life.

Places of Death

Because in modern society most dying occurs in hospitals, away from prying eyes, we are less apt than our ancestors to be reminded of it. Nevertheless, thousands of people die every day: The number of registered deaths in the United States alone in 1997 was over 2.3 million (Ventura, Anderson, Martin, & Smith, 1998). As illustrated in Fig. 10.7, both the overall death rate and the infant mortality rate are highest in the countries of Western, Eastern, and Middle Africa. However, the overall death rate in a population is not perfectly correlated with the infant mortality rate. For example, the overall death rate is higher but the infant mortality rate lower in Europe than in Asia and the Americas. This difference is due, in large measure, to the larger number of older people in European than in Asian and American countries.

With regard to the United States in particular, in 1997 the age-adjusted death rate per 100,000 population was an estimated 478.1 and the infant mortality rate was 7.1 (Ventura et al., 1998). The *age-adjusted death rate,* which takes into account the dependency of death rate on chronological age, is higher for males than for females in all race/ethnic groups in the United States. Among both men and women, it is highest for Blacks and lowest for Asian/Pacific Islanders (see Fig. 10.8). Infant and maternal mortality also vary with race—being higher for Blacks than for Whites. In addition to the total death rate, the death rates for various demographic groups have been declining in recent years (Anderson, Kochanek, & Murphy, 1997).

Of all the states or districts, the District of Columbia had both the highest crude death rate and the highest age-adjusted death rate in 1997. Alaska had the lowest crude death rate in that year, but the age-adjusted death rate was lowest in Hawaii. These differences are associated with the different race/ethnic makeup and lifestyles of the populations of these two geographical regions (Ventura et al., 1998).

Causes of Death

The major causes of death throughout the world vary with the particular geographical region. Although the countries in Western, Eastern, and Middle Africa consist of relatively young populations, they also have poorer nutrition and sanitation and consequently higher rates of infectious diseases than most other countries. Be that as it may, infectious diseases are responsible for fewer deaths than noncommunicable diseases such as cardiovascular diseases, cancer, and diabetes in all parts of the world except India and sub-Saharan Africa. The principal reason for the large number of deaths due to these noncommunicable diseases is the aging of the populations of both developed and underdeveloped countries. Changes in lifestyle (diet, smoking, etc.) are other contributing factors in the rise of heart disease, cancer, and other fatal disorders (Maugh, 1996).

Other changes during this century that have influenced the rank order of various causes of death are advances in sanitation, nutrition, and health care. Medical breakthroughs in the treatment of acute illness such as pneumonia, tuberculosis, and gastroenteritis have led to a decline in these conditions. However, the fact that people are living longer and are subjected to pollutants and other problems of modern living has led to a replacement of the killer diseases of yesteryear (pneumonia, influenza, etc.) with chronic conditions such as heart disease, cancer, and stroke. These are the first, second, and third causes of death today, whereas pneumonia and influenza have been relegated to sixth place and diabetes to seventh.

The relationship of chronological age to the frequency and cause of death varies with gender and race/ethnicity. For all races and both sexes combined, approximately three fourths of the persons who died in the United States in 1996 and 1997 were 65 years and older. The 10 major causes of death in 1996, in order of frequency, were: diseases of heart, malignant neoplasms (cancer), cerebrovascular diseases (stroke), chronic obstructive pulmonary diseases, accidents and adverse effects, pneumonia and influenza, diabetes mellitus, HIV infection, suicide, and chronic liver disease and cirrhosis. This is the order for all demographic groups com-

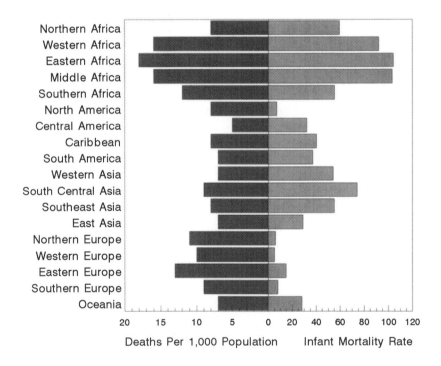

FIG. 10.7. Overall death rates and infant mortality rates for regions throughout the world. (Based on data in Population Reference Bureau, 1998.)

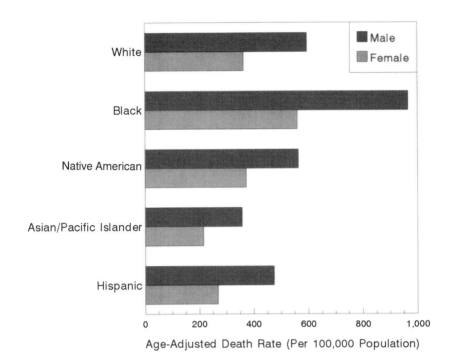

FIG. 10.8.   Age-adjusted death rates for five ethnic groups in 1997. (Based on data in Ventura, Anderson, Martin, & Smith, 1998.)

bined, but the order varies with age, sex, and race. For example, in 1996, accidents and adverse effects ranked Number 1 among causes of death for males up through age 44. Malignant neoplasms were the primary cause of death among females from age 25 to 64. For Black males, homicide and legal invention was the number one cause of death for those in the 15 to 24 year age group, and HIV infection was number one for Black males and females in the 25 to 44 year age group (Peters, Kochanek, & Murphy, 1998). Of particular interest in regard to group differences are variations in the homicide and suicide rates with age, sex, and race/ethnicity. As illustrated in Fig. 10.9, both the homicide and suicide rates are higher in males than females, but the suicide rate is higher in Whites than for Blacks.

The Dying Process

As with other human activities, there are individual and group differences in the dying process. Many people simply "go gently into that good night," sedated and unaware, whereas others consciously "rage against the dying of the light." Some people die quickly, even instantly, from a wound or

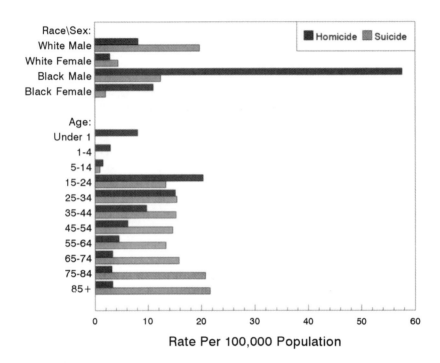

Rate Per 100,000 Population

FIG. 10.9.   Homicide and suicide rates by sex, race, and chronological age. (Based on data in Anderson, Kochanek, & Murphy, 1997.)

heart attack, whereas others experience a slow dying trajectory, lingering on for weeks or months through the miracles of modern medicine (Glaser & Strauss, 1968; Mauksch, 1975). To a great extent, the time of death depends on the nature of the patient's physical condition and the available medical treatments, but this is not to deny the importance of psychological factors. The results of observational and correlational studies suggest that some people can either hasten or delay death by means of their own thoughts. They can be scared to death, simply give up and die, or hang on until some personally significant date or event has occurred (Phillips & Smith, 1990).

The ways in which dying patients are treated, the encouragement given to them, and the choices or voices permitted them also seem to lengthen their stay on earth (Rodin & Langer, 1977). Hospices, which emphasize comfort and pain control and fewer heroic efforts to keep patients alive, are often better places than hospitals for terminally ill patients. Still not all dying patients want or should receive the same sort of treatment. Some are happy dying in the traditional way with their relatives and friends at the bedside, whereas others simply wish, like Tolstoy's Ivan Ilych, to be left alone with their thoughts and pain. Sensitive, effective health personnel, family members, friends, and spiritual advisers recognize that, as at other times of life and insofar as possible, dying patients should be allowed to make their own decisions and do what they can for themselves without interference from well-meaning but often misguided caregivers. For example, if they wish to sign a living will, they should be permitted to do so. If they do not wish to talk with a clergyman or have prayers said over them, their desire should be respected.

According to Kübler-Ross (1969), it is appropriate and desirable for dying individuals to go through a series of psychological stages, including denial, anger, bargaining, preparatory depression, and finally acceptance, although obviously not all dying patients do so. Other stage theories have been proposed to describe the dying process (e.g., Pattison, 1977), but thanatologists have also emphasized the individuality of a person's reactions to death and ways of dealing with it (Shneidman, 1987).

Funerals

Funeral rituals and methods of corpse disposal have varied extensively with historical period, culture, social class, and religion. Compared with Protestants, Jews, nonaffiliated respondents, and Unitarians, Catholics have more favorable attitudes toward funerals and are more likely to hold funerals in churches, but they are less impressed by cosmeticizing or beautifying the corpse. In contrast to Roman Catholics, Protestants are just as likely to hold funerals in a funeral home as in a church (Khleif, 1976). In both religions, the contemporary trend has been away from large church funerals and toward simpler funerals or memorial services.

The *wake,* which is a carryover of the ancient custom of filling the house of the dead with entertainment to "rouse the ghost," is favored more in lower or middle than in upper socioeconomic classes and by Blacks more than Whites (Salomone, 1968). Reflective of the overall trend toward toning down the more emotion-arousing features of the funeral service, wakes have become less popular. In all Western countries, neither the funeral service nor the procession from the place of the service to the final resting place is as emotional and flamboyant as it was in previous times (Norbeck, 1995). To Aries (1981), this is simply another manifestation of the denial of death that has characterized Western culture during the 20th century.

Methods of corpse disposal have also changed dramatically in this century. At different times and places, corpses have been disposed of by being interred, exposed to the open air, buried in water, consumed, or cremated. In the United States, approximately four fifths of the corpses are still buried in the ground. The remainder are cremated—a process that is gradually replacing burial. Cremation is least popular in the South, somewhat most popular in the Mountain region, and most popular of all in the Pacific states, where over 40% of the corpses are disposed of in this manner. Cremation is also quite popular in Canada, and Western Canada in particular, but even more so in Japan and many other Asian countries.

One factor that increased the popularity of cremation in the United States and other countries with large Catholic populations was the removal in the 1970s of the centuries-old objection of the Roman Catholic church to the practice. Whereas most Christian denominations now find either burial or cremation acceptable, Orthodox Jews and Muslims emphasize in-ground burial and Hindus and Buddhists prefer cremation.

Bereavement

The process of *mourning,* the culturally prescribed pattern of behavior by which grief is expressed, has varied with time and culture. Traditional mourning practices, such as wearing black, restricting one's social activities, and flying flags at half mast, are still seen but have become less common over the years. In Victorian England, the duration of mourning varied with one's relationship to the deceased: 12 months for a parent and 9 months for a grandparent, uncle, or aunt. The Victorians frowned on conspicuous displays of emotion during mourning and stressed calmness and fortitude in the face of death—an attitude adopted by the upper classes in America. The mourning process is even more involved in Orthodox Judaism, consisting of three periods: shivah, shloshim, and avelut. During the 7 days immediately after the funeral (*shivah*), mourners in the deceased's home sit on low stools and do not wear leather shoes. Men let the hair on their faces and heads grow, females refrain from using cosmetics, and all mourners avoid any sort of pleasures (bathing, sex, fresh clothing, etc.). Mourners can read only Job, Lamentations, parts of Jeremiah dealing with grief, and sections of the Torah concerned with mourning. The second period of mourning (*shloshim*) lasts from the end of shivah to the 30th day after burial. During this time, mourners cannot attend parties, get married, shave, or cut their hair. At the end of the shloshim period, mourning is considered to be over for all relatives except the mother and father of the deceased, who continue to mourn until 12 months after burial. During this last period (*avelut*), the parents continue to display their grief and avoid happy events, theaters, and concerts (Donin, 1972).

Regardless of the survivor's religious persuasion, grief is sometimes expressed before the loss of a loved one (anticipatory grief), and it is not always expressed immediately afterward. In fact, some people never go through the process of grieving but remain emotionally calm and collected throughout the wake, funeral, and postfuneral period. Other survivors express intense emotion and may take years to recover, if ever.

The intensity of grieving also varies with the age, sex, and personality of the bereaved, in addition to the sociocultural context, the relationship of the bereaved to the deceased, and the extent to which the death was expected.Understandably, death is most shocking when it occurs suddenly and survivors have no opportunity to prepare. Like adults, children experience grief, but they tend to work through it more quickly. The loss of a child or spouse is particularly traumatic for most adults. Older widows typically grieve less than younger ones, although many older widows experience strong feelings of grief for several months after the funeral (Wisocki & Averill, 1987).

The sex of the survivor is also a factor in grieving. Men are expected to react less emotionally than women and be able to cope without having to depend so much on other people for emotional support. According to Glick, Weiss, and Parkes (1974), the death of a loved one means different things to men and women: Men tend to feel dismembered, whereas women tend to feel abandoned. The SES and race/ethnicity of the survivor are also related to the intensity of the grief experience, but not in a straightforward manner. For example, the popular stereotype that, compared with working-class widows, those of higher social status show less overt emotion and experience less difficulty coping was not confirmed in Lopata's (1973) Chicago study.

As with responses to any crisis or tragedy, the manner of expressing grief is also affected by the personality of the bereaved. Most people show some combination of anxiety, fear, depression, guilt, and anger in response to the loss of a loved one—emotions that can be quite intense and even pathological in some cases. Also symptomatic of so-called *pathological grief* are *regression* (behaving childishly), *hallucinations* (hearing or seeing the deceased), *obsessional review* (constantly going over the events prior to the death), *overidentification* (talking and acting like the deceased), *idealization* or *sanctification* (remembering only good things about the deceased), and *mummification* (keeping all the deceased's possessions, as if he or she were still alive). Stress-related illnesses, suicide attempts, and *anniversary reactions* (reexperiencing feelings of grief on the anniversary of the death) may also occur in unresolved grief reactions.

SUMMARY

The human drama, from the cradle to the grave, consists of a series of events that are reacted to and shaped in various ways depending on the personality and circumstances of the individual. The more memorable of these events involve developmental tasks to be accomplished, crises to be overcome, and goals to be attained. Because this is one chapter rather than an entire textbook on human development across the life span, the topics selected for inclusion—education, occupation, expenditures, poverty, marriage and divorce, familial and extrafamilial relationships, religion, crime, prejudice, and death and bereavement—have not been dealt with at great length. The precise nature of the tasks subsumed under these topics and how they are accomplished depend on the physical and mental abilities of the individual and the society and culture in which he or she is a functioning member. In addition to obtaining both a general and special education, most people find it necessary to perform some sort of remunerative work to survive and prosper. Consequently, the chapter begins with a brief discussion of education and employment and how the fruits of one's study and labor are spent. The relationships of age, gender, racial/ethic, and certain other demographic differences to education, employment, and expenditures are also described.

The next topic is marriage and the family. Although a substantial majority of Americans continue to marry, the percentage has declined and the average age of first marriage has increased in recent years. Couples, whether blessed by marital union or not, are still having children, but the average age of parents has increased and varies with race/ethnicity and SES. Cohabitation and divorce are also quite common in our society, and a small percentage of people are gays or lesbians.

The high rate of divorce and the living conditions of children are only two of many social problems. Poverty, malnutrition, disease, crime, terrorism, armed conflict, and social prejudice are others. The annual crime rate in the United States varies not only with the specific crime (violent, property, etc.), but also with age, sex, race/ethnicity, marital status, income, geographical region, urban/rural residence, and other demographic variables. Economic prosperity and other factors have led to a decline in the crime rate in this country during the past few years, but hate crimes have continued to be a source of concern to the general public and to law enforcement officials in particular.

Despite material and social progress supported by legislation, minority groups in the United States are still subject to prejudice and discrimination. Black–White relationships, although improved, remain a source of concern and conflict in a nation committed to a social and political philosophy of establishing unity in diversity.

Dying has been characterized as the final developmental task, but one to which most people look forward the least. The overall death rate and the rate of infant mortality vary widely with geographical region. The countries of Eastern, Western, and Middle Africa, where malnutrition and infectious diseases are widespread, have the highest death rates of all. The primary causes of death in Western countries are heart disease, cancer, and stroke, but pneumonia, influenza, and other major killers of yesteryear have by no means disappeared.

Most people die in hospitals or nursing homes rather than in their own homes or in the streets. There are extensive individual differences in the attitudes of people toward dying and the rate and manner in which they die. Funeral rituals vary with religion and culture, and the general trend has been toward making them less elaborate and emotional. Burial remains the most popular method of corpse disposal in Western countries, but cremation has been gaining ground.

As with reactions to other highly stressful situations, the process of bereavement varies with the individual and the social group to which he or she belongs. The mourning process is generally not as involved or time-consuming as it once was, and survivors are encouraged to recuperate and get on with their lives. In some cases, however, grief is extremely intense, persistent, and even pathological.

SUGGESTED READINGS

Aiken, L. R. (1994). *Death, dying, and bereavement* (3rd ed.). Needham Heights, MA: Allyn & Bacon.

Gatz, M., & Cotton, B. (1994). Age as a dimension of diversity: The experience of being old. In E. J. Trickett, R. J. Watts, & D. Birman (Eds.), *Human diversity* (pp. 312–333). San Francisco: Jossey-Bass.

Jones, J. M. (1994). Our similarities are different: Toward a psychology of affirmative diversity. In E. J. Trickett, R. J. Watts, & D. Birman (Eds.), *Human diversity* (pp. 27–45). San Francisco: Jossey-Bass.

Lonner, W. J. (1994). Culture and human diversity. In E. J. Trickett, R. J. Watts, & D. Birman (Eds.), *Human diversity* (pp. 230–243). San Francisco: Jossey-Bass.

Masters, W. H., Johnson, V. E., & Kolodny, R. C. (1994). *Heterosexuality.* New York: Harper/Collins.

Rubin, J. Z., Pruitt, D. G., & Kim, S. H. (1994). *Social conflict: Escalation, stalemate, and settlement.* New York: McGraw-Hill.

Russell, C. (1996). *The official guide to racial and ethnic diversity.* Ithaca, NY: New Strategist Publications.

Triandis, H. (1994). *Culture and social behavior.* New York: McGraw-Hill.

Glossary

Ability test. A test that measures the extent to which a person is capable of performing a certain task or occupation.

Academic aptitude. The ability to learn school-type tasks; also called *scholastic aptitude*. Many intelligence tests are basically measures of academic aptitude.

Accident-prone personality. A now largely discredited notion that a particular personality type is associated with a greater tendency to have accidents.

Acculturation. Process of cultural change in people who are immersed in a new culture.

Acetylcholine. Neurotransmitter found particularly at the synapses of parasympathetic nerve fibers.

Adaptation. Evolutionary process in which the environment remains fairly constant and a species that is better adjusted to it is produced.

Adaptive behavior. The extent to which a person is able to interact effectively and appropriately with the environment.

Adrenal glands. Endocrine glands located on top of the kidneys and consisting of two parts: medulla and cortex.

Affective disorders. Mental disorders characterized by extreme disturbance of mood and emotion; includes depression and bipolar disorder.

Age-adjusted death rate. Death rate computed by applying the age-specific death rates for age groups to the standard (1940) population distribution by age.

Ageism. Discrimination against elderly adults simply because they are old.

Age norm. The average or expected characteristics or behaviors of a person of a particular chronological age.

Age-specific death rate. Crude death rate computed on a designated chronological age group.

Agoraphobia. An abnormal fear of being alone or in open, public places where escape might be difficult in case of a panic attack.

Alarm reaction. The first stage of Selye's general adaptation syndrome, in which the body is mobilized for fight or flight by increased activity of the sympathetic nervous system and the resulting muscular and glandular changes.

Alternate-forms reliability. An index of reliability determined by correlating the scores of individuals on one form of a test with their scores on another form.

Amygdala. Part of the limbic system consisting of a set of nuclei at the base of the temporal lobe; involved in emotional expression.

Analysis of variance (ANOVA). Statistical procedure involving variance comparisons for computing F ratios to determine the significance or differences among the means of several groups.

Androgens. Male sex hormones: testosterone and androsterone. See *estrogens.*

Anecdotal record. A written record of behavioral observations of a specified individual. Care must be taken to differentiate between observation and interpretation if the record is to be objective.

Anorexia nervosa. An eating disorder characterized by a pathological fear of being fat and consequent excessive dieting and emaciation; occurs primarily in adolescent girls.

Anthropometry. Measurement of the size and proportions of the human body.

Anticipatory grief. Grieving or mourning by a survivor that begins even before the death of a loved one.

Anxiety disorders. Mental disorders characterized by chronic feelings of apprehension or uneasiness. This diagnostic category includes generalized anxiety disorder, panic disorder, obsessive–compulsive disorder, posttraumatic stress disorder, and phobic disorder.

Aptitude. Capability of learning to perform a particular task or skill. Traditionally aptitude was thought to depend more on inborn potential than on actual practice.

Aptitude test. A measure of the ability to profit from additional training or experience—that is, become proficient in a skill or other ability.

Archival research. Research conducted with written records of events and preserved by an institution or cultural organization.

Arithmetic mean. A measure of the average or central tendency of a group of scores; computed by dividing the sum of the scores by the number of scores. See *median* and *mode.*

Assessment. Appraising the presence or magnitude of one or more personal characteristics. Assessing human behavior and mental processes includes such procedures as observations, interviews, rating scales, check-lists, inventories, projective techniques, and tests.

Assortative mating. Nonrandom mating between individuals possessing similar characteristics.

Attachment. Development by a young child or animal of a close, lasting relationship with another person; bonding.

Attitude. Tendency to respond positively or negatively to some object, person, or situation.

Attitude scale. A paper-and-pencil instrument consisting of a series of statements concerning an institution, situation, person, event, and so on. The examinee responds to each statement by endorsing it or indicating his or her degree of agreement or disagreement with it.

Attribution. Judgment that the causes of certain outcomes are internal or external to the person.

Autonomic nervous system. That part of the peripheral nervous system consisting of sympathetic and parasympathetic divisions.

Autosomal gene. A gene on any other chromosome than the sex chromosomes (X and Y).

Baseline time. Time required to respond to a single stimulus, such as a light or sound; same as simple reaction time or Donders A reaction time.

Base rate. Proportion of individuals having a specified condition who are identified or selected without the use of new selection procedures.

B-cells. Lymphocytes that are important in the production of antibodies.

Behavior genetics. Study of the inheritance of behavioral characteristics.

Bereavement. Loss of a loved one by death.

Bigotry. Intolerance of any creed, belief, or opinion that differs from one's own.

Bipolar disorder. Mental disorder in which the individual's mood fluctuates between extreme depression and elation.

Body mass index (BMI). A measure of relative weight computed as the ratio of the body weight in kilograms to the square of the height in meters. A person with a BMI of 25 to 30 is considered overweight and one with a BMI above 30 is obese.

Broca's area. Area in the left frontal portion of the cerebral cortex; concerned with the control of speech. Patients with damage to Broca's area have difficulty enunciating words correctly and speak in a slow, labored manner. See *Wernicke's area.*

Burnout. Emotional and behavioral impairment resulting from high levels of stress in occupational situations and precipitated by overwork; characterized by emotional exhaustion, lessened productivity, and feelings of depersonalization.

Canonical correlation. Multivariate statistical procedure for determining the relationships among several independent and several dependent variables.

Catecholamines. Group of neurotransmitters including epinephrine, norepinephrine, and dopamine.

Central nervous system. Part of the nervous system that is encased in bone; the brain and spinal cord. See *Peripheral nervous system.*

Central tendency. Average or central score in a group of scores; the most representative score (e.g., *arithmetic mean, median,* and *mode*).

Cephalic index. Ratio of the greatest breadth of the head to its greatest length from front to back, multiplied by 100.

Cerebellum. Largest structure in the hindbrain; concerned with motor coordination.

Cerebral cortex. Gray matter on the surface of the cerebral hemispheres; consists of a series of four to six layers made up of neurons that give it a gray appearance.

Cerebral hemispheres. Bilateral pair of structures making up the telencephalon of the brain; the neural seat of sensation, movement, and various higher order functions of the nervous system.

Checklist. List of words, phrases, or statements descriptive of personal characteristics; respondents endorse (check) those items that are characteristic of themselves (self-ratings) or other people (other-ratings).

Classification. The use of test scores and other assessment procedures to assign a person to one category rather than another.

Claustrophobia. An abnormal fear of narrow or enclosed places.

Close-coupled relationship. An enduring monogamous relationship between homosexuals. See *open-coupled relationship.*

Coefficient alpha. An internal-consistency reliability coefficient appropriate for tests composed of dichotomous or multipoint items; the expected correlation of one test with a parallel form containing the same number of items.

Coefficient of alienation. The proportion of variability in the Y (dependent) variable that cannot be accounted for by variation in the X (independent) variable; one minus the coefficient of determination.

Coefficient of determination. The proportion of the variability in the Y (dependent) variable that can be accounted for by variation in the X (independent) variable; the square of the correlation coefficient between X and Y.

Coefficient of equivalence. A reliability coefficient (correlation) obtained by administering a test to the same group of examinees on two different occasions. See *test–retest reliability.*

Coefficient of internal consistency. Reliability coefficient based on estimates of the internal consistency of a test (e.g., *split-half coefficient* and *coefficient alpha*).

Coefficient of stability. A reliability coefficient (correlation) obtained by administering a test to the same group of examinees on two different occasions. See *test–retest reliability.*

Coefficient of stability and equivalence. A reliability coefficient obtained by administering two forms of a test to a group of people on two different occasions.

Cognition. Having to do with the processes of intellect; remembering, thinking, problem solving, and the like.

Cognitive assessment. Measurement of intellective processes, such as perception, memory, thinking, judgment, and reasoning.

Cohort. A group of people of the same age, class membership, or culture (e.g., all people born in 1950).

Cohort sequential design. Developmental research design in which successive cohorts are compared over the same age ranges. For example, changes in attitude or ability from age 60 to 70 in a group born in 1910 are compared with changes in attitude from age 60 to 70 in a group born in 1920.

Collectivism. Cultural orientation that stresses interdependence, cooperation, and group harmony as opposed to personal goals. See *individualism.*

Communality. Proportion of variance in a measured variable accounted for by variance that the variable has in common with other variables.

Companionate marriage. Marital partnership in which the couple share interests and a love for each other.

Concordance rate. The degree to which other people have the same characteristic as a specific individual (*proband* or *index case*). The extent to which the characteristic is genetically based is determined by comparing the concordance rates for the proband's relatives with those of the general population.

Concurrent validity. The extent to which scores obtained by a group of people on a particular psychometric instrument are related to their scores determined simultaneously on another measure (*criterion*) of the same characteristic that the instrument is supposed to measure.

Confidence interval. A range of values within which one can be fairly certain (usually 95% or 99% confident) that a person's true score (or difference between scores) on a test or a criterion variable falls. See *standard error of measurement* and *standard error of estimate.*

Confirmatory research. Research investigation design to test or confirm the correctness of some proposition or hypothesis.

Confounded variable. Variable that covaries with the independent variable, thus making its effect on the dependent variable unclear.

Confounding. Situation in which two measures or characteristics vary in such a way that the independent effect of each cannot be determined. Age and cohort differences are confounded in cross-sectional research, and age and time of measurement are confounded in longitudinal research.

Congruent validity. Validity of a test or other psychometric instrument determined by the correlation between the test scores and scores on a criterion measure obtained in the same time frame as the test scores.

Construct. An abstract variable or concept designed to explain or interpret the relationship between two or more observable variables.

Construct validity. The extent to which scores on a psychometric instrument designed to measure a certain characteristic are related to measures of behavior in situations in which the characteristic is supposed to be an important determinant of behavior.

Content validity. The extent to which a group of people who are experts in the material with which a test deals agree that the test or other psychometric instrument measures what it was designed to measure.

Convergent thinking. Using facts and reason to produce a single correct answer to a problem. See *divergent thinking.*

Convergent validity. Situation in which an assessment instrument has high correlations with other measures or methods of measuring the same construct. See *discriminant validity.*

Coping. Controlling, reducing, or learning to tolerate stress-provoking events.

Corpus callosum. White band of nerve fibers connecting the two cerebral hemispheres.

Correlation. The degree of relationship between two variables signified by an index (a correlation coefficient) ranging from −1.00 to +1.00.

Correlation coefficient. A numerical index of the degree of relationship between two variables. Correlation coefficients usually range from −1.00 (perfect negative relationship) to .00 (total absence of a relationship) to +1.00 (perfect positive relationship). Two common types of correlation coefficients are the product-moment coefficient and the point-biserial coefficient.

Cremation. Process of reducing a dead body to cremains (ashes) by means of heat or direct flame.

Criterion. A standard or variable with which scores on a psychometric instrument are compared or against which they are evaluated. The validity of a test or other psychometric procedure used in selecting or classifying people is determined by its ability to predict a specified criterion of behavior in the situation for which people are being selected or classified.

Criterion-related validity. The extent to which a test or other assessment instrument measures what it was designed to measure, as indicated by the correlation of test scores with some criterion measure of behavior.

Crossing over. Exchanging of parts between two chromosomes during the replication process.

Cross-sectional study. Comparisons of the physical and psychological characteristics of different age groups of people. See *longitudinal study.*

Cross-sequential design. Developmental research design in which two or more successive cohorts are studied longitudinally. For example, the changes in attitude or ability from 1970 to 1990 in groups of individuals born in 1920, 1940, and 1960 are compared.

Cross-validation. Readministering an assessment instrument that has been found to be a valid predictor of a criterion for one group of persons to a second group of persons to determine whether the instrument is also valid for that group.

Crude birth rate. Number of births per 1,000 or 100,000 population in a given time period, typically a year.

Crude death rate. Number of deaths per 1,000 or 100,000 population during a particular period of time, usually 1 year.

Crystallized ability. R. B. Cattell's term for mental ability (knowledge, skills) acquired through experience and education and specific to certain fields, such as school learning, and applied in tasks where habits have become fixed. See *fluid ability.*

Cultural determinism. The idea that individual choices and actions are culturally determined.

Culture. A composite of behavior patterns, mores, attitudes, institutions, and organizations handed down from generation to generation.

Culture shock. Feelings of strangeness and anxiety on being exposed to a culture different from one's own.

Daily hassles. Everyday events that are annoying and produce a certain amount of stress.

Delirium. State of mental confusion characterized by clouding of consciousness, disorientation, restlessness, excitement, and frequently hallucinations.

Demography. The science of vital and social statistics (births, marriages, diseases, etc.) of populations.

Dependent variable. The variable in an experiment that changes as a function of changes in the independent variable. Variations in magnitude of the dependent variable, plotted on the Y axis of a graph, can be viewed as the experimental effect. See *independent variable.*

Depression. Mood disorder characterized by dejection, loss of interest in things, negative thoughts (including suicidal thoughts), and various physical symptoms (e.g., loss of appetite, insomnia, fatigue).

Descriptive research. Research designed simply to describe some object or event without attempting to explain it. See *inferential statistics.*

Descriptive statistics. Statistical procedures for describing a sample of data without attempting to generalize to a larger population of values.

Developmental studies. Research investigations (longitudinal, cross-sectional, etc.) designed to assess and evaluate changes in groups of people over time.

Deviation IQ. Intelligence quotient (IQ) score obtained by converting raw scores on an intelligence test to a score distribution having a mean of 100 and a standard deviation of 15 or 16.

Diathesis stress model. Concept that abnormal behaviors and mental disorders are the consequence of biological, psychological, and sociological predisposition factors being acted on by immediate, precipitating stress.

Differential association. Theory that criminal behavior results from the socialization of the individual into a system of values conducive to law violations.

Differential psychology. As pioneered by William Stern, the psychological study of individual and group differences.

Discriminant analysis. Multivariate statistical procedure for determining mathematical functions to predict scores on a weighted combination of variables from scores on another weighted combination of variables.

Discriminant validity. Situation in which a psychometric instrument has low correlations with other measures of (or methods of measuring) different psychological constructs.

Discrimination. Differential attitudes toward and treatment of people because of their membership in or affiliation with a particular sociocultural or ethnic group.

Disease-prone personality. As described by Friedman and Booth-Kewley (1987), a personality involving depression, anger/hostility, anxiety, and perhaps other personality variables.

Disordinal interaction. Research result in which the direction of the relationship between an independent and a dependent variable varies with the value of a third variable. See *ordinal interaction.*

Dissociative disorder. Mental disorder in which the individual avoids stress by escaping from his or her identify, as in psychological amnesia, fugue, somnambulism, or multiple personality.

Divergent thinking. Creative thinking involving more than one solution to a problem. See *convergent thinking.*

Dizygotic twins. Fraternal twins produced by coincident pregnancies (fertilization of two eggs by two sperm cells). See *monozygotic twins.*

DNA. Deoxyribonucleic acid. A nucleic acid polymer shaped as a double helix that forms the basic hereditary material of all living organisms. Most DNA is found in chromosomes.

Dominant gene. A gene that has an effect on a phenotypic characteristic even when the genotype is heterozygous.

Down's syndrome. Type of mental retardation resulting from a third chromosome in position number 21.

Dyscalculia (acalculia). Inability to perform arithmetical operations.

Dysgenic hypothesis. Hypothesis that the intellectual abilities of the population are deteriorating due to the relatively greater birth rate among women of lower intelligence.

Dyslexia. Reading disorder associated with an impairment in the ability to interpret spatial relationships or integrate auditory and visual information.

Educable mentally retarded (EMR). Children characterized by a mild degree of mental retardation (IQ = 51–69). Such children are capable of obtaining a third- to sixth-grade education and learning to read, write, and perform elementary arithmetic operations. See *trainable mentally retarded.*

Electroencephalograph (EEG). Record of electrical waves, ranging in frequency from 1 to 13 Hz, obtained from the scalp of the brain.

Electromyograph (EMG). Record of the electrical activity of the muscles.

Emergency reaction. Physiological response of the body to emergency situations; purveyed by the sympathetic nervous system and the adrenal glands.

Emotional intelligence. A type of social intelligence involving the ability to monitor one's own and others' emotions, discriminate among them, and use the information to guide one's own thinking.

Epidemiological studies. Prospective or retrospective investigations designed to determine the risk factors associated with particular diseases.

Epinephrine (adrenalin). A neurotransmitter, one of the catecholamines, involved in emergency reactions of the body.

Epistasis. Interaction of two genes that produces a phenotypic effect that is unpredictable from the effects of either gene alone.

Ergonomics. Science concerned with the relationships between humans and machines.

Estrogens. Female sex hormones secreted by the ovaries. See *androgens.*

Ethnic group. A group of people who share the same language and customs but not necessarily the same racial makeup.

Ethnic identity (ethnicity). The part of a person's identity that is defined by language, history, customs, and other aspects of his or her ethnic heritage.

Eugenics. The science of improving the qualities of a species, especially humans, by careful selection of parents.

Evolution. Change in the gene pool of a population over successive generations.

Experiment. Systematic scientific procedure for determining the cause of a relationship between two (independent and dependent) variables while controlling for extraneous variables.

Explanatory research. In contrast to exploratory research, research designed to provide an explanation for some phenomenon. See *exploratory research.*

Explanatory styles. As defined by Seligman (1991), the ways in which people explain good and bad past events, leading to a general attitude of optimism or pessimism.

Exploratory research. Relatively open-ended scientific investigation designed to discover possible relationships among and causes of certain natural phenomena. See *explanatory research.*

External validity. Generalizability of the results of a research study from a sample to a specified target population. See *internal validity.*

Extraneous variable. Variable that can interfere with a clear understanding of the relationship between an independent and a dependent variable.

Face validity. The extent to which the appearance or content of the materials (items, etc.) on a test or other psychometric instrument is such that the instrument appears to be a good measure of what it is supposed to measure.

Factitious disorder. Diagnostic category of mental disorders in which the individual feigns physical or psychological signs or symptoms to assume the sick role.

Factor. A dimension, trait, or characteristic of personality revealed by factor analyzing the matrix of correlations computed from the scores of a large number of people in several different tests or items.

Factor analysis. A mathematical procedure for analyzing a matrix of correlations among measurements to determine what factors (constructs) are sufficient to explain the correlations.

Factor loadings. In factor analysis, the resulting correlations (weights) between tests (or other variables) and the extracted factors.

Factor rotation. A mathematical procedure applied to a factor matrix for the purpose of simplifying the matrix for interpretation purposes by increasing the number of high and low factor loadings in the matrix. Factor rotation may be either *orthogonal*, in which case the resulting factors are at right angles to each other, or *oblique,* in which the resulting factor axes form acute or obtuse angles with each other.

False-negative error. Decision error in which an assessment or diagnostic procedure incorrectly identifies or predicts a maladaptive outcome (poor performance or psychopathology).

False-positive error. Decision error in which an assessment or diagnostic procedure incorrectly identifies or predicts an adaptive outcome (good performance or absence of psychopathology).

Fertility rate. Average number of children per woman of childbearing age in a given population.

Field dependence. A perceptual style in which the perceiver relies principally on cues from the surrounding visual environment, rather than on kinesthetic (gravitational) cues.

Field independence. A perceptual style in which the perceiver relies primarily on kinesthetic (gravitational) cues rather than on visual cues from the surrounding environment.

Field research. Research conducted outside the laboratory in a real-life situation.

Five-factor model (Big Five). A model of human personality based on the results of factor analysis that characterizes personality as a composite of five factors: neuroticism, extraversion, openness, agreeableness, and conscientiousness.

Fluid ability. R. B. Cattell's term for inherent, genetically determined mental ability, as seen in problem-solving or novel responses. See *crystallized ability.*

Flynn effect. An observed increase in the mean score on intelligence tests during the 20th century.

Forensic anthropology. The application of anthropological knowledge to questions of civil and criminal law.

Frequency distribution. A table of score intervals and the number of cases (scores) falling within each interval.

Frontal lobe. Portion of the cerebral cortex in the frontal lobes anterior to the central fissure.

g factor. A single general factor of intelligence postulated by Charles Spearman to account for the high correlations among tests of different cognitive abilities.

Gender identity. An individual's view of him or herself with regard to gender; the introspective part of *gender role.*

Gender role. A culture-specific pattern of behavior that is considered appropriate to a particular gender.

Gender schema. Internalized beliefs about what men and women are and how they are supposed to behave.

Gene. A microscopic particle consisting of DNA that determines hereditary characteristics.

General adaptation syndrome (GAS). Hans Selye's three-stage bodily stress response (alarm reaction, resistance, exhaustion) resulting form exposure to a stressor.

Genetics. The science of heredity.

Genotype. The underlying genetic structure of a characteristic.

Glial cells. Supporting cells that constitute a substantial part of the brain. Although glial cells are not neurons, they are thought to play a role in neuronal transmission.

Gonads. Male (testes) and female (ovaries) sex glands.

Grade norm. The average of the scores on a test made by a group of children at a given grade level.

Grief. Severe mental distress resulting from loss or affliction; acute sorrow or painful regret.

Group marriage. A communal arrangement in which a number of legally married couples share living quarters, duties, and sexual partners.

Gyrus. Convolution (fold) in the cerebral cortex.

Hardiness. A personality characteristic, including commitment, challenge, and control, associated with a lower rate of stress-related illness.

Hate crime. A crime motivated by preformed, negative bias against persons, property, or organizations based solely on race, religion, ethnicity/national origin, sexual orientation, or disability.

Health psychology. A branch of psychology concerned with research and applications directed toward the maintenance of health and the prevention of illness.

Hemisphericity. Individual differences in the level of activation of the two cerebral hemispheres.

Heritability index (coefficient) (h^2). Ratio of the test score variance attributable to heredity to the variance attributable to both heredity and environment.

Heterozygous. Two dissimilar genes underlying a particular characteristic.

Homozygous. Two identical genes underlying a particular characteristic.

Hormones. Chemicals secreted by endocrine glands.

Hypothalamus. Small neural structure located below the thalamus and above the brainstem. Contains groups of neurons that regulate motivated behavior (eating, drinking, sex, emotions), as well as endocrine functions and the maintenance of homeostasis.

Identification. Taking on the personal characteristics of another person, as when a developing child identifies with a significant other person. Also, in psychoanalytic theory, an ego defense mechanism for coping with anxiety.

Identification time. The difference between Donders C reaction time and Donders A reaction time; time required to identify a stimulus.

Identity. The gradual emergence and continual change in an individual's sense of self.

Identity crisis. In Erikson's theory of psychosocial developmental stages, the period, especially during adolescence, characterized by a strong concern with the acquisition of a sense of self. An identity crisis may end in either a sense of identity or identity diffusion.

Independent variable. The variable whose effects (on the *dependent variable*) are attempting to be determined in an experiment.

Index case. A person identified as having a particular disorder or characteristic, with which other persons can be compared or linked in studies of inheritance.

Individualism. Cultural orientation that emphasizes independence, autonomy, and self-reliance over group allegiance. See *collectivism*.

Individuating information. Information that assists in defining a person as an individual rather than as a member of a social group or category.

Infant mortality. Death before the age of 1 year.

Inferential statistics. Procedures for estimating population parameters from sample statistics; constructing confidence limits for the parameters and conducting statistical tests of hypotheses concerning the parameters. See *descriptive statistics*.

Informed consent. Consenting to participate in a research investigation after being told the nature of the investigation, how the results will be used, and that the participant is free to withdraw at any time.

Intelligence. Many definitions of this term have been offered, such as "the ability to judge well, understand well, and reason well" (A. Binet) and "the capacity for abstract thinking" (L. M. Terman). In general, what is measured by intelligence tests is the ability to succeed in school-type tasks.

Intelligence quotient (IQ). A derived score, used originally in scoring the Stanford–Binet Intelligence Scale. A ratio IQ is computed by dividing the examinee's mental age (MA), as determined from a score on an intelligence test, by his or her chronological age (CA) and multiplying the resulting quotient by 100. A *deviation IQ* is computed by multiplying the z score corresponding to a raw score on an intelligence test by the standard deviation of the deviation IQs and adding 100 to the product.

Intelligence test. A psychological test designed to measure an individual's aptitude for scholastic work or other kinds of activities involving verbal ability and problem solving.

Interest inventory. A test or checklist, such as the Strong Interest Inventory or the Kuder General Interest Survey, designed to assess individual preferences for certain activities and topics.

Internal consistency. The extent to which all items on a test measure the same variable or construct. The reliability of a test computed by the Spearman–Brown, Kuder–Richardson, or Cronbach-alpha formulas is a measure of the test's internal consistency.

Internal validity. Extent to which the results of an experiment are free from errors of measurement. See *external validity.*

Interpersonal intelligence. Ability to detect the moods of other people and lead them.

Interval scale. A measurement scale on which equality of numerical differences implies equality of differences in the attribute or characteristic being measured. The scale of temperature (Celsius, Fahrenheit) and, presumably, standard score scales (z, T), are examples of interval scales.

Intrapersonal intelligence. Knowing one's own feelings and understanding how to use that self-knowledge productively.

Inventory. A set of questions or statements to which the individual responds (e.g., by indicating agreement or disagreement); designed to provide a measure of personality, interest, attitude, or behavior.

Ipsative measurement. Test item format (e.g., forced choice) in which the variables being measured are compared with each other so that a person's score on one variable is affected by his or her scores on other variables measured by the instrument.

Islets of Langerhans. Specialized pancreatic cells that secrete hormones (insulin, glucagon) involved in the maintenance of the body's blood sugar level.

Just-world belief. Believing that people generally get what they deserve in this world.

Lake Wobegon effect. Tendency for an increasing number of students in school districts throughout the United States to score above the national norms on standardized achievement tests.

Law of filial regression. Tendency of the physical and mental characteristics of offspring to be less extreme than those of their parents; regression toward the mean.

Learned helplessness. Apathy or inactivity resulting from repeated inability to cope with stressful situations.

Learning disability. Difficulty in learning to read, write, spell, or perform arithmetic or other specific academic skills, but not deficient in general mental ability.

Levels of measurement. Precision of measurement, ranging from nominal to ordinal, interval and ratio scales (levels), in order of increasing precision.

Life expectancy. The average life span of people born in a certain year; probable length of life of an individual.

Life span. Longevity of an individual or the longest period of life of a member of a given species.

Lifestyle. Relatively permanent pattern of activities, including work, leisure, and associated social activities, characterizing an individual.

Limbic system. A set of structures in and around the midbrain (amygdala, hippocampus, septum, etc.) that regulate motivation and emotion, including waking and sleeping, excitement and quiet, feeding and mating.

Linkage. The joint transmission of genes located near each other on a chromosome.

Locus of control. Generalized belief concerning the causes of events in a person's life—whether the causes are internal or external, within or outside the person.

Longitudinal study. Studying the development of the same individual(s) at different ages over a period of years. See *cross-sectional study.*

Measurement. Procedures for determining (or indexing) the amount or quantity of some construct or entity; assignment of numbers to objects or events.

Median. Score point in a distribution of scores below and above which 50% of the scores fall; a measure of the average or central tendency of a group of measures. See *arithmetic mean* and *mode.*

Medulla oblongata. Part of hindbrain consisting of a bulge in the spinal cord as it enters the skull, at which major nerve tracts cross over to the opposite side; also important in vital reflexes.

Melting pot. Social/national concept of integration in which different ethnic groups are combined to produce a single mainstream culture. See *mosaicism.*

Mental chronometry. Measurement of the time required for mental (psychological) events to take place.

Mentally gifted. A person who is significantly above average in intellectual functioning, having an IQ of 130 or 140 and above.

Mentally retarded. A person who is significantly below average in intellectual functioning, having an IQ below 70 or 75.

Mental test. Term first used by J. M. Cattell to refer to psychological, especially intelligence, tests.

Mode. The most frequently occurring score in a group of scores. See *arithmetic mean* and *median.*

Moderator variable. Demographic or personality variable (e.g., age, sex, cognitive style, compulsivity) affecting the correlation between two other variables (e.g, aptitude and achievement).

Monozygotic twins. Identical twins produced by the same egg and sperm. See *dizygotic twins.*

Morbidity. Illness, injury, or disability.

Mortality. Death, in particular within a large population of people.

Mosaicism. Social/national concept in which each cultural group retains its own identity and tolerates differences among groups. See *melting pot.*

Mourning. Manifestation of sorrow or lamentation for the death of a person; traditionally indicated by wearing black clothes or a black arm band, hanging flags at half mast, and other cultural rituals. The period during which people mourn.

Multiculturalism. Diversity of racial and ethnic groups within a nation or other political body.

Multiple abstract variance analysis (MAVA). Statistical procedure, devised by R. B. Cattell, for determining the relative effects of heredity and environment on a particular personality characteristic.

Multiple aptitude battery. A battery of conormed tests designed to assess mental abilities.

Multiple correlation coefficient (R). A measure of the overall degree of relationship, varying between -1.00 and $+1.00$, of several variables with a single criterion variable. For example, the multiple correlation of a group of scholastic aptitude tests with school grades is typically around .60 to .70—a moderate degree of correlation.

Multiple-regression analysis. Statistical method for analyzing the contributions of two or more independent variables in predicting a dependent variable.

Multitrait-multimethod matrix. Matrix of correlation coefficients resulting from correlating measures of the same trait by the same method, different traits by the same method, the same trait by different methods, and different traits by different methods. The relative magnitudes of the four types of correlations are compared in evaluating the construct validity of a test.

Multivariate analysis of variance (MANOVA). Inferential statistical procedures for comparing the means of two or more groups on several dependent variables; an extension of univariate analysis of variance to multiple dependent variables.

Mutation. Change in a gene during reproduction.

Natural selection. Concept in theory of evolution that animals possessing certain characteristics will adapt better than others to certain environments and thereby survive to pass on their genetic characteristics to their offspring, while animals that do not have those characteristics have a lower chance of surviving long enough to reproduce and pass on their genes.

Neuron. The basic building block of the nervous system consisting of dendrites, cell body, axon, and end bulbs. The function of a neuron is to transmit and store electrochemical information.

Neurotransmitter. A chemical released at a synapse that affects the transmission of a nerve impulse across the synapse by changing the resting potential of a postsynaptic neuron.

Nominal scale. The lowest type of measurement in which numbers are used merely as descriptors or names of things, rather than designating order or amount.

Norepinephrine (noradrenalin). Hormone secreted by the adrenal medulla that causes bodily reactions similar to those produced by the sympathetic nervous system.

Norm group. Sample of people on whom a test is standardized.

Normal distribution. A smooth, bell-shaped frequency distribution of scores, symmetrical about the mean, and described by an exact mathematical equation. The test scores of a large group of examinees are frequently distributed in an approximately normal fashion.

Norms. A list of scores and the corresponding percentile ranks, standard scores, or other transformed scores of a group of examinees in a given demographic group (age, sex, race, geographical region, etc.) on a psychological test or other assessment device.

Oblique rotation. A factor rotation procedure in which the factor axes are allowed to form acute or obtuse angles with each other. Consequently, the factors are correlated. See *orthogonal rotation.*

Observation method. Observing behavior in a controlled or uncontrolled situation and making a formal or informal record of the observations.

Obsessive–compulsive disorder. A neurotic disorder in which the primary symptoms are obsessions (undesirable thoughts) and compulsions (repetitive acts).

Occipital lobe. Area of the cerebral cortex lying at the back of the head; especially important in vision.

Open-coupled relationship. A relationship in which two homosexuals live together but have other lovers as well. See *close-coupled relationship.*

Open marriage. A legally sanctioned union in which the partners find it perfectly acceptable to have sexual relationships with other people.

Operational definition. A definition that tells what to do or what procedure to follow to experience the thing being defined.

Ordinal interaction. Research result in which the magnitude of the relationship between an independent and a dependent variable varies with the value of a third variable. See *disordinal interaction.*

Ordinal scale. Type of measurement scale on which the numbers refer merely to the ranks of objects or events arranged in order of merit (e.g., numbers referring to order of finishing in a contest).

Organismic variable. Physical or psychological characteristics of subjects used in a research study; may be made an explicit part of the research design.

Orthogonal rotation. In factor analysis, a rotation that maintains the independence of factors—that is, the angles between factors are kept at 90 degrees and hence the factors are uncorrelated. See *Oblique rotation.*

Overweight. Weight exceeding the individual's desirable range by 10% to 20%; a *body mass index* of 25 or above.

Panic disorder. The manifestation of anxiety through panic attacks.

Parallel forms reliability. An index of reliability determined by correlating the scores made by a group of individuals on one form of a parallel test with their scores on a second form of the test.

Parasympathetic compensation. Compensatory activity of the parasympathetic nervous system in response to overactivity of the sympathetic nervous system.

Parasympathetic nervous system. Part of the autonomic nervous system arising from nerve fibers in the cranial and sacral regions of the spinal column; concerned with digestion and other vegetative functions of the body. See *sympathetic nervous system.*

Parathyroid glands. Two pairs of endocrine glands situated near the thyroid gland that secrete parahormone, a hormone that helps regulate the calcium–potassium balance of the blood.

Parietal lobe. Portion of the cerebral cortex located behind the central fissure and between the frontal and occipital lobes; contains neural structures for experiencing somesthetic sensations.

Participant observation. A research technique used primarily by cultural anthropologists in which an observer attempts to minimize the intrusiveness of his or her person and observational activities by becoming part of the group being observed (e.g., by dressing and acting like other members of the group).

Pathological grief. Grief in which the typical symptoms persist in intensified form or become noteworthy by their complete absence.

Penetrance. The degree to which a gene is expressed.

Percentile. The pth percentile is the score at or below which p percent of the scores of a specified group of individuals fall.

Percentile norms. A list of raw scores and the corresponding percentages of the test standardization group whose scores fall below the given percentile.

Percentile rank. The percentage of scores falling below a given score in a frequency distribution or group of scores; the percentage corresponding to the given score.

Peripheral nervous system. Part of the nervous system lying outside the brain and spinal cord; the autonomic nervous system and the peripheral nerves. See *central nervous system.*

Personal equation. Individual differences in reaction time first reported by 18th-century astronomers and studied extensively by psychologists during the late 19th century.

Personality. Sum total of the qualities, traits, and behaviors characterizing a person and by which, together with his or her physical attributes, the person is recognized as a unique individual.

Personality assessment. Description and analysis of personality by means of various techniques, including observing, interviewing, and administering checklists, rating scales, personality inventories, and projective techniques.

Personality disorders. A group of maladaptive behavioral syndromes originating in childhood but not characterized by psychoneurotic or psychotic symptomatology.

Personality inventory. A self-report inventory or questionnaire consisting of statements concerning personal characteristics and behaviors. On a true–false inventory, the respondent indicates whether each item is self-descriptive; on a multiple-choice or forced-choice inventory, the respondent selects the words, phrases, or statements that are self-descriptive.

Phobia. An irrational, persisting fear of something as in agoraphobia or claustrophobia.

Pineal gland. Endocrine gland situated at the base of the brain and involved in regulating the sleep–wakefulness cycle.

Pituitary gland. Endocrine gland situated below the hypothalamus that secretes growth hormone and various middle-man hormones regulating the secretions of other endocrine glands.

Placebo effect. Change in behavior resulting from the administration of a chemically inert substance to people who believe they are receiving an active drug.

Pleiotropy. Multiple phenotypic effects produced by a single gene.

Polygraph. So-called *lie-detection machine,* which measures heart rate, blood pressure, respiration rate, and the galvanic skin response.

Changes in these responses from baseline levels are considered to be indicative of lying.

Pons. Portion of the hindbrain consisting principally of motor fiber tracts connected to the cerebellum and spinal cord.

Postcentral gyrus. Area in the parietal lobe posterior to the central fissure that is concerned with somesthetic sensitivity.

Posttraumatic stress disorder (PTSD). A persisting anxiety reaction precipitated by a severely stressful experience, such as military combat, characterized by a reexperiencing of the stressful event and an avoidance of stimuli associated with it. Other symptoms include feelings of estrangement, recurring dreams and nightmares, and a tendency to be easily startled.

Poverty. Having little or no money, goods, or means of support. The official U.S. government definition of poverty includes a set of money income thresholds varying with the size and composition of the family.

Practical intelligence. Ability to solve problems of daily life for which there may be no clear-cut answers.

Precentral gyrus. Area in the frontal lobe just anterior to the central fissure that controls the movements of striated muscles.

Predictive validity. Extent to which scores on a test are predictive of performance on some criterion measure assessed at a later time; usually expressed as a correlation between the test (predictor variable) and the criterion variable.

Prejudice. Generalized negative feelings toward members of an outgroup in the absence of any rational justification for those feelings.

Prenatal. Occurring while the individual is still in the womb.

Primary memory. Short-term memory (STM) lasting up to half a minute, as in remembering a specific telephone number only until it has been dialed. Retention of five to seven bits of information in temporary memory storage.

Proband. See *index case.*

Probandwise concordance rate. Statistical measure of genetic influence computed by dividing twice the number of concordant pairs in the sample by the sum of the number of concordant and discordant pairs.

Progressive muscle relaxation. Alternate tightening and relaxing of specific muscle groups as a way of reducing stress.

Prospective study. Research investigation that follows up, over time, people having different characteristics or lifestyles to determine which ones develop a particular condition or disorder. See *retrospective study.*

Psychobiography. Analysis of the personalities of individuals by studying their personal histories.

Psychohistory. Study of psychological factors contributing to historical events and persons.

Psychometrics. Theory and research pertaining to the measurement of psychological (cognitive, affective, and psychomotor) characteristics.

Psychoneuroimmunology. A field of research that explores the interactions among psychological factors, the nervous system, and the immune system.

Psychophysiological disorder. A disorder characterized by physical symptoms produced by a combination of psychosocial and physiological variables.

Psychosocial stages. Erikson's modification of Freud's theory of psychosexual stages; emphasizes environmental and social problems, as contrasted with biological factors, in the progression of developmental stages from infancy to old age.

Psychosomatic disorder. Physical illness based on psychological stress, such as duodenal ulcers or tension headache.

Psychosomatic medicine. Branch of medicine concerned with the treatment of illnesses caused by stress and other mental states.

Pupillometrics. Measuring pupillary diameter as an indicator of pleasure or interest in a specific stimulus.

Quality of life. Personal appraisal of the extent to which one's life is satisfying and meaningful.

Quasi-experimental design. Nonexperimental design in which treatment conditions may be manipulated but subjects are not randomly assigned to them; also known as a *post hoc study.*

Race. A group of people with distinct, biologically determined, physical characteristics, including a distinctive skin color, body build, and physiological characteristics.

Racism. Prejudice and discrimination against other people simply because they belong to a different racial or ethnic group from one's own.

Random sample. A sample of observations (e.g., test scores) drawn from a population in such a way that every member of the target population has an equal chance of being selected in the sample.

Range. A crude measure of the spread or variability of a group of scores computed by subtracting the lowest score from the highest score.

Rapport. A warm, friendly relationship between examiner and examinee in a psychological testing situation.

Rating scale. A list of words or statements concerning traits or characteristics, sometimes in the form of a continuous line divided into sections corresponding to degrees of the characteristics, on which the rater indicates judgments of either his or her own behavior or characteristics or the behavior or characteristics of another person (ratee). The rater indicates how or to what degree the behavior or characteristic is possessed by the ratee.

Ratio IQ. Intelligence quotient computed by dividing a person's mental age score on an intelligence test by his or her chronological age in months and multiplying the resulting quotient by 100.

Ratio scale. A scale of measurement, having a true zero, on which equal numerical ratios imply equal ratios of the attribute being measured. Psychological variables are typically not measured on ratio scales, but height, weight, energy, and many other physical variables are.

Recessive gene. A gene that has an effect on an individual's phenotype only when there are two copies of the gene in each cell.

Recombination. Reassortment of genes during reproduction, which may produce a characteristic not observed in the parents.

Redintegration. Recognition response triggered by only part of a familiar stimulus complex.

Reform movement. Social movement during the late 19th and early 20th centuries that encouraged social surveys of cities and communities with the objective of instituting social reforms.

Regression effect. The tendency for people who score at the lower or higher end of a distribution of test scores to score closer to the mean on retesting.

Regression equation. A linear equation for forecasting criterion scores from scores on one or more predictor variables; a procedure often used in selection programs or actuarial prediction and diagnosis.

Regression toward the mean. Tendency for test scores or other psychometric measures to be closer to the mean on retesting; the more extreme the original score is, the closer it will be to the mean on retesting.

Reliability. The extent to which a psychological assessment device measures anything consistently. A reliable instrument is relatively free from errors of measurement, so the scores obtained on the instrument are close in numerical value to the true scores of examinees.

Reliability coefficient. A numerical index, between .00 and 1.00, of the reliability of an assessment instrument. Methods for determining reliability include test–retest, parallel forms, and internal consistency.

Representative sample. A group of individuals whose characteristics are similar to those of the population of individuals for whom a test is intended.

Retrospective study. Comparisons of the incidence of a disorder or other condition in two or more groups of people having different backgrounds, behaviors, or other characteristics. See *prospective study*.

RIASEC model. John Holland's model of person–environment interest/personality types consisting of realistic, investigative, artistic, social, enterprising, and conventional themes.

Risk factors. Characteristics or conditions occurring more frequently than average in individuals who develop particular diseases.

Role. A social behavior pattern that an individual is expected to display under certain conditions or in certain situations; the rights, obligations, and behaviors expected of an individual having a certain social or occupational status.

Savant. Mentally retarded individual who displays an extraordinary level of ability in one or more areas involving exceptional memory.

Scapegoating. A form of displaced aggression in which hostility is expressed toward some person or group of people other than the direct cause of the frustration.

Schizophrenia. Severe mental disorder characterized by withdrawal from reality and disturbances of thinking, emotion, and behavior; a breakdown of integrated personality functioning.

Seasonal affective disorder (SAD). Disorder affecting certain individuals who live in temperate or polar regions characterized by depression in the winter months alternating with a more positive mood in the summer.

Secondary memory. In contrast to primary and tertiary memory, memory that lasts from a few minutes to several hours.

Selection time. The difference between Donders B and Donders C reaction time; time required to determine which of two stimuli should be responded to.

Selective attrition. Tendency for a large number of low scorers than high scorers on a test administered in a longitudinal study to drop out of the study.

Self-efficacy. Confidence that one can succeed at something if one desires.

Self-fulfilling prophecy. Tendency for a person's expectations and attitudes regarding future events or outcomes to have an influence on their occurrence.

Self-healing personality. Personality consisting of adaptive traits such as hardiness and optimism.

Separation distress. Emotional distress displayed on separation from one's primary caregivers, typically the parents.

Septum. Nucleus in the limbic system that is thought to play a role in the expression of emotions (pleasure, rage, etc.).

Sex-limited gene. Gene that expresses its effects in only one sex.

Sex-linked gene. Gene that is present on either the X or Y chromosome.

Sexism. Stereotyping of and discrimination against persons of a particular sex.

Sexual orientation. An enduring sexual preference for members of the same sex (homosexuality), the opposite sex (heterosexuality), or both sexes (bisexuality).

Skewness. Degree of asymmetry in a frequency distribution. In a positively skewed distribution, there are more scores to the left of the mode (low scores); this is true when the test is too difficult for the examinees. In a negatively skewed distribution, there are more scores to the right of the mode (high scores); this is true when the test is too easy for the examinees.

Social class. Classification of people in a society according to a composite of economic, educational, occupational, and other indicators of status.

Somatoform disorder. Anxiety-based disorder in which the patient complains of bodily symptoms that suggest a physical problem but which has no detectable organic basis.

Somatotrophin. Growth hormone (GH) secreted by the anterior lobe of the pituitary gland. Oversecretion of GH can lead to giantism or acromegaly and undersecretion to dwarfism.

Somatotype. Classification of body build (physique) in W. H. Sheldon's three-component system: endomorphy, mesomorphy, and ectomorphy.

Special children. Children with physical, psychological, cognitive, or social problems that make the fulfillment of their needs and potentials more difficult than for other children.

Speciation. Independent development of different species produced by their evolution in different environments.

Specific learning disability. See *learning disability.*

Stacking. Form of discrimination in which members of a particular racial or ethnic group are consistently assigned to either peripheral or central positions on a sports team.

Stage of exhaustion. The last stage of Selye's general adaption syndrome, in which the capacity to withstand stressors declines and the person can become permanently incapacitated if stress continues.

Stage of resistance. Second stage in Selye's general adaptation syndrome; signs of the alarm reaction diminish while activity of the adrenal cortex and other indicators of settling in by the body for a long-term siege become prominent.

Standard deviation. The square root of the variance; a statistical measure of the dispersion or spread of a group of scores about the mean. See *variance.*

Standard error of estimate. The standard deviation of obtained criterion scores around the predicted criterion score; used to estimate a range of probable scores on a criterion variable for an individual whose score on the predictor variable is equal to a specified value.

Standard error of measurement. An estimate of the standard deviation of the normal distribution of test scores that an examinee would theoretically obtain by taking a test an infinite number of times. If an examinee's obtained test score is X, then the chances are two out of three that he or she is one of a group of people whose true scores on the test fall within one standard error of measurement of X.

Standardization. Administering a carefully constructed test to a large, representative sample of people under standard conditions for the purpose of determining norms.

Standardization sample. Subset of a target population on which a test is standardized.

Standard scores. A group of scores, such as z scores, T scores, or stanine scores, having a desired mean and standard deviation. Standard scores are computed by transforming raw scores to z scores, multiplying the z scores by the desired standard deviation, and then adding the desired mean to the product.

Standardized test. A test that has been carefully constructed by professionals and administered with standard directions and under standard conditions to a representative sample of people for the purpose of obtaining norms.

Stanine. A standard score scale consisting of Scores 1 through 9. Stanine scores have a mean of 5 and a standard deviation of approximately 2.

Statistic. A number used to describe some characteristic of a sample of test scores, such as the arithmetic mean or standard deviation.

Stereotype. Oversimplification and overgeneralization of the physical and behavioral characteristics of the members of a particular group.

Strange situation procedure. Research method for studying attachment in infants; involves the alternating presence of a stranger in the same room with the infant's mother and observation of the infant's reactions.

Stratified random sampling. A sampling procedure in which the population is divided into strata (e.g., men and women; Blacks and Whites, lower class, middle class, upper class) and samples are selected at random from the strata; sample sizes within strata are proportional to strata sizes.

Stress. A response to a stressor associated with psychological or physiological tension or imbalance in an organism; state resulting from perception by the individual that his or her resources are insufficient to meet the demands of a situation.

Stressor. A stimulus or situation that produces stress.

Structured interview. Interviewing procedure in which the interviewee is asked a predetermined set of questions.

Subject variable. See *organismic variable.*

Sympathetic nervous system. Division of the autonomic nervous system arising from chain ganglia in the thoracic and lumbar regions of the spinal column; helps prepare the organism physiologically for fight-or-flight responses precipitated by emergency situations. See *parasympathetic nervous system.*

Taboo. A practice that is forbidden and improper or unacceptable by a society and severely punished for its violation.

Tardive dyskinesia. Involuntary movements of the tongue, lips, jaw, and extremities resulting from excessive use of phenothiazines.

T-cells. Type of lymphocytes that either attack antigens directly or regulate other immune functions.

Temporal lobe. Area of the cerebral cortex located on the left and right sides of the brain below the lateral fissure and anterior to the occipital lobe; tonotopically organized for pitch sensitivity.

Terminal drop. Decline in intellectual functions (intelligence, memory, cognitive organization), sensorimotor abilities, and personality during the last few months of life.

Test. A psychometric instrument for evaluating the cognitive abilities, personality traits, psychomotor abilities, and other characteristics of an individual.

Test–retest reliability. A method of assessing the reliability of a test by administering it to the same group of examinees on two different occasions and computing the correlations between their scores on the two occasions.

Thymus gland. Endocrine gland located below the thyroid gland that secretes a hormone (thymosin) that contributes to lymphocyte formation and thereby the immune response of the body.

Thyroid gland. Double-lobed endocrine gland situated on either side of the windpipe; it secretes hormones that regulate growth and maturation.

Time-lag design. Developmental research procedure for examining several cohorts, each in a different time period.

Time-sequential design. Developmental research procedure in which two groups of people of different ages are compared at two different times to evaluate the interaction between age and time of measurement.

Tradition. A belief, custom, or legend that is handed down, orally or by practice, from generation to generation.

Traditional marriage. A marriage in which the husband is the dominant partner and decision maker and the wife is the principal housekeeper and child rearer.

Trainable mentally retarded (TMR). Children in the moderately retarded range of IQs (approximately 36–50) who usually cannot learn to read and write but can perform unskilled tasks under supervision. See *educable mentally retarded.*

T scores. Converted, normalized standard scores having a mean of 50 and a standard deviation of 10. *Z* scores are also standard scores with a mean of 50 and a standard deviation of 10, but in contrast to *T* scores they are not normalized.

t test. Parametric statistical test of the difference between the means of two independent groups or the mean of the differences between measures on two dependent (correlated) groups.

Type A behavior pattern. A pattern of behavior characterized by a combination of behaviors, including aggressiveness, competitiveness, hostility, quick actions, and constant striving; associated with a high incidence of coronary heart disease.

Type B behavior pattern. Pattern of behavior characterized by a relaxed, easygoing, patient, noncompetitive life style; associated with a low incidence of coronary heart disease.

Unobtrusive observations. Observations made without interfering with or otherwise influencing the behavior to be observed.

Validity. The extent to which an assessment instrument measures what it was designed to measure. Validity can be assessed in several ways: analyzing the instrument's content (*content validity*), relating scores on the test to a criterion (*predictive* and *concurrent validity*), and studying the extent to which the test is a measure of a certain psychological construct (*construct validity*).

Variability. The degree of spread or deviation of a group of scores around their average value. Measures of variability include the range, semi-interquartile range, variance, and standard deviation.

Variable. In contrast to a *constant,* any quantity that can assume more than one state or numerical value.

Variance. A measure of variability of test scores, computed as the sum of the squares of the deviations of raw scores from the arithmetic mean, divided by one less than the number of scores; the square of the standard deviation.

Vital statistics. Statistics concerning human life, the conditions affecting it, and the maintenance of the population (e.g., births, marriages, divorces, and deaths) during a specified time period.

Wernicke's area. Area in the left cerebral hemisphere concerned with the understanding of language. Patients with damage to Wernicke's area can hear words but fail to understand their meanings. See *Broca's area.*

Word association test. A projective test on which the examinee responds to each of several words presented by the examiner with the first word that comes to mind. Unusual responses or slow responding to certain words may be indicative of conflicts or other emotional problems associated with those words.

Working memory. Active memory for manipulating information for the next stage of memory processing.

X chromosome. One or two chromosomes in the 23rd (sex-determining) position contained in the cells of mammals; female reproductive cells have two X chromosomes in the 23rd position, but male cells have only one.

Y chromosome. One of two chromosomes in the 23rd position of male reproductive (sperm) cells.

References

Ackerman, D. (1991). *A natural history of the senses*. New York: Random House.

Adams, P. F., & Marano, M. A. (1995). Current estimates from the national interview survey, 1994. *Vital and Health Statistics 10*(193). Washington, DC: National Center for Health Statistics.

Adorno, T. W., Frenkel-Brunswik, E., Levinson, D., & Sanford, N. (1950). *The authoritarian personality*. New York: Harper.

af-Klinteberg, B. (1996). Biology, norms, and personality: A developmental perspective. *Neuropsychobiology, 34,* 146–154.

af-Klinteberg, B. (1997). Hyperactive behaviour and aggressiveness as early risk indicators for violence: Variable and person approaches. *Studies on Crime and Crime Prevention, 6(1),* 21–34.

Ahammer, L. M. (1973). Social-learning theory as a framework for the study of adult personality development. In P. B. Baltes & K. W. Schaie (Eds.), *Life-span developmental psychology: Personality and socialization* (pp. 256–294). New York: Academic Press.

Ahern, G. L., & Schwartz, G. E. (1985). Differential lateralization for positive and negative emotion in the human brain: EEG spectral analysis. *Neuropsychologists, 23,* 745–756.

Aiken, L. R. (1963). The relationships of dress to selected measures of personality in undergraduate women. *The Journal of Social Psychology, 59,* 119–128.

Aiken, L. R. (1995). *Personality assessment methods and practices* (2nd ed.). Göttingen, GE: Hogrefe & Huber.

Aiken, L. R. (1996a). *Assessment of intellectual functioning* (2nd ed.). New York: Plenum.

Aiken, L. R. (1996b). *Rating scales and checklists: Evaluating behavior, personality, and attitudes*. New York: Wiley.

Aiken, L. R. (1997a). *Assessment of adult personality*. New York: Springer.

Aiken, L. R. (1997b). *Psychological testing and assessment* (9th ed.). Newton, MA: Allyn & Bacon.

Aiken, L. R. (1997c). *Questionnaires and inventories: Surveying opinions and assessing personality*. New York: Wiley

Aiken, L. R. (1998). *Tests and examinations: Measuring abilities and performance*. New York: Wiley.

Ainsworth, M. D. S. (1967). *Infancy in Uganda: Infant care and the growth of love*. Baltimore: Johns Hopkins University Press.

Ainsworth, M. D. (1989). Attachments beyond infancy. *American Psychologist, 44,* 709–717.

Ainsworth, M. D., Blehar, M. C., Waters, E., & Wall, S. (1978). *Patterns of attachment.* Hillsdale, NJ: Lawrence Erlbaum Associates.

Aizenberg, R., & Treas, J. (1985). The family in late life: Psychosocial and demographic considerations. In J. Birren & K. Schaie (Eds.), *Handbook of the psychology of aging* (2nd ed., pp. 169–189). New York: Van Nostrand Reinhold.

Alderton, D. L. (1994). Mechanical ability. In R. J. Sternberg (Ed.), *Encyclopedia of human intelligence* (pp. 697–700). New York: Macmillan.

Alexander, F., & French, T. M. (1948). *Studies in psychosomatic medicine.* New York: Ronald.

Alexander, T. (1994). Cultural determinism. In R. J. Corsini (Ed.), *Encyclopedia of psychology* (Vol. 1, pp. 369–370). New York: Macmillan.

Allen, L. S., Hines, M., Shyne, J. E., & Gorski, R. A. (1989). Two sexually dimorphic cell groups in the human brain. *Journal of Neuroscience, 9,* 497–506.

Allen, M. G. (1976). Twin studies of affective illness. *Archives of General Psychiatry, 33,* 1476–1478.

Alm, P. O., af-Klinteberg, B., Humble, K., & Leppert, J. (1996). Psychopathy, platelet MAO activity and criminality among former juvenile delinquents. *Acta Psychiatrica Scandinavia, 94,* 105–111.

Altus, W. D. (1966). Birth order and its sequelae. *Science, 151,* 44–49.

Amabile, T. M., & Hennessey, B. A. (1992). The motivation for creativity in children. In A. K. Boggiano & T. S. Pittman (Eds.), *Achievement and motivation: A social-developmental perspective* (pp. 54–74). New York: Cambridge University Press.

American Association of Mental Retardation. (1992). *Mental retardation: Definition, classification, and systems of supports* (9th ed.). Washington, DC: Author.

American Psychiatric Association. (1994). *Diagnostic and statistical manual of mental disorders* (4th ed.). Washington, DC: Author.

Anastasi, A. (1958). *Differential psychology: Individual and group differences in behavior.* New York: Macmillan.

Anastasi, A., & Urbina, S. (1997). *Psychological testing* (7th ed.). Englewood Cliffs, NJ: Prentice-Hall.

Anderson, A. E., & DiDomenico, L. (1992). Diet vs. shape content of popular male and female magazines: A dose-response relationship to the incidence of eating disorders? *International Journal of Eating Disorders, 11,* 283–287.

Anderson, R. N., Kochanek, K. D., & Murphy, S. L. (1997). Report of final mortality statistics, 1995. *Monthly Vital Statistics Report, 45(11),* Suppl. 2. Hyattsville, MD: National Center for Health Statistics.

Andreasen, N. C. (1987). Creativity and mental illness: Prevalence rates in writers and their first-degree relatives. *American Journal of Psychiatry, 144,* 1288–1297.

Andreasen, N. C., Arndt, S., Alliger, R., Miller, D., & Flaum, M. (1995). Symptoms of schizophrenia: Methods, meanings, and mechanisms. *Archives of General Psychiatry, 52,* 341–351.

Antonucci, T. C. (1985). Personal characteristics, social support, and social behavior. In R. Binstock & E. Shanas (Eds.), *Handbook of aging and the social sciences* (pp. 94–128). New York: Van Nostrand Reinhold.

Archer, J. (1991). The influence of testosterone on human aggression. *British Journal of Psychology, 82,* 1–28.

Aries, P. (1981). *The hour of our death.* New York: Knopf.

Arnett, J. (1990). Drunk driving, sensation seeking, and egocentrism among adolescents. *Personality and Individual Differences, 11,* 541–546.

Arthur, W., Jr., & Graziano, W. G. (1996). The five-factor model, conscientiousness, and driving accident involvement. *Journal of Personality, 64,* 593–618.

Austin, G. R., & Garber, H. (Eds.). (1982). *The rise and fall of national test scores.* New York: Academic Press.

Bachman, R. B., Dillaway, H., & Lachs, M. S. (1998). Violence against the elderly: A comparative analysis of robbery and assault across age and gender groups. *Research on Aging, 20*(2), 183–198.

Baller, W. R., Charles, D. C., & Miller, E. L. (1967). Mid-life attainment of the mentally retarded: A longitudinal study. *Genetic Psychology Monographs, 75,* 235–329.

Baltes, P. B., & Willis, S. L. (1982). Plasticity and enhancement of intellectual functioning in old age: Penn States' Adult Development and Enrichment Program (ADEPT). In F. I. M. Craik & S. E. Trehub (Eds.), *Aging and cognitive processes* (pp. 353–389). New York: Plenum.

Bandura, A. (1977). *Social learning theory.* Englewood Cliffs, NJ: Prentice-Hall.

Bandura, A. (1989). Human agency in social cognitive theory. *American Psychologist, 44,* 1175–1184.

Baron, R. S., Cutrona, C. E., Hicklin, D., Russell, D. W., & Lubaroff, D. M. (1990). Social support and immune function among spouses of cancer patients. *Journal of Personality and Social Psychology, 59,* 344–352.

Barrick, M. R., & Mount, M. K. (1991). The big five personality dimensions and job performance: A meta-analysis. *Personnel Psychology, 44,* 1–26.

Barry, H., Child, I., & Bacon, M. (1959). Relation of child training to subsistence economy. *American Anthropologist, 61,* 51–63.

Baumrind, D. (1971). Current patterns of parental authority. *Developmental Psychology Monographs, 1,* 1–103.

Baumrind, D. (1978). Parental disciplinary patterns and social competence in children. *Youth and Society, 9,* 239–276.

Baumrind, D. (1993). The average expectable environment is not good enough: A response to Scarr. *Child Development, 64,* 1299–1317.

Bayley, N., & Oden, M. H. (1955). The maintenance of intellectual ability in gifted adults. *Journal of Gerontology, 10,* 91–107.

Bean, F., & Tienda, M. (1987). *The Hispanic population in the United States.* New York: Russell Sage.

Beck, A. T. (1993). Cognitive therapy: Past, present, and future. *Journal of Counseling and Clinical Psychology, 61,* 194–198.

Bell, A., & Zubek, J. (1960). The effect of age on the intellectual performance of mental defectives. *Journal of Gerontology, 15,* 285–295.

Bell, A. P., & Weinberg, M. S. (1978). *Homosexualities: A study of diversity among men and women.* New York: Simon & Schuster.

Benedict, R. F. (1946). *The chrysanthemum and the sword: Patterns of Japanese culture.* Boston: Houghton Mifflin.

Benjamin, J., Li, L., Patterson, C., Greenberg, B. D., Murphy, D. L., & Hamer, D. H. (1996). Population and familial association between the D4 dopamine receptor gene and measures of Novelty Seeking. *Nature Genetics, 12,* 81–84.

Bennett, K. A. (1993). *A field guide for human skeletal identification* (2nd ed.). Springfield, IL: C. C. Thomas.

Ben-Porath, Y. S., Shondrick, D. D., & Stafford, K. P. (1995). MMPI-2 and race in a forensic diagnostic sample. *Criminal Justice and Behavior, 22,* 19–32.

Berg, I. A. (1967). *Response set in personality assessment.* Chicago: Aldine.

Berkman, L., & Syme, S. L. (1979). Social networks, host resistance, and mortality: A nine-year follow-up study of Alameda County residents. *American Journal of Epidemiology, 109,* 186–204.

Berliner, D. C., & Biddle, B. J. (1995). *The manufactured crisis: Myths, fraud, and the attack on America's public schools.* Reading, MA: Addison-Wesley.

Berscheid, E. (1981). An overview of the psychological effects of physical attractiveness and some comments upon the psychological effects of knowledge of the effects of physical attractiveness. In G. W. Lucker, K. Ribbens, & J. A. McNamara (Eds.), *Psychological aspects of facial form* (Craniofacial growth series). Ann Arbor: Center for Human Growth and Development, University of Michigan.

Best, D. L., & Williams, J. E. (1993). A cross-cultural viewpoint. In A. E. Beall & R. J. Sternberg (Eds.), *The psychology of gender* (pp. 215–248). New York: Guilford.

Biederman, I., & Kaplan, R. (1970). Stimulus discriminability and S-R compatibility: Evidence for independent effects in choice reaction time. *Journal of Experimental Psychology, 86,* 434–439.

Biernat, M. (1991). Gender stereotypes and the relationship between masculinity and femininity: A developmental analysis. *Journal of Personality and Social Psychology, 61,* 351–365.

Binet, A., & Henri, V. (1896). La psychologie individuelle [Individual psychology]. *L'Année Psychologique, 2,* 411–465.

Blacks in sports. (1992, August). *Ebony,* p. 26.

Blackwood, D. H., Jr., He, L., Morris, S. W., McLean, A., Whitton, C., Thomson, M., Walker, M. T., Woodburn, K., Sharp, C. M., Wright, A. F., Shibasaki, Y., St. Clair, D. M., Porteous, D. J., & Muir, W. J. (1996). A locus for bipolar affective disorder on chromosome 4p. *Nature Genetics, 12,* 427–430.

Blanchard, E. B., Andrasik, F., & Arena, J. G. (1984). Personality and chronic headache. In B. A. Maher & W. B. Maher (Eds.), *Progress in experimental personality research: Vol 13. Normal personality processes* (pp. 303–364). New York: Academic Press.

Block, J. (1995). A contrarian view of the five-factor approach to personality description. *Psychological Bulletin, 117,* 187–215.

Blum, K., Cull, J. G., Braverman, E. R., & Comings, D. E. (1996). Reward deficiency syndrome. *American Scientist, 84,* 132–145.

Bogdan, R. (1986). Exhibiting mentally retarded people for amusement and profit, 1850–1940. *American Journal of Mental Deficiency, 91*(2), 120–126.

Bolger, N., & Zuckerman, A. (1995). A framework for studying personality in the stress process. *Journal of Personality & Social Psychology, 69,* 890–902.

Bostic, J. Q., & Tallent-Runnels, M. K. (1991). Cognitive styles: A factor analysis of six dimensions with implications for consolidation. *Perceptual and Motor Skills, 72,* 1299–1306.

Bouchard, T. J. (1994). Genes, environment, and personality. *Science, 264,* 1700–1701.

Bouchard, T. J., Jr. (1997). IQ similarity in twins reared apart: Findings and response to critics. In R. J. Sternberg & E. L. Grigorenko (Eds.), *Intelligence, heredity, and environment* (pp. 126–160). New York: Cambridge University Press.

Bouchard, T. J., Jr., Lykken, D. T., McGue, M., Segal, N. L., & Tellegen, A. (1990). Sources of human psychological differences: The Minnesota Study of Twins Reared Apart. *Science, 250,* 223–228.

Bowlby, J. (1982/1969). *Attachment and loss: Vol. 1. Attachment.* New York: Basic Books.

Bowlby, J. (1973). *Attachment and loss: Vol. 2. Separation: Anxiety and anger.* New York: Basic Books.

Bradbury, T. N., & Miller, G. A. (1985). Season of birth in schizophrenia: A review of evidence, methodology, and etiology. *Psychological Bulletin, 98,* 569–594.

Brand, P. A., Rothblum, E. D., & Solomon, L. J. (1992). A comparison of lesbians, gay men, and heterosexuals on weight and restrained eating. *International Journal of Eating Disorders, 11,* 253–259.

Breier, A., Charney, D. S., & Heninger, G. R. (1984). Major depression in patients with agoraphobia and panic disorder. *Archives of General Psychiatry, 41,* 1129–1135.

Brigham, C. C. (1923). *A study of American intelligence.* Princeton, NJ: Princeton University Press.

Brigham, C. C. (1930). Intelligence tests of immigrant groups. *Psychological Review, 37,* 158–165.

Brody, N. (1992). *Intelligence* (2nd ed.). San Diego: Academic Press.

Bronisch, T. (1996). The relationship between suicidality and depression. *Archives of Suicide Research, 2*(4), 235–254.

Brooks-Gunn, J., Klebanov, P. K., & Duncan, G. J. (1996). Ethnic differences in children's intelligence test scores: Role of economic deprivation, home environment, and maternal characteristics. *Child Development, 67,* 396–408.

Brown, J. D., & McGill, K. L. (1989). The cost of good fortune: When positive life events produce negative health consequences. *Journal of Personality and Social Psychology, 57,* 1103–1110.

Brown, P. (1988). *The body and society: Men, women, and sexual renunciation in early Christianity.* New York: Columbia University Press.

Bullock, W. A., & Gilliland, K. (1993). Eysenck's arousal theory of introversion–extraversion: A converging measures investigation. *Journal of Personality and Social Psychology, 64,* 113–123.

Buss, A. H. (1980). *Self-consciousness and social anxiety.* San Francisco, CA: Freeman.

Buss, A. H. (1994). The strategies of human mating. *American Scientist, 82,* 238–249.

Buss, A. H., & Plomin, R. (1984). *Temperament: Early developing personality traits.* Hillsdale, NJ: Lawrence Erlbaum Associates.

Buss, A. H., & Plomin, R. (1986). The EAS approach to temperament. In R. Plomin & J. Dunn (Eds.), *The study of temperament: Changes, continuities and challenges* (pp. 67–79). Hillsdale, NJ: Lawrence Erlbaum Associates.

Buss, D. M. (1989). Sex differences in human mate preferences: Evolutionary hypotheses tests in 37 cultures. *Behavioral and Brain Sciences, 12,* 1–14.

Buss, D. M., Abbott, M., Angleitner, A., & Asherian, A. (1990). International preferences in selecting mates: A study of 37 cultures. *Journal of Cross-Cultural Psychology, 21,* 5–47.

Butcher, J. N., & Rouse, S. V. (1996). Personality: Individual differences in clinical assessment. *Annual Review of Psychology, 47,* 87–111.

Butler, R. N. (1974). Successful aging. *Mental Health, 58*(3), 7–12.

Butler, R. N., & Lewis, M. I. (1982). *Aging and mental health* (3rd ed.). St. Louis: Mosby.

Byrne, D. (1971). *The attraction paradigm.* New York: Academic Press.

Cahan, S., & Ganor, Y. (1993). Cognitive gender differences among Israeli children. *Megamot, 34,* 521–537.

Caldwell, C. B., & Gottesman, I. I. (1991). Sex differences in the risk for alcoholism: A twin study. *Behavior Genetics, 21*, 563 (Abstract).

Campbell, D. P. (1965). A cross-sectional and longitudinal study of scholastic abilities over twenty-five years. *Journal of Counseling Psychology, 12*, 55–61.

Cannell, J. J. (1989). *The Lake Wobegon Report: How public educators cheat on achievement tests.* Albuquerque, NM: Friends for Education.

Carnegie Council on Adolescent Development. (1989, June). *Turning points: Preparing American youth for the 21st century* (Report of the Task Force on Education of Young Adolescents). New York: Carnegie Corporation.

Carroll, J. B. (1993). *Human cognitive abilities: A survey of factor-analytic studies.* New York: Cambridge University Press.

Carson, R. C., & Butcher, J. N. (1996). *Abnormal psychology and modern life* (10th ed.). Reading, MA: Addison-Wesley.

Carstensen, I. L. (1993). Motivation for social contact across the life span: A theory of socioemotional selectivity. In J. E. Jacobs (Ed.), *Nebraska Symposium on Motivation: Vol. 40. Developmental perspectives on motivation* (pp. 209–254). Lincoln: University of Nebraska Press.

Carstensen, I. L. (1995). Evidence for a lifespan theory of socioemotional selectivity. *Current Directions in Psychological Science, 4*, 151–156.

Case, R. B., Moss, A. J., Case, N., McDermott, M., & Eberly, S. (1992). Living alone after myocardial infarction: Impact on prognosis. *Journal of the American Medical Association, 267*, 515–519.

Cash, T. F. (1990). Losing hair, losing points?: The effects of male pattern baldness on social impression formation. *Journal of Applied Social Psychology, 20*, 154–167.

Caspi, A., Begg, D., Dickson, N., Harrington, H. L., Langley, J., Moffitt, T. E., & Silva, P. A. (1997). Personality differences predict health-risk behaviors in young adulthood: Evidence from a longitudinal study. *Journal of Personality and Social Psychology, 73*, 1052–1063.

Caspi, A., Herbener, E. S., & Ozer, D. J. (1992). Shared experiences and the similarity of personalities: A longitudinal study of married couples. *Journal of Personality & Social Psychology, 62*, 281–291.

Cattell, R. B. (1963). Theory of fluid and crystallized intelligence: A critical experiment. *Journal of Educational Psychology, 54*, 1–22.

Cattell, R. B. (1982). *The inheritance of personality and ability.* New York: Academic Press.

Ceci, S. J., & Williams, W. M. (1997). Schooling, intelligence, and income. *American Psychologist, 52*, 1051–1058.

Center for Disease Control. (1998, May 1). Self-reported frequent mental distress among adults—United States, 1993–1996. *Morbidity and Mortality Weekly Report*, Vol. 47/No. 16. Atlanta, GA: Author.

Charles, D. C., & James, S. T. (1964). Stability of average intelligence. *Journal of Genetic Psychology, 105*, 105–111.

Cherney, S. S., Fulker, D. W., Corley, R., Plomin, R., & DeFries, J. C. (1994). Continuity and change in infant shyness from 14 to 20 months. *Behavior Genetics, 24*, 365–380.

Christensen, H., Mackinnon, A., Jorm, A. F., Henderson, A. S., Scott, L. R., & Korten, S. E. (1994). Age differences and interindividual variation in cognition in community-dwelling elderly. *Psychology and Aging, 9*, 381–390.

Clark, L. F. (1993). Stress and the cognitive-conversational benefits of social interaction. *Journal of Social and Clinical Psychology, 12*, 25–55.

Clark, T. (1990). International marketing and national character: A review and proposal for an integrative theory. *Journal of Marketing, 54*(4), 66–79.

Clarke, S., Krafsik, R., Van der Loos, H., & Innocenti, G. M. (1989). Forms and measures of adult and developing human corpus callosum: Is there sexual dimorphism? *Journal of Comparative Neurology, 280,* 213–230.

Cloward, R. A., & Ohlin, L. E. (1960). *Delinquency and opportunity: A theory of delinquent gangs.* New York: The Free Press.

Coakley, J. J. (1982). *Sport in society: Issues and controversies* (2nd ed.). St. Louis, MO: Mosby.

Coakley, J. J. (1990). *Sport in society: Issues and controversies.* St. Louis, MO: Times Mirror/Mosby.

Cohen, S., & Williamson, G. M. (1991). Stress and infectious disease in humans. *Psychological Bulletin, 109,* 5–24.

Collins, J. G., & LeClere, F. B. (1997). *Health and selected socioeconomic characteristics of the family: United States, 1988–90.* (PHS) 97–1523. GPO stock number 017–022–01361–4. Washington, DC: National Center for Health Statistics.

Collins, M. A., & Zebrowitz, L. A. (1995). The contributions of appearance to occupational outcomes in civilian and military settings. *Journal of Applied Social Psychology, 25,* 129–163.

Conger, R. (1980). Juvenile delinquency: Behavior restraint or behavior facilitation? In T. Hirschi & M. Gottfredson (Eds.), *Understanding crime: Current theory and research* (pp. 131–142). Newbury Park, CA: Sage.

Congress, E. P., & Lyons, B. P. (1992). Cultural differences in health beliefs: Implications for social work practice in health care settings. *Social Work in Health Care, 17*(3), 81–96.

Cooley, C. H. (1922). *Human nature and the social order.* New York: Scribner.

Cooper, C. L., Kirkcaldy, B. D., & Brown, J. (1994). A model of job stress and physical health: The role of individual differences. *Personality and Individual Differences, 16,* 653–655.

Costa, P. T., Jr., & McCrae, R. R. (1986). Personality stability and its implications for clinical psychology. *Clinical Psychology Review, 6,* 407–423.

Costa, P. T., Jr., & McCrae, R. R. (1994). Stability and change in personality from adolescence through adulthood. In C. F. Halverson, Jr., G. A. Kohnstamm, & R. P. Martin (Eds.), *The developing structure of temperament and personality from infancy to adulthood* (pp. 139–150). Hillsdale, NJ: Lawrence Erlbaum Associates.

Court-Brown, W. M. (1968). *The development of knowledge about males with an XYY sex chromosome complement.* Unpublished paper, Medical Research Council, Western General Hospital, Edinburgh, Scotland.

Cowan, C. P., & Cowan, P. A. (1992). *When partners become parents.* New York: Basic Books.

Cox, R. P. (1996). An exploration of the demographic and social correlates of criminal behavior among adolescent males. *Journal of Adolescent Health, 19*(1), 17–24.

Craik, F. I. M., & McDowd, J. M. (1987). Age differences in recall and recognition. *Journal of Experimental Psychology: Learning, Memory, and Cognition, 13,* 474–479.

Crain-Thoreson, C., & Dale, P. S. (1992). Do early talkers become early readers? Linguistic precocity, preschool language, and emergent literacy. *Developmental Psychology, 28,* 421–429.

Creer, T. L., & Kotses, H. (1983). Asthma: Psychological aspects and management. In E. Middleton, Jr., C. Reed, & E. Ellis (Eds.), *Allergy: Principles and practice* (2nd ed.). St. Louis: Mosby.

Crocker, A. G., & Hodgins, S. (1997). The criminality of noninstitutionalized mentally retarded persons: Evidence from a birth cohort followed to age 30. *Criminal Justice & Behavior, 24,* 432–454.

Cronbach, L. J. (1970). *Essentials of psychological testing* (3rd ed.). New York: Harper & Row.

Culbertson, F. M. (1997). Depression and gender. *American Psychologist, 52,* 25–31.

Cunningham, M. R. (1986). Measuring the physical in physical attractiveness: Quasi-experiments on the sociobiology of female facial beauty. *Journal of Personality and Social Psychology, 50,* 925–935.

Cunningham, M. R., Roberts, A. R., Barbeen, A. P., & Druen, P. B. (1995). "Their ideas of beauty are, on the whole, the same as ours": Consistency and variability in the cross-cultural perception of female physical attractiveness. *Journal of Personality & Social Psychology, 68,* 261–279.

Dabbs, J. M., Carr, T. S., Frady, R. L., & Riad, J. K. (1995). Testosterone, crime, and misbehavior among 692 male prison inmates. *Personality & Individual Differences, 18,* 627–633.

Daderman, A., & af-Klinteberg, B. (1997). *Personality dimensions characterizing severely conduct disordered male juvenile delinquents.* Reports from the Department of Psychology, U. Stockholm (No. 831831 al-21).

Dahlstrom, W. G., & Gynther, M. D. (1986). Previous MMPI research on Black Americans. In W. G. Dahlstrom, D. Lachar, & L. E. Dahlstrom (Eds.), *MMPI patterns of American minorities* (pp. 24–49). Minneapolis: University of Minnesota Press.

Dai, X., Ryan, J. J., Paolo, A. M., & Harrington, R. G. (1991). Sex differences on the Wechsler Adult Intelligence Scale—Revised for China. *Psychological Assessment, 3,* 282–284.

Darwin, C. (1859). *The origin of species.* New York: Modern Library.

Das, J. P., Naglieri, J. A., & Kirby, J. P. (1994). *Assessment of cognitive processes: The PASS theory of intelligence.* Boston: Allyn & Bacon.

Davidson, R. J. (1991). Biological approaches to the study of personality. In V. J. Derlega, B. A. Winstead, & W. H. Jones (Eds.), *Personality: Contemporary theory and research* (pp. 87–112). Chicago: Nelson-Hall.

Davidson, R. J. (1993). The neuropsychology of emotional and affective style. In M. Lewis & J. M. Haviland (Eds.), *Handbook of emotions* (pp. 143–154). New York: Guilford.

Davies, N. (1998). *Europe: A history.* New York: Oxford University Press.

Davis, C., & Cowles, M. (1988). A laboratory study of temperament and arousal: A test of Gale's hypothesis. *Journal of Research in Personality, 22,* 101–116.

Davis, C., Kennedy, S. H., Ralevski, E., Dionne, M., Brewer, H., Neitzert, C., & Ratusny, D. (1995). Obsessive–compulsive and physical activity in anorexia nervosa and high-level exercising. *Journal of Psychosomatic Research, 39,* 967–976.

Davis, J. A., & Smith, T. W. (1994). *General Social Surveys, 1972–1994.* Chicago: National Opinion Research Center.

Day, J., & Curry, A. (1995). *Educational attainment in the United States: March 1995. Current Population Reports* (P20-489). Washington, DC: U.S. Department of Commerce.

Day, J., & Curry, A. (1997). *Educational attainment in the United States: March 1996. Current Population Reports* (P20-493). Washington, DC: U.S. Department of Commerce.

Deary, I. J., Ramsey, H., Wilson, J. A., & Riad, M. (1988). Simulated salivation: Correlations with personality and time of day effects. *Personality and Individual Differences, 9,* 903–909.

Dennis, W., & Najarian, P. (1957). Infant development under environmental handicap. *Psychological Monographs, 71,* No. 7.

De Pascalis, V., & Montirosso, R. (1988). Extroversion, neuroticism and individual differences in event-related potentials. *Personality and Individual Differences, 9,* 353–360.

Detterman, D. K., & Thompson, L. A. (1997). What is so special about special education? *American Psychologist, 52,* 1082–1090.

Diamond, M. (1993). Homosexuality and bisexuality in different populations. *Archives of Sexual Behavior, 22,* 291–310.

Dinklage, D., & Barkley, R. A. (1992). Disorders of attention in children. In F. Boller & J. Fragman (Series Eds.) & S. J. Segalowitz & I. Rapin (Vol. Eds.), *Handbook of neuropsychology: Vol. 7. Child neuropsychology* (pp. 279–307). Amsterdam: Elsevier Science.

Donin, H. H. (1972). *To be a Jew: A guide to Jewish observance in contemporary life.* New York: Basic Books.

Doppelt, J. E., & Wallace, W. L. (1955). Standardization of the Wechsler Adult Intelligence Scale for older persons. *Journal of Abnormal and Social Psychology, 51,* 312–330.

Driesen, N. R., & Raz, N. (1995). The influence of sex, age, and handedness on corpus callosum morphology: A meta-analysis. *Psychobiology, 23,* 240–247.

Duberman, L. (1974). *Marriage and its alternatives.* New York: Praeger.

Dunbar, E. (1943). *Psychosomatic diagnosis.* New York: Harper & Row.

Dunn, S. M., & Tuttle, J. R. (1981). The myth of the diabetic personality. *Diabetes Care, 4,* 640–646.

Dykens, E. M., Hodapp, R. M., & Leckman, J. F. (1994). *Behavior and development in fragile X syndrome.* Newbury Park, CA: Sage.

Eagly, A. H., Ashmore, R. D., Makhijani, M. G., & Longo, L. C. (1991). What is beautiful is good, but … : A meta-analytic review of research on the physical attractiveness stereotype. *Psychological Bulletin, 110,* 107–128.

Eaton, W., & Von Bargen, D. (1981). Asynchronous development of gender understanding in preschool children. *Child Development, 52,* 1020–1027.

Ebstein, R. P., Novick, O., Umansky, R., Priel, B., Osher, Y., Blaine, D., Bennett, E. R., Nemanov, L., Katz, M., & Belmaker, R. H. (1996). Dopamine D4 receptor (D4DR) exon III polymorphism associated with the personality trait of Novelty Seeking. *Nature Genetics, 12,* 78–80.

Edelbrock, C., Rende, R., Plomin, R., & Thompson, L. A. (1995). A twin study of competence and problem behavior in childhood and early adolescence. *Journal of Child Psychology and Psychiatry, 36,* 775–785.

Edmonds, R. (1982). Programs of school improvement: An overview. *Educational Leadership, 40,* 4–11.

Edwards, E. D. (1983). Native American elders: Current social issues and social policy implications. In R. L. McNeely & J. L. Cohen (Eds.), *Aging in minority groups* (pp. 74–82). Beverly Hills, CA: Sage.

Eisdorfer, C. (1963). The WAIS performance of the aged: A retest evaluation. *Journal of Gerontology, 18,* 169–172.

Eisenman, R. (1992). Birth order, development and personality. *Acta Paedopsychiatrica International Journal of Child and Adolescent Psychiatry, 55,* 25–27.

Elam, S. M. (Ed.). (1978). *A decade of Gallup polls on attitudes toward education: 1969–1978.* Bloomington, IN: Phi Delta Kappa.

Elder, G. H., Jr. (1969). Appearance and education in marriage mobility. *American Sociological Review, 34,* 519–533.

Ellis, L., & Ames, M. A. (1987). Neurohormonal functioning and sexual orientation: A theory of homosexuality–heterosexuality. *Psychological Bulletin, 101,* 233–258.

Engle, R. W. (1994). Memory. In R. J. Sternberg (Ed.), *Encyclopedia of human intelligence* (pp. 700–704). New York: Macmillan.

Epstein, S., Pacini, R., Denes-Raj, V., & Heier, H. (1996). Individual differences in intuitive-experiential and analyical-rational thinking styles. *Journal of Personality & Social Psychology, 71,* 390–405.

Ericsson, K. A. (1985). Memory skill. *Canadian Journal of Psychology, 39,* 188–231.

Eronen, M. (1995). Mental disorders and homicidal behavior in female subjects. *American Journal of Psychiatry, 152,* 1216–1218.

Eronen, M., Hakola, P., & Tiihonen, J. (1996). Mental disorders and homicidal behavior in Finland. *Archives of General Psychiatry, 53,* 497–501.

Esquirol, J. E. D. (1945/1838). *Mental maladies.* Philadelphia, PA: Lea & Blanchard.

Evans, D., Funkenstein, H., Albert, M., Scherr, P., Cook, N., Chown, M., Hebert, L., Hennckens, C., & Taylor, D. (1989). Prevalence of Alzheimer's disease in a community population of older people. *Journal of the American Medical Association, 262,* 2551–2556.

Ewen, R. B. (1998). *An introduction to theories of personality* (5th ed.). Mahwah, NJ: Lawrence Erlbaum Associates.

Eysenck, H. J. (1962). Conditioning and personality. *British Journal of Psychology, 53,* 299–305.

Eysenck, H. J. (1967). *The biological basis of personality.* Springfield, IL: C. C. Thomas.

Eysenck, H. J., & Eysenck, S. B. G. (1975). *Manual of the Eysenck Personality Questionnaire.* San Diego: Educational and Industrial Testing Service.

Eysenck, H. J. (1982). *Personality, genetics, and behavior.* New York: Praeger.

Eysenck, H. J. (1990). Biological dimensions of personality. In L. A. Pervin (Ed.), *Handbook of personality theory and research* (pp. 244–276). New York: Guilford.

Eysenck, H. J. (1995). *Genius: The natural history of creativity.* Cambridge, England: Cambridge University Press.

Eysenck, H. J., & Rachman, S. (1965). *The causes of neurosis.* San Diego: Robert R. Knapp.

Ezrin, C. (1977). Psychiatric aspects of endocrine and metabolic disorders. In E. D. Wittkower & H. Warnes (Eds.), *Psychosomatic medicine: Its clinical applications* (pp. 280–295). New York: Harper & Row.

Feingold, A. (1990). Gender differences in effects of physical attractiveness on romantic attraction: A comparison across five research paradigms. *Journal of Personality and Social Psychology, 59,* 981–993.

Feingold, A. (1992a). Good-looking people are not what we think. *Psychological Bulletin, 111,* 304–341.

Feingold, A. (1992b). Gender differences in mate selection preferences: A test of the parental investment model. *Psychological Bulletin, 112,* 125–139.

Feingold, A. (1992c). Sex differences in variability in intellectual abilities: A new look at an old controversy. *Review of Educational Research, 62,* 61–84.

Feingold, A. (1994). Gender differences in variability in intellectual abilities: A cross-cultural perspective. *Sex Roles, 30,* 81–92.

Feldman, D. H., & Goldsmith, L. T. (1991). *Nature's gambit: Child prodigies and the development of human potential.* New York: Teachers College Press.

Felton, B. J., & Revenson, T. A. (1987). Age differences in coping with chronic illness. *Psychology and Aging, 2,* 164–170.

Ferguson, D. M. (1997). Structural equation models in developmental research. *Journal of Child Psychology & Psychiatry & Allied Disciplines, 38,* 877–887.

Filsinger, E. E. (1984). Social class. In R. J. Corsini (Ed.), *Encyclopedia of psychology* (Vol. 3, pp. 332–333). New York: Wiley.

Fink, H. K. (1994). Genetic disorders. In R. J. Corsini (Ed.), *Encyclopedia of psychology* (2nd ed., Vol. 2, pp. 57–61). New York: Wiley.

Flanagan, D. P., Genshaft, J. L., & Harrison, P. L. (Ed.). (1997). *Contemporary intellectual assessment: Theories, tests, and issues.* New York: Guilford.

Floderus-Myrhed, B., Pedersen, N., & Rasmuson, I. (1980). Assessment of heritability for personality based on a short form of the Eysenck Personality Inventory: A study of 12,898 twin pairs. *Behavior Genetics, 10,* 153–162.

Flynn, J. R. (1987). Massive IQ gains in 14 nations: What IQ tests really measure. *Psychological Bulletin, 101,* 171–191.

Flynn, J. R. (1991). *Asian-Americans: Achievement beyond IQ.* Hillsdale, NJ: Lawrence Erlbaum Associates.

Flynn, J. R. (1998). IQ gains over time: Toward finding the causes. In E. Neisser (Ed.), *The rising curve: Long-term gains in IQ and related measures* (pp. 25–66) Washington, DC: American Psychological Association.

Folkman, S., Lazarus, R., Pimley, S., & Novacek, J. (1987). Age differences in stress and coping processes. *Psychology and Aging, 2,* 171–184.

Folkman, S. L., & Lazarus, R. S. (1980). An analysis of coping in a middle-aged community sample. *Journal of Health and Social Behavior, 21,* 219–239.

Ford, M. E. (1986). For all practical purposes: Criteria for defining and evaluating practical intelligence. In R. J. Sternberg & R. K. Wagner (Eds.), *Practical intelligence: Nature and origins of competence in the everyday world* (pp. 183–200). New York: Cambridge University Press.

Ford, M. E. (1994). Social intelligence. In R. J. Sternberg (Ed.), *Encyclopedia of human intelligence* (pp. 974–978). New York: Macmillan.

Forster, A. (1994). Learning disability. In R. J. Sternberg (Ed.), *Encyclopedia of human intelligence* (pp. 647–652). New York: Macmillan.

Fox, M., Gibbs, M., & Auerbach, D. (1985). Age and gender dimensions of friendship. *Psychology of Women Quarterly, 9,* 489–502.

Fozard, J. L., Vercruyssen, M., Reynolds, S. L., Hancock, P. A., & Quilter, R. E. (1994). Age changes and changes in reaction time: The Baltimore Longitudinal Study of Aging. *Journal of Gerontology, 49*(4), P179–P189.

Frankenberger, W. (1984). A survey of state guidelines for identification of mental retardation. *Mental Retardation, 22,* 17–20.

Freimer, N. B., Reus, V. I., Escamilla, M. A., McInnes, L. A., Spesny, M., Leon, P., Service, S. K., Smith, L. B., Silva, S., Rojas, E., Gallegos, A., Meza, L., Fournier, E., Baharloo, S., Blankenship, K., Tyler, D. J., Batki, S., Vinogradov, S., Weissenbach, J., Barondes, S. H., & Sandkuijl, L. A. (1996). Genetic mapping using haplotype, association and linkage methods suggests a locus for severe bipolar disorder (BP1) at 18q22-q23. *Nature Genetics, 12,* 436–441.

Friedman, H. S. (Ed.). (1990). *Personality and disease.* New York: Wiley.

Friedman, H. S. (1991). *The self-healing personality.* New York: Holt.

Friedman, H. S., & Booth-Kewley, S. (1987). Personality, Type A behavior, and coronary heart disease: The role of emotional expression. *Journal of Personality and Social Psychology, 53,* 783–792.

Fromm, E. (1941). *Escape from freedom.* New York: Holt, Rinehart & Winston.

Frueh, B. C., Smith, D. W., & Libet, J. M. (1996). Racial differences on psychological measures in combat veterans seeking treatment for PTSD. *Journal of Personality Assessment, 66,* 41–53.

Fulker, D. W., & Cardon, L. R. (1994). A sib-pair approach to interval mapping of quantitative trait loci. *American Journal of Human Genetics, 54,* 1092–1103.

Funk, S. C. (1992). Hardiness: A review of theory and research. *Health Psychology, 11,* 335–345.

Furnham, A. (1992). *Psychology at work.* London: Routledge.

Furnham, A., & Rawles, R. (1995). Sex differences in the estimation of intelligence. *Journal of Social Behavior and Personality, 10,* 741–748.

Gale, A., & Eysenck, M. W. (1992). *Handbook of individual differences: Biological perspectives.* New York: Wiley.

Galton, F. (1962). *Hereditary genius: An inquiry into its laws and consequences.* London: Collins. (Original work published 1869)

Galton, F. (1874). *English men of science: Their nature and nurture.* London: Macmillan.

Galton, F. (1907). *Inquiries into human faculty and its development.* London: Macmillan. (Original work published 1883)

Gardner, H. (1983). *Frames of mind: The theory of multiple intelligences.* New York: Basic Books.

Gardner, H. (1994). Multiple intelligences theory. In R. J. Sternberg (Ed.), *Encyclopedia of human intelligence* (pp. 740–742). New York: Macmillan.

Gardner, H. (1997). Failing to act: Regrets of Terman's geniuses. *Journal of Creative Behavior, 31*(2), 120–124.

Geary, D. C. (1998). *Male, female: The evolution of human sex differences.* Washington, DC: American Psychological Association.

Geberth, V. J., & Turco, R. N. (1997). Antisocial personality disorder, sexual sadism, malignant narcissism, and serial murder. *Journal of Forensic Sciences, 42,* 49–60.

Geen, R. G. (1984). Preferred stimulation levels in introverts and extraverts: Effects on arousal and performance. *Journal of Personality and Social Psychology, 46,* 1303–1312.

Gettelman, T. E., & Thompson, J. K. (1993). Actual differences and stereotypical perceptions in body image and eating disturbance: A comparison of male and female heterosexual and homosexual samples. *Sex Roles, 29,* 545–562.

Gill, K., & Keats, D. M. (1980). Elements of intellectual competence: Judgments by Australian and Malay university students. *Journal of Cross-Cultural Psychology, 11,* 233–243.

Ginns, E. I., Ott, J., Egeland, J. A., Allen, C. R., Fann, C. S. J., Pauls, D. L., Weissenbach, J., Carulli, J. P., Falls, K. M., Keith, T. P., & Paul, S. M. (1996). A genome-wide search for chromosomal loci linked to bipolar affective disorder in the Old Order Amish. *Nature Genetics, 12,* 431–435.

Glaser, B. G., & Strauss, A. L. (1968). *Time for dying.* Chicago: Aldine.

Glenn, N. D., & Supancic, M. (1984). The social and demographic correlates of divorce and separation in the United States: An update and reconsider. *Journal of Marriage and the Family, 46,* 563–575.

Glick, I. O., Weiss, R. S., & Parkes, C. M. (1974). *The first year of bereavement.* New York: Wiley.

Glueck, S., & Glueck, E. (1950). *Unraveling juvenile delinquency.* Cambridge, MA: Harvard University Press.

Glueck, S., & Glueck, E. (1956). *Physique and delinquency.* New York: Harper & Row.

Goldberg, L. R. (1994). Basic research on personality structure: Implications of the emerging consensus for applications to selection and classification. In M. G. Rumsey, C. B. Walker, & J. H. Harris (Eds.), *Personnel selection and classification* (pp. 247–259). Hillsdale, NJ: Lawrence Erlbaum Associates.

Goldfarb, W. (1955). Emotional and intellectual consequences of psychological deprivation in infancy. In E. Hoch & J. Zubin (Eds.), *Psychopathology in childhood* (pp. 105–119). New York: Grune.

Goleman, D. (1987a, April 7). The bully: New research depicts a paranoid, lifelong loser. *New York Times,* pp. 19, 23.

Goleman, D. (1987b, July 7). Brain defect tied to utter amorality of the psychopath. *New York Times,* pp. 13, 16.

Gonzalez, M. C. (1993). Native American perspectives on the lifespan. In R. Kastenbaum (Ed.), *Encyclopedia of adult development* (pp. 360–364). Phoenix, AZ: Oryx.

Gorer, G. (1964/1948). *The American people: A study in national character* (rev. ed.). New York: Norton.

Gorer, G. (1955). *Exploring English character.* New York: Criterion Books.

Gorer, G., & Rickman, J. (1963/1949). *The people of Great Russia: A psychological study.* New York: Norton.

Gottesman, I. I. (1991). *Schizophrenia genesis: The origins of madness.* New York: Freeman.

Gove, W. R. (1980). *The labeling of deviance* (2nd ed.). Beverly Hills, CA: Sage.

Graves, E. J., & Gillum, B. S. (1996). *1994 Summary: National Hospital Discharge Survey, Advance data from vital and health statistics* (no. 278). Hyattsville, MD: National Center for Health Statistics.

Greenfield, P. M. (1998). The cultural evolution of IQ. In U. Neisser (Ed.), *The rising curve: Long-term gains in IQ and related measures* (pp. 81–123). Washington, DC: American Psychological Association.

Griffin, P. (1993–1994). Homophobia in sport: Addressing the needs of lesbian and gay high school athletes (Special Issue). *High School Journal, 77*(1–2), 80–87.

Grissmer, D. W., Kirby, S. N., Berends, M., & Williamson, S. (1994). *Student achievement and the changing American family.* Santa Monica, CA: RAND.

Guilford, J. P. (1967). *The nature of human intelligence.* New York: McGraw-Hill.

Guilford, J. P., & Hoepfner, R. (1971). *The analysis of intelligence.* New York: McGraw-Hill.

Gur, R. C., & Reivich, M. (1980). Cognitive task effects on hemispheric blood flow in humans: Evidence for individual differences in hemispheric activation. *Brain and Language, 9,* 78–92.

Gynther, M. D. (1981). Is the MMPI an appropriate assessment device for Blacks? *Journal of Black Psychology, 7,* 67–75.

Habib, M., Gayraud, D., Oliva, A., Regis, J., Salamon, G., & Khalil, R. (1991). Effects of handedness and sex on the morphology of the corpus callosum: A study with brain magnetic resonance imaging. *Brain and Cognition, 16,* 41–61.

Hall, C. S. (1938). The inheritance of emotionality. *Sigma Xi Quarterly, 26,* 17–27.

Halpern, D. F. (1994). Gender differences in intellectual abilities. In R. J. Sternberg (Ed.), *Encyclopedia of human intelligence* (pp. 463–467). New York: Macmillan.

Halpern, D. F. (1997). Sex differences in intelligence: Implications for education. *American Psychologist, 52,* 1091–1101.

Hamid, P. N., & Loh, D. (1995). Gender stereotyping in estimates of intelligence in Chinese students. *Journal of Social Psychology, 135,* 407–409.

Hampson, E. (1990). Variations in sex-related cognitive abilities across the menstrual cycle. *Brain and Cognition, 14,* 26–43.

Hansen, C. (1989). A causal model of the relationship among accidents, biodata, personality, and cognitive factors. *Journal of Applied Psychology, 74,* 81–90.

Harasty, J., Double, K. L., Halliday, G. M., Kril, J. J., & McRitchie, D. A. (1997). Language-associated cortical regions are proportionally larger in the female brain. *Archives of Neurology, 54,* 171–176.

Harlow, H. F. (1958). The nature of love. *American Psychologist, 13,* 673–685.

Harlow, H. F., & Zimmerman, R. R. (1959). Affectional responses in the infant monkey. *Science, 130,* 421–432.

Harrell, T. W., & Harrell, M. S. (1945). Army General Classification Test Scores for civilian occupations. *Educational and Psychological Measurement, 5,* 229–342.

Harrison, A. A., & Saeed, L. (1977). Let's make a deal: An analysis of revelations and stipulations in lonely hearts advertisements. *Journal of Personality and Social Psychology, 354,* 257–264.

Hartung, C. M., & Widiger, T. A. (1998). Gender differences in the diagnosis of mental disorders: Conclusions and controversies of the DSM–IV. *Pschyological Bulletin, 123,* 260–278.

Haskins, R. (1989). Beyond metaphor: The efficacy of early childhood education. *American Psychologist, 44,* 274–282.

Hatfield, E., & Sprecher, S. (1986). *Mirror, mirror. ... The importance of looks in everyday life.* Albany, NY: State University of New York Press.

Hathaway, S. R., & McKinley, J. C. (1989). *MMPI–2.* Minneapolis: University of Minnesota Press.

Hedges, L. V., & Nowell, A. (1995, July 7). Sex differences in mental test scores, variability, and numbers of high-scoring individuals. *Science, 269,* 41–45.

Heinrichs, R. W. (1993). Schizophrenia and the brain. *American Psychologist, 48,* 221–233.

Helson, R., & Moane, G. (1987). Personality change in women from college to midlife. *Journal of Personality and Social Psychology, 53,* 176–186.

Henriques, J. B., & Davidson, R. J. (1989). Affective disorders. In G. Turpin (Ed.), *Handbook of clinical psychophysiology* (pp. 357–393). London: Wiley.

Henry, B., Caspi, A., Moffitt, T. E., & Silva, P. A. (1996). Temperamental and familial predictors of violent and nonviolent criminal convictions: Age 3 to age 18. *Developmental Psychology, 32,* 614–623.

Henss, R. (1987). Zur Beurteilerübereinstimmmung bei der Einschätzung der Physischen Attraktivität junger and alter Menschen (Consensus in judging the attractiveness of young and older people). *Zeitschrift für Sozialpsychologie, 18,* 118–130.

Herbert, T. B., & Cohen, S. (1993). Depression and immunity: A meta-analytic review. *Psychological Bulletin, 113,* 472–486.

Herrnstein, R. J., & Murray, C. (1994). *The bell curve.* New York: The Free Press.

Hess, B. (1971). *Amicability.* Unpublished doctoral dissertation, Rutgers University, New Brunswick, NJ.

Hill, C. D., Rogers, R., & Bickford, M. E. (1996). Predicting aggressive and socially disruptive behavior in a maximum security forensic psychiatric hospital. *Journal of Forensic Sciences, 41,* 56–59.

Hill, R. D., Storandt, M., & Malley, M. (1993). The impact of long-term exercise training on psychological function in older adults. *Journal of Gerontology: Psychological Sciences, 48,* 12–48.

Hirsch, N. D. M. (1926). A study of natio-racial mental differences. *Genetic Psychology Monographs, 1,* 231–406.

Høag, P. (1995). *Smilla's sense of snow.* New York: Dell.

Hobbs, N. (1963). A psychologist in the Peace Corps. *American Psychologist, 18,* 47–55.

Hodes, R. L., Cook, E. W., & Lang, P. (1985). Individual differences in autonomic response: Conditioned association or conditioned fear? *Psychophysiology, 22,* 545–560.

Hodgins, S. (1997). An overview of research on the prediction of dangerousness. *Nordic Journal of Psychiatry, 51* (Suppl. 39), 33–38, 73–95.

Hodgins, S., Mednick, S., Brennan, P. A., Schulsinger, F., & Engberg, M. (1998). "Mental disorder and crime": Commentary reply. *Archives of General Psychiatry, 55,* 87–88.

Hogan, R., Hogan, J., & Roberts, B. W. (1996). Personality measurement and employment decisions. *American Psychologist, 51,* 469–477.

Holden, R. J., Pakula, I. S., & Mooney, P. A. (1997). A neuroimmunological model of antisocial and borderline personality disorders. *Human Psychopharmacology Clinical & Experimental, 12,* 291–308.

Holland, J. L. (1985). *Making vocational choices: A theory of careers: A theory of vocational personalities and work environments* (2nd ed.). Englewood Cliffs, NJ: Prentice-Hall.

Holland, J. L. (1996). Exploring careers with a typology: What we have learned and some new directions. *American Psychologist, 51,* 397–406.

Hollingworth, L. S. (1942). *Children above 180 IQ, Stanford-Binet origin and development.* Yonkers, NY: World Book.

Hoover, D. W. (1993). Community studies. In M. K Clayton, E. J. Gorn, & P. W. Williams (Eds.), *Encyclopedia of American social history* (Vol. 1., pp. 297–305). New York: Scribner's.

Horn, J. L. (1982). The theory of fluid and crystallized intelligence in relation to concepts of cognitive psychology and aging in adulthood. In F. I. M. Craik & S. Trehub (Eds.), *Advances in the study of communication and affect: Volume 8. Aging and cognitive processes* (pp. 237–278). New York: Plenum.

Horn, J. L., & Hofer, S. M. (1992). Major abilities and development in the adult period. In R. J. Sternberg & C. A. Berg (Eds.), *Intellectual development* (pp. 44–99). Cambridge, England: Cambridge University Press.

Howard, J. H., Cunningham, D. A., & Rechnitzer, P. A. (1987). Personality and fitness decline in middle-aged men. *International Journal of Sport Psychology, 18,* 100–111.

Howe, M. J. A. (1989). *Fragments of genius: The strange feats of idiots savants.* London: Routledge.

Hoyer, W. J., & Plude, D. J. (1980). Attentional and perceptual processes in the study of cognitive aging. In L. Poon (Ed.), *Aging in the 1980s* (pp. 227–238). Washington, DC: American Psychological Association.

Hultsch, D. F., & Dixon, R. A. (1990). Learning and memory in aging. In J. E. Birren & K. W. Schaie (Eds.), *Handbook of aging and the social sciences* (2nd ed., pp. 554–585). New York: Van Nostrand Reinhold.

Humphreys, L. G., & Davey, T. C. (1988). Continuity in intellectual growth from 12 months to 9 years. *Intelligence, 12,* 183–197.

Hunt, J. McV. (1961). *Intelligence and experience.* New York: Ronald.

Hunter, E. J. (1981). *Wartime stress: Family adjustment to loss* (USIU Report No. TR-USIU-81–07). San Diego: United States International University.

Hunter, J. E., & Schmidt, F. L. (1996). Intelligence and job performance: Economic and social implications. *Psychology, Public Policy, & Law, 2,* 447–472.

Hunter, J. E., Schmidt, F. L., & Hunter, R. (1979). Differential validity of employment tests by race: A comprehensive review and analysis. *Psychological Bulletin, 86,* 721–735.

Hurlock, E. B. (1994). Dress. In R. J. Corsini (Ed.), *Encyclopedia of psychology* (Vol. 1, pp. 437–439). New York: Macmillan.

Huyck, M. H. (1982). From gregariousness to intimacy: Marriage and friendship over the adult years. In T. M. Field, A. Huston, H. C. Quay, L. Troll, & G. E. Finley (Eds.), *Review of human development* (pp. 471–484). New York: Wiley.

Hyde, J. S., Fennema, E., & Lamon, S. J. (1990). Gender differences in mathematics performance: A meta-analysis. *Psychological Bulletin, 107,* 139–153.

Innocenti, G. M. (1994). Some new trends in the study of the corpus callosum. *Behavioral and Brain Research, 64,* 1–8.

International Society for the Study of Individual Differences. (1997). *Personality and Individual Differences, 22,* iii–iv.

Jackson, D. N. (1989a). *Basic Personality Inventory manual.* London, Ontario, Canada: Sigma Assessment Systems.

Jackson, D. N. (1989b). *Personality Research Form manual.* London, Ontario, Canada: Sigma Assessment Systems.

Jackson, D. N. (1994). *Jackson Personality Inventory—Revised manual.* Port Huron, MI: Sigma Assessment Systems.

Jackson, J. F. (1993). Human behavioral genetics, Scarr's theory, and her views on interventions: A critical review and commentary on their implications for African American children. *Child Development, 64,* 1318–1332.

Jackson, L. A., & McGill, O. D. (1996). Body type preferences and body characteristics associated with attractive and unattractive bodies by African Americans and Anglo Americans. *Sex Roles, 35,* 295–307.

Jackson, N. E. (1992). Precocious reading of English: Origins, structure, and predictive significance. In P. S. Klein & A. J. Tannenbaum (Eds.), *To be young and gifted* (pp. 171–203). Norwood, NJ: Ablex.

Jacobson, J. W., & Mullick, J. A. (1992). A new definition of mental retardation or a new definition of practice? *Psychology in Mental Retardation and Developmental Disabilities, 18,* 9–14.

Jamison, K. R. (1984). Manic-depressive illness and accomplishment: Creativity, leadership, and social class. In F. K. Goodwin & K. R. Jamison (Eds.), *Manic-depressive illness.* New York: Oxford University Press.

Jamison, K. R. (1989). Mood disorders and patterns of creativity in British writers and artists. *Psychiatry, 52,* 125–134.

Jamison, K. R. (1993). *Touched with fire: Manic-depressive illness and the artistic temperament.* New York: The Free Press.

Jancke, L., & Steinmetz, H. (1994). Interhemispheric-transfer time and corpus callosum size. *Neuroreport, 5,* 2385–2388.

Janos, P. M., & Robinson, N. M. (1985). Psychosocial development in intellectual gifted children. In F. D. Horowitz & M. O'Brien (Eds.), *The gifted and talented: Developmental perspectives* (pp. 149–195). Washington, DC: American Psychological Association.

Janowsky, J. S., Oviatt, S. K., & Orwoll, E. S. (1994). Testosterone influences spatial cognition in older men. *Behavioral Neuroscience, 108,* 325–332.

Janus, S. S., & Janus, C. L. (1993). *The Janus Report on sexual behavior.* New York: Wiley.

Jensen, A. R. (1985). Methodological and statistical techniques for the chonometric study of mental abilities. In C. R. Reynolds & V. L. Willson (Eds.), *Methodological and statistical advances in the study of individual differences* (pp. 51–116). New York: Plenum.

Jensen, A. R., & Johnson, R. W. (1994). Race and sex differences in head size and IQ. *Intelligence, 18,* 309–333.

Jensen, A. R., & Sinha, S. N. (1991). Physical correlates of human intelligence. In P. A. Vernon (Ed.), *Biological approaches to the study of human intelligence* (pp. 139–242). Norwood, NJ: Ablex.

Johnson, E. (1991, November 18). I'll deal with it (Interview with "Magic" Johnson). *Sports Illustrated, 75,* 16–45.

Johnson, S. C., Pinkston, J. B., Bigler, E. D., & Blatter, D. D. (1996). Corpus callosum morphology in normal controls and traumatic brain injury: Sex differences, mechanisms of injury, and neuropsychological correlates. *Neuropsychology, 10,* 408–415.

Jonassen, D. H., & Grabowski, B. L. (1993). *Handbook of individual differences, learning, and instruction.* Hillsdale, NJ: Lawrence Erlbaum Associates.

Jones, A. E. (1997). Reflection-impulsivity and wholist-analyic: Two fledglings? ... or is R-I a cuckoo? *Educational Psychology, 17*(1–2), 65–77.

Jones, H. E., & Conrad, H. S. (1933). The growth and decline of intelligence: A study of a homogeneous group. *Genetic Psychology Monographs, 13,* 223–298.

Jones, J. M. (1994). Our similarities are different: Toward a psychology of affirmative diversity. In E. J. Trickett, R. J. Watts, & D. Birman (Eds.), *Human diversity* (pp. 27–45). San Francisco: Jossey-Bass.

Jones, R. L. (1991). *Black psychology* (3rd ed.). Berkeley, CA: Cobb & Henry.

Jutai, J. W., Hare, R. D., & Connolly, J. F. (1987). Psychopathy and event-related brain potentials (ERPs) associated with attention to speech stimuli. *Personality and Individual Differences, 8,* 175–184.

Kagan, J. (1966). Reflection-impulsivity: The generality and dynamics of conceptual tempo. *Journal of Abnormal Psychology, 71,* 17–24.

Kagan, J. (1994). *Galen's prophecy: Temperament in human nature.* New York: Basic Books.

Kagan, J., Reznick, J. S., & Snidman, N. (1988). Biological bases of childhood shyness. *Science, 240,* 167–171.

Kalat, J. W. (1998). *Biological psychology* (6th ed.). Pacific Grove, CA: Brooks/Cole.

Kalish, R. A., & Reynolds, D. K. (1981). *Death and ethnicity: A psychocultural study.* Farmingdale, NY: Baywood.

Kamen-Siegel, L., Rodin, J., Seligman, M. E. P., & Dwyer, J. (1991). Explanatory style and cell-mediated immunity in elderly men and women. *Health Psychology, 10,* 229–235.

Kardiner, A. (1946/1939). *The individual and his society.* New York: Columbia University Press.

Kardiner, A. (1959/1945). *The psychological frontier of society.* New York: Columbia University Press.

Kaufman, A. S. (1990). *Assessing adolescent and adult intelligence.* Needham Heights, MA: Allyn & Bacon.

Kempen, G. I. J. M., Jelicic, M., & Ormel, J. (1997). Personality, chronic medical morbidity, and health-related quality. *Health Psychology, 16,* 539–546.

Kermoian, R., & Leiderman, P. H. (1986). Infant attachment to mother and child caretaker in an East African community (Special Issue: Cross-cultural human development). *International Journal of Behavioral Development, 9,* 455–469.

Khleif, B. (1976). The sociology of the mortuary: Religion, sex, age and kinship variables. In V. R. Pine, A. H. Kutscher, D. Peretz, R. J. Slater, R. DeBellis, & D. J. Cherico (Eds.), *Acute grief and the funeral.* Springfield, IL: C. C. Thomas.

Kidd, J. W. (1983). The 1984 A.A.M.D. definition and classification of mental retardation: The apparent impact of the CEC-MR position. *Education and Training of the Mentally Retarded, 18,* 243–244.

Kiecolt-Glaser, J. K., & Glaser, R. (1992). Psychoneuroimmunology: Can psychology interventions modulate immunity? *Journal of Consulting and Clinical Psychology, 60,* 569–575.

Kiecolt-Glaser, J. K., & Glaser, R. (1993). Mind and immunity. In D. Goleman & J. Gurin (Eds.), *Mind body medicine* (pp. 39–61). Yonkers, NY: Consumer Reports Books.

Kilbride, H. W., Johnson, D. L., & Streissguth, A. P. (1977). Social class, birth order, and newborn experience. *Child Development, 48,* 1686–1688.

Kimura, D., & Hampson, E. (1994). Cognitive pattern in men and women is influenced by fluctuations in sex hormones. *Psychological Science, 3,* 57–61.

Kobasa, S. C. (1979). Stressful life events, personality, and health: An inquiry into hardiness. *Journal of Personality and Social Psychology, 37,* 1–11.

Kobasa, S. C., Maddi, S., & Kahn, S. (1982). Hardiness and health: A prospective study. *Journal of Personality and Social Psychology, 42,* 168–177.

Kohlberg, L. (1966). A cognitive-development analysis of children's sex-role concepts and attitudes. In E. Maccoby (Ed.), *The development of sex differences* (pp. 82–173). Sanford, CA: Stanford University Press.

Kolb, B., & Whishaw, I. Q. (1996). *Fundamentals of human neuropsychology* (4th ed.). New York: Freeman.

Kowalski, R. M. (1993). Inferring sexual interest from behavioral cues: Effects of gender and sexually relevant attitudes. *Sex Rules, 29,* 13–36.

Krech, D., Crutchfield, R., & Livson, N. (1969). *Elements of psychology* (2nd ed.). New York: Knopf.

Kretschmer, E. (1925). *Physique and character.* New York: Harcourt, Brace.

Kreutzer, J. S., Marwitz, J. H., & Witol, A. D. (1995). Interrelationships between crime, substance abuse, and aggressive behaviours among persons with traumatic brain injury. *Brain Injury, 9,* 757–768.

Kristiansson, M. (1995). Incurable psychopaths? *Bulletin of the American Academy of Psychiatry & the Law, 23,* 555–562.

Kroemer, K., Kroemer, H., & Kroemer-Elbert, K. (1994). *Ergonomics: How to design for ease and efficiency.* Englewood Cliffs, NJ: Prentice-Hall.

Krueger, R. F., Schutte, P. S., Caspi, A., Moffitt, T. E., Campbell, K., & Silva, P. A. (1994). Personality traits are linked to crime among men and women: Evidence from a birth cohort. *Journal of Abnormal Psychology, 103,* 328–338.

Kübler-Ross, E. (1969). *On death and dying.* New York: Macmillan.

Kurdek, L. A., & Schmitt, J. P. (1986). Early development of relationship quality in heterosexual married, heterosexual cohabiting, gay, and lesbian couples. *Developmental Psychology, 22,* 305–309.

Lamison-White, L. (1997, September). *Poverty in the United States: 1996. Current Population Reports* (P60-198). Washington, DC: U.S. Bureau of the Census.

Lancer, I., & Rim, Y. (1984). Intelligence, family size and sibling age spacing. *Personality & Individual Differences, 5,* 151–157.

Landau, T. (1989). *About faces: The evolution of the human face.* New York: Anchor.

Lander, E. S., & Schork, N. J. (1994). Genetic dissection of complex traits. *Science, 265,* 2037–2048.

Langlois, J. H., Roggman, L. A., Casey, R. J., Ritter, J. M., Rieser-Danner, L. A., & Jenkins, V. Y. (1987). Infant preferences for attractive faces: Rudiments of a stereotype? *Developmental Psychology, 23,* 363–369.

Lanyon, R. I. (1973). *Psychological Screening Inventory: Manual* (2nd ed.). Port Huron, MI: Research Psychologists Press/Sigma Assessment Systems.

Lanyon, R. I. (1978). *Psychological Screening Inventory: Manual* (2nd ed.). Port Huron, MI: Research Psychologists Press/Sigma Assessment Systems.

Larsen, R. J., & Kasimatis, M. (1991). Day-to-day symptoms: Individual differences in the occurrence, duration, and emotional concomitants of minor daily illnesses. *Journal of Personality, 59,* 415–420.

Laumann, E. O., Gagnon, J. H., Michael, R. T., & Michaels, S. (1994). *The social organization of sexuality: Sexual practices in the United States.* Chicago: The University of Chicago Press.

Law, D. J., Pellegrino, J. W., & Hunt, E. B. (1993). Comparing the tortoise and the hare: Gender difference and experience in dynamic spatial reasoning tasks. *Psychological Science, 4,* 35–40.

Leinbach, M. D., & Fagot, B. I. (1993). Categorical habituation to male and female faces: Gender schematic processes in infancy. *Infant Behavior and Development, 16,* 317–332.

Leites, N. S. (1990). Early signs of giftedness. *Soviet Psychology, 28*(5), 25–41.

Lemert, E. M. (1972). *Human deviance, social problems, and social control* (2nd ed.). Englewood Cliffs, NJ: Prentice-Hall.

Lentzer, H. R., Pamuk, E. R., Rhodenhiser, E. P., Rothberg, R., & Powell-Griner, E. (1992). The quality of life in the year before death. *American Journal of Public Health, 82,* 1093–1098.

Leonard, C. M., , L. J., Mercado, L. R., Brown, S. R., Breier, J. I., & Agee, O. F. (1996). Cerebral asymmetry and cognitive development in children: A magnetic resonance imaging study. *Psychological Science, 7,* 89–95.

Lerner, R. M., & Busch-Rossnagel, N. (Eds.). (1981). *Individuals as producers of their own development.* New York: Academic Press.

LeUnes, A. D., & Nation, J. R. (1989). *Sport psychology: An introduction.* Chicago: Nelson Hall.

LeVay, S. (1991). A difference in hypothalamic structure between heterosexual and homosexual men. *Science, 253,* 1034–1037.

LeVay, S., & Mamer, D. H. (1994). Evidence for a biological influence in male homosexuality. *Scientific American, 270*(5), 44–49.

Levin, H. (1987). Accelerating schools for disadvantaged students. *Educational Leadership, 44*(6), 19–21.

Lewis, D. O., Pincus, J. H., Bard, B., & Richardson, E. (1988). Neuropsychiatric, psychoeducational, and family characteristics of juveniles on death row. *American Journal of Psychiatry, 145,* 584–589.

Lewis, M., & Jaskir, J. (1983). Infant intelligence and its relation to birth order and birth spacing. *Infant Behavior & Development, 6,* 117–120.

Licinio, J., Wong, M. L., & Gold, P. W. (1996). The hypothalamic-pituitary-adrenal axis in anorexia nervosa. *Psychiatry Research, 62,* 75–83.

Lieberman, M. A. (1965). Psychological correlates of impending death: Some preliminary observations. *Journal of Gerontology, 20,* 71–84.

Lindfors, B. (1984). P. T. Barnum and Africa. *Studies in Popular Culture, 7,* 18–25.

Linn, M. L., & Hyde, J. S. (1989). Gender, mathematics, and science. *Educational Researcher, 18*(8), 17.

Lipsey, M. W., & Wilson, D. B. (1993). The efficacy of psychological, educational, and behavioral treatment: Confirmation from meta-analyses. *American Psychologist, 48,* 1181–1209.

Livson, N., & Peskin, H. (1980). Perspectives on adolescence from longitudinal research. In J. Adelson (Ed.), *Handbook of adolescent psychology* (pp. 47–98). New York: Wiley.

Loehlin, J. C., Horn, J. M., & Willerman, L. (1997). Heredity, environment, and IQ in the Texas Adoption Project. In R. J. Sternberg & E. L. Grigorenko (Eds.), *Intelligence, heredity, and environment* (pp. 105–125). New York: Cambridge University Press.

Loevinger, J. (1996). In defense of the individuality of personality theories. *Psychological Inquiry, 7,* 344–346.

Lopata, H. Z. (1973). *Widowhood in an American city.* Cambridge, MA: Schenckman.

Lubinski, D. J., & Dawis, R. V. (1995). *Assessing individual differences in human behavior.* Palo Alto, CA: Davies-Black.

Luria, A. R. (1966). *Higher cortical functions in man.* New York: Basic Books.

Luster, T., & McAdoo, H. P. (1994). Factors related to the achievement and adjustment of young African-American children. *Child Development, 65,* 1080–1094.

Lynam, D. R. (1996). Early identification of chronic offenders: Who is the fledgling psychopath? *Psychological Bulletin, 120,* 209–234.

Lynn, R. (1987). The intelligence of the mongoloids: A psychometric, evolutionary, and neurological theory. *Personality and Individual Differences, 8,* 813–844.

Lynn, R. (1994). Sex differences in intelligence and brain size: A paradox resolved. *Personality and Individual Differences, 17,* 257–271.

Lynn, R. (1998). In support of the nutrition theory. In U. Neisser (Ed.), *The rising curve: Long-term gains in IQ and related measures* (pp. 207–215). Washington, DC: American Psychological Association.

Lynn, R., & Hampson, S. (1986). The structure of Japanese abilities: An analysis in terms of the hierarchical model of intelligence. *Current Psychological Research and Reviews, 4,* 309–322.

Maccoby, E. E., & Martin, J. A. (1983). Socialization in the context of the family: Parent–child interaction. In P. H. Mussen (Ed.), *Handbook of child psychology: Vol. 4. Socialization, personality, and social development* (pp. 1–101). New York: Wiley.

MacKinnon, D. W. (1962). The nature and nurture of creative talent. *American Psychologist, 17,* 484–495.

MacPhee, D., Ramey, C. T., & Yeates, K. O. (1984). Home environment and early cognitive development: Implications for intervention. In A. W. Gottfried (Ed.), *Home environment and early cognitive development: Longitudinal research* (pp. 343–369). Orlando, FL: Academic Press.

Madden, P. A. F., Heath, A. C., Rosenthal, N. E., & Martin, N. G. (1996). Seasonal changes in mood and behavior. *Archives of General Psychiatry, 53,* 47–55.

Maddi, S. R. (1996). *Personality theories: A comparative analysis* (6th ed.). Pacific Grove, CA: Brooks/Cole.

Magnavita, N., Narda, R., Sani, L., Carbone, A., De-Lorenzo, G., & Sacco, A. (1997). Type A behaviour pattern and traffic accidents. *British Journal of Medical Psychology, 70,* 103–107.

Mainstream Science on Intelligence. (1994, December 13). *The Wall Street Journal,* p. A18.

Major, B., Carrington, P. I., & Carnevale, P. J. D. (1984). Physical attractiveness and self-esteem: Attribution for praise from an other-sex evaluator. *Personality and Social Psychology Bulletin, 10,* 43–50.

Malinowski, B. (1927). *Sex and repression in savage society.* New York: Harcourt, Brace.

Maltsberger, J. T. (1997). Ecstatic suicide. *Archives of Suicide Research, 3,* 283–301.

Manly, B. F. J. (1994). *Multivariate statistical methods: A primer* (2nd ed.). London & New York: Chapman & Hall.

Markides, K. S., Liang, J., & Jackson, J. S. (1990). Race, ethnicity and aging: Conceptual and methodological issues. In R. H. Binstock & L. K. George (Eds.), *Handbook of aging and the social sciences* (3rd ed., pp. 112–129). San Diego: Academic Press.

Markus, H., & Kitayama, S. (1991). Culture and the self: Implications for cognition, emotion, and motivation. *Psychological Review, 98,* 224–253.

Martin, A. (1997). On teenagers and tattoos. *Journal of the American Academy of Child & Adolescent Psychiatry, 36,* 860–861.

Martin, C. L., Wood, C. H., & Little, J. K. (1990). The development of gender stereotype components. *Child Development, 61,* 1891–1904.

Martorell, R. (1998). Nutrition and the worldwide rise in IQ scores. In U. Neisser (Ed.), *The rising curve: Long-term gains in IQ and related measures* (pp. 183–206). Washington, DC: American Psychological Association.

Matas, L., Arend, R. A., & Sroufe, L. A. (1978). Continuity of adaptation in the second year: The relationship between quality of attachment and later competence. *Child Development, 49,* 483–494.

Maugh, T. H. (1996, September 16). Worldwide study finds big shift in causes of death. *Los Angeles Times,* pp. A1, A14.

Maugh, T. H. (1997, February, 28). Study finds piano lessons boost youths' reasoning. *Los Angeles Times,* p. A3.

Mauksch, H. O. (1975). The organizational context of dying. In E. Kübler-Ross (Ed.), *Death: The final stage of growth* (pp. 7–24). Englewood Cliffs, NJ: Prentice-Hall.

Mayer, J. D., & Geher, G. (1996). Emotional intelligence and the identification of emotion. *Intelligence, 22,* 89–114.

Mayer, J. D., & Salovey, P. (1993). The intelligence of emotional intelligence. *Intelligence, 17,* 433–442.

Mayer, J. D., & Salovey, P. (1995). Emotional intelligence and the construction and regulation of feelings. *Applied & Preventive Psychology, 4,* 197–208.

McAuley, E. (1992). Understanding exercise behavior: A self-efficacy perspective. In G. C. Roberts (Ed.), *Understanding motivation in exercise and sport* (pp. 107–128). Champaign, IL: Human Kinetics.

McAuley, E., Courneya, K. S., & Lettunich, J. (1991). Effects of acute and long-term exercise on self-efficacy responses in sedentary, middle-aged males and females. *The Gerontologist, 31,* 534–542.

McAuley, E., Lox, L., & Duncan, T. E. (1993). Long-term maintenance of exercise, self-efficacy, and physiological change in older adults. *Psychological Sciences, 48,* P218–P224.

McCall, R. B. (1979). The development of intellectual functioning in infancy and the prediction of later IQ. In J.D. Osofsky (Ed.), *Handbook of infant development* (pp. 707–741). New York: Wiley.

McCrae, R. R., & Costa, P. T., Jr. (1982). Self-concept and the stability of personality: Cross-sectional comparisons of self-reports and ratings. *Journal of Personality and Social Psychology, 43,* 1282–1292.

McCrae, R. R., & Costa, P. T., Jr. (1984). *Emerging lives, enduring dispositions.* Boston: Little, Brown.

McCrae, R. R., & Costa, P. T., Jr. (1987). Validation of the five-factor model of personality across instruments and observers. *Journal of Personality and Social Psychology, 52,* 138–155.

McDonald, A. S., & Davey, G. C. L. (1996). Psychiatric disorders and accidental injury. *Clinical Psychology Review, 16,* 105–127.

McGue, M., & Lykken, D. T. (1992). Genetic influence on risk of divorce. *Psychological Science, 3,* 368–373.

McGuire, F. L. (1976). Personality factors in highway accidents. *Human Factors, 18,* 433–442.

McKenney, J., & Keen, P. G. W. (1974). How managers' minds work. *Harvard Business Review, 52,* 79–90.

McKenzie, C. (1995). A study of serial murder. *International Journal of Offender Therapy & Comparative Criminology, 39*(1), 3–10.

McNeil, J. K., LeBlanc, E. M., & Joyner, M. (1991). The effects of exercise on depressive symptoms in the moderately depressed elderly. *Psychology and Aging, 6,* 487–488.

Mead, M. (1969/1935). *Sex and temperament in three primitive societies.* New York: Dell.

Melamed, T. (1994). Correlates of physical features: Some gender differences. *Personality and Individual Differences, 17,* 689–691.

Miller, E. M. (1994). Intelligence and brain myelination: A hypothesis. *Personality and Individual Differences, 17,* 803–832.

Miller, L. K. (1989). *Musical savants: Exceptional skill in the mentally retarded.* Hillsdale, NJ: Lawrence Erlbaum Associates.

Miller, W. B. (1958). Lower-class culture as a generating milieu of gang delinquency. *Journal of Social Issues, 14,* 5–19.

Moffatt, S. D., & Hampson, E. (1996). A curvilinear relationship between testosterone and spatial cognition in humans: Possible influence of hand preference. *Psychoneuroendocrinology, 21,* 323–337.

Moghaddam, F. M., Taylor, D. M., & Wright, S. C. (1993). *Social psychology in cross-cultural perspective.* New York: Freeman.

Molfese, V. J., DiLalla, L. F., & Bunce, D. (1997). Prediction of the intelligence test scores of 3- to 8–year-old children by home environment, socioeconomic status, and biomedical risks. *Merrill-Palmer Quarterly, 43,* 219–234.

Monaghan, E. P., & Glickman, S. E. (1992). Hormones and aggressive behavior. In J. B. Becker, S. M. Breedlove, & D. Crews (Eds.), *Behavioral endocrinology* (pp. 261–285). Cambridge, MA: MIT Press.

Monahan, J. (1996). Violence prediction: The past twenty and the next twenty years. *Criminal Justice & Behavior, 23,* 107–120.

Montag, I., & Comrey, A. (1987). Internality and externality as correlates of involvement in fatal driving accidents. *Journal of Applied Psychology, 72,* 339–343.

Morris, T. W., & Levinson, E. M. (1995). Relationship between intelligence and occupational adjustment and functioning: A literature review. *Journal of Counseling and Development, 73,* 503–514.

Morrison, A. M., & Von Glinow, M. A. (1990). Women and minorities in management. *American Psychologist, 45,* 200–208.

Muth, J., & Cash, T. F. (1997). Body-image attitudes: What difference does gender make? *Journal of Applied Social Psychology, 27,* 1438–1452.

National Center for Educational Statistics. (1996). *National assessment of educational progress (NAEP), 1994 long-term trend assessment.* Washington, DC: U.S. Department of Education.

National Center for Health Statistics. (1991). *Current estimates from the National Health Interview Survey, 1990. Vital and Health Statistics* (Series 10, No. 181). Washington, DC: U.S. Government Printing Office.

National Center for Health Statistics. (1995). *Health, United States, 1994.* Hyattsville, MD: Public Health Service.

National Center for Health Statistics (1996). *NHANES III reference manuals and reports* [CD-ROM]. Hyattsville, MD: U.S. Department of Health and Human Services, Public Health Service, CDC.

National Institute of Mental Health. (1998, May 11). *Mental illness in America: The National Institute of Mental Health agenda.* Washington, DC: Author.

National Research Council and Institute of Medicine, Committee on the Health & Safety Implications of Child Labor. (1998). *Protecting youth at work: Health, safety, and development of working children and adolescents in the United States.* Washington, DC: Author.

National Safety Council. (1998). *Accident facts, 1997 edition.* Itasca, IL: Author.

Needleman, H. L., Schell, A., Bellinger, D., Leviton, A., & Allred, E. N. (1990). The long-term effects of exposure to low doses of lead in childhood. *New England Journal of Medicine, 322*(2), 83–88.

Neisser, U. (1998). *The rising curve: Long-term gains in IQ and related measures.* Washington, DC: American Psychological Association.

Neisser, U., Boodoo, G., Bouchard, T. J., Jr., Boykin, A. W. Brody, N., Ceci, S. J., Halpern, D. F., Loehlin, J. C., Perloff, R., Sternberg, R. J., & Urbina, S. (1996). Intelligence: Knowns and unknowns. *American Psychologist, 51,* 77–101.

Newport, F., & Saad, L. (1997, March). Religious faith is widespread but many skip church. *The Gallup Poll Monthly,* pp. 20–29.

Nichols, S. L., & Newman, J. P. (1986). Effects of punishment on response latency in extroverts. *Journal of Personality and Social Psychology, 50,* 624–630.

Niemcryk, S. J., Jenkins, C. D., Rose, R. M., & Hurst, M. W. (1987). The prospective impact of psychosocial variables on rates of illness and injury in professional employees. *Journal of Occupational Medicine, 29,* 645–652.

Nietzel, M. T. (1979). *Crime and its modification: A social learning perspective.* New York: Pergamon.

Nisbet, J. D. (1957). Intelligence and age: Retesting after twenty-four years inteval. *British Journal of Educational Psychology, 27,* 190–193.

Norbeck, E. (1995). Funeral. *Encyclopedia Americana, 12,* 168.

Ochse, R. (1991). The relation between creative genius and psychopathology: An historical perspective and a new explanation. *South African Journal of Psychology, 21*(1), 45–53.

Ogden, C. L., Troiano, R. P., Briefel, R. R., Kuczmarski, R. J., Flegal, K., & Johnson, C. L. (1997). Prevalence of overweight among preschool children in the United States, 1971 through 1994. *Pediatrics, 99*(4).

Oglesby, C. A. (1983). Interactions between gender identity and sport. In J. M. Sislva & R. S. Weinberg (Eds.), *Psychological foundations of sport* (pp. 387–399). Champaign, IL: Human Kinetics.

Oglesby, C. A. (1998). *Encyclopedia of women in sport in America* (pp. 136–138, 182–183). Phoenix, AZ: Oryx Press.

O'Gorman, J. G. (1983). Habituation and personality. In A. Gale & J. A. Edwards (Eds.), *Physiological correlates of human behavior: Vol. 3. Individual differences and psychopathology* (pp. 45–61). London: Academic Press.

Ohman, A. (1986). Face the beast and fear the face: Animal and social fears as prototypes for evolutionary analyses of emotion. *Psychophysiology, 23*, 123–145.

O'Leary, A. (1990). Stress, emotion, and human immune function. *Psychological Bulletin, 108*, 363–382.

Olin, J. T., Schneider, L. S., Eaton, E. M., Zemensky, M. F., & Pollack, V. E. (1992). The Geriatric Depression Scale and the Beck Depression Inventory as screening instruments in an older adult outpatient population. *Psychological Assessment, 4*, 190–192.

Oliver, J. M., Cole, N. H., & Hollingsworth, H. (1991). Learning disabilities as functions of familial learning problems and developmental problems. *Exceptional Children, 57*, 427–440.

Oliver, M. B., & Hyde, J. S. (1993). Gender differences in sexuality: A meta-analysis. *Psychological Bulletin, 114*, 29–51.

Ord, J. G. (1971). *Mental tests for pre-literates*. London: Ginn.

Ortar, G. (1963). Is a verbal test cross-cultural? *Scripta Hierosolymitana (Hebrew University, Jerusalem), 13*, 329–335.

Ortner, S. (1974). Is female to male as nature is to culture? In M. Rosaldo & L. Lamphere (Eds.), *Women, culture and society* (pp. 67–87). Stanford, CA: Stanford University Press.

Osborn, D. R. (1996). Beauty is as beauty does?: Makeup and posture effects on physical attractiveness judgments. *Journal of Applied Social Psychology, 26*, 31–51.

Ostendorf, F., & Angleitner, A. (1994). The five-factor taxonomy: Robust dimensions of personality description. *Psychologica Belgica, 34*, 175–194.

Overman, W. H., Bachevalier, J., Schuhmann, E., & Ryan, P. (1996). Cognitive gender differences in very young children parallel biologically based cognitive gender differences in monkeys. *Behavioral Neuroscience, 110*, 673–684.

Owens, W. A., Jr. (1953). Age and mental abilities: A longitudinal study. *Genetic Psychology Monographs, 48*, 3–54.

Owens, W. A., Jr. (1966). Age and mental abilities: A second adult follow-up. *Journal of Educational Psychology, 57*, 311–325.

Pagano, R. R. (1994). *Understanding statistics in the behavioral sciences* (4th ed.). Minneapolis/St. Paul: West.

Parkes, K. R. (1994). Personality and coping as moderators of work stress processes: Models, methods and measures. Special Issue: A healthier work environment. *Work and Stress, 8*, 110–129.

Pattison, E. M. (1977). Death throughout the life cycle. In E. M. Pattison (Ed.), *The experience of dying* (pp. 18–27). Englewood Cliffs, NJ: Prentice-Hall.

Pearce-McCall, D., & Newman, J. P. (1986). Expectations of success following noncontingent punishment in introverts and extroverts. *Journal of Personality and Social Psychology, 50,* 439–446.

Pedersen, D. M., & Kono, D. M. (1990). Perceived effects on femininity of the participation of women in spot. *Perceptual and Motor Skills, 71,* 783–792.

Pedersen, N. L., Plomin, R., Nesselroade, J. R., & McClearn, G. E. (1992). A quantitative genetic analysis of cognitive abilities during the second half of the life span. *Psychological Science, 3,* 346–353.

Penev, P. D., Zee, P. C., & Turek, F. W. (1997). Serotonin in the spotlight. *Nature, 385,* 123.

Pennington, B. F. (1991). *Diagnosing learning disorders: A neuropsychological framework.* New York: Guilford.

Peplau, L., & Gordon, S. L. (1985). Women and men in love: Sex differences in close heterosexual relationships. In V. O'Leary, R. K. Unger, & B. S. Wallston (Eds.), *Women, gender, and social psychology* (pp. 257–292). Hillsdale, NJ: Lawrence Erlbaum Associates.

Perkins, C. A., Klaus, P. A., Bastian, L. D., & Cohen, R. L. (1996). *Criminal victimization in the United States, 1993.* Washington, DC: Bureau of Justice Statistics.

Perry, A. (1986). Type A behavior pattern and motor vehicle drivers' behavior. *Perceptual and Motor Skills, 63,* 875–878.

Peters, K. D., Kochanek, K. D., & Murphy, S. L. (1998). Deaths: Final data for 1996. *National Vital Statistics Reports* (Vol. 47, No. 9). Hyattsville, MD: National Center for Health Statistics.

Peterson, C., Seligman, M. E. P., & Vaillant, G. E. (1988). Pessimistic explanatory style is a risk factor for physical illness: A thirty-five-year longitudinal study. *Journal of Personality and Social Psychology, 55,* 23–27.

Phillips, D. P., & Smith, D. G. (1990). Postponement of death until symbolically meaningful occasions. *Journal of the American Medical Association, 263,* 1947–1951.

Phinney, J. S. (1990). Ethnic identity in adolescents and adults: Review of research. *Psychological Bulletin, 108,* 499–514.

Piaget, J. (1952). *The origins of intelligence in children.* New York: International Universities Press.

Piaget, J. (1954). *The construction of reality in the child.* Margaret Cook (Trans.). New York: Basic Books.

Plomin, R. (1994). *Genetics and experiences: The interplay between nature and nurture.* Thousand Oaks, CA: Sage.

Plomin, R. (1997). Identifying genes for cognitive abilities and disabilities. In R. J. Sternberg & E. L. Grigorenko (Eds.), *Intelligence, heredity, and environment* (pp. 89–104). New York: Cambridge University Press.

Plomin, R., Chipuer, H. M., & Neiderhiser, J. M. (1994). Behavioral genetic evidence for the importance of nonshared environment. In E. M. Hetherington, D. Reiss, & R. Plomin (Eds.), *Separate social worlds of siblings: The impact of nonshared environment on development* (pp. 1–31). Hillsdale, NJ: Lawrence Erlbaum Associates.

Plomin, R., Emde, R., Braungart, J. M., Campos, J., Corley, R., Fulker, D. W., Kagan, J., Reznick, S., Robinson, J., Zahn-Waxler, C., & DeFries, J. C. (1993). Genetic change and continuity from 14 to 20 months: The MacArthur Loongitudinal Twin Study. *Child Development, 64,* 1354–1376.

Plomin, R., & McClearn, G. E. (Eds.). (1993). *Nature, nurture, and psychology.* Washington, DC: American Psychological Association.

Plomin, R., & Saudino, K. J. (1994). Quantitative genetics and molecular genetics. In J. E. Bates & T. D. Wachs (Eds.), *Temperament: Individual differences at the interface of biology and behavior* (pp. 143–171). Washington, DC: APA Books.

Polich, J., & Martin, S. (1992). P300, cognitive capability, and personality: A correlational study of university undergraduates. *Personality and Individual Differences, 13,* 533–543.

Population Reference Bureau. (1998). *1998 World Population Data Sheet.* Washington, DC: Author.

Pritchard, W. S. (1989). P300 and EPQ/STPI personality traits. *Personality and Individual Differences, 10,* 15–24.

Quinsey, V. L. (1995). The prediction and explanation of criminal violence. *International Journal of Law & Psychiatry, 18,* 117–127.

Rajecki, D. W., Bledsoe, S. B., & Rasmussen, J. L. (1991). Successful personal ads: Gender differences and similarities in offers, stipulations, and outcomes. *Basic and Applied Social Psychology, 12,* 457–469.

Ramey, C. T., & Campbell, F. A. (1991). *Poverty, early childhood education and academic competence: The Abecedarian Project.* Cambridge, England: Cambridge University Press.

Reedy, M. N., Birren, J. E., & Schaie, K. W. (1981). Age and sex differences in satisfying love relationships across the adult life span. *Human Development, 24,* 52–66.

Reichs, K. J. (1998). *Forensic osteology: Advances in the identification of human remains* (2nd ed.). Springfield, IL: C. C. Thomas.

Reilly, J., & Mulhern, G. (1995). Gender differences in self-estimated IQ: The need for care in interpreting group data. *Personality and Individual Differences, 18,* 189–192.

Reimanis, G., & Green, R. F. (1971). Imminence of death and intellectual decrement in aging. *Developmental Psychology, 5,* 270–272.

Reynolds, C. R. (1990). Conceptual and technical problems in learning disability diagnosis. In C. R. Reynolds & R. W. Kamphaus (Eds.), *Handbook of psychological and educational assessment of children: Intelligence and achievement* (pp. 571–593). New York: Guilford.

Reynolds, C. R., Chastain, R. L., Kaufman, A. S., & McLean, J. E. (1987). Demographic characteristics and IQ among adults: Analysis of the WAIS-R standardization sample as a function of the stratification variables. *Journal of School Psychology, 25,* 323–342.

Ribble, M. A. (1944). Infantile experience in relation to personality development. In J. M. Hunt (Ed.), *Personality and the behavior disorders* (Vol. 2, pp. 621–651). New York: Ronald.

Rice, M. E. (1997). Violent offender research and implications for the criminal justice system. *American Psychologist, 4,* 414–423.

Riding, R. J., & Read, G. (1996). Cognitive style and pupil learning preferences. *Educational Psychology, 16*(1), 81–106.

Riegel, K. F., & Riegel, R. M. (1972). Development, drop, and death. *Developmental Psychology, 6,* 306–319.

Robinson, J. L., Kagan, J., Reznick, J. S., & Corley, R. (1992). The heritability of inhibited and uninhibited behavior: A twin study. *Developmental Psychology, 28,* 1030–1037.

Rodin, J., & Langer, E. (1977). Long-term effects of a control-relevant intervention with institutionalized aged. *Journal of Personality and Social Psychology, 35,* 897–902.

Romanes, G. J. (1883). *Animal intelligence.* New York: Appleton.

Rose, R. J., & Ditto, W. B. (1983). A developmental genetic analysis of common fears from early adolescence to early adulthood. *Child Development, 54,* 361–368.

Rose, R. J., Koskenvuo, M., Kaprio, J., Sarna, S., & Langinvainio, H. (1988). Shared genes, shared experiences, and similarity of personality: Data from 14,288 adult Finnish co-twins. *Journal of Personality and Social Psychology, 54,* 161–171.

Rosenthal, R., Hall, J. A., DiMatteo, M. R., Rogers, P. L., & Archer, D. (1979). *Sensitivity to nonverbal communication: The PONS test.* Baltimore, MD: Johns Hopkins University Press.

Rotella, R. J., & Murray, M. M. (1991). Homophobia, the world of sport, and sport psychology consulting. *Sport Psychologist, 5,* 355–364.

Rotter, J. B. (1966). Generalized expectancies for internal versus external control of reinforcement. *Psychological Monographs, 81* (1, Whole No. 609).

Rourke, B. P. (Ed.). (1989). *Nonverbal learning disabilities: The syndrome and the model.* New York: Guilford.

Rourke, M. (1998, June 21). Redefining religion in America. *Los Angeles Times,* pp. A1, A30–A31.

Rubin, L. B. (1985). *Just friends: The role of friendship in our lives.* New York: Harper & Row.

Rubin, Z. (1981, May). Does personality really change after 20? *Psychology Today,* pp. 18–27.

Rubin, Z., Hill, C. T., Peplau, L. A., & Dunkel-Schetter, C. (1980). Self-disclosure in dating couples: Sex roles and the ethic of openness. *Journal of Marriage and the Family, 42,* 30.

Rushton, J. P., & Erdle, S. (1987). Evidence for aggressive (and delinquent) personality. *British Journal of Social Psychology, 26,* 87–89.

Rushton, J. P., Fulker, D. W., Neale, M. C., Nias, D. K. B., & Eysenck, H. J. (1986). Altruism and aggression: The heritability of individual differences. *Journal of Personality and Social Psychology, 50,* 1192–1198.

Rushton, J. P., & Osborne, R. T. (1995). Genetic and environmental contributions to cranial capacity in Black and White adolescents. *Intelligence, 20,* 1–13.

Russell, C. (1996). *The official guide to racial and ethnic diversity.* Ithaca, NY: New Strategist Publications.

Rutter, M. (1979). Maternal deprivation, 1972–1978: New findings, new concepts, new approaches. *Child Development, 50,* 1192–1198.

Ryckman, R. M. (1997). *Theories of personality* (6th ed.). Pacific Grove, CA: Brooks/Cole.

Salomone, J. J. (1968). An empirical report on some controversial American funeral practices. *Sociological Symposium, 1,* 47–56.

Saluter, A. F. (1996). *Marital status and living arrangements: March 1995* (PPL-52). Washington, DC: U.S. Bureau of the Census, Fertility & Family Statistics Branch, Population Division.

Saluter, A. F., & Lugaila, T. A. (1998, March). *Marital status and living arrangements: March 1996. Current Population Reports* (P20-496). Washington, DC: U.S. Bureau of the Census.

Samenow, S. E. (1984). *Inside the criminal mind.* New York: Times Books.

Samenow, S. E. (1996). The criminal personality. In S. E. Samenow (Ed.), *The Hatherleigh guide to psychiatric disorders* (pp. 137–152). New York: Hatherleigh.

Sapadin, L. A. (1988). Friendship and gender: Perspectives of professional men and women. *Journal of Social and Personal Relationships, 5,* 387–403.

Sattler, J. M. (1988). *Assessment of children* (3rd ed.). San Diego: Jerome M. Sattler.

Saudino, K. J., & Eaton, W. O. (1995). Continuity and change in objectively assessed temperament: A longitudinal twin study of activity level. *British Journal of Developmental Psychology, 13,* 81–95.

Saudino, K. J., & Plomin, R. (1996). Personality and behavioral genetics: Where have we been and where are we going? *Journal of Research in Personality, 30,* 335–347.

Scarr, S. (1992). Developmental theories for the 1990s: Development and individual differences. *Child Development, 63,* 1–19.

Scarr, S. (1993). Biological and cultural diversity: The legacy of Darwin for development. *Child Development, 64,* 1333–1353.

Scarr, S., & Weinberg, R. A. (1976). I.Q. test performance of black children adopted by white families. *American Psychologist, 31,* 726–739.

Scarr, S., & Weinberg, R. A. (1978). The influence of "family background" on intellectual attainment. *American Sociological Review, 43,* 674–692.

Scarr, S., Weinberg, R. A., & Waldman, I. D. (1993). IQ correlations in transracial adoptive families. *Intelligence, 17,* 541–555.

Schaffer, H. R., & Emerson, P. E. (1964). The development of social attachments in infancy. *Monographs of the Society for Research in Child Development, 29* (3, Serial No. 94).

Schaie, K. W. (1977). Quasi-experimental research designs in the psychology of aging. In J. E. Birren & K. W. Schaie (Eds.), *Handbook of the psychology of aging* (pp. 39–59). New York: Van Nostrand Reinhold.

Schaie, K. W. (1990). The optimization of cognitive functioning in old age: Prediction based on cohort-sequential and longitudinal data. In P. B. Baltes & M. Baltes (Eds.), *Longitudinal research and the study of successful (optimal) aging* (pp. 94–117). Cambridge, England: Cambridge University Press.

Schaie, K. W. (1994). The course of adult intellectual development. *American Psychologist, 49,* 304–313.

Schaie, K. W., & Willis, S. L. (1986). Can decline in adult cognitive functioning be reversed? *Developmental Psychology, 22,* 223–232.

Scheier, M. F., & Carver, C. S. (1985). Optimism, coping, and health: Assessment and implications of generalized outcome expectancies. *Health Psychology, 4,* 219–247.

Scheier, M. F., & Carver, C. S. (1992). Effects of optimism on psychological and physical well-being: The influence of generalized outcome expectancies on health. *Journal of Personality, 55,* 169–210.

Schindler, R. M., & Holbrook, M. B. (1993). Critical periods in the development of men's and women's tastes in personal appearance. *Psychology & Marketing, 10,* 549–564.

Schlaug, G., Jaencke, L., Huang, Y., & Steinmetz, H. (1995). In vivo evidence of structural brain asymmetry in musicians. *Science, 267,* 699–701.

Schou, M. (1997). Forty years of lithium treatment. *Archives of General Psychiatry, 54,* 9–13.

Schultz, D. P., & Schultz, S. E. (1993). *Psychology and work today* (6th ed.). New York: Macmillan.

Schwartz, G. E., Davidson, R. J., & Maer, F. (1975). Right hemisphere lateralization for emotion in the human brain: Interactions with cognition. *Science, 190,* 286–288.

Seguin, E. (1907/1866). *Idiocy: Its treatment by the physiological method.* New York: Teachers College, Columbia University.

Selfe, L. (1977). *Nadia: A case of extraordinary drawing ability in an autistic child.* London: Academic Press.

Seligman, M. E. P. (1991). *Learned optimism.* New York: Alfred A. Knopf.

Selye, H. (1976). *The stress of life* (rev. ed.). New York: McGraw-Hill.

Serin, R. C., & Amos, N. L. (1995). The role of psychopathy in the assessment of dangerous. *International Journal of Law & Psychiatry, 18,* 231–238.

Shavelson, R. J. (1996). *Statistical reasoning for the behavioral sciences* (3rd ed.). Needham Heights, MA: Allyn & Bacon.

Shaw, L., & Sichel, H. S. (1971). *Accident proneness: Research on the occurrence, causation, and prevention of road accidents.* New York: Pergamon.

Shaywitz, B. A., Shaywitz, S. E., Pugh, K. R., Constable, R. T., Skudlarski, P., Fulbright, R. K., Bronen, R. A., Fletcher, J. M., Shankweller, D. P., Katz, L., & Gore, J. C. (1995). Sex differences in the functional organization of the brain for language. *Nature, 373,* 607–609.

Shea, C. (1994, September 7). "Gender gap" on examinations shrank again this year. *Chronicle of Higher Education,* p. A54.

Sheldon, W. H., Stevens, S. S., & Tucker, W. B. (1940). *The varieties of human physique.* New York: Harper & Row.

Sheldon, W. H., & Stevens, S. S. (1942). *The varieties of temperament.* New York: Harper & Row.

Shneidman, E. S. (1987, March). At the point of no return. *Psychology Today,* pp. 54–58.

Siever, M. D. (1994). Sexual orientation and gender as factors in socioculturally acquired vulnerability to body dissatisfaction and eating disorders: Special Section: Mental health of lesbians and gay men. *Journal of Consulting and Clinical Psychology, 62,* 252–260.

Sigman, M., & Whaley, S. E. (1998). The role of nutrition in the development of intelligence. In U. Neisser (Ed.), *The rising curve: Long-term gains in IQ and related measures* (pp. 155–182). Washington, DC: American Psychological Association.

Sigurdsson, J. F., & Gudjonsson, G. H. (1996). Psychological characteristics of juvenile alcohol and drug users. *Journal of Adolescence, 19,* 41–46.

Simmons, A. M. (1998, September 30). Where fat is a mark of beauty. *Los Angeles Times,* A1, A12.

Singh, D. (1995a). Female health, attractiveness, and desirability for relationships: Role of breast asymmetry and waist-to-hip ratio. *Ethology and Sociobiology, 16,* 465–481.

Singh, D. (1995b). Female judgment of male attractiveness and desirability for relationships: Role of waist-to-hip ratio and financial status. *Journal of Personality & Social Psychology, 69,* 1089–1101.

Singh, D., & Young, R. K. (1995). Body weight, waist-to-hip ratio, breasts, and hips: Role in judgments of female attractiveness and desirability for relationships. *Ethology and Sociobiology, 16,* 483–507.

Skodak, M., & Skeels, H. M. (1949). A final follow-up study of one hundred adopted children. *Journal of Genetic Psychology, 75,* 85–125.

Slavin, R. E., & Braddock, J. H., III (1993, Summer). Ability grouping: On the wrong track. *The College Board Review,* pp. 11–18.

Sorrentino, R. M., Holmes, J. G., Lhanna, S. E., & Sharp, A. (1995). Uncertainty orientation and trust in close relationships: Individual differences in cognitive styles. *Journal of Personality & Social Psychology, 68,* 314–327.

Spearman, C. E. (1927). *The abilities of man.* London: Macmillan.

Spergel, P., Ehrlich, G. E., & Glass, D. (1978). The rheumatoid arthritic personality: A psychodiagnostic myth. *Psychosomatics, 19,* 79–86.

Spitz, H. (1986). *The raising of intelligence: A selection of attempts to raise retarded intelligence.* Hillsdale, NJ: Lawrence Erlbaum Associates.

Spitz, R. R. (1946). Analitic depression. *Psychoanalytic Study of the Child, 2,* 313–342.

Sprecher, S. (1989). The importance to males and females of physical attractiveness, earning potential, and expressiveness in initial attraction. *Sex Roles, 21,* 591–607.

Sroufe, A. (1985). Attachment classification from the perspective of infant-caregiver relationship and infant temperament. *Child Development, 56,* 1–14.

Sroufe, A., Fox, N., & Pancake, V. (1983). Attachment and dependency in developmental perspective. *Child Development, 54,* 1615–1627.

Stacy, A. W., Sussman, S., Dent, C. W., & Burton, D. (1992). Moderators of peer social influence in adolescent smoking. *Personality and Social Psychology Bulletin, 18,* 163–172.

Stanley, J. C., Keating, D. P., & Fox, L. H. (Eds.). (1974). *Mathematical talent: Discovery, description, and development.* Baltimore, MD: Johns Hopkins University Press.

Starkstein, S. E., & Robinson, R. G. (1986). Cerebral lateralization in depression. *American Journal of Psychiatry, 143,* 1631.

Steelman, L. C., & Doby, J. T. (1983). Family size and birth order as factors on the IQ performance of Black and White children. *Sociology of Education, 56,* 101–109.

Stelmack, R. M. (1990). Biological bases of extraversion: Psychophysiological evidence. *Journal of Personality, 58,* 293–311.

Stelmack, R. M., & Houlihan, M. (1995). Event-related potentials, personality, and intelligence: Concepts, issues, and evidence. In D. H. Saklofske & M. Zeidner (Eds.), *International handbook of personality and intelligence* (pp. 349–365). New York: Plenum.

Stelmack, R. M., Houlihan, M., & McGarry-Roberts, P. S. (1993). Personality, reaction time, and event-related potentials. *Journal of Personality and Social Psychology, 65,* 399–409.

Stelmack, R. M., & Michaud-Achorn, A. (1985). Extraversion, attention, and habituation of the auditory evoked response. *Journal of Research in Personality, 19,* 416–428.

Stenberg, G., Rosen, I., & Risberg, J. (1988). Personality and augmenting/reducing in visual and auditory evoked potentials. *Personality and Individual Differences, 9,* 571–580.

Stenberg, G., Rosen, I., & Risberg, J. (1990). Attention and personality in augmenting/reducing of visual evoked potentials. *Personality and Individual Differences, 11,* 1243–1254.

Stern, W. (1921/1911). *Die differentielle Psychologie in ihren methodischen Grundlagen* [Methodological foundations of differential psychology]. Leipzig: Barth.

Sternberg, R. J. (1985). *Beyond IQ: A triarchic theory of human intelligence.* New York: Cambridge University Press.

Sternberg, R. J. (1986). A triangular theory of love. *Psychological Review, 93,* 119–135.

Sternberg, R. J. (1988). Mental self-government: A theory of intellectual styles and their development. *Human Development, 31,* 197–224.

Sternberg, R. J. (Ed.). (1994a). *Encyclopedia of human intelligence*. New York: Macmillan.

Sternberg, R. J. (1994b). Practical intelligence. In R. J. Sternberg (Ed.), *Encyclopedia of human intelligence* (pp. 821–828). New York: Macmillan.

Sternberg, R. J. (1997). Human abilities. *Annual Review of Psychology, 49*, 479–502.

Sternberg, R. J., & Grigorenko, E. L. (Eds.). (1997). *Intelligence, heredity, and environment*. New York: Cambridge University Press.

Sternberg, R. J., & Lubart, T. I. (1991). An investment theory of creativity and its development. *Human Development, 34*, 1–31.

Sternberg, R. J., & Lubart, T. I. (1992). Buy low and sell high: An investment approach to creativity. *Psychological Science, 1*, 1–5.

Sternberg, S. (1969). Memory scanning: Mental processes revealed by reaction time experiments. *American Scientist, 57*, 421–457.

Sutherland, E. H. (1939). *Principles of criminology*. Philadelphia: Lippincott.

Suzuki, L. A., & Gutkin, T. B. (1993, August). *Racial/ethnic ability patterns on the WISC-R and theories of intelligence*. Paper presented at the 101st annual convention of the American Psychological Association, Toronto, Ontario, Canada.

Takahashi, K. (1986). Examining the Strange Situation procedure with Japanese mothers and 12–month-old infants. *Developmental Psychology, 22*, 265–270.

Tannen, D. (1990). *You just don't understand: Women and men in conversation*. New York: Morrow.

Taylor, P. J., Leese, M., Williams, D., Butwell, M., Daly, R., & Larkin, E. (1998). Mental disorder and violence: A special (high security) hospital study. *British Journal of Psychiatry, 172*, 218–226.

Taylor, R. L., & Richards, S. B. (1991). Patterns of intellectual differences of Black, Hispanic, and White children. *Psychology in the Schools, 28*, 5–8.

Taylor, S. E. (1990). Health psychology: The science and the field. *American Psychologist, 45*, 40–50.

Temoshuk, L. (1992). *The Type C connection: The behavioral links to cancer and your health*. New York: Random House.

Terman, L., & Oden, M. H. (1947). *Genetic studies of genius: Vol. 4. The gifted child grows up*. Stanford, CA: Stanford University Press.

Terman, L., & Oden, M. H. (1959). *Genetic studies of genius: Vol. 5. The gifted group at mid-life: Thirty-five years' follow-up of the superior child*. Stanford, CA: Stanford University Press.

Tett, R., Jackson, D., & Rothstein, M. (1991). Personality measures as predictors of job performance: A meta-analytic review. *Personnel Psychology, 44*, 703–735.

The best in their field. (1993, July). *Hispanic Business*, pp. 52–56.

Thomas, A., Chess, S., & Birch, H. (1968). *Temperament and behavior disorders in children*. New York: New York University Press.

Thomas, G. E., Alexander, K. L., & Eckland, B. K. (1979). Access to higher education: The importance of race, sex, social class, and academic credentials. *School Review, 87*, 133–156.

Thorndike, E. L. (1911). *Animal intelligence*. New York: Macmillan. (Original work published 1898.)

Thorndike, R. L., Hagen, E. P., & Sattler, J. M. (1986). *The Stanford-Binet Intelligence Scale: Fourth Edition, Technical manual*. Chicago: Riverside.

Thurstone, L. L. (1938). Primary mental abilities. *Psychometric Monographs* (No. 1). Chicago: University of Chicago Press.

Tiihonen, J., Hakola, P., & Eronen, M. (1995). Homicidal behaviour and mental disorders. *British Journal of Psychiatry, 167*, 821.

Tokar, D. M., & Swanson, J. L. (1995). Evaluation of the correspondence between Holland's vocational personality typology and the five factor model of personality. *Journal of Vocational Behavior, 46,* 89–108.

Tomarken, A. J., Davidson, R. J., Wheeler, R. E., & Doss, R. C. (1992). Individual differences in anterior brain asymmetry and fundamental dimensions of emotion. *Journal of Personality and Social Psychology, 62,* 676–687.

Tramontana, M. G., Hooper, S. R., & Selzer, S. C. (1988). Research on the preschool prediction of later academic achievement: A review. *Developmental Review, 8,* 89–146.

Treffert, D. A. (1989). *Extraordinary people.* London: Bamtam.

Triandis, H. C. (1989). The self and social behavior in differing cultural contexts. *Psychological Review, 96,* 506–520.

Trickett, E. J., Watts, R. J., & Birman, D. (Eds.). (1994). *Human diversity.* San Francisco: Jossey-Bass.

Trimpop, R., & Kircaldy, B. (1997). Personality predictors of driving accidents. *Personality and Individual Differences, 23,* 147–152.

Trivers, R. (1971). Parental investment and sexual selection. In B. Campbell (Ed.), *Sexual selection and the descent of man* (pp. 136–179). Chicago: Aldine.

Trivers, R. (1985). *Social evolution.* Menlo Park, CA: Benjamin/Cummings.

Troiano, R. P., Flegal, K., Kuczmarski, R. J., Campbell, S. M., & Johnson, C. L. (1995). Overweight prevalence and trends for children and adolescents. *Archives of Pediatric & Adolescent Medicine, 149,* 1085–1091.

Tryon, R. C. (1940). Genetic differences in maze learning in rats. *Yearbook of the National Society for Studies in Education, 39,* 111–119.

Tuddenham, R. D., Blumenkrantz, J., & Wilkin, W. R. (1968). Age changes in AGCT: A longitudinal study of average adults. *Journal of Counseling and Clinical Psychology, 32,* 659–663.

Tyler, L. E. (1978). *Individuality.* San Francisco: Jossey-Bass.

U.S. Bureau of the Census. (1992). *Marriage, divorce and remarriage in the 1990's. Current Population Reports* (P23-180). Washington, DC: U.S. Government Printing Office.

U.S. Bureau of the Census. (1995). *Population profile of the United States: 1995* (Current Population Reports, Series P23–180). Washington DC: U.S. Government Printing Office.

U.S. Bureau of the Census. (1997a). *Money income in the United States: 1996 (With separate data on valuation of non-cash benefits). Current Population Reports* (P60-197). Washington, DC: U.S. Government Printing Office.

U.S. Bureau of the Census. (1997b). *Statistical abstract of the United States: 1997* (117th ed.). Washington, DC: Author.

U.S. Bureau of the Census (1998). *Statistical abstract of the United States: 1998* (118th ed.). Washington, DC: Author.

U.S. Bureau of Labor Statistics. (1997, November). *Employment and earnings.* Washington, DC: U.S. Government Printing Office.

U.S. Department of Defense, (1993). *ASVAB 18/19 technical manual.* North Chicago, IL: U.S. Military Entrance Processing Command.

U.S. Department of Education, Office for Civil Rights. (1997, July 22). *1994 elementary and secondary school civil rights compliance report: Projected values for the nation.* Unpublished table.

U.S. Department of Justice, Federal Bureau of Investigation. (1997). *Crime in the United States, 1996. Uniform Crime Reports.* Washington, DC: U.S. Government Printing Office.

U.S. Department of Justice, Federal Bureau of Investigation. (1998). *Hate crime statistics 1997*. Washington, DC: U.S. Government Printing Office.

U.S. Department of Justice, Bureau of Justice Statistics. (1997, November). *Criminal victimization 1996*. Washington, DC: U.S. Government Printing Office.

U.S. Department of Labor, Bureau of Labor Statistics. (1998). *Consumer expenditures in 1997*. Washington, DC: Author.

Vaillant, G. E. (1979). Natural history of male psychologic health: Effects of mental health on physical health. *New England Journal of Medicine, 30,* 1249–1254.

Van Ijzendoorn, M. H., & Kroonenberg, P. M. (1988). Cross-cultural patterns of attachment: A meta-analysis of the strange situation. *Child Development, 59,* 147–156.

Ventura, S. J., Anderson, R. N., Martin, J. A., & Smith, B. L. (1998). Births and deaths: Preliminary data for 1997. *National Vital Statistics Reports* (Vol. 47, No. 4). Hyattsville, MD: National Center for Health Statistics.

Ventura, S. J., Martin, J. A., Curtin, S. C., & Mathews, T. J. (1998). *Report of final natality statistics, 1996. Monthly Vital Statistics Report* (vol. 46, no. 11, suppl. 2). Hyattsville, MD: National Center for Health Statistics.

Ventura, S. J., Peters, K. D., Martin, J. A., & Maurer, J. D. (1997). *Births and deaths: United States, 1996. Monthly Vital Statistics Report* (vol. 46 no. 1, supp. 2). Hyattsville, MD: National Center for Health Statistics.

Vernon, P. A. (Ed.). (1994). *The neuropsychology of individual differences*. San Diego: Academic Press.

Vernon, P. E. (1960). *The structure of human abilities* (rev. ed.). London: Methuen.

Vrij, A., Van-Schie, E., & Cherryman, J. (1996). Reducing ethnic prejudice through public communication programs: A social-psychological perspective. *Journal of Psychology, 130,* 413–420.

Vuckovic, N., Misic-Pavkov, G., & Doroski, M. (1997). Forensic-psychiatric characteristics of murder: Alcoholic aspect. *Psihijatrija Danas, 29*(1–2), 97–110.

Wagner, M. E., Schubert, H. J., & Schubert, D. S. (1985). Family size effects: A review. *Journal of Genetic Psychology, 146,* 65–78.

Wagner, R. K. (1997). Intelligence, training, and employment. *American Psychologist, 52,* 1059–1069.

Waters, E., Wippman, J., & Sroufe, L. A. (1979). Attachment, positive affect, and competence in the peer group: Two studies in construct validation. *Child Development, 50,* 821–829.

Watson, D., & Pennebaker, J. W. (1989). Health complaints, stress, and distress: Exploring the central role of negative affectivity. *Psychological Review, 96,* 234–254.

Watson, J. D., & Crick, F. H. C. (1953). Molecular structure of nucleic acids. *Nature, 171,* 737–738.

Webb, J. T., & Meckstroth, B. (1982). *Guiding the gifted child*. Columbus: Ohio Psychology Publishing.

Wechsler, D. (1981). *WAIS-R manual*. New York: The Psychological Corporation.

Weinberger, D. R. (1996). On the plausibility of "the neurodevelopmental hypothesis" of schizophrenia. *Neuropsychopharmacology, 14,* 1S-11S.

Weisse, C. S. (1992). Depression and immunocompetence: A review of the literature. *Psychological Bulletin, 111,* 475–489.

Weissman, M. M., Leckman, J. F., Merikangas, K. R., Gammon, G. D., & Prusoff, B. A. (1984). Depression and anxiety disorders in parents and children: Results from the Yale family study. *Archives of General Psychiatry, 41,* 845–852.

Wengler, L., & Rosén, A-S. (1995). Optimism, self-esteem, mood and subjective health. *Personality and Individual Differences, 18,* 653–661.

Whitam, F. L., Diamond, M., & Martin, J. (1993). Homosexual orientation in twins: A report on 61 pairs and three triplet sets. *Archives of Sexual Behavior, 22,* 187–206.

Whitbourne, S. K. (1985). *The aging human body: Physiological changes and psychological consequences.* New York: Springer-Verlag.

White, N., & Cunningham, W. R. (1988). Is terminal drop pervasive or specific? *Journal of Gerontology: Psychological Sciences, 43,* P141–P144.

Whiting, B. B., & Edwards, C. P. (1988). *Children of different worlds: The formation of social behavior.* Cambridge, MA: Harvard University Press.

Wiggins, J. S. (1973). *Personality and prediction: Principles of personality assessment.* Reading, MA: Addison-Wesley.

Willerman, L., Schultz, R., Rutledge, J. N., & Bigler, E. D. (1991). In vivo brain size and intelligence. *Intelligence, 15,* 223–228.

Willerman, L., Schultz, R., Rutledge, J. N., & Bigler, E. D. (1992). Hemispheric size asymmetry predicts relative verbal and nonverbal intelligence differently in the sexes: An MRI study of structure-function relations. *Intelligence, 16,* 315–328.

Williams, J. E., & Best, D. L. (1982). *Measuring sex stereotypes: A thirty-national study.* Beverly Hills, CA: Sage.

Williams, W. M., & Ceci, S. J. (1997). Are Americans becoming more or less alike? Trends in race, class, and ability differences in intelligence. *American Psychologist, 52,* 1226–1235.

Willis, S. L. (1990). Introduction to the special section on cognitive training in later adulthood. *Developmental Psychology, 26,* 875–878.

Wilson, G. (1978). Introversion/extroversion. In H. London & J. E. Exner (Eds.), *Dimensions of personality* (pp. 217–261). New York: Wiley.

Wilson, M. A., & Languis, M. L. (1990). A topographic study of differences in the P300 between introverts and extraverts. *Brain Topography, 2,* 269–274.

Winner, E. (1996). *Gifted children: Myths and realities.* New York: Basic Books.

Winner, E. (1997). Exceptionally high intelligence and schooling. *American Psychologist, 52,* 1070–1081.

Wisocki, P. A., & Averill, J. R. (1987). The challenge of bereavement. In L. L. Carstensen & B. A. Edelstein (Eds.), *Handbook of clinical gerontology* (pp. 312–321). New York: Pergamon.

Witelson, S. F., Glezer, I. I., & Kigar, D. L. (1995). Women have greater density of neurons in posterior temporal cortex. *Journal of Neuroscience, 15,* 3418–3428.

Witkin, H. A., & Berry, J. W. (1975). Psychological differentiation in cross-cultural perspective. *Journal of Cross-Cultural Psychology, 6,* 4–87.

Witkin, H. A., & Goodenough, D. R. (1977). Field dependence and interpersonal behavior. *Psychological Bulletin, 84,* 661–689.

Witkin, H. A., Mednick, S. A., Schlolsinger, F., Bakkestrom, E., Christiansen, K. O., Goodenough, D. R., Hirschhorn, K., Lundstean, C., Owen, D. R., Philip, J., Rubin, D. B., & Stocking, M. (1976). XYY and XXY men: Criminality and aggression. *Science, 193,* 547–555.

Witkin, H. A., Moore, C., Goodenough, D. R., & Cox, P. (1977). Field dependent and field independent cognitive styles and their educational implications. *Review of Educational Research, 47,* 1–64.

Witkin, H. A., Price-Williams, D., Bertini, M., Bjorn, C., Oltman, P. K., Ramirez, M., & Van Meel, J. (1973). *Social conformity and psychological differentiation.* Princeton, NJ: Educational Testing Service.

Wober, M. (1974). Towards an understanding of the Uganda concept of intelligence. In J. W. Berry & P. R. Dasen (Eds.), *Culture and cognition: Readings in cross-cultural psychology* (pp. 261–280). London: Methuen.

Woll, S. (1986). So many to choose from: Decision strategies in videodating. *Journal of Social and Personal Relationships, 3,* 43–52.

Wolpe, J. (1982). *The practice of behavior therapy* (3rd ed.). New York: Pergamon.

Wooten, K. C, Barner, B. O., & Silver, N. C. (1994). The influence of cognitive style upon work environment preferences. *Perceptual and Motor Skills, 79,* 307–314.

Wright, P. (1989). Gender differences in adults' same- and cross-gender friendships. In R. S. Adams & R. Bleiszner (Eds.), *Older adult friendship* (pp. 197–221). Newbury Park, CA: Sage.

Wright, P. M., Kacmar, K. M., McMahan, G. C., & Deleeuw, K. (1995). P=f(M × A): Cognitive ability as a moderator of the relationship between personality and job performance. *Journal of Management, 21,* 1129–1139.

Wrightsman, L. S. (1994a). *Adult personality development: Vol. 1. Theories and concepts.* Thousand Oaks, CA: Sage.

Wrightsman, L. S. (1994b). *Psychology and the legal system* (3rd ed.). Pacific Grove, CA: Brooks/Cole.

Yang, S.-Y., & Sternberg, R. J. (1997). Taiwanese Chinese people's conceptions of intelligence. *Intelligence, 25,* 21–36.

Yerkes, R. M. (Ed.). (1921). Psychological examining in the United States Army. *Memoirs of the National Academy of Sciences, 15.*

Yochelson, S., & Samenow, S. E. (1976). *The criminal personality: Vol. 1. A profile for change.* New York: Jason Aronson.

Zajonc, R. B. (1976). Family configuration and intelligence. *Science, 192,* 227–236.

Zajonc, R. B. (1986). The decline and rise of scholastic aptitude scores. *American Psychologist, 41,* 862–867.

Zedeck, S. (1971). Problems with the use of "moderator" variables. *Psychological Bulletin, 76,* 295–310.

Zigler, E., & Berman, W. (1983). Discerning the future of early childhood intervention. *Journal of Marriage and the Family, 53,* 773–786.

Zigler, E., & Hodapp, R. M. (1986). *Understanding mental retardation.* New York: Cambridge University Press.

Zuckerman, M. (1994). *Behavioral expressions and biosocial bases of sensation seeking.* New York: Cambridge University Press.

Zuckerman, M. (1995). Good and bad humors: Biochemical bases of personality and its disorders. *Psychological Science, 6,* 325–332.

Author Index

Subject Index